A Chinese Literary Mind

A Chinese Literary Mind

CULTURE, CREATIVITY, AND
RHETORIC IN *WENXIN DIAOLONG*

Edited by Zong-qi Cai

STANFORD UNIVERSITY PRESS

STANFORD, CALIFORNIA

2001

Stanford University Press
Stanford, California 2001
© 2001 by the Board of Trustees of the
Leland Stanford Junior University

Printed in the United States of America on acid-free,
archival-quality paper

Library of Congress Cataloging-in-Publication Data
A Chinese literary mind : culture, creativity, and rhetoric in
Wenxin Diaolong / edited by Zong-qi Cai
    p. cm.
  Includes bibliographical references and index.
  ISBN 0-8047-3618-9 (alk. paper)
  1. Liu Hsieh, ca. 465–ca. 522. Wen hsin tiao lung.
  2. Chinese literature—History and criticism— Theory,
etc. I. Cai Zong-qi
  PL2261.L483 C46 2000
  801'.95'0951—dc21   00-056358

Original printing 2001

Last figure below indicates year of this printing:

10 09 08 07 06 05 04 03 02 01

Typeset by Birdtrack Press in 11/14 Adobe Garamond and
Fang Song Medium

To Yu-kung Kao

Acknowledgments

The ten essays collected in this volume are revised versions of the papers presented at an international conference on *Wenxin diaolong* held at the University of Illinois, Urbana-Champaign, on April 11 and 12, 1997. The conference was generously funded by two institutions at the University of Illinois: the Center for East Asian and Pacific Studies and the College of Liberal Arts and Sciences. The Research Board of the University of Illinois provided a grant for hiring a graduate student to assist in the preparation of the conference volume. In addition to acknowledging financial support by these institutions, I must express my gratitude to the faculty, students, and staff at Illinois for providing support of many kinds. In particular, I want to thank Professor George T. Yu, the Center's director, for his unfailing support of our project from its conception to its fruition; Professor Peter N. Gregory for his invaluable suggestions concerning the conference and the volume; Dr. Xueqin Zheng and my wife, Jing Liao, for their indispensable help during the conference; and Pi-hsia Hsu, for her devoted assistance in the preparation of our final manuscript.

In addition to the papers collected in this volume, the conference benefited from insightful presentations by Professor John Hay of the University of California at Santa Cruz, Professor Qiu Shiyou of Zhongshan University (China), Professor Maureen Robertson of the University of Iowa, and Professor Zhang Shaokang of Beijing University. The essays by Professors Qiu and Zhang may be found in *Wenxin diaolong yanjiu* 文心雕龍研究 (Studies on *Wenxin diaolong*), vol. 3 (Beijing: Beijing University Press, 1998).

I wish to thank the editorial staff at Stanford University Press for their professional guidance. I am particularly thankful to Helen Tartar for her valuable advice and enthusiastic support, Mary Severance and Matt Stevens for their careful supervision of the production process, and Lisl Hampton for her meticulous copyediting.

Z. C.

Contents

Contributors

Zong-qi Cai is associate professor of Chinese and Comparative Literature at the University of Illinois, Urbana-Champaign. He is the author of *The Matrix of Lyric Transformation: Poetic Modes and Self-Presentation in Early Chinese Pentasyllabic Poetry* (Michigan, 1996), and *Configurations of Comparative Poetics: Three Perspectives on Western and Chinese Literary Criticism* (Hawaii, forthcoming).

Kang-i Sun Chang is professor of Chinese Literature at Yale University. Her scholarly publications include *The Evolution of Chinese Tz'u Poetry* (Princeton, 1980), *Six Dynasties Poetry* (Princeton, 1986), and *The Late Ming Poet Ch'en Tzu-lung: Crises of Love and Loyalism* (Yale, 1991). She is the coeditor (with Ellen Widmer) of *Writing Women in Late Imperial China* (Stanford, 1997) and is also the compiler and coeditor (with Haun Saussy) of *Women Writers of Traditional China: An Anthology of Poetry and Criticism* (Stanford, 1999).

Ronald Egan is professor of Chinese Literature at the University of California, Santa Barbara. He is the author of *Word, Image, and Deed in the Life of Su Shi* (Harvard, 1994). He is also the translator of a selection of essays by the contemporary scholar Qian Zhongshu, entitled *Limited Views: Essays on Ideas and Letters by Qian Zhongshu* (Harvard, 1998).

Wai-yee Li is professor of Chinese Literature at Harvard University. She is the author of *Enchantment and Disenchantment: Love and Illusion in Chinese Literature* (Princeton, 1993) and *The Readability of the Past in Early Chinese Historiography* (forthcoming).

Shuen-fu Lin is professor of Chinese Literature at the University of Michigan, Ann Arbor. He is the author of *The Transformation of the Chinese Lyrical Tradition: Chiang Kuei and Southern Sung Tz'u Poetry* (Princeton, 1978). He is also coeditor (with Stephen Owen) of *The Vitality of the Lyric Voice: Shih Poetry from the Late Han to the T'ang* (Princeton, 1986) and cotranslator (with Larry Schulz) of *The Tower of Myriad Mirrors: A Supplement to Journey to the West* (by Tung Yüeh), second edition (Michigan, 2000).

Richard John Lynn is professor of Chinese Literature, Department of East Asian Studies, at the University of Toronto, Canada. His publications include *Kuan Yün-shih* (Twayne, 1980), *Chinese Literature: A Draft Bibliography in Western European Languages* (Australian National University, 1980), *Guide to Chinese Poetry and Drama* (G. K. Hall, 1984), *The Classic of Changes: A New Translation of the I Ching as Interpreted by Wang Bi* (Columbia, 1994; CD-ROM, 1996), and *The Classic of the Way and Virtue: A New Translation of the Taodejing of Laozi as Interpreted by Wang Bi (226–49)* (Columbia, 1999). He is the editor of James J. Y. Liu, *Language—Paradox—Poetics: A Chinese Perspective* (Princeton, 1998). Current works in progress include *History and Connoisseurship of Chinese Soapstone (Shoushanshi) Carvings*, an annotated translation of Yan Yu's *Canglang shihua*, and a book-length study of the poet Huang Zunxian's literary experiences in Japan (1877–82).

Victor H. Mair is professor of Asian and Middle Eastern Studies at the University of Pennsylvania. A specialist on Sino-Indian and Sino-Iranian cultural relations, he also has a deep interest in Chinese lexicography. He is the editor of *The Columbia Anthology of Traditional Chinese Literature* (1994) and *The Columbia History of Chinese Literature* (forthcoming). He is also an editor of the *ABC Chinese-English Dictionary* and is preparing the first etymological dictionary of Chinese words. In addition, he is the author or translator of numerous books, articles, and reviews dealing with Chinese languages, literature, and religion.

Stephen Owen is James Bryant Conant University Professor of Chinese at Harvard University. His most recent books include *An Anthology of Chinese Literature: Beginnings to 1911* (Norton, 1996) and *The End of the Chinese Middle Ages: Essays in the Mid-Tang Literary Culture* (Stanford, 1997).

Andrew H. Plaks is professor of East Asian Studies and Comparative Literature at Princeton University. He is the author of *Archetype and Allegory in the Dream of the Red Chamber* (Princeton, 1976) and *The Four Masterworks of the Ming Novel: Ssu ta ch'i-shu* (Princeton, 1987). He is the editor of *Chinese Narrative: Critical and Theoretical Essays* (Princeton, 1977).

Zhang Shaokang is professor of Chinese Literature in the Department of Chinese at Beijing University. He is the president of the Chinese *Wenxin diaolong* Association. His publications include *Wenxin diaolong xintan* 文心雕龍新探 (New investigations on *Wenxin diaolong*) (Qi-Lu shushe, 1987), *Zhongguo gudai wenxue chuangzuolun* 中國古代文學創作論 (Ancient Chinese theories of literary creation) (Beijing University, 1983), and *Zhongguo wenxue lilun piping fazhanshi* 中國文學理論批評發展史 (A history of the development of Chinese literary theory and criticism) (Beijing University, 1995).

A Chinese Literary Mind

Introduction

ZONG-QI CAI

A scholar of no great distinction in his own day, Liu Xie was born into a family of modest means—that of commoners or a decayed aristocratic line. In his early life he received a solid education in Confucian classics and showed a strong interest in Buddhism. He did not marry, probably due to both his Buddhist beliefs and his lack of financial resources for a respectable marriage. It is generally believed that he composed *Wenxin diaolong* during the Zhong-xing reign (501–2) of the Qi dynasty (479–502) in a bid to gain patronage from the court and to achieve fame as a writer of ornate prose, a highly prized genre at that time. The story goes that one day he posed as a peddler and stopped the carriage of Shen Yue 沈約 (441–513), the towering literary master of the time, to present this work to him. Shen Yue did stop to glance over Liu's work and expressed his approval on the spot. Liu's endeavor for literary fame was, however, only modestly successful. In his lifetime he did not fulfill his dream of achieving literary eminence, even though Shen Yue and Xiao Tong 蕭統 (501–31), the crown prince of the Liang and the compiler of the renowned *Wen xuan* 文選 (Anthology of refined literature), did speak well of his literary talents. Later in life, Liu devoted himself instead to editing Buddhist sutras and writing Buddhist treatises in a monastery, where he was granted imperial permission to take Buddhist vows shortly before his death.

Although Liu Xie was not influential in his own time and remained so for many centuries, his magnum opus was certainly not ignored. We find an abundance of references to *Wenxin diaolong* in historical texts as well as writings on literature. *Wenxin diaolong* is believed to have been transmitted to Japan by the middle of the eighth century and to Korea by the ninth century. Nonetheless, it did not register the kind of importance accorded other critical works such as *Shi pin* 詩品 (The grading of poets) by Liu's contemporary Zhong Hong 鍾嶸 (?–518). Only in the Qing dynasty did it begin to receive more serious critical attention. For its ascent to the apex of traditional Chinese literary criticism, it had to wait until this century, when critical studies of it would reach epic proportions. It is estimated that by 1992 as many as 140 books and 2,419 articles were published on *Wenxin diaolong* in the Chinese Mainland, Taiwan, Hong Kong, Singapore, Japan, and Korea. In addition to these publications, there has been a plethora of regional and international symposiums and conferences devoted exclusively to this masterwork (this is documented in chapter 10).

Today *Wenxin diaolong* reigns supreme in the field of traditional literary scholarship. There are more publications and conferences devoted to this work than all other texts except *Honglou Meng* 紅樓夢 (Dream of red chamber). The studies of *Wenxin diaolong* are now known in China as *longxue* 龍學 or "dragonology," a disciplinary or quasi-disciplinary title derived from *Long*, the last character of the book's title. *Longxue* reflects not only the traditional Chinese fondness of the dragon as an auspicious symbol but also an intention to rival *hongxue* 紅學 ("redology"), a title that was originally a bad joke but later became a much used title for the studies of the *Dream of the Red Chamber*. In contrast to the explosive interest in *Wenxin diaolong* in Asia, however, there has been a prolonged reticence about this masterwork on this side of the Pacific. After the publication of Vincent Y. Shih's English translation in 1957, there appeared only two Ph.D. dissertations and a few isolated articles in the following decades. Only very recently did we see a new translation of its major chapters with copious annotations and commentaries by Stephen Owen in his *Readings in Chinese Literary Thought*. To help fill this regrettable lacuna in the scholarship on *Wenxin diaolong*, we have undertaken a collaborative endeavor in preparing this first book-length critical study of the masterwork in the English language.

What is it about *Wenxin diaolong* that has attracted so much critical attention in this century? If there is one thing that accounts for its importance more than anything else, one may say it is its building of a grand critical system, marked by its extensive range and its intricate codification of diverse critical issues, topics, and views.

The extensive range of *Wenxin diaolong* may be shown by sheer statistics. In the space of fifty chapters, Liu Xie mentions more than 500 historical or legendary figures, cites about 500 titles, and comments on nearly 200 genres and subgenres. This bulk of references amounts to a compendium of major literary and cultural facts from the earliest times to his own day. But *Wenxin diaolong* is far more than a compendium of dry facts. All these references appear in the context of his wide-ranging critical investigations, which cover almost the entire domain of literary criticism. Liu formulated his comprehensive views on the origins of literature, literary history, tradition, individual talent, the creative process, the qualities of the author, genre transformation, rhetoric, literary form, the reception of literary works, and so forth.

Liu Xie's integration of diverse critical issues, topics, and views into a grand critical system has been one of the most intriguing subjects of investigation in the *Wenxin diaolong* scholarship of this century. Liu Xie himself is so conscious of his critical system that he reflects upon his construction of it in the last chapter. In explaining the title *Wenxin diaolong*, he sets forth the three broadest areas of his work. For him, *wenxin* denotes the use of the mind in composing a work, and thus it encompasses all issues and topics pertaining to the creative and, by extension, receptive processes. *Diaolong*, literally translated as "the carving of dragons," describes the shaping of the beautiful configurations of a written work, and hence it covers all the issues and topics relating to rhetoric. Moreover, Liu tries to disassociate the phrase *diaolong* from the pejorative sense of mere craft by relating it to the broader cosmological and cultural configurations. By this phrase Liu means to include his discussions of the origins and nature of literature as well.

In addition, Liu explains the organization of the fifty chapters. The first five chapters offer an exhaustive examination of what he calls the "pivot of literature" (文之樞紐) (*WXDL* 50/105).[1] They trace the development of literature from its ultimate origin in the cosmological Tao, to its germination in the Confucian canons, and to its first flowering in the belletristic traditions of *Chuci*. Chapters 6 to 25 investigate all major belletristic and nonbelletristic genres and subgenres under two broad categories: writings with rhyme (*wen* 文) and writings without rhyme (*bi* 筆). The second half of the book shifts from specific genres to general critical issues. Chapters 26 through 49 are each developed around one or two important critical issues. The fiftieth chapter explains the intricate organization of the fifty chapters modeled on the symbolic numerology of fifty in *Yi jing* 易經 (Book of changes). By comparing his work with the *Book of Changes*, he apparently intends to bring our attention to his self-conscious endeavor to construct a grand critical system that emulates the cosmological system of the *Book of Changes* both in its completeness and in its dynamic integration of multifarious components.

In examining Liu's critical system, most scholars dwell upon the organization of the fifty chapters and come up with many competing ways to regroup the chapters along the broad outlines sketched by Liu. In so doing, they hope to shed light on the interrelationships of the fifty chapters as a unified whole. Alternatively, we may go beyond the issue of chapter organization and explore the inner workings of Liu's critical system from a new perspective. Let us conceive of Liu's critical system in terms of a dynamic interplay of diachronic and synchronic studies, theoretical and practical criticism.

Diachronic studies encompass Liu's extensive discussions on cultural and literary transformations on different levels: overall cultural transformation (chapters 1–3), general literary history (chapters 29, 45), and specific genre histories (chapters 5–25). Synchronic studies include his views on the creative process (chapters 26, 46), the qualities of the author (chapters 27, 42, 47, 49), the interactive relationship between feelings and language (chapters 28, 30–32), the reception of literary works (chapter 48), and rhetoric (chapters 33–41, 43–44). In pursuing these diachronic and synchronic studies, Liu moves freely between the two poles of theoretical and practical criticism. Sometimes he elucidates theoretical principles in abstract terms, and sometimes he offers impressionistic remarks on the styles of periods and authors. For the most part, he focuses on theoretical discussion and practical criticism in alternate chapters, but it is not uncommon for him to shift back and forth within a single chapter.

It is true that Liu Xie himself does not employ the terms used here to describe his critical system. But Liu's reflections on his own mode of thought and discourse amount to an elucidation of the critical system shown above.

He tells us he aims to "trace the origins [of both *wen* and *bi* categories] and describe their growth and mutation" [原始表末] (*WXDL* 50/109). In other words, he seeks an exhaustive diachronic coverage in his studies of both categories of genres. In the meantime, he seeks to "define terms and illuminate their meanings, select representative works for each chapter, and lay out the principles [of *wen* and *bi* writings] in order to bring out their unifying features" [釋名以章義，選文以定篇，敷理以舉統] (*WXDL* 18/ 37). This remark is a perfect description of his synchronic investigation of diverse genres and subgenres. Speaking of theoretical inquiry, he stresses the importance of "penetrating thought to the realm of the subtle spirit" [銳思於機神之區] (*WXDL* 18/76) and "searching into the depth and grasping the ultimate" [鉤深取極] (*WXDL* 18/106). This search for deep-lying truth and principles doubtless comes close to what we nowadays call theoretical criticism. Liu Xie believes that direct aesthetic engagement with the objects of investigation is a prerequisite for theoretical inquiry. "Only after one has played a thousand tunes," he says, "can one have a knowledge of sounds" [操千曲而後曉聲] (*WXDL* 48/76). All his impressionistic remarks on individual authors and texts apparently spring from such an aesthetic engagement and thus may be considered an exercise of practical criticism. On account of his construction of this grand system, modern scholars have elevated Liu to the pedestal of critical preeminence. Lu Xun 魯迅 (1881–1936), for instance, claims that "in the East there is Liu Yanhe's 劉彥和 [Liu Xie's] *Literary Mind*, and in the West there is Aristotle's *Poetics*."

In studying *Wenxin diaolong*, we have two major objectives. The first is to present a critical introduction to its three broad areas of focus: cultural traditions, literary creation, and rhetorical art. We explore these areas in four interlocking sets of papers. The second objective is to examine these areas from new perspectives. As newcomers to the study of *Wenxin diaolong*, we believe that we have the advantage of looking at this masterwork through unjaded eyes. By introducing new critical perspectives and raising new issues, we hope to make our own contributions to the current scholarship on *Wenxin diaolong*.

In exploring Liu Xie's discussion of cultural traditions, the essays in Part I focus on the relationship between *Wenxin diaolong* and broader literary and critical traditions. Kang-i Sun Chang's essay discusses the significance of *Wenxin diaolong* in the context of canon formation. In undertaking this grand project of literary criticism, she argues, Liu Xie aims to elevate literature to a canonical status comparable to that of the Confucian classics. To Liu Xie, the best way to achieve this goal is to establish a link between literary tradition and the Confucian classics. Liu conceives of such a connection in terms of shared revelations of the Tao through beautiful configurations of writing (*wen*). He seeks on the one hand to reassess the canonicity of the Confucian classics in terms of their *wen* and on the other hand to classify all the major genres of writing according to the particular stylistic features they inherited from a given classic. In order to justify his canonization of literature, he not only places *wen* at the center of the entire cultural configuration, but he also views it as the Tao's manifestation that is equal to, if not more potent than, heaven and earth. Considering the supreme importance of *wen*, he deems it appropriate to recognize the value of even ancient apocryphal texts on the basis of their *wen* (belletristic) merits. For the same reason, he elevates Qu Yuan's 屈原 (ca. 339–ca. 278 B.C.) works, censured by many as morally incorrect and rhetorically excessive, to a position next to *Shijing* 詩經 (Book of poetry). In conclusion, Chang examines the extent to which Liu Xie's goal of "self-canonization" led him to undertake his grand project. By conferring canonical status upon literature, Chang observes, Liu hopes to have the same status conferred upon himself and hence to share the literary immortality enjoyed by the writers he discusses. This hope of self-canonization was eventually fulfilled, though not until nearly one and a half millennia after his death.

My own contribution examines *Wenxin diaolong* with a view to understanding the systematics of traditional Chinese literary criticism. I begin with a discussion of three major concepts of literature developed from the earliest times through the Han and an account of Liu Xie's comprehensive concept of literature. I argue that if we compare these four concepts of literature we can see a common denominator—literature as a harmonizing process. This process arises in the heart (*xin* 心) of a composer or author when he responds to various external processes on physiological, psychological, moral, intuitive, or intellectual levels. As he makes known his responses by dancing, playing music, singing, speaking, or writing, this process moves from the inner to the outer worlds and helps bring about the harmony between men and various ongoing external processes. We can also perceive two prominent *differentiae*. The first is that literature as a process is conceived rather differently. In *Yao dian* 堯典 (Canon of yao), it is depicted as an auxiliary part of a dance-centered religious performance. In *Zuo zhuan* 左傳 (Zuo commentary) and *Guo yu* 國語 (Speeches of the states), it is seen as a relatively more important but nonetheless auxiliary part of a music-centered courtly ceremony. In *Shi* daxiu 詩大序 (Great Preface to the *Book of Poetry*), it is taken to be the central part of the verbalization-centered social intercourse. In *Wenxin diaolong*, it is conceived as a largely autonomous, text-centered, belletristic pursuit. The second *differentia* is that the origins, formation, and functions of literature are all explained in terms of interaction and harmonization with different ongoing processes—the numinous spirits, natural forces, ethical sociopolitical forces, or the mysterious Tao. The common denominator and two *differentiae* testify not only to the interrelatedness of the four concepts but also to the systematics of traditional Chinese criticism as a whole.

The essays in Part II broaden the investigation of cultural traditions by bringing our attention to the intellectual foundations of *Wenxin diaolong*. Victor H. Mair takes up one of the most difficult and controversial issues in the studies of *Wenxin diaolong*: the relationship between this masterwork and Buddhism, which was flourishing in Liu's time. He shows us that over the last couple of decades *Wenxin diaolong* specialists in Asia have taken three different positions concerning the role of Buddhism in *Wenxin diaolong*: Buddhism was effectively absent from the text; it played a prominent role; and it was present but played no significant role. In examining these three positions, Mair makes a special effort to expose the polemics that have bedeviled them, especially the first and second. Although the first and second positions are diametrically opposed to each other, they are motivated by the same misguided national pride or blatant cultural prejudice. By declaring the Buddhist elements immaterial in *Wenxin diaolong*, the former seeks to defend the foremost icon of Chinese critical traditions. By the same token, in denouncing *Wenxin diaolong* as a camouflaged Buddhist text intended to subvert Confucianism, the latter aims to preserve the purity of the same traditions. Apparently, both polemics are predicated on the same premise that Buddhism is a foreign and inimical religion. By expunging all these polemics, Mair argues, we can arrive at a new position on this old issue. According to him, the role of Buddhism in *Wenxin diaolong* is vital because from Buddhist sources Liu obtained his basic epistemological model, his analytical methods, his organizational schemes, and many key concepts. This role of Buddhism should not be considered to be at variance with the equally vital role of native Confucianism. Rather, the two should be seen to coexist and often complement each other to the beneficial effect of enhancing the complexity of this masterwork. The compatibility of the two, Mair notes, is aptly indicated by the title itself, of which the first half, *wenxin*, bespeaks the Buddhist concept of mind and the second half, *diaolong*, conveys the longstanding Confucian concerns with language and rhetoric.

Richard John Lynn's essay examines the relationship of *Wenxin diaolong* to the writings of Wang Bi 王弼 (226–49), the neo-Taoist philosopher. Wang's writings are no less important a source of ideas, terms, and epistemological models for Liu Xie than Buddhist scriptures. Liu's debt to Wang Bi is best seen in his adoption of three key terms, *yi* 意 (concept, ontological entity), *xiang* 象 (image), and *yan* 言 (words, speech), which lie at the heart of the latter's onto-epistemological inquiries. After a close study of Wang's use of these three terms in his annotations to *Laozi* and the *Book of Changes*, Lynn examines Liu's use of these terms in *Wenxin diaolong*. In chapter 1, "Yuan Dao" 原道 (Tao as the source), Liu uses *xiang* in the sense of concrete configurations of *wen* and *yan* as the embodiment of *xiang*. This reminds us of Wang's use of *yan*, *xiang*, and *yi* as vehicles for conveying an ascending degree of reality. In chapter 26, "Shensi" 神思 (Spirit and thought), Liu not only uses the three terms but actually arranges them with a tripartite hierarchy similar to the one established by Wang Bi. However, while Wang Bi emphasizes the gaps between them in a descending scale of ontological validity from *yi* to *xiang* to *yan*, Liu stresses the possibility of closing these gaps and embodying ontological reality in language. To illustrate this essential difference between Wang's and Liu's interpretations of the tripartite hierarchy, Lynn compares Wang's disapproval and Liu's approval of Han scholars' reliance on *xiang* to explain the *Book of Changes*. By endorsing the Han scholars' views, Liu intends to affirm the power of images and words to embody what is beyond the sensory realm. This comparison of Wang's and Liu's uses of the three terms can help us establish a proper conceptual frame for understanding Liu's theory of literary creation, the core issue to be fully explored in Part III.

In exploring the issue of the literary mind, the essays in Part III seek to understand Liu Xie's theory of literary creation from two different contemprary perspectives. Egan offers a close reading of chapter 26, "Shensi," the core of Liu's theory of literary creation. Liu's idea of *shen* 神 in this chapter, Egan argues, is derived from and largely identical to the ancient idea of *daimon*, the subtlest element of the human psyche that corresponds to the manifold divinities of the natural world. Like the ancients, Liu conceives of the operation of *shen* in terms of a flight of the mind out of the physical body to roam afar in defiance of time and space—a flight reminiscent of the soul's wandering in a shamanistic journey. Unlike shamanistic experience, however, Liu believes that the writer's "daimonic roaming" is aided and in many ways controlled by his sensory perception and linguistic cognition. In other words, Liu's idea of *si* 思 (creative process) is an interaction between "transcendental" roaming and experiential perception, linguistic exercise, and reasoning (*li* 理). It is out of this interaction that *yi* 意, or authorial intent, is an envisaging (*yixiang* 意象) of the work-to-be. Although Liu's application of the ancient idea of daimonic roaming to literary creativity was not new, strictly speaking, the privileged place he gave to daimonic thinking in his treatise is a significant innovation in the critical tradition. He elevates this manner of thinking above all others, showing his preference for a literary mind that "ventures forth." Moreover, in his comments on the way this thinking works Liu repeatedly emphasizes the detachment of the author's mind from his immediate surroundings and even broaches the possibility of transcending the limits and realities of the physical world. Such ideas are of particular interest for their divergence from what later came to be dominant assumptions in literary criticism about the inseparability of author, biographical experience, and literature. To Liu, daimonic thinking can work its magic on not only the formless, insubstantial *yi*, but also on the substantial *yan*, referents to empirical realities. Because of his daimonic thinking, the writer can dislodge words from their hackneyed referents and create them anew by interweaving them into beautiful patterns (*wen*) unrivaled by the real world. In the light of all these operations of daimonic thinking in both metaphysical and physical realms, Liu departs from Wang Bi's position and argues for the possibility of fusing *yi*, *xiang*, and *yan*. This firm belief in, and thorough elucidation of, the transforming power of daimonic thinking, Egan concludes, is the defining feature of Liu's theory of literary creation.

After Egan's close reading of the "Shensi" chapter within early Chinese intellectual and literary traditions, we move to Shuen-fu Lin's investigation of Liu's theory of literary creation in a broader framework that includes a comparative dimension. Modern scholars of *Wenxin diaolong* generally interpret the term *shensi* as referring to the mental faculty called *xiangxiang* 想象, which is the modern Chinese equivalent of imagination in English. In equating *shensi* with imagination, these scholars emphasize *shensi*'s connotations of the ideas of artistic creativity, invention, and novelty derived from the nineteenth-century Western Romantic views of art and imagination. *Xiangxiang* is actually a very old term, going at least as far back as *Chuci* 楚辭, (The songs of Chu). Literally, it means "to visualize an image of someone or something." It is therefore basically identical in literal meaning with imagination, which, as Mary Warnock defines it, is "that which creates mental images."[2] Interestingly, however, the word *xiangxiang* did not become a key term in Chinese criticism and aesthetics until modern times. Lin draws our attention to the fact that in early usage the word *si* 思 in *shensi* entails both the sense of "purely intellectual thought" and of "to cherish the memories of." This second sense involves the ability to evoke mental images of things not present physically. Even though *shensi* or daimonic thinking does not completely correspond to the dominant Western notion of imagination, it embodies both aspects of "image-producing faculty" and "unifying artistic creativity." Lin directs our attention to the bodily basis for Liu's comments on the importance of a writer's intent-pneuma (*zhiqi* 志氣) and on the interactions between his mind-heart (*xin* 心) and things (*wu* 物) in the external world.

Lin also demonstrates that Liu is also fully aware of the significance of imagination's organizing power when he discusses the shaping (*guiju* 規矩) and carving (*kelou* 刻鏤) functions of daimonic thinking in literary creation. Liu's concept of *shensi* is indeed comparable to Coleridge's "shaping spirit of imagination." Although he describes imagination as something that is not bound by any temporal and spatial restrictions, Liu does recognize its structuring function. In his theory, therefore, there is no dichotomy between mind and body, cognition and emotion, and reason and imagination. Another of Liu's contributions is his insistence on the cultivation of imagination in the creative process, from the preparatory stage to the execution of a literary work. Coleridge regards the poet's creative imagination as genius which, once lost, cannot be regained. Although Liu acknowledges that daimonic thinking defies adequate explanation and description when it reaches the highest order, he nevertheless emphasizes the necessity of continuous culti-vation. Thus he offers his reader the optimistic notion that a writer's power of the imagination is not simply something he is endowed with, but some-thing he shares with fellow human beings and that requires continuous effort to bring to fruition.

Part IV explores Liu Xie's theory of rhetorical art. As in Part III, the first essay is a close reading of the most important chapter of *Wenxin diaolong* on the issue under discussion. In examining the chapter in question ("Lici" 麗 辭 [Parallel phrasing]), Andrew H. Plaks first identifies it as one primary locus classicus for the notion of rhetorical parallelism that lies at the heart of Liu Xie's rhetoric theory and represents the essence and glory of Chinese literary art at large. As is shown later in the Tang regulated poetry (*lüshi* 律 詩), rhetorical parallelism developed in China with a degree of subtlety and complexity unrivaled by other classical literatures. This supreme achievement of rhetorical parallelism, Plaks argues, is due both to Chinese cosmological thinking modeled on *yin* and *yang* opposites and to the Chinese linguistic structures that are particularly conducive to the formation of units of equal lengths. Considering its paramount importance in Chinese literary art, Liu's systematic discussion of rhetorical parallelism, the first ever in Chinese poetics, is of great significance. In elucidating the nature of rhetorical parallelism, Liu adopts a microscheme of diachronic and synchronic, theoretical and prac-tical criticisms. He traces the genealogy of parallel constructions from antiq-uity to his own time, describing it as a trajectory from spontaneous doubling to ever more self-conscious crafting of parallel forms. He offers practical comments on many well-known examples of parallel phrasing, singling out those in *Shijing* and *Zuozhuan* as models of parallel forms for later poetry and prose, respectively. Liu also provides a synchronic, theoretical categoriza-tion of parallelism into two related pairs: semantic and textual, straight and antithetical. In defining these pairs, he aims to distinguish their aesthetic value based on their varying degrees of interface of symmetry and difference.

As we move from Plaks's to Stephen Owen's paper, we cannot help noticing a stimulating semblance of "antithetical parallelism" at work. The two papers are symmetrical in subject matter but they are somewhat asymmetrical with regard to the angles of their critical judgments. While Plaks applauds Liu Xie's endeavors to illuminate the aesthetic qualities and potentials of paral-lelism in belletristic writings, Owen, turning attention to Liu Xie's own writing, sees parallelism primarily as a procedure of analysis and textual production, with implicit claims of authority not dissimilar to the discursive procedures of Aristotelian logic. Owen "whimsically" calls such formal procedures for developing a topic the "discourse machine." While this discourse machine usually produces acceptable statements, it not infrequently generates propositions that conflict with received judgments and common sense. To these latter Owen gives the name "Liu Xie," the writer as the locus of opinions that are independent of his discursive procedures. Thus Owen explains the text of *Wenxin diaolong* not as the work of a "thinker" explaining his "ideas," but as a dialectic between the discourse machine and "Liu Xie"; the former produces propositions according to the rules of parallel exposition, and the latter qualifies, corrects, and redirects propositions that conflict with received judgments and common sense. Owen finds this dialectical move of qualification, correction, and redirection on all levels of the work, from individual sentences to whole chapters. One particularly noteworthy example, Owen observes, occurs in chapter 29, "Tongbian" 通變 (Continuity and variation), a binome lying at the core of the cosmological system of the *Book of Changes* and denoting the opposite yet complementary thrusts of continuity and change at work in all cosmological binarisms. *Bian* in this binome refers to change only in the purely positive sense. Once, however, the exposition of "continuity and variation" turns to literary history, it comes into conflict with a powerfully held conviction that literature has been in a steady process of decline since antiquity. Another, negative sense of *bian* as deviation comes to the fore and turns the chapter in an altogether different direction. Through such examples Owen seeks to demonstrate that *Wenxin diaolong* is not a "container" of Liu Xie's thought but rather an animate process by which discursive procedures and ideological assumptions interact to develop a series of concepts and problems.

In her contribution, Wai-yee Li offers another explanation of Liu Xie's yoking of two opposite versions of literary history. She focuses on Liu's conflicting perspectives on *wen* as immanent order and rhetorical excess. Li suggests that when he views literary history from the former perspective in chapter 29, "Tongbian," Liu naturally praises the unadorned works in pre-Han and Han literature for their adherence to the immanent order and censures the works of the post-Han periods for their extravagant rhetoric that undermines order. However, when Liu surveys literary history from the

latter perspective in chapter 45, "Shixu" 時序 (Times and changes), he un-
hesitatingly sets aside his motto of "revering the [unadorned] classics" and
lavishes his praise on the writers of the (Liu) Song period for their rhetorical
exuberance. Whereas the tone of this celebration of Song literature is open
and defiant, Li notes that Liu's criticism of it in chapter 29, "Tongbian," is
relatively restrained. Seen in this light, Liu's condemnation of post-Han
literature may not be wholehearted, or at least equivocal enough to allow its
placement alongside the scheme of the positive *tongbian*. Hence his conflation
of two conflicting versions of literary history. In Li's opinion, Liu's ambivalent
perspective on *wen* constitutes a broad conceptual paradigm within which
one may situate not only Liu's contradictory versions of literary history but
many of the customary shifts of emphasis between opposing poles that can
be found in his thought: between natural order and rhetorical exuberance in
his evaluation of literary styles, between spontaneity and technical mastery
in his discussion of the creative process, and between natural origins and
human endeavor in his account of literature's genesis. In following Wai-yee
Li's argument, we actually traverse all of the three areas explored above.

Looking back on our discussion, we note that our own work seems to
have taken on some of the systematic coherence of *Wenxin diaolong*: "Beginning and end come together perfectly, with an orderly texture and sequence"
[首尾圓和，條貫統序] (*WXDL* 32/43–44). While each chapter in this
volume can stand alone as a self-contained essay, these contributions form a
unified whole. Along with the unity of our critical concerns and efforts,
there is a healthy tension of differences and disagreements. Some of us stress
Liu Xie's intellectual grounding in the Confucian traditions while others are
interested in the Buddhist influence on his modes of discourse and thought.
Some seek to demonstrate the systematic coherence of *Wenxin diaolong*, and
others bring our attention to gaps, discontinuities, and contradictions on
various levels of Liu's discourse. The dynamic interplay of resonance and
dissonance and of agreements and disagreements serves to keep our minds
open to new critical horizons.

To challenge us to forge ahead along this path of investigation, Steven
Owen raised two thought-provoking questions in his concluding remarks
at our 1997 conference. First, he asked why Liu Xie chose to write a grand
composition on the model of the *śāstra*, a rigorously analytical form of discourse developed in Indian Buddhism, as had never been used and would

not be used again in Chinese literary criticism. Second, he wondered what it is about *Wenxin diaolong* that led to its relative obscurity in pre-Qing times and its absolute preeminence in the studies of literary criticism in our day. These questions should have been asked and addressed long ago but have so far evaded the critical attention of Asian scholars of *Wenxin diaolong*. To pursue these important questions and illuminate these "blind spots" in the *Wenxin diaolong* scholarship, we and our readers will have to go forth from this book on a new journey of critical inquiry.

PART ONE

Literary and Critical Traditions

CHAPTER ONE

Liu Xie's Idea of Canonicity

KANG-I SUN CHANG

When we think about the Chinese notion of canonicity, we think first of Liu Xie, because he is particularly conscious of the power of the canon and the normative values it carries for literary and cultural history. There is no doubt that Liu Xie desired to have his *Wenxin diaolong* included in the canon. In fact, his anxieties about canonical inclusion were so great that he once dreamt of "holding ritual vessels, of red lacquer, going off southward with Confucius" (*WXDL* 50/34–35).[1] To join Confucius means joining the grandiose process of cultural transmission, of handing down the essentials of the great classical tradition.

However, the question of Liu Xie's attitude toward the Confucian classics has always generated a great deal of controversy. On the one hand, some scholars have assumed that Liu Xie devoted the first few chapters of his *Wenxin dialong* to the Confucian classics because he wished to use the moral teachings of the ancient sage as a corrective for the prevailing decadence that Liu Xie had witnessed among the literary circles of his time. On the other hand, some modern scholars, knowing Liu Xie's primary devotion to literature, have claimed that Liu Xie was not a true supporter of Confucian classics and that he only paid lip service to Confucian teaching.[2] The problem of both of these positions, I believe, lies in their shared misconception that there is a dichotomy between Confucian classics and literature; this mistaken notion has led many people to overlook Liu Xie's innovative approach to the Confucian tradition and his understanding of its role in the literary canon.

First, Liu Xie ardently believed in the Five Classics as the source of literature. Unlike most Confucian scholars in his time, Liu Xie insisted that the classics were the finest models of literature not just in content but also in style. To a certain extent his interpretation of the Confucian tradition attempts to redefine the literary significance of the classics as largely a matter of style and of the effective rendering of concrete reality. For example, in his chapter on *zongjing* 宗經, he draws on the work of an earlier author, Yang Xiong, who compared the literary style of the Confucian texts to the "carving jade" and noted that the Five Classics are "replete with *wen*" (*WXDL* 3/111–12).[3] Throughout *Wenxin diaolong*, Liu Xie maintains that the most essential aspect of a sage is that he knows how to convey Tao and human emotions creatively through beautiful language. In other words, a sage would need to be first of all a distinguished author.[4] In fact, he believes it is Confucius's literary achievement, as seen in his powerful verbal expressions that are "richer than the mountain and sea," that eventually makes him immortal (*WXDL* 2/98).

Using Confucius as the classic model of literary creativity, Liu Xie begins to evaluate other ancient philosophers and essayists with more than usual attention to their resources of language. He says the works of Mencius and Xunzi are particularly distinguished for their "elegant style": that of Lie Zi for "its vigorous spirit and colorful imagery," that of Zou Zi 鄒子 for "its wild imagination, and powerful expressions," and that of Huainan Zi 淮南子 for the "wide-ranging references and beautiful phrases" (*WXDL* 17/108–9, 112–13ff., 131). Again, Liu Xie claims that because of their distinguished writings and especially "their brilliance in words," these outstanding talents were able to attain literary immortality and forever shine "like the sun and moon" (*WXDL* 17/9–12).

Most interestingly, in his attempt to emphasize the centrality of literary art in ancient civilization, Liu Xie went so far as to canonize the apocrypha, which had been conventionally attributed to some prehistorical, mythical figures. In his chapter on *zhengwei* 正緯, Liu Xie invites the reader to re-evaluate the position of the apocrypha from a literary perspective, rather than dwelling on the old question of "true or false." Liu Xie realizes that such writings are of questionable authorship and that they do not represent the teachings of the sage. Nonetheless, he calls our attention to these texts' remarkable use of the "rich and brilliant language" and concludes that although these apocryphal writings "add nothing to the classics, they are a great help to literary composition" (*WXDL* 4/98–100).[5]

It is important to note that there is something significantly new with Liu Xie's approach to ancient classics and the apocrypha. His recognition of the literary quality of these texts is quite creative. Indeed, few writers before Liu Xie had been as concerned to give a new definition of *wen* (literature). Instead of carrying out the pedagogical work of classical commentaries, as did Ma Rong (79–166), Zheng Xuan (127–200), and some other Confucian scholars (*WXDL* 50/44), Liu Xie produced an original work of literary criticism in which he attempts to present his ideas about *wen*. In this sense, he was perhaps the first critic in ancient China to be so conscious of the importance of a clearly defined literary tradition. As T. S. Eliot pointed out, true classicism requires a "maturity of mind," a "consciousness of history."[6]

In Liu Xie's thought, "history" means a true literary history that traces back to the origins of *wen*. Thus, throughout *Wenxin diaolong*, Liu Xie attempts to show both the cosmological significance of the *wen* (as realized in the natural patterns) and the literary *wen* (as reflected in the writings of the sages). He assumes that *wen* comes from the original Tao, which only the mind (*xin*) of the sage is able to comprehend and bring out its true quality. From the Tao to the sages and then to *wen*, there seems to be a compelling connection. Thus, Liu Xie seems to argue that *wen* is not just literary but also cultural. By extension, a poet or literary critic should be not only a promoter of pure literature but also a bearer of humanism if he is to follow the example of the sage.

Liu Xie's interpretive approach elevates literature to an unprecedented position, a position as high as the authoritative Confucian classics. Liu Xie canonized literature, but he adopted a procedure that was radically different from those of others before him. Instead of using moral principles as a means of evaluating (or elevating) literature, as had many scholars before him, Liu Xie applies literary aesthetics to the Confucius classics, thus making literary quality the prime criterion for judging all canons. Liu Xie's use of new criteria touches on the essential nature of canonicity in the sense that evaluative criteria for canonization are always changing in response to the needs of the present.

This last point becomes especially pertinent when we consider Liu Xie's canonization of *Chuci* (楚 辭), an anthology of poems originated in the Chu region. In sharp contrast to the Confucian *Classic of Poetry*, the *Shijing* 詩經 in which poems are primarily anonymous, *Chuci* is associated with the poet Qu Yuan 屈原 (d. 278 B.C.?). Qu Yuan was China's first poet to become known by name, and his great poem "Lisao" 離騷 stands at the head of the anthology. Qu Yuan was the first writer in the Chinese tradition to deal honestly and revealingly about his feelings in his poetry.[7] To Liu Xie, *Chuci* is the first truly "literary" canon because of the personal and essentially literary character of the poems. But *Chuci* is not important only in the history of literature; for Liu Xie, it is paradigmatic of the essential nature of *wen* itself. This can be demonstrated by the fact that the chapter "Biansao" 辨 騷, which includes comments on "Lisao" and other pieces of *Chuci*, forms part of the beginning portion of *Wenxin diaolong* where Liu Xie lays out his general ideas about *wen*.[8] Thus, this essay focuses on Liu Xie's reading in order to draw out his theory of canonization.

It should be mentioned that *Chuci*'s "canonical" status was somewhat questionable for Liu Xie's contemporaries, especially the orthodox Confucians. In fact, many scholars and historians before Liu Xie had already confronted a series of problems in their continual attempt to come to terms with this important collection of poems; in many ways they violated the classic style, but their literary quality made them worthy of serious recognition. In his chapter entitled "Biansao," Liu Xie sums up the various appraisals of *Chuci* throughout the ages:

昔漢武愛騷，而淮南作傳，以為國風好色而不淫，小雅怨誹而 不亂，若離騷者，可謂兼之…班固以為露才揚己，忿懟沉江； 羿澆二姚，與左氏不合…王逸以為詩人提耳，屈原婉順，離騷 之文，依經立義，馳虯乘鷖，則時乘六龍；崑崙流沙，則禹貢 敷土…及漢宣嗟嘆，以為皆合經傳，揚雄諷味，亦言體同詩 雅…(*WXDL* 5/9–14, 19–22, 29–36, 41–44)

Long ago Emperor Wu of the Han loved reading the *Sao*, and Prince An of Huainan wrote an exegesis of it. To the prince, while the "Guofeng" expresses passion without excess, and the "Xiaoya" social complaint without rebelliousness, the "Lisao" may be said to contain qualities of both. . . . Ban Gu, however, was critical of Qu Yuan, thinking that the poet was showing off his talents and making an exhibition of himself in his works, that he drowned himself in the river out of resentment and bitterness, that the stories of Yi and Jiao and the two Yao beauties are not consistent with the records in the *Zuozhuan*. . . . Later, Wang Yi observed that the ancient poets [in the *Shijing*] preached by overbearing force while Qu Yuan was humble and unassuming, and that the ideas in the "Lisao" are based on the classics: for example, the driving of dragons in fours and the riding of the phoenixes are based on "He then rides on six dragons . . . " [taken from the *Book of Changes*] and references to Kun-dun and Liu sha are based on the "Division of Lan" in the "Yugong" [of the *Book of History*]. . . . Similarly, Emperor Xuan of the Han admired the *Sao* for its consistency with the classics, and Yang Xiong repeatedly chanted and appreciated the *Sao*, claiming that its style is the same as the Odes.[9]

Clearly, these comments are all based on the Confucian moral code—the same kind of criterion adopted by the commentary tradition of the *Shijing*, the *Classic of Poetry*. In their common desire to canonize *Chuci*, commentators such as Emperor Wu and Emperor Xuan of the Han, Wang Yi, and Yang Xiong apparently went out of their way to argue that Qu Yuan upholds the basic Confucian value of moderation and that *Chuci* is essentially no different from the *Shijing*. Conversely, Ban Gu argues that the Chu poet erred because of his violation of the "moderation" requirement, as may be seen in Qu Yuan's eagerness to express sorrow and indignation to excess. To Liu Xie, the judgments of these famous readers of *Chuci* all seem extremely contrived, if not completely unacceptable. Thus, he comments: "[E]ither in commendation or in censure all have been quite arbitrary, and both blame and praise have been exaggerated. Their discriminations are not precise, and their evaluations unreliable."[10]

Liu Xie's formulation of a new critical standard in literary canonicity is thus to a certain extent a reaction against his predecessors' evaluations of *Chuci*. He has offered a new way of reading *Chuci*, based on objective analysis while taking special contexts into consideration. Liu begins by demonstrating the four ways in which the songs' evocation of the sage kings is in accordance with the classics. First, Qu Yuan praises the virtues of the historical sage kings, Yao and Shun, in the style of the "Diangao" in the *Book of History*. Second, Qu Yuan condemns the immoral acts of the wicked kings, Jie and Zhou, as a way of remonstration. Third, Qu Yuan uses the dragons and rainbows as symbols of virtue and sycophants, adopting the devices of allegory and metaphor. Finally, Qu Yuan expresses the sentiments of a loyal but rejected subject. In all these respects, Liu Xie concludes, *Chuci* is in perfect harmony with the spirit of *feng* 風 and *ya* 雅 of the *Shijing*, the great Confucian canon of poetry.

In addition to these so-called similarities between *Chuci* and the classics, Liu Xie also points out four ways in which *Chuci* differs greatly from the classical models. First, it makes frequent references to fantastic rides on clouds and dragons and long mythical journeys in pursuit of goddesses, stories that seem "bizarre and far-fetched." Second, it contains narratives about Gonggong overturning heaven, Houyi shooting down the nine suns, the nine-headed uprooter of trees, and the three-eyed Earth god, tales that are "incredible and strange." Third, Qu Yuan's desire to drown himself by following the examples of Peng Xian 彭咸 and Wu Zixu 伍子胥 makes him seem rather "cowardly and narrow in vision." Finally, the songs include accounts of men and women enjoying music and drinking together night and day, indulging in "licentiousness and excess."

Without a doubt, these "excessive" elements in *Chuci* violate the classical principle of moderation and restraint. There is no question that these violations would have been objectionable to the sensibilities of orthodox Confucians. But, instead of elaborating upon the moral implications of these differences, as most traditional scholars would have done, Liu Xie merely lists them in a rather matter-of-fact way, without comment. He then pursues an interpretation rarely attempted by earlier critics: he evaluates *Chuci*, not in view of the classical standards, but according to the poet's own creative strength. It is clear that on formal grounds, as Liu Xie has taken pains to demonstrate, *Chuci* is a singularly unclassical collection of poems. However, he believes that it is precisely because *Chuci* departs creatively from the classical models that it deserves to be recognized as a new canon.

觀其骨鯁所樹，肌膚所附，雖取鎔經旨，亦自鑄偉辭。

When we examine the bone structure of the [*Chuci*] and the musculature and integument which the structure sustains, we can see that although the work absorbs the basic ideas of the classics, it is also constituted of magnificent literary expressions that are the original creation of the author himself. (*WXDL* 5/96–99)[11]

Although *Chuci* also contains other poets' works, it is clear that Liu Xie is referring mainly to Qu Yuan's originality here. The general assumption is that other poets in Qu Yuan's school merely followed in Qu Yuan's footsteps. For Liu Xie, the key to *Chuci*'s literary strength lies in Qu Yuan's (and his followers') amazing resources of language, which are so extensive that many of the limits of the poetic language seem to have been reached.

故騷經九章，朗麗以哀志；九歌九辯，綺靡以傷情，遠遊天問，瑰詭而慧巧，招魂招隱，豔耀而深華；卜居標放言之致，漁父寄獨往之才。故能氣往轢古，辭來切今，驚采絕豔，難與並能矣。

Thus, the "Lisao" and "Jiu zhang," brilliant and beautiful, communicate frustrated desire; "Jiu Ge" and "Jiu Bian", delicate and lyrical, express grief; the "Yuanyou" and "Tianwen", odd and eccentric, exhibit great artfulness; and the "Zhaohun" and "Dazhao", gorgeous and dazzling, are imbued with profound beauty. The "Buju" reveals the true manner of one in exile; and the "Yufu" manifests the unique talent of a recluse. It is for these reasons that their vigor excels that of the ancients and their language is unmatched in the present day. With their startling grace and unique beauty in diction, they are indeed unsurpassed. (*WXDL* 5/99–113)[12]

Indeed, Liu Xie's respect for Qu Yuan almost reaches the level of hero worship. He celebrates the literary accomplishments of the ancient poet by stylizing and idealizing him. Qu Yuan inspires the reader's admiration by revealing a "distant" world, a world drastically different from that of the "familiar" *Shijing*.

不有屈原，	Without Qu Yuan
豈見離騷。	How could there be "Lisao"?
驚才風逸，	His startling talent as free as wind,
壯采煙高。	His beautiful diction as lofty as mist.[13]
山川無極，	Mountains and streams have no bounds,
情理實勞。	His emotions and ideas are those of a great sufferer.
金相玉式，	His poetry is of gold and jade,
豔溢錙毫。	Even the smallest details overflow with beauty.

(*WXDL* 5/142–50)

It should be mentioned that Liu Xie's canonization of Qu Yuan and *Chuci* has always been regarded as rather problematic by Chinese scholars. This is because for generations many scholars have assumed that the above-mentioned four differences are evidence of Liu Xie's disapproval of *Chuci*. Yet these erudite people can also see that Liu Xie clearly puts Qu Yuan's work in the company of the classics and considers the Chu poet a "great hero" in the field of poetry. They wonder why there is such a jump from serious reservations to enthusiastic praise. Indeed, this question has been left unanswered for years. Only recently, when this issue again became the center of dispute in *Wenxin diaolong* scholarship in China, have scholars found it necessary to reread Liu Xie's original text concerning *Chuci*.

However, these rereadings, perhaps with the single exception of Wang Dajin's 王達津, still focus on the Confucianist/anti-Confucianist dilemma and have not yet reached any real breakthroughs in their interpretations.[14] If we view this from new perspective, what may seem contradictory can indeed become consistent. The key is to put aside Confucianism and mainly consider Liu Xie's attempt to establish the canon in a literary tradition. It is crucial to ask ourselves what makes an author and his works canonical. This question is as important today as it was in Liu Xie's time. Harold Bloom said, "One mark of an originality that can win canonical status for a literary work is a strangeness that we either never altogether assimilate, or that becomes such a given that we are blinded to its idiosyncrasies."[15] In Qu Yuan and *Chuci* as a whole, there is a certain quality of canonical strangeness, what Liu Xie calls "guiyi" 詭異 or "jueguai" 譎怪, which has become such an intertextual phenomenon that one is naturally overwhelmed by it. In fact, Liu Xie was not the first to canonize Qu Yuan. Long before Liu Xie, someone had already called the "Lisao" a *jing* (canonical text), and the Han scholar Wang Yi also tried to canonize Qu Yuan by linking *Chuci* to the *Shijing*.[16] Or, we may say that Qu Yuan canonized himself by producing truly impressive works which constantly demand rereading in different times. Again, Harold Bloom's comment on the Western canon well illuminates the fact that there is a universally shared criterion of canonicity: "One ancient test for the canonical remains fiercely valid: unless it demands rereading, the work does not qualify."[17]

Although Liu Xie was not the first person to bring the Chu poet to the canonical position, he was nonetheless responsible for creating new literary criteria in interpreting *Chuci*. For the first time, *Chuci* is viewed as a purely literary canon, which represents the true voice of a master poet with whom later writers can identify themselves. By focusing on *Chuci*, Liu Xie expanded the canon to include a much wider spectrum of styles and subjects. He also demonstrated how a tradition can exercise great force upon a poet, and how the poet in turn can change and influence that tradition. In other words, in his *Wenxin diaolong* Liu Xie constructed a powerful dynamic between tradition and individual talent.[18] He has shown why a poet might turn to the classics for literary models, and he has also explained why the poet needs to break away from tradition. Without the maintenance of classical values, poetry runs the risk of losing its direction and proper standards. But mere repetitions of the old could kill literary innovation and eventually cause the death of literature itself. Thus, Liu Xie claims that the main purpose of his *Wenxin diaolong* is not only to demonstrate how the literary mind "has its origin in the Tao, takes the sage as its model, finds the main forms in the classics, and consults the ancient apocrypha," but also how it may "show changes in the *Sao*" (*WXDL* 50/99–104).

Certainly we can see many "changes" in *Chuci*, which represents a completely different generic style from the *Shijing*. Judged by classical standards, the *Sao* style, both in diction and syntax, is overly refined and extremely sensory. Nothing of the sort is to be found in the ancient classics. However, in Liu Xie's view it is precisely this quality of "strangeness" that allows Qu Yuan to give expression to the impulsive and dramatic, most often in matters concerned with frustrated desires. Most important, Qu Yuan was writing in a new genre, which always allows for a different set of stylistic manipulations that are conditioned by the special contexts of a new era or place. Indeed, in reading *Wenxin diaolong* we get a strong sense of Liu Xie's generic discrimination in literature, which takes both literary origins and formal innovations into consideration. In the case of *Chuci*, Liu Xie relies precisely on this consciousness of genre for his literary revaluation. He says: "Although [*Chuci*] may be said to be a mere gambler [*botu* 博徒] in the world of *ya* and *Song*, it is a great hero [*yingjie* 英傑] in the realm of *fu*" (*WXDL* 5/94–95).

Clearly Liu Xie witnesses in *Chuci* the awakening of a new spirit and a new kind of rhetorical stylization. He believes that *Chuci* matches and in some way even surpasses its classical models especially in terms of its literary influence. For generations, as Liu Xie explains in his chapter "Biansao,"

Chuci has served as a popular model for emulation. One may say that the most remarkable achievement of *Chuci* lies perhaps in its power to attract all types of readers. As Wendell Harris points out, "canons are made up of readings, not of disembodied texts."[19] In the case of *Chuci*, the work has been canonized largely because of the favorable reception of readers through time. Although readers might differ in background and abilities, they all seem to have the same goal in mind—they wish to learn from the great *Chuci*.

> 故才高者菀其鴻裁，中巧者獵其豔辭，吟諷者銜其山川，童蒙者
> 拾其香草。

> Thus great talents borrow large conceptions from it; the mediocre but skill-ful writers steal sensory diction from it. Those who love to chant poetry sing its descriptions of mountains and streams; young poetic novices re-member the names of fragrant grasses by reading it. (*WXDL* 5/130–33)

The notion of literary influence through reading was by no means a new concept for Liu Xie's contemporaries. But few people in his time would have conceived of such a creative strategy of interpretation, a way of reading that powerfully links the notion of reader's response to that of canonicity in literature. The idea is that a great literary work such as *Chuci* is primarily canonized by readers, whose power is so overwhelming that the work in question simply has to enter the canon. By this Liu Xie seems to suggest that pure literary canons are still different from classical Confucian canons. Whereas the process of classical canonization has a tendency toward closure, literary canonicity is essentially open-ended, always anticipating the demands of new readers and the formation of new genres, new lists of great works, and new ranges of criteria. Of course, compared to the wide distinction between literary canons and biblical canons in the Western tradition the relationship between Chinese literary works and Confucian classics is much more fluid.[20] Both literary canons and Confucian canons have the same basis in *wen*, and despite their minor differences there is always a sense of continuity between the two.

With this in mind, Liu Xie maintains that the Confucian classics should always serve as the anchor around which literature evolves and changes. If we return to Liu Xie's analysis, we see that despite its strange and exotic tendencies, *Chuci*'s stylistic departure from the classics does not violate the integrity of the classical ideal. Liu Xie seems to suggest that the four differences he finds, mainly the bizarre descriptions of long fantastic journeys to mythical realms and the persistent erotic search for the goddesses, are complementary, rather than contrary, to the classical ideal of the *Shijing* world. This is because, as Liu Xie argues, *Chuci* contains both the quality of the strange (奇) and that of genuineness (*zhen* 真); it employs beautiful language (*hua* 華) but does not neglect substantive content (*shi* 實).[21] To the ancients, *zhen* and *shi* are the two principal qualities characterizing the works of the sages; all else are considered rather minor by comparison. By embracing these two important qualities, as it does in the four instances mentioned above, *Chuci* clearly marks the spirit of classical antiquity. On another level, Liu Xie seems to argue that *Chuci*'s real contribution lies in its innovative mixture of "proper" content and exotic style—the two elements in poetry that were hitherto thought to be mutually exclusive.[22] In other words, Qu Yuan has created a new genre of poetry that contains serious substance but is also known for its use of flowery and sensuous language. According to Liu Xie, even this new mixed style typical of the Chu poet is built upon the classical ideal of Confucius, whose elegant style of writing is characterized by "both beautiful language and meaningful substance" (*WXDL* 2/84–85).

Clearly, for Liu Xie the key to all good writing is a proper balance between form and substance. In learning from Qu Yuan, however, one often encounters the problem of turning one's attention from content and toward the fantastic and sensual imagery. Perhaps this is understandable because his text, full of vivid sensory depiction of external scenes, especially of the magical, provides ample opportunity for visualization. But the danger is that the dense texture of meaning might pale before the power of sensory appearance, such that the reader sees only one side of Qu Yuan. Keenly aware of this danger, Liu Xie advises the imitators of Qu Yuan to exercise self-control. He explains that the best way is to "lean on the *Ya* and *Song* [in the *Shijing*] as one would lean on the crossbar of a carriage, and to harness the poetry of Chu as one harnesses a horse" (*WXDL* 5/134–35).[23]

As T. S. Eliot says, "a man may be a great artist, and yet have a bad influence."[24] Much of what Liu Xie says about the problems of literature during the Six Dynasties might be taken as a reference to Qu Yuan's "bad influence"; for example, he laments in the chapter "Tongbian" 通變:

楚漢侈而豔，魏晉淺而綺，宋初訛而新。從質及訛，彌近彌澹。

The Chu and Han works were excessive and sensuous, the Wei and Jin were shallow and decorative. In the Liu-Song dynasty, things first became deceptive and a hunger for novelty appeared. From substantive plainness [*zhi*] on to falseness—the nearer we come to our own times, the more insipid literature becomes. (*WXDL* 29/49–54)[25]

In Liu Xie's view, the main problem with his contemporaries and immediate predecessors is that by modeling themselves after the tradition of *Chuci*, they learned only the rhetorical art of *qi* (strangeness) from Qu Yuan without observing the classical requirement of *zhen* (genuineness). According to Liu Xie, the ancient writers "created their writings for the sake of expressing their emotion" (*wei qing er zao wen* 為情而造文), while later poets "created their emotions for the sake of writing *wen*" (*wei wen er zao qing* 為文而造情).[26] In other words, ancient poets sang of their true emotions, while more recent poets wrote about false emotions that were merely decorated with colorful language. For Liu Xie, *zhen* remains the essential criterion for judging the works of his contemporaries, who had been "attracted by sophistry and artistry" and had an overwhelming "tendency toward pretentiousness."[27] The result was that most writers of the Six Dynasties focused on "pursuing the novel and the strange" at the risk of "losing touch with the proper way" (*WXDL* 30/130).[28] Their hunger for novelty was so great that they devoted all their energies to "the competition of inventing the wondrous [*qi*] by a single line" (*WXDL* 6/145).[29]

Despite Liu Xie's powerful rhetoric and argument, however, one cannot help thinking that perhaps he was also under the influence of a common notion of "historical regression" in literature, the assumption that present works are necessarily inferior to those of the past. In his enthusiasm to elevate the position of the ancient poet Qu Yuan, whose poetry is thought to have maintained a good balance between *qi* and *zhen* and between *hua* and *shi*, Liu Xie completely neglected the literary accomplishments of his contemporaries and immediate predecessors. Likewise, we may question whether Liu Xie's basic idea of the Five Classics as the perfect model of literature might not also come from this one-sided view of "regression," which was shared by many intellectuals and scholars in traditional China.

However, the so-called historical regression in literature is to a certain extent a reflection of the psychological paradox on the part of the creative writer. We can say that writing itself is an experience of continual battles between theory and practice, between the norm and its variations, and between the ideal and the personal. Liu Xie looks up to the classical ideal of moderation and tries to use it as a yardstick for literary criticism. But his own style of writing, no doubt influenced by the "period taste" of the times, betrays a strong preference for overly ornate language, in sharp contrast to the plain style of the classics. Such disparity, or tension, between the ideal and the practical is of course quite common to writers. In fact, in these experiences of paradox and tension an author can somehow comprehend all the varieties of poetic mode and can therefore enable himself to produce works that are at once old and new, grand and small.

On another level we can also see that Liu Xie's inordinate respect for classical models recalls an essential conception of canonicity in all cultures. In his article, "An Idea and Ideal of a Literary Canon," Charles Altieri calls our attention particularly to the importance of establishing normative models through idealizations of classical authors. He says, "Our judges for ideals must be those whom we admire as ideal figures or those whom these ideal figures admired."[30] Indeed, Liu Xie's unqualified admiration for Confucius and Qu Yuan reminds us of Longinus's idealization of figures such as Homer and Plato. Longinus writes:

> Accordingly it is well that we ourselves also, when elaborating anything which requires lofty expression and elevated conception, should shape some idea in our minds as to how perchance Homer would have said this very thing, or how it would have been raised to the sublime by Plato or Demosthenes or by the historian Thucydides. For those personages, presenting themselves to us and inflaming our ardor and as it were illuminating our path, will carry our minds in a mysterious way to the high standards of sublimity which are imaged within us.[31]

Like Longinus, Liu Xie was greatly inspired by the canonical figures in antiquity who, though perhaps existing only in Liu's own imaginative projections, had given him the reason to write the monumental *Wenxin diaolong* and also the interests and high standards he needed to ennoble his project. As he says in his afterword ["Xu zhi" 序 志], he took his "brush in hand" and mixed his ink, beginning to write his discourse on literature only after realizing that "we have gone long and far from the Sage, and the normative forms of literature have divided and scattered" (*WXDL* 50/56–57, 70–71).[32]

In writing his *Wenxin diaolong* Liu Xie was keenly aware of his predecessors and a literary posterity to judge him. He was intensely conscious of his connection with other writers through time; he recognized and accepted his role as a cultural transmitter in carrying on the great tradition. One of his anxious expectations was that his work in literary criticism, though perhaps unappreciated by his contemporaries, would be recognized by future generations. Since he was so deeply enlightened by the ancient sages, he hoped that his book would do the same for literary posterity without "beclouding the vision" of future readers.[33] However, he knew that true understanding in literature does not occur often, perhaps "only once in a thousand years." In his chapter, "The one who knows the tone" ("Zhiyin" 知音), he speaks of Qu Yuan as someone who was misunderstood by his own contemporaries; as Qu Yuan once said, "the crowd does not understand my rare luster" (*WXDL* 48/118).[34] Liu Xie comments that "only one who knows the tone can perceive what is rare" (*WXDL* 48/119).[35] The implication is that Liu Xie, who truly understands the rare qualities and aspirations of the Chu poet, is the *zhiyin* of Qu Yuan. Reading *Wenxin diaolong*, one gets the impression that Qu Yuan is Liu Xie's real model for emulation, because Liu's book is written in an ornamental style similar to that of *Chuci*. It seems as though Liu Xie and Qu Yuan are calling to each other by mutual rereadings through time.

The hope that one's work will reach and address more than one's present-day audience is familiar to modern readers. In his poem "The Living Hand" John Keats speaks of how his own hand comes back into life after his death. Alfred Tennyson, in his elegy "In Memoriam," also writes vividly of pressing the hand of his dead friend as a way of celebrating the eternal connection beyond this life.[36] These examples refer to the writers' wish to reach one another through time in recognition of their literary power. Instead of using the hand as a metaphor for immortality, Liu Xie stresses the power of the heart or mind (*xin*). To Liu Xie, the literary mind is the only kind of mind that endures, because through writing, one writer's mind touches another's and one finds true immortality. In particular, Liu Xie speaks of Confucius as one "whose mind still shines after a thousand years" (*WXDL* 2/100). Liu concludes *Wenxin diaolong* with a personal wish for literary immortality: "If literature truly carries mind, / Then my mind has found a lodging" (*WXDL*

50/170–71).[37] In fact, such a vision of literary immortality has deep roots in the Chinese tradition, and the example of the Grand Historian Sima Qian immediately comes to mind—precisely because of his wish to reach the minds of future readers through writing, Sima Qian decided not to take his own life in the face of a severe personal trauma.

But Liu Xie's rhetoric of immortality has a special implication for us today: It tells us that the canon is primarily a manifestation of a desire to be remembered, to be included in a cultural memory. Liu stresses rereading or revisionism. In evaluating the ancient sages and Qu Yuan, Liu Xie deliberately argues for a new approach by offering a revised set of aesthetic criteria, while recognizing the power of past standards and future judgments.[38] He truly understands the complex workings of the literary mind and a writer's need for otherness, the need to be heard across time through the canon.

The Making of a Critical System: Concepts of Literature in *Wenxin diaolong* and Earlier Texts

ZONG-QI CAI

Liu Xie's *Wenxin diaolong* is often hailed as the most systematic work of literary criticism in premodern China—unrivaled both in its scope and in the richness of its insights. The discussion of Liu Xie's building of a critical system is one of the most fruitful areas of scholarship in the studies of *Wenxin diaolong*.[1] However, there is a conspicuous dearth of studies that approach this systematic work with a view to understanding the inner coherence or systematics of traditional Chinese literary criticism. Here I propose to examine *Wenxin diaolong* with this broad view in mind, focusing on the concept of literature. I will begin by examining three major concepts of literature developed from the earliest times through the Han dynasty, and I will then consider how Liu Xie synthesizes earlier critical concerns and formulates his comprehensive concept of literature.[2] To demonstrate the interrelatedness of these four concepts, I will identify and discuss their common denominator and *differentia*. Through this interrelatedness, I will argue, we can gain insight into the systematics of traditional Chinese literary criticism as a whole.

THE RELIGIOUS CONCEPT OF LITERATURE
IN THE *BOOK OF DOCUMENTS*

The earliest concept of literature is generally traced to the statement "Shi yan zhi" 詩言志 [Poetry expresses the heart's intent], attributed to legendary emperor Shun 舜 during a conversation with his music official Kui 夔. This statement is recorded in "Canon of Yao," chapter 1 of the *Book of Documents*, one of the six Confucian classics.[3] Although few believe that this statement actually came from the mouth of the legendary emperor, most scholars agree that it conveys the earliest known concept of literature.

> 帝曰。夔。命女典樂。教胄子。直而溫。寬而栗。剛而無虐。
> 簡而無傲。詩言志。歌永言。聲依永。律和聲。八音克諧。無
> 相奪倫。神人以和。夔曰。於予擊石拊石。百獸率舞。

I bid you, Kui, the emperor said, to preside over music and educate our sons, [so that they will be] straightforward yet gentle, congenial yet digni-fied, strong but not ruthless, and simple but not arrogant. Poetry expresses the heart's intent [*zhi*];[4] singing prolongs the utterance of that expression. The notes accord with the prolonged utterance, and are harmonized by the pitch tubes. The eight kinds of musical instruments attain to harmony and do not interfere with one another. Spirits and man are thereby brought into harmony.

    Oh! yes, replied Kui, I will strike and tap the stones, and a hundred beasts will follow one another to dance.[5]

Brief as they are, these remarks cover three main phases of an artistic process: its origins in the human heart, its external manifestations, its effects on the outside world. Poetry is seen as the initial part of a performance that aims to harmonize internal and external processes. During this performance, the performers seek to convey *zhi*, or the movement of the heart's intent, through poetic utterances, chanting, singing, music-playing, and dancing.[6] One desired result of this performance is the achievement of inner equilibrium, a mental state deemed conducive to the moral education of young people. By watching or participating in such a performative process, the young people can acquire a balanced, harmonious character. The more important goal of this performance, however, is to bring the affairs of men into accord with the spirits. Through an intensifying series of rhythmical bodily movements that culminates in the dance of a hundred beasts, the performers seek to please the spirits and achieve harmony with them. The dance of a hundred beasts ordered by Kui is generally believed to represent a form of totemic dance that involves the wearing of animal hides.[7] However, scholars such as Kong Yingda 孔穎達 (574–648) prefer to take "the dance of a hundred beasts" as a literal description. According to Kong, this description of animals being moved to dance in unison is intended to manifest the miraculous effects of the harmony between the spirits and men. He writes: "It is easy to move the spirits and men, but not birds and beasts. When even a hundred beasts follow one another to dance, one can see that the harmony between the spirits and men has been achieved."[8]

This dance, totemic or not, marks the center and high point of the entire performance, and it is most instrumental to the achievement of harmony between the spirits and men, even though it is explicitly mentioned by Kui, not Shun himself. In tracing the sequence of the "externalization" of *zhi*, we clearly perceive a crescendo from verbal utterance, to chanting, to music-playing, and to dancing. Marking a steady intensification of rhythmic bodily movements, this crescendo represents a scale of value largely based on the physical force of performance. Poetry, the least dynamic physically, is placed at the bottom. Dance, the most dynamic physically, constitutes the climax of the entire performance.

This emphasis on the velocity of physical movement is generally considered a salient feature of *religious* performances in most primitive traditions. It has been attributed by some to the desire of primitive people to imitate, respond to, or even have "control over the mysterious forces that are everywhere present in nature and life and that are potentially active in the affairs of man."[9] In Chinese high antiquity, dance must have played such a pivotal role in religious performances intended to evoke and tap into divine forces.[10] However, if we look through all the major texts about high antiquity, including the "Canon of Yao," we notice that accounts of ancient religious dance are outweighed, in sheer volume as well as in assigned importance, by accounts of music. Does this indicate that in high antiquity dance was not quite as important as is indicated by the "Shi yan zhi" statement? Or does it merely reflect the emphasis on music in the much later time of the Zhou, when most accounts of high antiquity were recorded in various chronicles and ritual texts?

To many scholars, the latter supposition is more plausible. To affirm the paramount importance of dance in ancient times, these scholars have sought to reinterpret ancient poems, especially the hymns in the *Book of Poetry*, primarily as records or scripts of religious dance. In his "Preface to the 'Nine Songs'" ("Jiuge xu" 九歌序) in the *Songs of Chu* (*Chuci*), Wang Yi 王逸 (ca. 89–158) writes: "In the city of Ying in southern Chu of the old days, which lies in the area between the Ruan and Xiang rivers, the populace believed in ghosts and were fond of sacrificial services. In performing sacrificial services, they invariably sang songs and performed drum dances in order to please various spirits."[11] Later, Ruan Yuan 阮元 (1764–1849), in explaining the meaning of *song* 頌 (hymns), the most ancient section of the *Book of Poetry*, writes that "*song* is none other than appearance [*rong* 容]" and that "various segments of the three *song* or hymns are all appearances of dance, and are therefore called *song*. Like musical plays after the Yuan, its songs, its dance, and its [playing of] musical instruments are all actions and gestures."[12] With this explanation, Ruan apparently intends to stress poetry's complete integration with, or rather subordination to, dance in those religious hymns of high antiquity. Over the centuries, many Chinese scholars have accepted and further developed Ruan Yuan's view on *song*'s relationship to dance. Liang Qichao (1873–1929) contends that "*song* is dance music or drama script."[13] Chow Tse-tsung traces *song* to a particular ritualistic *weng*-dance.[14] Most recently, Ye Shuxian boldly (and perhaps a bit too imaginatively) identifies *song* with various types of primitive dance, including those associated with fertility, burial, and even head-hunting.[15] In discussing the origins of Chinese poetry and drama, Zhang Binglin (1869–1936), Chen Mengjia (1911–66), Wang Guowei (1877–1927), and Liu Shipei (1884–1919) also stress the pivotal importance of religious dance for the birth of these two literary forms.[16]

In short, the "Shi yan zhi" statement in "Canon of Yao" expresses a distinctively religious concept of literature. It is marked by a subordination of poetry to dance, by a recognition of poetry's auxiliary role in evoking the numinous spirits, and by an overriding concern with the harmony between the numinous spirits and man. Although the importance of dance-centered religious performance was to disappear in later times, this statement remains, as Zhu Ziqing says, "the pioneering outline" (*kai shan gangling* 開 山 綱 領) of Chinese literary criticism.[17] It was to wield an enduring influence on the development of traditional Chinese literary criticism for one simple reason. It set forth the core belief of literature as a process—one that arises from inward responses to the outer realms, manifests itself in different artistic forms, and in turn harmonizes various processes in the realms of heaven, earth, and man.[18] This core belief provides the basic conceptual model for understanding literature for millennia to come.

THE HUMANISTIC CONCEPT OF LITERATURE IN THE
ZUO COMMENTARY AND SPEECHES OF THE STATES

In developing the "Shi yan zhi" statement into their own concepts of literature, later critics tend to redefine literature as a process, reprioritize the forms of *zhi*'s outer manifestation, and reassess literature's functions in terms of its impact on different external phenomena. This long, continual process of reappropriating the "Shi yan zhi" statement was already well under way in the Spring and Autumn period or even earlier.

The statement occurs many times in the *Zuo Commentary* (*Zuo zhuan* 左傳) and *Speeches of the States* (*Guo yu* 國 語). In repeating this statement, however, the Eastern Zhou chroniclers seek to express a concept of literature quite different from the religious concept of literature presented in the "Canon of Yao." They begin to redefine poetry as an integral part of a music-centered performance during court ceremonies. Music, incorporating songs and poetry, had already replaced dance as the primary expressive form of *zhi* by this time.[19] As Zhu Ziqing points out, people at this time "express *zhi* with music, express *zhi* with songs, and express *zhi* with poems. . . . To communicate with one another through music and songs is for them a way of life."[20] Considering this dominance of music, it is little wonder that "music-words" (*yueyu* 樂 語) became an all-important subject of education. Of the six types of music-words (*xing* 興, *dao* 道, *feng* 諷, *song* 誦, *yan* 言, *yu* 語) mentioned in *Rituals of Zhou*,[21] Zhu explains, the first and second seem to be the music of multiple instruments, the third and fourth solo music, and the fifth and sixth citations of words of songs in daily life.[22]

The dominance of music and the subordination of poetry are also reflected in the two major types of poetry of the time, *xianshi* 獻 詩 (or *caishi* 采 詩) and *fushi* 賦 詩. Both are sung aloud to music on courtly occasions.[23] The first type consists of poems originally composed and sung by ordinary people and later collected and set to music by musicians for submission to the ruler. The second type includes poems, mostly those of the *Book of Poetry*, selected by feudal lords or officials to be presented with music on diplomatic occasions for the purpose of expressing their own *zhi* and the *zhi* of their states.[24]

The primary goal of the music-centered courtly performances in the *Zuo Commentary* and *Speeches of the States* is to harmonize sociopolitical or natural processes, not to please the numinous spirits, as in "Canon of Yao." In this regard, three specific functions are discussed in these two texts. The first function is to enable the ruler to gauge popular sentiment and the state of governance.[25] In the *Zuo Commentary*, Duke Xiang 29th year (512 B.C.), Ji Zha 季 札 (fl. 512 B.C.) comments on the musical performance of all the major groups of poems in the *Book of Poetry*, correlating their aesthetic qualities with the conditions of governance and popular sentiment in the place and time of their origins. For him, the character of excess in music and poetry, as shown in the airs of Zheng, signifies moral decay and sociopolitical disorder. Conversely, the character of the mean betokens the moral virtues of the people and proper governance by the rulers. It manifests itself in various virtues not taken to excess: "grave but not despondent," "pensive but not timid," "straightforward but not overbearing," and so on. Ji Zha considers the hymns of Zhou to embody the ideal of abiding by the mean (*zhizhong* 制 中) and cites as many as thirteen different virtues kept to the mean in these hymns. In addition to commenting on the poems, he observes the general correlation between music ("five sounds") and ethico-sociopolitical realities ("eight winds").[26]

The second function is to help shape the moral character of the members of the ruling class. If the "Canon of Yao" passage has touched upon the edifying effect of music and poetry, Yan Zi 晏 子 (?–500 B.C.)[27] offers an explanation of music's power to transform man in the *Zuo Commentary*, Duke Xiang 22nd year (519 B.C.). Like Ji Zha, he pursues a correlative argument. He argues that elements of music arise from the myriad categories of things and naturally become their symbolic correlates. "There are the breath," says he, "the two types of dance, the three subjects, the four objects, the five notes, the six pitch tubes, the seven sounds, the eight winds, and the nine songs—together these nine things form [the substance for music]" [一氣, 二體, 三類, 四物, 五聲, 六律, 七音, 八風, 九歌, 以相成也].[28] So intricately bound up with the inherent order of things, he contends, music can bring into play the multifarious opposites and harmonize them in the course of performance. Moreover, such a harmonious music performance can induce a corresponding mental equilibrium in the mind of the listener and render him virtuous and harmonious. "There are the qualities of clear and turbid," he continues, "big and small, long and short, fast and unhurried, hard and soft, plaintive and joyful, slow and speedy, high and low, outgoing and incoming, comprehensive and scattered—all these qualities complement one another. A gentleman listens to such music, and thereby attains the peace of mind. When he has peace of mind, his virtues become harmonious" [清濁大小, 短長疾徐, 哀樂剛柔, 遲速高下, 出入周疏, 以相濟也. 君子聽之, 以平其心, 心平德和].[29]

The third and the most important function is to bring about harmony between nature and man. For the people of the Spring and Autumn period, the harmonization of human affairs is often merely part of broader endeavors to achieve the all-important harmony with natural processes and forces that decisively impact the survival and well-being of man. In "Speeches of Zhou," the entertainer Zhoujiu 州鳩 in 522 B.C. gives an excellent exposition of how music, songs, and poetry bring about such harmony. In an attempt to dissuade him from violating the rules for making musical instruments, he explains to King Jing 景王 (r. 544–520 B.C.) the inherent relationship between music and natural processes. Zhoujiu, too, pursues a correlative argument. He begins by reaffirming the relationship between governance and music through their common principles of harmony and peacefulness. "Governance manifests itself in music. Music arises from harmony. Harmony arises from peaceful accord. Pitches are to harmonize music. Musical scales are to bring pitches in accord" [夫政象樂, 樂從和, 和從平。 聲以和樂, 律以平聲].[30] To demonstrate the correlation between music and natural processes, he first shows how harmonious music serves to regulate the "eight winds."[31] Thanks to such music, he says, "the cosmic breath [qi] hence does not impede the yin, nor dispel the yang. Yin and yang follow each other in order, wind and rain arrive with the season, living things grow well and flourish, people are benefited and brought into harmony. All things are in place and music is brought to completion. Neither those above nor those below are worn out. This is called the rectification of music" [於是乎氣無 滯陰。亦無散陽。陰陽序次。風雨時至。嘉生繁祉。人民龢 利。物備而樂成。上下不罷。故曰樂正。].[32] Moreover, Zhoujiu believes that through harmonious music man can achieve harmony with natural processes and numinous spirits. "Therefore," he concludes, "we chant with the virtue of the mean, and we sing with the notes of the mean. The virtue and notes are not violated in order to bring harmony between the spirits and man. Thus the spirits are put at ease and the commoners are made to listen" [於是乎道之以中德。詠之以中音。德音不愆。以 合神人。神是以寧。民是以聽。].[33]

In sum, the reformulation of the "Shi yan zhi" statement in the *Zuo Commentary* and *Speeches of the States* gives birth to a new, humanistic concept of literature. In elevating the status of music and in rethinking the functions of music and poetry, the speakers in these two texts consistently display an overriding concern with sociopolitical and natural processes that immediately affect the conditions of human existence. These humanistic concerns form a striking contrast to the overriding concern with the numinous spirits in earlier times. It is true that the people of the Spring and Autumn period continue to discuss harmony between the spirits and men. But as shown in Zhoujiu's remarks on music, this harmony is not the direct result of the magical invocation of divinities through powerful rhythmical dance, chanting, and singing. Rather, it is the indirect consequence arising from the harmonization of natural and sociopolitical processes through rituals and music. In view of this ascendancy of humanistic concerns over religious ones, it seems appropriate to use the term "humanistic" to characterize the new concept of literature expressed in the *Zuo Commentary* and *Speeches of the States*.

THE DIDACTIC CONCEPT OF LITERATURE
IN THE "GREAT PREFACE"

The "Shi yan zhi" statement goes through yet another significant reformulation in Han times, developing into a full-fledged didactic concept of literature in the "[Great] Preface to the Mao Text of the *Book of Poetry*" (*Mao Shi xu* 毛 詩序).[34] The "Great Preface" is, as Stephen Owen says, "the most authoritative statement on the nature and function of poetry in traditional China."[35] What distinguishes it from earlier discussions of poetry is its elevation of poetic verbalization over music and songs and its reassessment of poetry's functions in purely didactic terms.

To begin with, let us see how poetry is redefined in relation to music and songs in the "Great Preface." Elaborating on the "Shi yan zhi" statement, the author goes to great lengths to stress the central importance of *yan* 言, or words. "Poetry is where the heart's intent goes," he writes. "What is still in the heart is 'intent'; what is expressed in words is 'poetry.' Emotions are stirred inside and manifest themselves in words" [詩者，志之所之也，在心為志，發言為詩]. He apparently believes that what is in the heart, be it called *zhi* or *qing*, manifests itself primarily in poetic verbalization. To support his elevation of words, he simply cites a passage from the "Record of Music" (*Yue ji* 樂記): "Emotions move within and take form in words. If words cannot express them adequately, we sigh them out. If sighing is not adequate, we sing them out. If singing is not adequate, we unconsciously move our hands to gesticulate, and stamp our feet to dance" [情動於中而形於言，言之不足故嗟嘆之，嗟嘆之不足故永歌之，永歌之不足，不知手之舞之，足之蹈之也].[36] In the "Record of Music" this passage occurs at the end and strikes us as an unimportant afterthought, but here it constitutes the cornerstone of his argument for the elevation of poetic verbalization over music and dance.[37]

A comparison of this passage with the "Canon of Yao" and "Speeches of Zhou" passages will show how it effectually reverses the conventional auxiliary role assigned to poetry. In the "Canon of Yao" passage, poetry is placed at the head of a continuum of other ritualistic activities: chanting, singing, and dancing. This placement gives the illusion that poetry initiates those activities and thus is of central importance. However, upon close examination, it is clear that poetry only prepares the reader for what is to come. Verbal utterances are merely the raw material to be transformed successively by chanting, singing, music-playing, and dancing. Thus, the succession of these activities indicates a process of the intensification of physical movements—from the normal exhalation in speaking to the prolonged exhalation in chanting and singing to the movement of the whole body in dancing.

This process does seem to imply an ascending scale of importance in proportion to the intensification of physiological movement. Poetry—or poetic verbalization—lies at the very bottom of this scale as it entails the least physiological movement and is farthest away from the point of culmination.

The "Speeches of Zhou" passage deals primarily with music and leaves out the discussion of dance. Nevertheless, it adopts a similar scale of value that sets music performance over verbalization and considers poetry-chanting to be merely a component part of music. In the "Great Preface," poetry is also placed before chanting, singing, and dancing. However, this same sequence of activities indicates a descending scale of importance. Now, at the center of these activities is poetry, the least physiologically prominent. All other activities are presented as complements to poetic verbalization. Chanting, singing, and dancing become necessary in a graduated manner only when poetic verbalization cannot adequately express emotions.[38] This marginalization of music and dance is evident throughout the "Great Preface." Dance is mentioned only in the passage cited above. Nor is music discussed for its own sake. Indeed, even when the author cites another passage from the "Record of Music" about *sheng* 聲 (sounds) and *yin* 音 (tones), he seems to refer exclusively to the emotive tonality of poetic verbalization. "Emotions are discharged in sounds. As those sounds assume a pattern, they are called 'tones.' The tones of a well-governed time are peaceful and joyful; the governance is marked by harmony. The tones of a time of chaos are woeful and filled with anger; the governance is deviant. The tones of a fallen state are sorrowful and contemplative; the people are in dire straits" [情發於聲,聲成文謂之音.治世之音安以樂,其政和.亂世之音怨以怒,其政乖.亡國之音哀以思,其民困].[39] In the "Record of Music," these remarks are immediately followed by a lengthy discussion of music's relationship to the ethico-socio-political order. By contrast, here they lead to praise of the transforming power of poetry in complete disassociation with music. It is quite clear that the words *sounds* and *tones* are now used in reference to the tonality of poetic verbalization rather than actual sounds and notes of music. For the first time in Chinese criticism, the author has established the importance of poetic verbalization over dance, music, and songs.[40]

In my opinion, this redefinition of literature as a verbalization-centered form of social intercourse arises in response to two profound changes taking place during the Warring States period and Han times: the gradual divorce of poetry from music, and the gradual shift in man's overriding focus from natural processes to human relationships. Toward the end of the Spring and Autumn period, these two changes had already gotten under way. For instance, in Confucius's discussion of poetry (*shi*), or rather the *Book of Poetry*, in *Analects*, we can find plenty of evidence of these two changes. In *Analects*, Confucius makes a total of nineteen references to the *Book of Poetry*.[41] In all but two of these references, he discusses the *Book of Poetry* separately from music. Not only does he recognize the independence of poetry from music and examine it in its own right, but he also puts it on a par with music. He declares, "Let a man be inspired by the *Poetry*, set straight by the rituals, and perfected by music."[42] The shift of his overriding concern to human relationships is no less prominent. In discussing the *Book of Poetry*, he completely leaves out any consideration of its impact on natural forces, focusing exclusively on its ethical, social, and political functions. For example, in his summary statement, he explains how *The Book of Poetry* can help regulate human relationships in the spirit of the mean and provide the norm of human interaction among equals, between fathers and sons, and between the ruler and his subjects. He says, "How come you, little ones, do not study the *Poetry*? The *Poetry* may help to inspire, to observe, to keep company and to express grievances. It may be used in the service of one's father at home and in the service of one's lord abroad" [小子何莫學夫詩? 詩可以興, 可以觀, 可以群, 可以怨, 邇之事父, 遠之事君].[43]

In later texts written during the Warring States period, we can observe the continuation of these two changes. In *Mencius* (*Meng Zi* 孟子) and *Strategies of the Warring States* (*Zhanguo ce* 戰國策), for instance, discussions of the *Book of Poetry* no longer occur in the immediate context of the music performance of the *Book of Poetry*, nor do they entail any serious consideration of music.[44] In contrast to the foregrounding of the relationship between nature and man in the *Zuo Commentary* and "Speeches of Zhou," in these two texts the overriding concern is with human relationships in the tradition of *Analects*. By the time of the first century A.D. when the "Great Preface" was written, poetry had become independent of music and the Confucian doctrine had been established as the state ideology. Under such circumstances, it is only too natural that the author of the "Great Preface" would redefine poetry as the verbalization-centered form of social intercourse and stress its ethical, social, and political functions.

The "Great Preface" offers a comprehensive examination of four different harmonizing functions of poetry. The first function is to harmonize an individual's inner and outer lives. By transforming emotions into words, the author contends that one can restore inward equilibrium and maintain outward moral decorum. In this regard, he writes that poetry "arises from emotion and ends in conformity to rituals" [發乎情，止乎禮儀].[45]

The second function is to foster harmony among the people of a given state. According to the author, one's emotional utterances resonate with those of others and therefore register the "tones of a well-governed time" or the "tones of a time of chaos" indicative of the conditions of state governance. Thanks to this moral empathy, the words of a person denote the air (*feng*) of an entire state.

The third function is to bring about harmony between the subjects and the ruler. In the author's opinion, the airs are a particularly desirable mode of communication with the rulers and his subjects. This is because they are "concerned mainly with patterning [of expressions] and allow for subtle remonstrance" [主文而譎諫].[46] Through highly suggestive airs, those who "express [their grievances] are not held culpable, and those who hear it find enough to warn themselves" [言之者無罪，聞之者足以戒].[47] This subtle form of communication enhances harmony between those above and those below without impairing the social hierarchy that separates them.

The fourth function of poetry is to exert moral influence over the populace. By using the airs as means of moral instruction, the ruler can show his people examples of good and bad government, moral and immoral conduct. Through these four functions, the author believes, poetry can not only rectify ethico-socio-political processes, but it can also bring about harmony between man and the numinous spirits. For this reason, he declares, "to move heaven and earth, and to win the sympathy of ghost and spirits, nothing is nearly comparable to poetry" [動天地，感鬼神，莫近於詩].[48]

The author of the "Great Preface" also touches upon the origin of poetry. He believes that poetic verbalizations arise in response to social and political realities and embody the pattern of orderliness or chaos of the outer world. Based on this belief, he identifies the four known genres in the *Book of Poetry*—airs (*feng* 風), great odes (*daya* 大雅), lesser odes (*xiaoya* 小雅), and hymns (*song* 頌)—with responses to different ethico-socio-political realities. According to him, an air is born of a single person's responses to the conditions of his own state. "Therefore, that which concerns the affairs of one state and is tied to the fundamental existence of one single person is called an air" [是 以一國之事，繫一人之本，謂之風].[49] An ode "recounts the events of the world and observes the customs within the four corners" [言天下之 事，形四方之風].[50] A hymn is the product of responses to grand virtues and accomplishments of a ruler, and it serves to "report his accomplishments to the divinities" [以其成功告於神明者也].[51] In addition to these four genres, he mentions "changed airs" (*bianfeng* 變風) and "changed odes" (*bianya* 變雅) as responses to the times of sociopolitical chaos and moral decay.

By elevating poetry over music, by realigning it with ethico-socio-political processes, and by reconceptualizing its functions in terms of the harmonization of those processes, the author has transformed the "Shi yan zhi" statement into a full-fledged didactic concept of literature. In my view, the rise of this didactic concept has as much to do with the changing contexts of discussing the *Book of Poetry* as with the broad social and political changes noted above. In the *Zuo Commentary* and "Speeches of Zhou," remarks on the *Book of Poetry* are made mostly by the dukes and their close attendants when commenting on ongoing courtly ceremonies. In such contexts, the speaker and the listener are in the presence of each other, and neither assumes a detached moralizing position. Thus, their remarks on poetry often strike us as descriptive rather than prescriptive. The speakers seek to understand the impact of music and poetry on sociopolitical and natural processes by means of correlative reasoning. By contrast, the author of the "Great Preface" casts himself in the role of an invisible implied speaker, addressing a broad audience ranging from commoners to the monarch. The inherent detachment of a writer enables him to go beyond the confines of ongoing courtly ceremonies and to reconceive the *Book of Poetry* as the verbalization-centered form of social intercourse as it is used in his own time. Moreover, this detachment allows him to stand on the high ground of Confucian morality and prescribe how the *Book of Poetry* should be used by ruler and subjects alike. As this didacticism permeates and unifies his entire argument, it seems fitting to characterize his concept of literature as a didactic one.

THE COMPREHENSIVE CONCEPT OF LITERATURE
IN *WENXIN DIAOLONG*

If the author of the "Great Preface" has developed the "Shi yan zhi" statement into a full-fledged didactic concept of literature, Liu Xie transforms this "pioneering outline" of Chinese literary criticism into a comprehensive concept of literature. His magnum opus, *Wenxin diaolong*, is ordinarily not placed in the lineage of the "Shi yan zhi" traditions as we know them today.[52] This is probably because of its lack of strong didacticism for which the "Shi yan zhi" traditions became known after the Han. Here, in linking *Wenxin diaolong* with the "Shi yan zhi" traditions, I mean not to associate it with the latter's didacticism, but rather to show how Liu Xie inherited from the latter the basic model of understanding literature as a harmonizing process. As we shall see presently, through this model Liu reconceptualizes all the major aspects of literature: its nature, its origins, its formation in the mind and language, and its functions.

In redefining literature as a process, Liu Xie takes the elevation of poetry over music as his point of departure, as does the author of the "Great Preface." While the latter surreptitiously reverses the dominance of music over poetry, Liu openly places poetry over music and expounds on the rationale of this elevation of poetry in explicit terms. "The body of music is sounds, and blind music masters must tune their instruments. The mind of music is poetry, and gentlemen should rectify their literary expressions. . . . Therefore we know that Ji Zha observed the language of songs, not merely listened to their sounds" [樂體在聲，瞽師務調其器：樂心在詩，君子宜正其文⋯故知季札觀辭，不直聽聲而已] (*WXDL* 7/99–101, 107–8).[53] Here Liu establishes the importance of poetry over music in a rather clever way. He accepts the traditional praise of music but adds that the miraculous power of music comes from its words rather than its sounds. This seemingly insignificant qualification amounts to nothing less than a negation of the traditional view of music. As sounds are traditionally considered the essence of music, his comparison of sounds to the body means a relegation of music itself to a secondary status. Moreover, by calling poetry the mind of music, he tactfully transfers the traditional praise of music to poetry. To underscore this elevation of poetry over music, he compares literary-minded gentlemen (*junzi* 君子) favorably with illiterate blind musicians working with instruments. In addition, he reinterprets the story of Ji Zha's observation of Zhou music, suggesting that Ji Zha cared more about the words than sounds of songs and music.

Unlike the author of the "Great Preface," however, Liu Xie does not consider poetry to be superior to music on the grounds of the efficacy of verbalization for rectifying intra- and interclass relationships. In his opinion, poetry—or, broadly speaking, literature—is characterized primarily by "patterns" (*wen* 文) of written words and secondarily by "tones" (*yin* 音) of verbalization. What makes literature superior to music is the visual impact of its written words, not the auditory effects of its verbalization, which are not dissimilar to those of music. In chapter 48, "Zhi yin" 知音 (An understanding critic), Liu seeks to establish the paramount importance of written words by comparing them favorably with sounds of music. "In reading a work of literature," he writes, "one opens a text and penetrates the feelings [of the author]. . . . Although we cannot see the faces of writers of a remote age, we may look into their works and immediately see their minds" [觀文者披文以入情. . . .世遠莫見其面，覘文輒見其心] (*WXDL* 48/97, 100–101). To Liu, written words, not fleeting sounds of verbalization or music, enable us to see into the minds of ancient writers. Moreover, writing has the power of making manifest what lies hidden in nature. "If one's mind is set on the mountains and rivers," he continues, "a zither can express his feelings. What is more, when the tip of a writing brush brings things into form, where [can] the basic principles remain hidden?" [夫志在山水，琴表其情，況形之筆端，理將焉匿] (*WXDL* 48/104–7).[54] In the dynamic processes of writing and reading, Liu believes, one can penetrate basic principles through a creative patterning of written words.

In light of this conception of literature as primarily the "patterning" of written words, Liu Xie reconceptualizes the origins of literature by way of a method unknown to earlier critics. Whereas earlier critics traced the origins of literature to *zhi* or the movement of the heart's intent in response to specific external processes, Liu Xie attributes the birth of literature to the natural manifestation of the Tao (the ultimate process), as well as to conscious human endeavors to transform an inward experience into a "pattern" of written words. Liu sets forth this view of the dual origins of literature in the opening paragraph of the first chapter of *Wenxin diaolong*, "*Yuan dao*" 原道 (The Tao as the source).

文之為德也大矣，與天地並生者何哉？夫玄黃色雜，方圓體
分，日月疊壁，以垂麗天之象；山川煥綺，以鋪理地之形：
此蓋道之文也。仰觀吐曜，俯察含章，高卑定位，故兩儀既
生矣。惟人參之，性靈所鍾，是謂三才；為五行之秀，實天
地之心。心生而言立，言立而文明，自然之道也。

The pattern [*wen*] as a power is very great. It is born together with heaven
and earth, and why is it so? With the black [of heaven] and the yellow [of
the earth], the myriad colors are compounded. With the squareness [of
earth] and the roundness [of heaven], all forms are distinguished. The sun
and the moon overlap each other like two jade disks, manifesting to those
below the magnificent image of heaven. Rivers and mountains are brilliantly adorned to display the orderly configurations of the earth. These
are the pattern of the Tao. As man looked up to see the radiance above
and looked down to observe the inner loveliness below, the positions of
high and low were determined and the two primary forms [heaven and
earth] came into being. Only human beings, endowed with intelligence,
can integrate with them. Together they are called the Triad. Human beings are the efflorescence of the Five Agents and are, in fact, the mind of
heaven and earth. When mind came into being, language was formed.
When language was formed, the pattern became manifest. This is the Tao,
the natural course of things. (*WXDL* 1/1–21)

If the origins of literature are only marginally discussed in earlier texts, Liu
makes this issue the sole focus of the first three chapters of *Wenxin diaolong*.
He argues that literature shares with heaven and earth the same origin as the
Tao, the ultimate process, and hence is an autonomous process that runs
parallel to heaven and earth. This argument is based on his identification of
literature's graphic form with the spatial configurations of heaven and earth
as analogous patterns (*wen*) of the Tao. He believes that heaven, earth, and
humans all manifest the Tao through spatial forms proper to themselves—
for heaven, the sun, moon, and other celestial images; for earth, mountains,
rivers, and other topographical shapes; and for humans, the graphic pattern
of words. Of these three analogous forms, he holds that the last is more
efficacious than the other two. It yields the most subtle secrets of the Tao
because it is the brainchild of humans who are the embodiment of the Five
Agents and the mind of heaven and earth.

Liu Xie is apparently aware that these claims are potentially contradictory. To say that the pattern of literature is identical with that of heaven or earth is to suggest it is unconsciously formed. To say that it is more refined because of human participation is to presume that it is *not* unconsciously formed. To resolve this contradiction, Liu Xie ingeniously uses the traditional myths about the origins of written characters. By recounting these myths, Liu Xie points to the dual sources of writing: the markings on the "Yellow River Diagram" and the "Luo River Writing" presented to humans by the tortoise and dragons, and the trigrams and hexagrams invented and elucidated by the ancient sages. The first source signifies the ultimate non-human origin of literature in the supreme ultimate. "The origins of human pattern began in the supreme ultimate. So it goes that the 'Yellow River Diagram' gave birth to the eight trigrams, and that the 'Luo River Writing' contained the nine divisions. In addition, there were the fruit of jade tablets inscribed with gold, and the flower of green strips with red words. For all these was anyone responsible? No. They also came from the principle of the spirit" [人文之元，肇自太極...若乃河圖孕乎八卦，洛書韞乎九疇，玉版金鏤之實，丹文綠牒之華，誰其尸之，亦神理而已] (*WXDL* 1/42–43, 52–57). By claiming that the "Yellow River Diagram" and the "Luo River Writing" gave birth to the eight trigrams and the nine divisions, Liu Xie makes it clear that the latter are a human elucidation of the former and that they should be regarded as a natural manifestation of the Tao analogous to the outer configurations of heaven and earth. The second source reveals the penultimate human origin of writing in the cosmological diagram drawn by the ancient sages.

幽贊神明，易象惟先.庖犧畫其始，仲尼翼其終。而乾坤兩位，獨制文言，言之文也，天地之心哉。

The Images of the *Book of Changes* were first to illuminate the numinous spirits that lie obscurely hidden. Fu Xi began [the *Book of Changes*] by marking [its eight trigrams] and Confucius completed it by adding the Wings [commentaries]. For the two trigrams of Qian and Kun, Confucius composed the "Patterned Words." The pattern of words is indeed the "mind of heaven and earth." (*WXDL* 1/44–51)

In Liu's opinion, the Images of the *Book of Changes* are superior to the "Yellow

River Diagram" because they do far more than provide a rough sketch of cosmic forces. They make known the innermost secrets of the Tao, establish the warp and woof of the universe, and perfect the laws of the human world (*WXDL* 1/96–109). On this basis, Liu Xie sees fit to claim the superiority of this "human pattern" to all naturally formed patterns in heaven and earth (*WXDL* 1/14–41).

By explaining the ultimate and penultimate origins of literature in this light, Liu Xie forestalls the potential contradiction arising from his view that the "human pattern" of writing is at once analogous with and superior to the patterns of heaven and earth. In exploring the origins of writing, Liu Xie seeks to exhibit the inherent links between the Tao and the human world, between the trigrams and hexagrams and the writings of subsequent ages. Because the ancient sages were endowed with plentiful intelligence, they could comprehend and give the subtlest revelation of the workings of the Tao in their writings. By the same token, the writings of subsequent ages could continue to manifest the Tao largely because they were derived from the luminous writings of the ancient sages. To set forth the crucial role of the sages' writings in the manifestation and transmission of the Tao, Liu writes:

故知道沿聖以垂文，聖因文而明道，旁通而無滯，日用而不匱。易曰：鼓天下之動者存乎辭。辭之所以能鼓天下者，乃道之文也。

Therefore we know that the Tao passed down its pattern [*wen*] through the sages and that the sages illuminated the Tao through their own writings [*wen*]. It penetrates everywhere unimpeded, and is applied day after day without being exhausted. The *Book of Changes* says, "That which can make the world move lies in language." That by which language can make the world move is the pattern [*wen*] of the Tao. (*WXDL* 1/110–17)

Liu Xie devotes much of the first chapter, as well as the second chapter, "Zhengsheng" 徵聖 (Applying the sages' [writings] as the touchstone) and the entirety of the third chapter, "Zongjing" 宗經 (Adopting the classics as the models) to the project of tracing the transmission of the Tao from the *Book of Changes* down to different literary genres of his own time. First, he establishes a sequence among the Confucian classics, extending from the

Book of Changes, to the *Book of Documents*, to the *Book of Poetry*, to the *Book of Rites*, and to the *Spring and Autumn Annals* (*WXDL* 1/74–95; 3/12–25). Then, he sets forth the distinctive modes of observation and expression (*WXDL* 2/42–59; 2/64–67; 3/35–74) and the resulting stylistic characteristics (*WXDL* 3/103–10) in these five classics. On the basis of its stylistic characteristics, he takes each of the five classics to be the source of given genres (*WXDL* 3/85–102). In this manner, he establishes an elaborate genealogy of literary genres, beginning with the five classics and ending with the multitude of belletristic and nonbelletristic genres of his own time.

Liu Xie's view on literary creation is no less radically different from those of Han and pre-Han critics.[55] If literature is to them part of a public, expressive, and performative process centered on dance, music, or verbalization, it means to Liu Xie a process of composing a written, belletristic work, a process that is largely private, contemplative, and creative. In discussing the expressive and performative processes, earlier critics tended to focus on the interaction with the processes of a given realm—the numinous, the natural, or the human. When Liu Xie looks into the contemplative-creative process, however, he carefully analyzes the interaction with external processes on *multiple* levels at different compositional stages.

Liu Xie devotes chapter 26, "Shensi" 神思 (Spirit and thought), and chapter 46, "Wuse" 物色 (The colors of nature), exclusively to the examination of the entire creative process. The opening passage of chapter 46 describes the arousal of emotion at the initial stage of literary composition. "Springs and autumns revolve around in succession. The yin force brings bleakness, and the yang force brightness. As the colors of nature are stirred into movement, the mind, too, is swayed. . . . When the colors of nature greet him, how can man remain unmoved" [春秋代序，陰陽慘舒，物色之動，心亦搖焉 . . . 物色相召，人誰獲安] (*WXDL* 46/1–4; 11–12). Liu contends that the writer responds to the ongoing processes of nature on a similar simple and psychological level. The cycle of seasons, along with the changing appearances of many things, engenders delight, pensiveness, melancholy, or sorrow in the heart of the writer. These responses awaken the writer's desire to write about what is inside his heart. "Thus when the poets feel moved by physical things," writes Liu Xie, "their categorical associations are endless. They linger around in the sphere of the myriad images, and meditate and chant gently in the domain of what they have seen and heard" [是

以詩人感物，聯類無窮，流連萬象之際，沈吟視聽之區] (*WXDL* 46/29–32).

In chapter 26, "Shensi," Liu Xie begins by examining how such a categorical association leads to the flight of the poet's spirit at the next stage. Now the writer is no longer responding to concrete physical things. Instead he is quietly contemplative and his innermost spirit wanders off to meet things or objects (*wu*) beyond the restrictions of time and space.

> 古人云：形在江海之上，心存魏闕之下。神思之謂也。文之思也，其神遠矣！故寂然凝慮，思接千載；悄焉動容，視通萬里。

> An ancient said, 'While [a person's] body is on the rivers and lakes, his mind remains at the foot of the high palace tower.' This is what is called 'spirit and thought.' In the thought process of literature, the spirit goes afar. As he silently reaches the state of mental concentration, his thought may trace back one thousand years. As he shows the slightest movement in his countenance, his vision may go through ten thousand *li*. (*WXDL* 26/1–10)

This outbound flight is often taken as the sole meaning of "spirit and thought." If we examine what immediately follows, however, we see that this flight is only the initial part of a reciprocal process. "In the midst of his chanting and singing, the sounds of pearls and jade issue forth. Right before his brows and lashes, the spectacle of windblown clouds spreads out. All this is made possible by the principle of thought" [吟詠之間，吐納珠玉之聲；眉睫之前，卷舒風雲之色：其思理之致乎] (*WXDL* 26/11–15). Having followed the flight across "ten thousand *li*" in the previous passage, here we trace the inbound flight, if you will, of faraway objects (*wu*) toward one's ear and eye; these opposing movements are complementary in the process of *shensi*. Given this, we should take the next line, "when the principle of thought is at its most miraculous, the spirit wanders with external things" [故思理為妙，神與物遊] (*WXDL* 26/16–17), to mean that one's spirit goes out into the world to mingle with external things and eventually returns with them to one's own mind. Liu's conception of *shensi* as a "double journey" is reaffirmed when he notes that the outbound flight is controlled by the psychological-moral process (*zhi*) and the physiological-moral process (*qi*).

"The spirit dwells in the bosom, intent [*zhi*] and vital breath [*qi*] control the pivot of its outlet" [神居胸臆，而志氣統其關鍵] (*WXDL* 26/18–19). Then he identifies the perceptual processes (aural and visual) and the intellectual processes (the conscious use of language) as crucial to mediating the influx of things from afar. "External things come in through the ear and the eye, with language controlling the hinge and trigger [for their influx]" [物沿耳目，而辭令管其樞機] (*WXDL* 26/20–21). To Liu, the success of *shensi* depends on a well-coordinated operation of all these processes impacting the double journey. "When the hinge and trigger allow passage, no external things can have hidden appearance. When the pivot of its outlet is closed, the spirit is impeded" [樞機方通，則物無隱貌；關鍵將塞，則神有遯心] (*WXDL* 26/22–25). The final result of *shensi*, Liu believes, is a mutual transformation of the inner (*shen* 神, *qing* 情) and the outer (*wu* 物, *xiang* 象) into *yixiang* 意象, or "idea-image,"[56] and a perfect embodiment of this idea-image in the medium of *yan* 言, or language (*WXDL* 26/48–64).[57]

To achieve this ideal result of *shensi*, Liu maintains, a writer must cultivate qualities essential to the smooth operation of these processes. The writer must learn to obtain the state of "the emptiness and stillness," a necessary condition for the outbound flight of his spirit. "Therefore in shaping and developing literary thought," Liu writes, "what is the most important is 'emptiness and stillness'" [是以陶鈞文思，貴在虛靜] (*WXDL* 26/26–27). To ensure a smooth passage of his spirit, the writer must "remove obstructions in the five viscera and cleanse the spirit" [疏瀹五藏，澡雪精神] (*WXDL* 26/28–29)—in other words, he must build up his vital energy and his moral character. To improve his intellectual capability, he must "accumulate learning and thus store up treasures" [積學以儲寶] (*WXDL* 26/30) and "contemplate the principles [of things] and thus enrich his talent" [酌理以富才] (*WXDL* 26/31). To sharpen his perceptual power, he must "examine and observe things to bring them to the fullest light" [研閱以窮照] (*WXDL* 26/32). Finally, in order to be able to put forth his idea-image in language, he must "follow the flow of ideas and feelings to search for felicitous expressions" [馴致以懌辭] (*WXDL* 26/33). After a writer has cultivated all these qualities, Liu believes, he will be able to effectively engage with the external processes on intuitive, physiological, moral, psychological, and intellectual levels. What emerges from this well-coordinated operation of *shensi* will be a great work of literature.

Liu Xie's views on the functions of literature also stand in sharp contrast to those held by earlier critics. If the discussion of the functions of literature is the most important part of Han and pre-Han critical texts, it is the least important part of Liu's concept of literature. None of the fifty chapters of *Wenxin diaolong* is devoted to this issue, while a great many chapters are written solely to discuss the origins and creation of literature. Unlike the author of the "Great Preface," Liu Xie does not expatiate on how literature can and should be used to rectify human relationships, harmonize natural forces and processes, and bring man in accord with the spirits. Instead, he merely acknowledges that "using poetry to eulogize good and correct evil deeds is a long-standing practice" [順美匡惡，其來久矣] (*WXDL* 6/32–33) and perfunctorily mentions these two edifying functions in a number of chapters.[58] On the theoretical level, Liu regards literature as an autonomous process whose value should be judged not by how it harmonizes certain socio-political processes but by how it embodies the Tao within its *wen* or beautiful configurations, and thereby "sets forth the warp and woof of the cosmos, perfects and unifies the lasting laws" [經緯區宇，彌綸彝憲] (*WXDL* 1/106–7).

Liu Xie's concept of literature is by any measure a remarkably comprehensive one. In formulating it, Liu has deftly assimilated and transformed earlier critical concerns with various external and internal processes. Let us first consider his treatment of external processes.[59] On the stratum of the ultimate cosmological process, we observe his transformation of the early religious obsession with *shen*, the numinous spirits, into an artistic engagement with *shen*, the mysterious operation of the Tao, in the mind as well as the outer world.[60] On the stratum of natural processes, we find that he keenly observes the relationship of literature with the yin and yang, the Five Agents, and concrete natural processes as do different speakers in the *Zuo Commentary* and *Speeches of the States*. However, he wants to explore the relevance of those natural processes for artistic creation, not the usefulness of literature in regulating those natural processes for the sake of growth and prosperity.[61] On the stratum of ethico-socio-political processes, we notice his shift of attention from practical didactic concerns of the "Great Preface" to a "metaphysical" task of embodying the ideal moral and social order in a bellestristic work.

Turning our attention to internal processes, we note that, on the stratum of suprasensory experience, Liu substitutes contemplative intuition for religious invocation as the means of contact with the ultimate reality. On the stratum of physiological experience, we observe his sublimation, if you will, of ritualistic bodily movements into an endeavor to cultivate and exercise *qi* for literary creation.[62] On the stratum of psychological experience, we see that he shifts his interest from the expression of *zhi*, the central concern of the "Great Preface," to the "artistic configurations of emotion" (*qingwen* 情文). On the stratum of moral experience, Liu relegates moral remonstration and teaching to peripheral significance, but he continues to stress the relevance of the author's moral character for literary creation.

Liu has made it possible for the reader to perceive different aspects of literature in terms of a complex multilevel interaction of internal and external processes. Most modern critics agree that Liu's grand scheme is centered upon the Tao, but they hold vastly different views about the nature of the Tao. Modern critics variously identify Liu's Tao with the human Tao in *Analects*, the naturalistic Tao in *Laozi* and *Zhuangzi*, the Buddhist Tao, and the synthesis of the Confucian and the Taoist Tao in *Commentaries to the Book of Changes* (*Yi zhuan* 易傳).[63] Following the last and the most prevailing of these views, I would argue that the Tao lying at the heart of *Wenxin diaolong* is identical to the Tao in the *Commentaries to the Book of Changes*, especially in the "Commentary on the Appended Phrases" ("Xici zhuan" 系辭傳).[64] In this "Commentary," we are told that "the *Book of Changes*, as a book, is broad and great and encompasses everything. It has the Tao of heaven in it, the Tao of man in it, and the Tao of earth in it."[65] By adopting this all-inclusive Tao as the center of reference in *Wenxin diaolong*, Liu Xie sets up an organismic scheme of human interaction with diverse external processes on five levels—physiological, psychological, moral, intuitive, and intellectual.[66]

By conceptualizing literature within this organismic scheme, Liu Xie aims to lay down normative principles of belletristic *wen*, in an earnest endeavor to emulate the establishment of the nonbelletristic *wen* by pre-Confucian sages and Confucius. In chapter 50, "Xu zhi" 序志 (Exposition of my intentions), the epilogue to the entire book, Liu writes that to be such a "systematizer" of literature is the only way for him to realize his childhood dream of "holding red-lacquer ritual vessels and following Confucius in a south-bound journey" (*WXDL* 50/34–35). He regrets that it is no longer possible to establish himself as a great Confucian exegete since "Ma Rong

[馬融 (79–166)], Zheng Xuan, and other Confucian scholars have already thoroughly expounded the Confucian classics" (*WXDL* 50/44–45). But thanks to the deficiencies of earlier literary critics, he sees the opportunity to achieve immortality through a codification of the principles of literature. To him, not being rigorously systematic is the greatest deficiency of his predecessors. He finds their writings to be "not comprehensive" (*buzhou* 不周), "careless and inadequate" (*shulue* 疏略), "fragmented and disorderly" (*suiluan* 碎亂), or "insufficient in the treatment of essentials" (*guayao* 寡要).[67] Thus, the best way to for Liu Xie to surpass his predecessors is to set down the principles of literature the most systematic way possible. To this end, he models "his principle of organizing chapters and his naming of chapters" on the symbolic numerology of fifty, or "the numerology of the great expansion" (*da yan zhi shu* 大衍之數) in the *Book of Changes* (*WXDL* 50/129–32).[68] In the *Book of Changes*, this numerology serves to signify the organismic totality of the universe: the supreme ultimate, heaven and earth, the sun and moon, the four seasons, the twelve months, and twenty-four *qi*, or ethers.[69] In adopting this numerology, Liu Xie doubtless wishes to construct a system to encompass the literary experience—from its ultimate cosmological origin to the minutest rhetorical details, from the entire literary tradition to individual talents, from nonbelletristic to belletristic genres and subgenres, from the creative to the receptive process, from the author's character to the reader's qualities, and so forth. We can assume that Liu Xie's comprehensive concept of literature and his critical system at large emerge from his consistent, self-conscious thinking about literature through the paradigm of the *Book of Changes*.

THE INTERRELATEDNESS OF THE FOUR CONCEPTS OF LITERATURE AND THE SYSTEMATICS OF TRADITIONAL CHINESE CRITICISM

Liu Xie's synthesis of earlier critical concerns is testimony to his critical acumen and the inherent affinities of the four concepts of literature. In conclusion, let me examine the interrelatedness of these concepts to gain insight into the systematics of traditional Chinese literary criticism as a whole.

If the four concepts share a common denominator, I would argue that it is the core belief that literature is a process that harmonizes various ongoing processes in the realms of heaven, earth, and man. According to early Chinese critics, this process arises in the heart (*xin*) of a composer or author when he responds to various external processes on physiological, psychological, moral, intuitive, or intellectual levels. As he makes known his responses by dancing, playing music, singing, speaking, or writing, this process moves from the inner to the outer worlds and helps bring about the harmony between men and nature. Simply put, literature is made up of three major phases— its origin in response to the world, its formation in the human heart and language, and its function to harmonize the external and internal worlds.[70]

Comparing the four concepts, we can also perceive two prominent *differentiae*. The first is that literature as a process is defined rather differently. It is an auxiliary part of a dance-centered, religious performance in "Canon of Yao." In the *Zuo Commentary* and "Speeches of Zhou," literature is a relatively more important but nonetheless auxiliary part of a music-centered, courtly ceremony. In the "Great Preface," it is the central part of verbalized social intercourse. Finally, in *Wenxin diaolong*, it is a largely autonomous, text-centered, belletristic pursuit.[71]

The second *differentia* is that the origins, formation, and functions of literature are explained in terms of interaction with different processes. In explaining the origins of literature, early critics trace it to the writer's inward response to external processes—to the numinous spirits in the "Canon of Yao," to the natural forces in the *Zuo Commentary* and "Speeches of Zhou," to the ethico-socio-political processes in the "Great Preface," and to the manifold processes of the Tao in *Wenxin diaolong*. In examining the formation of literature, these critics stress these interactions on different levels of human experience—on physiological and psychological levels in the "Canon of Yao," the *Zuo Commentary*, and the "Speeches of Zhou"; on psychological and moral levels in the "Great Preface"; and on all levels in *Wenxin diaolong*. In describing the functions of literature, they emphasize harmony with numinous spirits, attunement with natural forces, rectification of human relationships, and revelation of the mysterious Tao at work in all realms.

The connections among the four concepts reveal an intricate critical system. Such a system, of course, debunks the widely accepted belief that traditional

Chinese criticism does not have a coherent system. Traditional Chinese criticism strikes us as impressionistic, haphazard, and orderless only because we seek to understand it within the analytical framework grounded in the "truth-based," dualistic paradigms of Western critical thinking. Yet when we reexamine it within a "process-based" paradigm, we can see overwhelming evidence of the systematic coherence as delineated in the foregoing discussions.

Such a critical system can also help us understand the coherence of later Chinese criticism, on both the macro- and microcosmic scales. It is clear that the development of Chinese criticism after Liu Xie displays the same fundamentals that are at the core of early Chinese criticism. Later Chinese critics also cherish the belief of literature as a harmonizing process. They tend to express this belief through tenets centered on the Tao, such as "Poetry is to illuminate the Tao" (*shi yi ming Dao* 詩以明道), "Poetry is to carry the Tao" (*shi yi zai Dao* 詩以載道), "Poetry is to embody the Tao" (*shi yi guan Dao* 詩以貫道),[72] as well as through older tenets like "shi yan zhi," "shi yuan qing" 詩緣情, "and "yuan Dao" 原道. They also seek to redefine the nature of literature as a process, frequently reversing the relative importance of music and verbalization on the one hand and written composition on the other. Third, they also tend alternately to regard culture or nature as the ultimate reference for discussing the origins, formation, and functions of literature.

On the microcosmic scale, we can perceive the inner coherence in the discussions of specific critical subjects, such as literary creation, the classification of styles, the genealogy of literary schools, and others. For instance, we may explore the interrelatedness of *Twenty-Four Modes of Poetry* (*Er shi si shi pin* 二十四詩品), traditionally attributed to Sikong Tu 司空圖 (837–908), in terms of a complex pattern of interaction with different external processes on the physiological, psychological, intuitive, moral, or intellectual levels at different stages of literary creation or appreciation. Within a process-based paradigm, we may even attempt to reconstruct the nomenclature of many Chinese critical terms long censured for being elusive and not logically connected. For example, we may reconstruct the nomenclature of the *qi* 氣-related terms within an interactive scheme of internal and external processes.[73]

The goal of discerning a critical system in traditional Chinese criticism has excited and eluded us for decades. In examining the four concepts of literature, I have identified their common denominator and *differentiae* and thus revealed the systematic coherence of early Chinese criticism. Because we clearly see similar systematic coherence in critical writing of other periods, we may conceive of a process-based systematics in traditional Chinese criticism as a whole. To further develop ideas about this systematics and its utility for understanding traditional Chinese criticism will be an exciting and daunting task.

PART TWO

Intellectual Foundations

CHAPTER THREE

Buddhism in *The Literary Mind and Ornate Rhetoric*

VICTOR H. MAIR

> When [the writer's] mind is at rest, he may begin to formulate a
> pattern of sounds,
> and when his principles are correct, he may display literary
> decorativeness.
> In this manner, the substance will not be damaged by the literary
> adornment,
> and the mind will not be drowned in a mass of erudition.[1]
>
> 心定而後結意，理正而後摛藻，使文不滅質，博不溺心
>
> —Liu Xie, *Wenxin diaolong*, chapter 31

For the last couple of decades, a scholarly (and sometimes not so scholarly)
debate has raged over whether Buddhism played a significant role in the
composition of *Wenxin diaolong* (The literary mind and ornate rhetoric).
Its author, Liu Xie, nakedly and unabashedly employs the patently Buddhist
term *prajñā* in chapter 18 of *WXDL*. What could be more Buddhist than
prajñā, which signifies intuitive wisdom or highest knowledge?[2] Those who
insist that Buddhism is inconsequential to *WXDL* dismiss this occurrence
of *prajñā* as a fluke and maintain that it has no real bearing on Liu Xie's
overall concept of literature or on his detailed examination of its various
genres. Yet, it is worth observing that the expression *juejing* 絕境 (incomparable realm), with which Liu Xie identifies *prajñā*, is not without its own
Buddhist resonance. Indeed, particularly as applied by Wang Guowei 王國
維 (1877–1927), the related expression *jingjie* 境界 (realm—comparable to
Sanskrit *viṣaya*) later became one of the most important concepts in Chinese
literary criticism.[3] Furthermore, in the same passage where Liu Xie refers to

prajñā, he also speaks of *zhengli* 正理 (correct principle), arguably one of the most potent concepts in *WXDL*. The qualifier *zheng* (correct, true, right, just, exact) occurs often in *WXDL*.[4] We should note that *zheng* is a vital part of Buddhist religious and philosophical discourse, such as that about *zhengjue* 正覺 (true consciousness, i.e., *saṃbodhi*, the wisdom or omniscience of a Buddha), *zhengjian* 正見 (*samyagdṛṣṭi*, meaning "right views"), *zheng Dao* 正道 (the true Way), and so on, especially as contrasted with *pian* 偏 (partial, deviant). It turns out, then, that the notorious *prajñā* passage of *WXDL* may be characterized as fairly saturated with overt and implicit Buddhist references.

Part of the problem lies in the fact that—aside from this single and highly conspicuous usage of *prajñā*—there is supposedly not much else in *WXDL* that is overtly Buddhist. This relative absence of manifestly Buddhist language in *WXDL* has made it easy for opponents of a consequential Buddhist role in the formation of Liu Xie's critical conceptions to regard the occurrence of *prajñā* as an aberration. Whether this argument is legitimate, I leave for others to decide. My task, rather, is to delineate the battle lines in this sometimes hotly contested engagement and then to ask, "What does it all matter?" In other words, why do people get so exercised over the presence or absence of Buddhism in *WXDL*?

BUDDHISM AND CONFUCIANISM IN CONTEMPORARY CHINESE STUDIES ON *WENXIN DIAOLONG*

There is a wide spectrum of opinions concerning the role of Buddhism in *WXDL*: (a) for all intents and purposes, it was effectively absent from the text; (b) it played a prominent, even decisive, role; (c) it was present but played no significant role. Even among those who agree that Buddhism played a vital role in *WXDL*, there are two dramatically opposed ways of interpreting that perception: either the Buddhist elements in *WXDL* are said to have enhanced its standing as one of China's earliest and greatest monuments of literary criticism and theory, or it is argued that the Buddhist (read "Indian") aspects of *WXDL* totally vitiate and discredit it as an authentic exposition of Chinese literary theory. The latter argument has been most forcefully presented by Ma Hongshan of Xinjiang University.[5] Ma contends that Liu Xie was a thoroughgoing Buddhist from the time he was raised by the famous monk Sengyou 僧佑 until his death. Ma also maintains that *WXDL* is permeated with Buddhist ideology from start to finish and that Liu hypocritically traded on his Buddhist connections to secure a series of estimable official positions that he held in the Liang government between the ages of thirty-seven and fifty-four. According to Ma, Liu Xie wrote *WXDL* when he was in his thirties, and at that time he was still a careerist crypto-Buddhist. Indeed, Ma contends that Liu Xie declared his true affiliations only when he was near the end of his life.[6]

In paper after paper maligning Liu Xie, Ma Hongshan's central thesis is that the implicit intent of the Tao 道 of *WXDL* is "to control Confucianism with Buddhism [by] combining Buddhism and Confucianism" [以佛統儒，佛儒合一]. In each of his papers, Ma hammers away insistently at what he considers to be Liu Xie's hypocrisy and subversive aims. Obsessed with the nefarious Buddhist content, which he is convinced pervades *WXDL*, he cites earlier critics who harbored similar reservations about Liu Xie and his work. Even in his analysis of specific terms in *WXDL* such as *shenli* 神理 (spiritual principle), *ziran* 自然 (spontaneity), *taiji* 太極 (the absolute), *xuansheng* 玄聖 (mysteriously sage), and so forth, Ma declares that Liu is attempting to subvert Confucianism.[7]

In sum, Ma Hongshan holds that, in *WXDL*, Liu Xie merely makes a pretense of trying to seem Confucian, but that secretly and ardently he intends his book as a vehicle for spreading Buddhist ideology. The *WXDL*, perforce, is a devious and inferior work that must be exposed in its true character. One of the most noticeable features of Ma Hongshan's sustained denunciations of Liu Xie and *WXDL* is that they appear on the pages of some of China's most prestigious scholarly journals. For this to happen in the space of a few years at the end of the 1970s and the beginning of the 1980s would have required the support of powerful figures in the intellectual bureaucracy.

Throughout his critique of Liu Xie, Ma Hongshan makes the highly judgmental assumption that because *WXDL* is Buddhist, it deserves condemnation. It is hard to know what to make of such an assertion—coming from a late-twentieth-century critic in the People's Republic of China—except to say that it appears to recycle all of the old xenophobic Confucian fears about Buddhism as a foreign (and therefore superfluous or inimical) religion. We, of course, are free to take a more dispassionate and detached approach. But the issues raised by Ma Hongshan may be even more crucial than he himself imagined.

Many Chinese scholars were astonished and offended that Ma would vilify Liu Xie so harshly and attack *WXDL* with such vehemence, since the man and his book are central icons of the entire tradition of Chinese literary criticism and theory. The stakes are indubitably high. If *WXDL* is Buddhist (that is, bad), almost the whole history of Chinese literary criticism and theory is placed in jeopardy. It is no wonder that a number of Chinese scholars scrambled to defend *WXDL* vigorously. The nature of their collaborative defense, however, deserves to be pondered. They did not set out to demonstrate that Buddhism is good, but rather to prove that, whatever Buddhism there may be in *WXDL*, it is both innocuous and immaterial. Many of them simply hoped (and some tried to prove) that it was not really there at all.

One might wish to put forward the counterargument that the elevation of belles lettres in China during the Six Dynasties, in contrast to previous Confucian utilitarian attitudes toward writing, reflects the profound Indian aesthetic preoccupations of the time. But this is a still more outrageous proposition than Ma Hongshan's, so I will leave it aside for the moment in order to avoid stirring up an even angrier nest of hornets than did Professor Ma. I shall, however, consider such a possibility near the end of this essay.

One of the most influential individuals to come to the defense of Liu Xie and *WXDL* was Wang Yuanhua[8] of East China Normal University in Shanghai (formerly head of the Shanghai Bureau of Cultural Affairs). Wang acknowledges that Liu Xie died a Buddhist and that he is the author of two texts that are blatantly Buddhist: "Mie huo lun" 滅惑論 (Treatise on eliminating doubts), and *Liang Jian'an wang zao Shanshan Shicheng si shixiang bei* 梁建安王造 剡山石城寺石像碑 (Stele inscription for a stone statue at Shicheng Temple of Mt. Shan commissioned by the Liang Dynasty Prince of Jian'an).[9] These are the only two other extant works beside *WXDL* by Liu Xie.

Wang Yuanhua maintains that the difference between *WXDL* and the two overtly Buddhist pieces by Liu Xie is purely a matter of timing. Wang claims that Liu Xie underwent an ideological transformation around the beginning of the Tianjian 天監 (Heavenly Supervision) reign period (502 A.D.) when he became a scholar-official and that this represents the dividing line between his earlier and later periods. Before this division, by which time *WXDL* had presumably already been written, Liu Xie was supposedly a Confucian; after the division, when he wrote "Mie huo lun" and the Shicheng Temple stele inscription, he had allegedly converted to Buddhism.[10]

There are difficulties with this scenario. In the first place, one would have expected Liu Xie to be more Confucian *after* he entered officialdom than he had been before, although Wang apparently would agree with Ma Hongshan that Liu's acceptance of Buddhism was merely a cynical ploy to ingratiate himself with the emperor, who was well disposed to the religion, and with the powerful monks who were close to the ruler. Secondly, Liu Xie was surely already steeped in Buddhism prior to the initiation of his work on *WXDL*. We shall investigate additional problems with Wang Yuanhua's thesis that are shared by Pan Chonggui.

Kong Fan[11] also takes up Ma Hongshan's challenge to defend the integrity and value of *WXDL*, but he does so in a very different manner from that of Wang Yuanhua. Kong starts from the premise that during the Six Dynasties, Buddhism and Xuanxue 玄學 (abstruse learning) were in the ascendant. The similarities in their philosophies—for example, Buddhist *kong* 空 (emptiness, or Sanskrit *śūnyatā*) was analogous to Xuanxue *wu* 無 (nothingness, nonbeing)—allowed these two systems of thought to commingle until the distinction between them was blurred. Gradually, Buddhism displaced Xuanxue and became predominant. Kong chiefly attributes to Xuanxue the elements in *WXDL* shared by the two systems of thought. Furthermore, he stresses the Confucian lineaments of the book as a whole, so that Buddhism is essentially distilled out of Liu Xie's literary criticism and theory, which are thereby rescued from Ma Hongshan's damning assertions. Kong admits that Liu Xie was a devoted Buddhist but denies that his personal beliefs had any noticeable effect on *WXDL*. According to Kong, whatever is Buddhist about *WXDL* comes from Xuanxue.

Still another scholar who rushed to rescue Liu and *WXDL* from Ma Hongshan's charges of subversion was Li Qingjia.[12] Li, too, not only failed to find any presence of Buddhist elements to besmirch the pristine Confucian purity of *WXDL*, he further asserted that Liu Xie's masterwork was actually opposed to Buddhism. (Li, incidentally, consistently refers to Ma Hongshan as one of "those who subscribe to the identity of Buddhism and Confucianism.") One of the arguments adduced by Li against the possibility of Buddhist influence upon *WXDL* is the following: If Liu Xie were such a good Buddhist when he wrote his treatise, why did he not become a monk when he was living with Sengyou and assisting the celebrated monk in his various Buddhist compilation projects? Although this is a common argument among those who insist upon an absence of Buddhism in *WXDL*, it is spurious, since (like Xie Lingyun 謝靈運 [385–433] and many other Buddhist devotees of the age) he could have been a sincere lay Buddhist without becoming a monk. Furthermore, whether Liu Xie was a lay Buddhist or a Buddhist monk at a given stage in his life is irrelevant to the Buddhist content of *WXDL*. What matters is the Buddhist content (or lack thereof) of *WXDL* itself. Equally specious is Li's contention that *WXDL* has nothing to do with Buddhism because it was never listed in Buddhist bibliographies and because traditional Chinese bibliographies never identified it as a Buddhist treatise. Although Li devotes a considerable amount of effort to developing this argument, it is so infantile that a rebuttal is hardly required. The fact that *WXDL* is a work of literary criticism and theory does not preclude the possibility that it was significantly influenced by its author's Buddhist proclivities. The one contribution of Buddhism to *WXDL* admitted by Li is its superior organization and logic.

The latest salvo in the debate over Buddhism in *WXDL* was fired by Wang Chunhong,[13] who holds that Liu Xie wrote *WXDL* to restore the purity of Chinese writing, which was being threatened by the massive influence of Buddhist literature since the latter part of the Eastern Han period (25–220 A.D.). According to Wang, Liu Xie was concerned that the peculiar language and style of the Buddhist translators, almost all of whom were foreign up to his time, were seriously contaminating the work of even those authors who were not themselves Buddhists. (The language Wang Chunhong is referring to is that which I have called Buddhist Hybrid Chinese or Buddhist Hybrid Sinitic. BHC [or BHSi] is a special variety of classical Chinese [or Literary Sinitic] whose syntax is distorted by Indic and, to a lesser extent, Iranian or Tocharian grammar and whose vocabulary is liberally peppered with neologisms, calques, transcriptions, translated terms, and vernacular expressions. To a devout Confucian literatus steeped only in Han and earlier Chinese texts, BHC was an abomination; to the Buddhists, it was as familiar and lively as Marxist-Leninist-Engelsian translatese—with all of its Germanicisms and Slavicisms—was to a loyal communist cadre in mid-twentieth-century

People's Republic of China.) Curiously, however, Wang maintains that Liu Xie used a combination of Confucian concepts (for example, *zongjing* 宗經 [the classics as sources]) and Buddhist principles (for example, *zheng* 正 [correct, right, proper; Sanskrit *samyak*]) to combat these linguistic ills. Following Zhang Shaokang,[14] Wang strongly emphasizes the Buddhist origins of *shensi* 神思 (spiritual thought) and, to a lesser extent, *wuse* 物色 (the form [Sanskrit *rūpa*] of things), which he believes Liu Xie inherited from the distinguished monk Zongbing 宗炳 (375–443), as transmitted through the Vinaya school, to which Huiyuan 慧遠 (334–416) and his own master, Sengyou, adhered.

Wang also briefly examines the Buddhistic resonance of *xujing* 虛靜 (empty stillness), *yinxiu* 隱秀 (implicitness and explicitness), *tongbian* 通變 (comprehensive variability), *fenggu* 風骨 (wind and bones, i.e., animation and structure), *tixing* 體性 (bodily nature, used as a translation of Sanskrit *svabhāva* [innate disposition, state of being, natural state] and *ātmakatva* [self-nature]),[15] and other key terms in *WXDL*. Indeed, Wang believes that he is able to trace the basic concepts of virtually all of Liu Xie's theoretical chapters and of several of the chapters on stylistic features to Buddhist sources: "The formation of all the important literary ideas in Liu Xie's *The Literary Mind and Ornate Rhetoric* is inseparably related to covert Buddhist influences."[16] Unlike Ma Hongshan, Wang sees nothing insidious about this, but he accepts it as unavoidably due to the intellectual atmosphere of the age and to Liu Xie's personal religious affiliations.

AS IN CHINA, SO TOO IN HONG KONG AND TAIWAN

Before the controversy over the role of Buddhism in *WXDL* erupted in the People's Republic of China, two of the most distinguished Chinese scholars in Taiwan and Hong Kong were already dueling over the same subject. Maintaining that *WXDL* is permeated with Buddhist elements, Rao Zongyi[17] declares that what makes Liu's treatise unique are its strict organization and extraordinary insights. In the following paragraphs, I summarize other major points in Rao's short but seminal article on Buddhism in *WXDL*.

Liu Xie was versed in Buddhist texts and absorbed their modes of analysis and categories of thought. To be sure, the intellectual life of the Six Dynasties period was deeply imbued with Indian characteristics through Buddhism, many of which ineluctably affected Liu Xie. If one wants to understand the roots of thought in *WXDL*, one must not overlook Buddhism.

Liu Xie was orphaned while still young and chose never to marry. He lived with the learned *śramaṇa* (ascetic) Sengyou for more than ten years, during which period he studied Buddhism and became thoroughly conversant with its scriptures. Sengyou was one of the most celebrated Buddhist monks in Chinese history, and he published a number of highly important works. One of these was *Chu Sanzang ji ji* 出 三 藏 記 集 (Collected notes on the production of the Buddhist *Tripiṭaka*), arguably the most authoritative bibliography of Chinese Buddhist texts ever published. Liu Xie assisted Sengyou in its compilation.[18] Since *Chu Sanzang ji ji* includes many works of the Liang period, it must have been completed after *WXDL* was written. Sengyou died in the seventeenth year of the Tianjian reign period (518) of the Liang dynasty, and Liu Xie composed a stele inscription for him. Subsequently, Liu Xie received an imperial command to assist the *śramaṇa* Huizhen 慧 震 in collating *sūtras*. After his work was finished, he became a monk himself and changed his name to Huidi 慧 地.

Rao discusses the literary thought of Liu Xie under three headings.

1. Reliance on the Buddhist notion of *shen* 神 (spirit) to explain the source of literary creativity.

In *WXDL*, *shen* is contrasted with *xing* 形 (form) and is held to be superior because it transcends the confines of material existence.[19] In "Mie huo lun," Liu Xie states that Buddhist dharma concentrates on refining the spirit, while Taoist doctrine works at refining the form. Whereas form is finite and restricted, spirit is boundless and unrestrained. The evaluative distinction between Buddhist spirit and Taoist form was a commonplace from the Jin and Liu Song periods on.

2. The relationship of Liu Xie's thought to Indian logic and exposition.

There are noticeable affinities between Buddhist modes of expression and Liu Xie's thought as exemplified in *WXDL*, e.g., the *zan* 贊 (eulogy) at the end of each chapter, which is comparable to *gāthā*s at the conclusion of divisions in Buddhist texts,[20] a shared predilection for numbered lists of categories or stages in the exposition of an argument,[21] the very word *xin* 心 (mind), which reflects the Buddhist notion of *citta* or *hṛdaya* (mind) and which was often used in the titles of Buddhist texts from the Jin and Liu Song periods on (whereas the usage and meaning of *xin* in the title of *WXDL* have no clear precedent in pre-Buddhist texts),[22] the philosophically productive contrast between *ti* 體 (substance) and *yong* 用 (application) frequently elaborated by Buddhist authors (also occasionally adopted by Xuanxue proponents), and so forth.

3. Using Buddhist learning to explicate literary questions.

Technical matters in the *WXDL* pertaining to script (e.g., Siddham-like *lianbian* 聯邊 [joined sides] and *banzi* 半字 [semi-graph] in the "Lianzi" [Practice of the script] 練字 chapter), poetics (e.g., the distinction between prosodic effects of the Sanskritic *he* 和 [harmony] and Sinitic *yun* 韻 [rhyme] types), and so forth can only be fully comprehended through reference to Indian ideas and techniques current in China at the time *WXDL* was written. Even though such references to Buddhism are not as explicit as *prajñā*, they are equally specific in their application.

For Rao, Buddhist learning constitutes the heart of Liu Xie's conceptualization of literature. Consequently, only to one who has a clear recognition of Liu Xie's relationship to Buddhism will his ideas about the "literary mind" and all that it entails be entirely accessible.

Ignoring all of the evidence presented by Rao, Pan Chonggui[23] adopts a similar approach to that of Wang Yuanhua. Pan, too, emphasizes Liu Xie's alleged "conversion," but he prefers to begin by focusing on the obvious declarations of solidarity with Confucianism in *WXDL* and then to engage in a discussion of when Liu Xie "attached himself to the *śramaṇa* Sengyou," together with a minute analysis of the practice of writing Buddhist stele inscriptions in Liu Xie's day. Following the wording of his biography in scroll 50 of the *Liang History*, the vast majority of specialists believe that Liu Xie lived with Sengyou for over a decade as an orphaned youth.

勰早孤，篤志好學，家貧不婚娶，依沙門僧佑，與之居處，積十餘年，遂博通經論，因區別部類，錄而序之，今定林寺經藏，勰所定也[24]

Liu Xie was orphaned while still young, yet he had a firm resolve and delighted in learning. Because he came from a poor family, he did not marry, but attached himself to the *śramaṇa* Sengyou, with whom he dwelled for a total of more than ten years. Thereupon, he became broadly versed in the *sūtra*s and *śāstra*s, and consequently he classified them in groups and categories, recording and writing prefaces for them. The Buddhist canon preserved in the Dinglin Temple today was established by Liu Xie.

Pan, on the other hand, attempts to show that Liu Xie was recruited by Sengyou in his late twenties to work on the latter's many compilation projects, which constituted Liu's "attachment" to the famous monk (to my knowledge, this is the latest date put forward by anyone). In other words, according to Pan, Liu Xie was sought out by Sengyou to work on his compilation projects because he was already an accomplished literatus. As such, his views on literature would have been formed and impervious to the Buddhist blandishments of Sengyou.

Despite the inconclusive nature of Pan's contention concerning the actual period when Liu Xie was attached to Sengyou, let us accept—for the sake of argument—that he began this apprenticeship at age twenty-seven or twenty-eight. Even if this were so, it would still have been at least four or five years before Liu Xie, in his own words, "began to discuss literature" (as we will see in the next paragraph). This would have allowed plenty of time for him to be contaminated by Sengyou's Buddhist doctrines prior to his work on *WXDL*.

As a matter of fact, there is good reason to believe that Liu Xie began to write *WXDL* after he was thirty years old (i.e., in the year 495 or later), since he states unambiguously in the "Xuzhi" 序志 (Postface), "When I was past thirty, then I began to discuss literature" [齒在踰立乃始論文]. No one, not even Pan Chonggui himself, would assert that Liu Xie's attachment to Sengyou began after he was thirty years old. Therefore, we must accept that Liu Xie would have been exposed to Buddhist texts and ideas before he started to write *WXDL*. If, following the consensus view that *WXDL* was not completed until 502 (or, as some maintain, still later), Liu Xie would have been thirty-eight years old by that time. (It would seem very odd for the poor, orphaned youth who chose not to marry to wait until he was thirty-eight to forty-eight years old—already well into his middle age—to seek refuge with Sengyou.) For a work as mature and substantial as *WXDL*, it would be wholly reasonable to accept that Liu Xie was engaged in preparing and writing it during his thirties. In any event, it would have been impossible for him to remain ignorant of Buddhism throughout that decade.

There are other insurmountable obstacles to the acceptance of Pan's thesis. For instance, if Sengyou had sought the services of Liu Xie because he was already an accomplished literatus and if, as Pan assumes, Liu Xie had no previous contact with Buddhists, what special qualifications would he have had to work on Sengyou's projects? Second, after citing from *Gaoseng zhuan* 高僧傳 (Biographies of eminent monks) notices of more than three dozen stele inscriptions for Buddhist monks written by famous writers (including three by Liu Xie), Pan illogically claims that this proves Liu Xie's literary learning was already accomplished before 492 (after which time, by Pan's reckoning, but by no one else's, Liu attached himself to Sengyou). In fact, quite the contrary conclusion should be drawn, since none of the stele inscriptions for Buddhist monks written by Liu Xie date from before 492. (They are from 492 or later, 494, and 518; another not cited by Pan is from 516.) Third, Pan totally neglects the occurrence of *prajñā* and other explicit or implicit evidence of Buddhism in *WXDL*.

Pan Chonggui sets himself up as directly counterposed to the viewpoint of Rao Zongyi concerning the ideological heritage of *WXDL*. The former asserts that Liu Xie's masterwork is thoroughly Confucian, while the latter maintains that only by recognizing the Buddhist foundations of the text can one fully comprehend it. We are faced with starkly contrasting opinions firmly held by two of the most honored scholars in the Chinese-speaking world today. Is one wrong and the other right? Are they both wrong? Are they both right? As is true of almost every contestation, I believe that they are both right and they are both wrong, but Rao Zongyi is more right than he is wrong, and Pan Chonggui is more wrong than he is right.

Pan is correct because *WXDL* is superficially Confucian, but he is flagrantly incorrect with regard to the timing of Liu Xie's alleged conversion to Buddhism, and he is utterly oblivious to the Buddhist elements in *WXDL*. Rao is correct because he discerns the Buddhist underpinnings of *WXDL*, but he is slightly incorrect in failing to note that Liu Xie cloaked the superstructure of his tome in largely Confucian colors. For someone who insists that the author of *WXDL* be either purely Confucian or purely Buddhist, Liu Xie comes across as an ideological schizophrenic. For someone who is acquainted with the intellectual complexities of the age and who is aware that *WXDL* is a treatise on literary criticism and theory, not an exposition of Buddhist doctrine, however, it is entirely natural that Liu Xie wrote just the way he did.[25]

THE HEART OF THE MATTER

Liu Xie invented the expression *wenxin* 文心 (literary mind). Many readers of the text have remarked that it is an unusual collocation.[26] It would seem that Liu Xie himself was aware of the strangeness of this first half of the title of his book and strove to forestall suspicion by defining *wenxin* at the very beginning of the crucial "Xuzhi" chapter [Postface] somewhat awkwardly as *wei wen zhi yong xin* 為文之用心 (the using of the mind to make literature [?]) and dredging up two obscure texts entitled *Qin xin* 琴心 (Zither mind) and *Qiao xin* 巧心 (Clever mind), neither of which is of much help in trying to grasp the meaning of *wenxin*.

I suggest that a driving force behind Liu Xie's invention of *wenxin* was the Buddhist concept of mind (*xin*, Sanskrit *hṛdaya* or *citta*), which was extremely important in Six Dynasties thought and which had a decided impact upon the literary aesthetics of the period (e.g., Xie Lingyun's *shangxin* 賞心 [appreciative mind]).[27] Liu Xie emphasized the role of the mind even further, making it the source of literary creation, not merely appreciation. In his first chapter, "YuanTao" 原道 (The original Way), he offers one of the most remarkable statements in the whole of *WXDL*: "The mind is born and words are established; words are established and pattern/script/literature is manifested" [心生而言立，言立而文明]. In *WXDL*, Liu Xie returns again and again to the capacity of the mind to produce literature through the medium of language.[28]

The idea that the mind is the creative source of all phenomena, including literature, is Buddhist. Prior to the advent of Buddhism in China, *xin* signified the physical organ known as the heart, the locus of thought, the center, and so forth, but it never referred to that faculty which produces the universe and all that is in it.[29] This concept is epitomized in the expression *san jie [wei] yi xin* 三界 [唯] 一心 (The three worlds [i.e., all existence] are but one mind). This saying derives from a verse in the *Avataṃsaka sūtra (Huayan jing)* 華嚴經 (first translated into Chinese by Buddhabhadra in 418–

420), which continues: *xin wai wu bie fa, xin Fo ji zhongsheng, shi san wu chabie* 心外無別法，心佛及眾生，是三無差別 (Outside mind there are no other dharmas; there is no distinction among the mind, the Buddha, and all beings). This quintessential statement was reformulated countless times in a wide variety of Chinese Buddhist texts. The Sanskrit equivalent of *san jie [wei] yi xin* is *tribhava-cittamātra* (The three worlds [are] mind only) or, in more expanded form, *cittamātram idaṃ yad idaṃ traidhātukam*. In terms of its construction, *wenxin* functions as a compound of the *tatpuruṣa* type (determinative noun-compound class).[30]

A corroborative hint that *wenxin* is possessed of Buddhist nuances is to be found in the final "Xu zhi" chapter, where Liu Xie states: "The activity of the literary mind is based in the Way (Tao)" [文心之作也，本乎道]. This is mirrored by the first, foundation chapter, which is on "the original Way." The compelling question, then, is whose Way is this? Since all the major schools of thought in China took the Way as their fundamental cosmological and ethical principle, it could be Buddhist, Taoist, or Confucian; hence different scholars have claimed different ideological orientations for *WXDL*. It may be pertinent to observe that, in "Mie huo lun," Liu Xie unequivocally equates the Way (Tao) with bodhi (that is, Buddhist enlightenment).

In contrast to the uniqueness of *wenxin*, the other half of the book's title, *diaolong* 雕龍 (carved dragons), is a typical Chinese expression going back to the Warring States period and signifying an elaborate, mannered style.[31] Thus, the complete title of the book actually means something like "literary creativity [as contrasted with] ornate rhetoric." The former component of the title pertains to the fresh, Buddhistically imbued literary ideals of Shen Yue 沈約 (441–513) and his associates, while the latter component refers to the traditional, more Confucian practices espoused by Prince Zhaoming 昭明 (501–531), Zhong Rong 鍾嶸 (468–518), and others of their persuasion. We shall return to this epochal controversy in Chinese literary history momentarily. To be brief, we may summarize our views on the title of Liu Xie's magnum opus by stating that it neatly encapsulates the tensions between Buddhism and Confucianism that are operative in the book as a whole. In a word, *xin* is the key to *WXDL*.

If we admit the consensus view that *WXDL* was written around the end of the Qi dynasty (i.e., ca. 501–502), this means that it was composed around the time when Shen Yue's theory of the four tones was being popularized.

The poetry critic Zhong Rong was the most distinguished opponent of the theory, while Liu Xie was a strong supporter.[32] Liu Xie showed his interest in the tonal rules at many places in *WXDL*; so important did he consider them that he even devoted the better part of a chapter ("Shenglü" 聲律 [Musicality]) to them.[33] Liu Xie's strong support of the tonal rules in and of itself shows his Buddhist proclivities, since they were formulated by Shen Yue and his circle of associates under obvious Indian influence.[34] Shen Yue was definitely a lay Buddhist, and a very learned one at that.[35] Among other evidence of his Buddhist sincerity is a penitential text of the *uposatha* type that he wrote to confess his sins.[36]

It is particularly noteworthy that Liu Xie first sought and gained Shen Yue's approval *before* publishing *WXDL*. Moreover, he humbled himself by standing in front of Shen Yue's cart with his book, as though he were a peddler (乃負書候約於車前，狀若貨鬻者).[37] This means that Liu Xie publicly aligned himself with what we might call the Buddhistic school of literary theory, and that he did so directly in connection with the issuance of *WXDL*. I submit, therefore, that Liu Xie was in all likelihood at least partially conscious of the Buddhist foundations of his work.

To be sure, the primary motivation for Liu Xie to undertake *WXDL* at all—since he was apparently otherwise completely occupied with his Buddhist editorial and compositional chores—would seem to have been to throw his support behind Shen Yue and his camp. There is no firm evidence that he wrote any other secular piece, either before or after the age of thirty. It is somewhat ironic, therefore, that Liu Xie has become—in this century—the most outstanding exemplar of early Chinese literary criticism and theory.

Finally, Liu Xie's biography in the *Liang History* affirms that, "in writing, he was strong in Buddhist principles" [為文長於佛理]. It is impossible to rule out the applicability of this statement to the writing of *WXDL*.

INDIAN ARCHETYPES FOR *WENXIN DIAOLONG*

Stephen Owen observed that *WXDL* is divided into two main parts—one dealing primarily with specific genres and the other dealing chiefly with style, language, figures of speech, and so forth.[38] This prompted me to compare the structure and contents of *WXDL* with those of Sanskrit treatises on poetics. Adequate treatment of this subject would require a separate paper at least as lengthy as that by Mair and Mei on the Indian origins of regulated verse (*lüshi* 律詩) prosody. Here I shall only briefly raise some suggestive possibilities and point the way to future research.[39]

First, we must recognize that, while the dating of most early Indian texts and authors on poetics is highly vexed (as is the dating of early Indian history in general), the scientific analysis of poetic language began at least as early as Pāṇini (fl. 400 B.C.). In his *Aṣṭādhyāyī*, the great grammarian employs many of the standard terms used by later writers on poetics (for example, *alaṃkāra* [poetic ornament or embellishment, figure of speech], *upamā* [simile], *sāmānya* [equivalency, similitude], *sādṛśya* [resemblance], and so on). Furthermore, many of these terms are also to be found in the Vedas, the Upaniṣads, and the Brāhmaṇas, so we know that their roots lie deep in Indian antiquity.[40] That Pāṇini was not the sole originator of these usages is clear from the fact that he himself cites numerous predecessors.[41] Pāṇini's contemporaries and successors, such as Yāska (fl. 320 B.C.), Kātyāyana (probably fourth century B.C.), and Patañjali (second century B.C.), continued and elaborated the discourse on poetic language until, by the time of Bharata's famous *Nāṭyaśāstra* (ca. first–third centuries A.D.), a coherent system for the description, classification, and assessment of poetic literature had been established.[42] For the next two millennia, Indian treatises on poetics basically subscribed to the same model as that adopted by the *Nāṭyaśāstra*.[43]

Of the hundreds of Indian writers on poetics known by name in the centuries succeeding Bharata, we may focus on two representative individuals who have particular relevance for *WXDL*. They are Bhāmaha and Daṇḍin, both of whom may have lived as early as the late fifth or early sixth century and may thus conceivably have had a more or less direct impact upon Liu Xie.[44] Even if Bhāmaha and Daṇḍin are later than Liu Xie, they and other writers on poetics who followed them explicitly or implicitly refer to predecessors such as Medhāvin whose works would have been extant before Liu Xie's time.[45] (It cannot be stressed too heavily that the normal Indian process of the transmission of texts—from epics to *sūtras* and *śāstras* to poems—was an oral one; hence many works were never written down.[46] And those that were committed to writing for one reason or another were subject to all the ravages that a humid, bug-infested, tropical climate presented. A goodly percentage of the ancient Sanskrit manuscripts that survived have been found in the cooler climes of Kashmir and Nepal or the more arid environments of Rajasthan and Central Asia.) Furthermore, Bhāmaha is widely regarded as a Buddhist (or, at least, as having strong Buddhist affinities), so it is all the more likely that some form of his work (or that of an earlier confrere) would have been transmitted to China along with Buddhism and made available to Buddhist literati such as Liu Xie.

From Bharata to Bhāmaha and Daṇḍin, Indian authorities on poetics have customarily dealt with such matters as embellishments, figures of speech, faults or flaws, logic, meaning (ideas, intent), grammatical and rhetorical correctness, proper use of language, musicality (rules governing sounds), and prosody, all of which are treated in the second half of *WXDL*. They also discuss the peculiarly Indian aesthetic notion of *rasa* (sentiment, taste) and the psychological theory of *bhāva* (emotion), which are echoed in *WXDL* by *xing* 性 and *qing* 情. It is particularly intriguing that both Bhāmaha and Daṇḍin devote extensive coverage to the "body" (*śarīra*) of poetry.[47] Similarly, one of the most salient terms in *WXDL* is *ti* 體 (literally, "body"), which connotes meanings ranging from "style" to "substance," "form," and "genre," just as does the Sanskrit word. Finally, Indian works on poetics frequently survey the various literary genres, comparing and contrasting them with poetry (*kāvya*), which is the supreme manifestation of the literary impulse. The same holds true for *WXDL*.

For all of these reasons and others too tedious to mention, it is entirely appropriate to style the *WXDL* as a *śāstra*, the class of writing to which the works of the major Indian authors on poetics such as Bharata, Bhāmaha, and Daṇḍin belong.

We may further observe that, aside from *lun* 論, another common translation of *śāstra* in Chinese was *shengjiao* 聖教 (teaching of the sages) or *shengshuo* 聖說 (discourse of the sages). With this, we may compare the second chapter of *WXDL*, "Zhengsheng" 徵聖 (Evidence of the sages). As was the custom in Indian treatises (*śāstras*) on literature, Liu Xie begins *WXDL* with the philosophical, mythological, and moral premises that underlay his work. And, as did many of his Indian predecessors, he then moves on to an examination of specific genres and closes with an exposition of various literary devices and figures.

The proportion of emphasis upon and the order of the various components of literature discussed in *WXDL* are not exactly the same as in any single

Indian work on poetics that can be securely dated before Liu Xie, but the overall correspondences between Liu Xie's masterwork and the major Indian treatises on poetics are sufficient to warrant more detailed investigation. To be sure, the arrangement of and weight placed upon the diverse elements of Bhāmaha's *Kāvyālaṃkāra* (Ornamentation of poetry) and Daṇḍin's *Kāvyādarśa* (Mirror of poetry) on the one hand and Liu Xie's *WXDL* on the other are uncannily similar.[48] In the words of Edwin Gerow, the preeminent American authority on Indian poetics, both *Kāvyālaṃkāra* and *Kāvyādarśa* "begin with the usual attempt to situate *kāvya* in the universe of discourse: patronage and educational prerequisites, languages and other genres. The major thrust of both works follows: a discussion of the distinctive qualities (*guṇa*), forms (*alaṃkāra*), and debilitating detractions (*doṣa*) of poetic assertion. Poetry is language, and it is language caught in rather small compass. . . ."[49] In *WXDL*, we see replicated the identical Bhāmaha- and Daṇḍin-like progression from the religious and philosophical foundations of literature to its manifestations in various genres and thence, after a large shift toward more concrete realia, to the qualities, techniques, and devices of literary (especially poetic) compositions. Such a close set of complex three-way correspondences can scarcely be due to happenstance but must be the result of some sort of intimate linkage between the Indian and the Chinese traditions of poetics.

The *WXDL* is by no means a translation of any known Indian work. It is a Chinese text through and through; not only is it written in classical Chinese, its examples and citations are all masterfully drawn from Chinese literature in an impressive display of erudition. Furthermore, as Zong-qi Cai has shown so well,[50] in *WXDL* Liu Xie has created an integral system of literary theory and criticism in conformity with ancient Chinese traditions of thought and performance. At the same time, *WXDL* shares so many telling features with various Indian treatises on poetics that one can hardly escape the conclusion that it was substantially influenced, whether directly or indirectly, by Indian conceptions about *kāvya* and other types of literature that, like vast amounts of other cultural baggage, were quite naturally brought to China along with Buddhism.

Crass as his argument may sound, Ma Hongshan's contention that *WXDL* is superficially Confucian but fundamentally Buddhist is essentially correct. While I would not attribute this to any devious intent on the part of Liu

Xie, it is difficult to deny that the overall appearance and diction of *WXDL* are those of a Confucian treatise. However, when we dig beneath the surface to analyze its epistemology and methodology, we perceive that it is Buddhist to the core.[51] This should not be in the least disconcerting, since Liu Xie was a deeply learned Buddhist layman (later a monk) who lived in an age steeped in Buddhism.

In the "Xu zhi" chapter, which functions as a postface to *WXDL* and which was quoted *in extenso* in his biography in the *Liang History*, Liu Xie tells of a dream he had in which he followed Confucius south (*sui Zhongni er nan xing* 隨 仲 尼 而 南 行) and how impressed he was by the sage and his teachings. This would appear to be a clear statement of intent to stave off rebuke by the Confucian literary clique at court for any Buddhist sentiments that might unconsciously or accidentally surface in his opus. Considering the eclectic intellectual climate of the Six Dynasties, in which—to one degree or another—Confucianism, Buddhism, Taoism, and (during the early part of this period) Xuanxue[52] were simultaneously subscribed to by most scholars,[53] and particularly in light of Liu Xie's early Buddhist upbringing, it would have been virtually impossible for him to banish all traces of Buddhism from his writing. Yet we must admit that *WXDL* is basically a secular work dealing with secular literature. In it, Liu Xie does not mention a single Buddhist work of literature. I suspect that he felt the proper place for that was in the sort of large-scale Buddhist compilation projects in which he assisted Sengyou. Since *WXDL* was intended for the secular sphere, therefore, it is not surprising that Buddhism is seldom openly encountered in it. But this, by no means whatsoever, rules out the possibility that *WXDL* may have been conceived upon a Buddhist epistemology.

The most important Buddhist contributions to *WXDL* lie not in its use of such Buddhistic expressions as *yuantong* 圓 通 (perfect comprehension)[54] but in the mode of thought and systematic organization Liu Xie employed in writing it. *WXDL* was part of a sea change in Chinese aesthetics that took place during the Six Dynasties. This was a time when Buddhism was in the ascendancy, so it is inevitable that Buddhist ideas would have had a significant impact upon Chinese art and literature, as they did upon Chinese philosophy and religion. Like the celebrated "Six Laws" (*liu fa* 六 法) of painting formulated by Xie He 謝 赫 (fl. ca. 500–535?), which are perfectly analogous to the *ṣaḍaṅga* (six limbs) of Indian painting theory,[55] *WXDL* is an excellent example of the wedding of Indian ideas and methods with Chinese practice.

The Six Dynasties witnessed the increasing "belletricization" of Chinese literary criticism and theory that paralleled the Buddhicization of Chinese society during the same period and beyond. If we trace the development of Chinese literary criticism and theory from Cao Pi's 曹丕 (187–226) "Lun wen" 論文 (Essay on literature) through Lu Ji's 陸機 (261–303) "Wen fu" 文賦 (Rhapsody on literature), Liu Xie's *WXDL*, Kūkai's 空海 (774–835) *Bunkyō hifuron* 文鏡秘府論 (*Treatise/śāstra on the secret repository/kośa of the literary/kāvya mirror/ādarśa/darpaṇa*) to Yan Yu's 嚴羽 (fl. 1200) *Canglang shihua* 滄浪詩話 (Poetry talks by the recluse of Canglang River), where poetic inspiration is characterized as Zen/Chan/*dhyāna* 禪 (meditation[al insight]), we observe a fertile process of belletricization/Buddhicization that greatly enriched Chinese reflections upon and conceptualizations of literature. *WXDL* represents a key stage in that development and demonstrates how Indian notions about literature could be smoothly absorbed into Chinese discussions of the subject without entirely displacing or grossly distorting them.

In my estimation, the entire controversy over the existence or nonexistence of Buddhist elements in *WXDL* is a tempest in a teapot—insofar as the literary value and intellectual content of Liu Xie's masterpiece are concerned—yet it is extremely revealing about matters of nationalistic pride and cultural prejudice, which ideally should be absent from academic inquiries such as this.

Did Buddhism play a significant role in *WXDL*?[56] Yes, even if we ignore "the incomparable realm of *prajñā*" (which, [un]fortunately, we cannot). In sum and in essence, *WXDL* is precisely what Stephen Owen has claimed it to be: a "*śāstra* on literature,"[57] that is, a *sāhityaśāstra* or, better still, a *kāvyaśāstra*. Indeed, we might well render the entire title more fully as *Kāvyahṛdaya-alaṃkāraśāstra* (Treatise on the literary heart/mind and its embellishments).[58] There are ample Indian paradigms for such a rubric and for the poetics that it designates.

Wang Bi and Liu Xie's *Wenxin diaolong*: Terms and Concepts, Influence and Affiliations

RICHARD JOHN LYNN

The writings of Wang 王弼 (226–49) served as an important source for many of the concepts, terms, and epistemological and rhetorical models used by Liu Xie. When one compares various passages in Wang's writings with statements in *Wenxin diaolong*, it is obvious that Liu must have read Wang's essays and commentaries carefully and thought deeply about some passages. Explicit evidence for Liu's interest in Wang's writings occurs in *Wenxin diaolong* itself; in chapter 18, "Lunshuo" 論説 (On discourse and discussion), Liu Xie praises four works by Wang Bi—*Laozi zhu* 老子注 (Commentary to *Laozi*), *Laozi weizhi lilue* 老子微指例略 (General remarks on the subtle and profound meaning of the *Laozi*), *Zhouyi zhu* 周易注 (Commentary to the *Changes of the Zhou*), and *Zhouyi lueli* 周易略例 (General remarks on the *Changes of the Zhou*).

> When the Wei first became hegemonic, as the art of government conjoined the teachings of the School of Names and that of the Legalists, Fu Gu 傅嘏 [209–55] and Wang Can 王粲 [177–217] examined and assessed names and principles, but, by the Zhengshi era [240–48], an earnest wish had arisen to conserve the literary heritage, and, thanks to such figures as He Yan 何晏 [190–249], discourses on the Mysterious began to flourish. It was then that Dan [Laozi] and Zhou [Zhuangzi] so came to prevail that they even contended with Master Ni [Confucius] for supremacy! When

we carefully read. . . . the two *General Remarks* 兩 例 by Fusi [Wang Bi] [*Zhouyi lueli* and *Laozi weizhi lilue*], and the two *Discourses* 二 論 [*Wuwei lun* 無 為 論 (On nonpurposeful action) and *Wuming lun* 無 名 論 (On the nameless)] by Pingshu [He Yan] we discover that all express independent views based on original insight and argue with precision and tight organization. There is no doubt that these are outstanding examples of discourses. (*WXDL* 18:50–68)[1]

As for the commentary, its composition is a discourse broken into fragments, and, although the odds and ends of text that result differ [from that of the integral discourse], when the commentary is considered as a whole, it turns out to be much the same. . . . As for such works as Master Mao's [Mao Heng 毛 亨] exegesis on the *Classic of Poetry* 訓 詩, [Kong 孔] Anguo's 安 國 [second century B.C.] commentary to the *Classic of History*, Master Zheng's [Zheng Xuan] exegeses on the [three] *Rites*, and Wang Bi's commentary to the *Classic of Changes*, all these are concise but thoroughly lucid—worthy models indeed for exegetical writing! (*WXDL* 18/125–40)

Liu Xie does not refer to Wang Bi by name anywhere else in *Wenxin diaolong*. However, in many places throughout his work, he must have had Wang's writings in mind, at least indirectly, since the occurrence there of certain terms and concepts is distinctly reminiscent of Wang's writings some three centuries earlier. For instance, in this same chapter, Liu Xie also discusses writers whose works seem to belong to the same tradition as Wang Bi's commentary to the *Laozi*.

Next we come to Song Dai 宋 岱 [dates unknown][2] and Guo Xiang 郭 象 [d. 312], who applied their sharp wits to the realm of incipiency and the spirit, and to Yifu [Wang Yan 王 衍 (256–311)] and Pei Wei 裴 頠 [267–300], who disputed each other on the boundary between existence and nothingness. They all strode independently through their own times, and their footsteps echo down the ages. However, those who got bogged down in existence attached themselves completely to physical form and function, while those who prized nothingness devoted themselves exclusively to the obscure and immaterial. Each was merely sharp when it came to one of these biased ways of explanation or the other, so none arrived at the whole truth. It is indeed true that to set the fountainhead of ultimate spirituality in motion, one must dwell in the absolute realm of *prajña* 般 若! All those engaged in talk on the Left of the Yangzi [during the Eastern Jin era (317–420)] had the Mysterious 玄 as their sole concern. Although something new was added every day, for the most part it was just a continuation of what had been said before. (*WXDL* 18/74–91)

Terms such as *ji* 幾 (incipiency), *shen* 神 (spirit), *you* 有 (existence), *wu* 無 (nothingness), *xing* 形 (physical form), *yong* 用 (function), *jiliao* 寂寥 (the obscure and immaterial), and *xuan* 玄 (the Mysterious) were common throughout the discourse of intellectual thought during the Wei-Jin-Song-Qi-Liang eras (the third through sixth centuries). They first appeared in neo-Taoism and its critique of Confucianism and Legalism, then in the Taoist-Buddhist dialogue, and finally within the internal discourse of Buddhism itself. We can say that the initiation of this tradition of discourse and the setting of its parameters probably owes more to Wang Bi than to anyone else. It is remarkable how many of the assumptions and particular modes of argument that constitute the intellectual discourse of *Wenxin diaolong* seem to have been prefigured in the writings of Wang Bi. Although many significant texts intervene during the three centuries that divide Liu from Wang, it is likely that Liu Xie had read Wang's commentaries and discourses on the *Yijing* and *Taodejing* with great care. The purpose of this essay is to explore the depth and extent of this affinity.

For Liu, the most important parts of Wang's works seem to have been the fourth section of the *Zhouyi lueli* 周易略例 (General remarks on the *Changes of the Zhou*), *Ming xiang* 明象 (Clarifying the images), *Laozi zhilue* 老子指略 (Outline introduction to *Laozi*), and, as a challenge to be overcome, the first section of the *Laozi zhu* 老子注 (Commentary to *Laozi*). Wang's commentary to the *Changes* is also likely to have had an influence, but it is probably impossible to distinguish this from the general impact of the *Changes* on Liu's thought, which, given the many times Liu refers to the *Changes* throughout *Wenxin diaolong*, must have been considerable. Although Wang's commentary to the *Changes* had to share authority with Zheng Xuan's commentary, the *Zhouyi Zheng Kangcheng zhu* 周易鄭康成注, during most of the sixth century,[3] we saw above that Zheng's work is not mentioned in *Wenxin diaolong*, and it is Wang's *Zhouyi zhu* that earns Liu's praise—strong evidence for Liu's familiarity with and respect for it.

Let us now take a look at a passage in *Ming xiang*, in which Wang Bi explicates the relationships among images (*xiang* 象), words (*yan* 言), and ideas (*yi* 意). This passage seems to have had a profound effect on Liu Xie's own thinking.

> Images are the means to express ideas. Words [that is, the texts] are the means to explain the images. To yield up ideas completely there is nothing

better than the images, and to yield up the meaning of the images there is nothing better than words. The words are generated by the images, thus one can ponder the words and so observe what the images are. The images are generated by ideas, thus one can ponder the images and so observe what the ideas are. The ideas are yielded up completely by the images, and the images are made explicit by the words. Thus, since the words are the means to explain the images, once one gets the images, he forgets the words, and, since the images are the means to allow us to concentrate on the ideas, once one gets the ideas, he forgets the images. Similarly, "the rabbit snare exists for the sake of the rabbit, once one gets the rabbit, he forgets the snare, and the fish trap exists for the sake of fish; once one gets the fish he forgets the trap."[4] If this is so, then the words are snares for the images, and the images are traps for the ideas.

Therefore someone who stays fixed on the words will not be one to get the images, and someone who stays fixed on the images will not be one to get the ideas. The images are generated by the ideas, but if one stays fixed on the images themselves, then what he stays fixed on will not be images as we mean them here. The words are generated by the images, but if one stays fixed on the words themselves, then what he stays fixed on will not be words as we mean them here. If this is so, then someone who forgets the images will be one to get the ideas, and someone who forgets the words will be one to get the images. Getting the ideas is in fact a matter of forgetting the images, and getting the images is in fact a matter of forgetting the words. Thus, although the images were established in order to yield up ideas completely, as images they may be forgotten. Although the number of strokes were doubled[5] in order to yield up all the innate tendencies of things, as strokes they may be forgotten.

This is why anything that corresponds analogously to an idea can serve as its image, and any concept that fits with an idea can serve as corroboration of its nature. If the concept involved really has to do with dynamism, why must it be only presented in terms of the horse? And if the analogy used really has to do with compliance, why must it be only presented in terms of the cow? If its lines really do fit with the idea of compliance, why is it necessary that *Kun* [Hexagram 2] represent only the cow, and if its concept really corresponds to the idea of dynamism, why is it necessary that *Qian* [Hexagram 1] represent only the horse? Yet there are some who have convicted *Qian* of horsiness. They made a legal case out of its texts and brought this accusation against its hexagram, and, in doing so, they may have come up with a horse, but *Qian* itself got lost in the process! . . . This is all due to the fact that by concentrating on the images one forgets about the ideas. If one were instead to forget about the images in order to seek the ideas they represent, the concepts involved would then become evident as a matter of course.[6]

Overall, Wang Bi's *Ming xiang* can be read, first, as a long exposition on a brief passage in the "Xici zhuan" 繫辭傳 (Commentary on the appended phrases) of the *Classic of Changes*, Part 1, 12:

> The Master said: "Writing does not exhaust words, and words do not exhaust ideas. If this is so, does this mean that the ideas of the sages cannot be discerned?" The Master said: "The sages established images in order to express their ideas exhaustively. They established the hexagrams in order to treat exhaustively the true innate tendency of things and their counter-tendencies to spuriousness. They attached phrases to the hexagrams in order to exhaust what they had to say. . . ."[7]

This all seems straightforward, except for the distinction in Wang's thought between *yi* 意 (idea) and *yi* 義 (concept). However, it is possible to clarify this distinction by referring to other passages in Wang's writings. In his commentary to the *Wenyan* (Commentary to the words of the text) to Top Yang in *Qian* 乾, Hexagram 1 (Pure Yang), Wang states:

> [T]he *Changes* consist of images, and what images are produced from are concepts. One first has to have a particular concept, which one then brings to light by using some concrete thing to exemplify it. Thus one uses the dragon to express *Qian* and the mare to illustrate *Kun*. One follows the concept inherent in a matter and chooses an image for it accordingly.[8]

In his commentary to the *Xiang zhuan* 象傳 (Commentary on the images) to First Yin in *Xie* 解 Hexagram 40 (Release), Wang equates concept with principle (*li* 理). First, the passage from *Xiang zhuan*: "To be on the borderline between hard and soft as a concept means 'there is no blame' [或有過咎，非其理也。義猶理也]. Wang comments: "When something incurs blame, it means that it does not measure up to the principle involved. Concept here is the same as principle."[9] In discussing this passage in Wang Bi's writings, Feng Youlan 馮友蘭 concludes: "Both terms [*concept* and *principle*], therefore, would seem to be his designations for the primary principles which underlay the phenomenal world, whereas by 'ideas' he would seem to mean these same objective principles as they are mentally imprinted in men's minds."[10] If, as Feng suggests, "ideas" are individual and particular mental experiences of general "concepts," then it seems that Tang Junyi says something similar in his own analysis of Wang Bi's terminology: "When ideas are made known, they become concepts" [意之所知即義].[11] That is, once ideas are articulated (rendered in knowable form), they are concepts. Ideas are private and personal; concepts are public and general. An individual's experience of a concept or principle is, first, as an idea that, in order to be shared with and communicated to others, has to be put in a knowable form, as a concept or principle. Therefore, ideas become concepts, when starting from the individual (subjective), and concepts or principles become ideas when starting from the general (objective). However, Feng Youlan also notes that Wang Bi does not always seem to maintain this distinction. He concludes: "It would thus appear that what he calls 'ideas' and what he calls 'concepts' are essentially the same."[12] As proof, Feng cites two brief statements by Wang. The first is from the beginning of *Ming xiang*, and the second is from his commentary to the *Wenyan* (Commentary on the words of the text) to Top Yang in *Qian* 乾, Hexagram 1 (Pure Yang) (both quoted above): "Images are the means to express ideas" [夫象者，出意者也]; and "what images are produced from are concepts" [象之所生，生於義也]. I do not think Feng is correct, for it is not necessary to interpret 意 and 義 as "essentially the same." The two statements, taken together, suggest the following paradigm: 義 (concepts equal principles 理) are manifested in 象 (images), and these images then evoke 意 (ideas) in those who behold them. This is in accordance with the distinction defined by Tang Junyi and, earlier, by Feng himself. The distinction, I believe, is useful, so I shall maintain it throughout this study.

Before comparing these statements concerning the relationship among ideas (*yi* 意), concepts (*yi* 義), images (*xiang* 象), and words (*yan* 言) in Wang Bi's writings with appropriate passages in the *Wenxin diaolong*, we should note the important place *xiang* 象 (images) have in the first chapter of Liu's work, "Yuan Tao" (The Tao as source). In "Yuan Tao" these terms are discussed as: (1) manifestations of the pattern of Heaven (*tianwen* 天文): the sun, moon, and constellations of stars and planets; (2) manifestation of the pattern of man (*renwen* 人文) in the *Classic of Changes*: descriptive and prescriptive models for individual and social human behavior; and (3) manifestations of the Tao as revealed in the "Yellow River Diagram" and the "Luo River Writing" and codified by the sages: the trigrams, hexagrams, basic texts, and exegetical "Wings" of the *Classic of Changes*. It is likely that Liu Xie based most of his comments relating to *xiang* directly on the "Xici zhuan" 繫辭傳 (Commentary on the appended phrases) and other parts of the

Classic of Changes and not on Wang's commentary. However, Liu's comments are worth reviewing, since they are so fundamental to understanding the range of meanings of *xiang* in *Wenxin diaolong* as a whole.

> *Wen* 文 [pattern] as power is indeed great! But how is it born together with Heaven and Earth? Out of [Heaven's] black and [Earth's] yellow, all colors are compounded; out of [Heaven's] squareness and [Earth's] roundness, all bodies form characteristic shapes; the sun and the moon endlessly alternate their disks of jade and so suspend images that cohere to Heaven; and mountains and rivers shine forth their elegant weave and so set out forms that configure Earth. Such is the pattern of the Tao. (*WXDL* 1/1–8)

> The origin of the pattern of man lies in the great ultimate.[13] Mysteriously assisted by the numinous and the bright [the gods], the images of the *Changes* led the way.[14] Bao Xi [Fu Xi] made strokes for its beginning [i.e., created the trigrams], and Zhongni [Confucius] added "Wings" [the exegetical texts] for its final development. However, it was only for the two positions *Qian* [Heaven or Pure Yang] and *Kun* [Earth or Pure Yin] that he made the *Wenyan* 文言 [Commentary on the words of the text], for the pattern of words [*wen zhi yan* 文之言] is indeed the mind of Heaven and Earth [*Tiandi zhi xin* 天地之心]! As for such things as the "Yellow River Diagram" begot with the Eight Trigrams, the "Luo River Writing" furnished with the Nine Categories, solid figuration as in jade tablets inlaid with gold, and flowery surface delineation as on green plaques inscribed with red script, who was ever in charge of them? For these can only be examples of numinous striation! (*WXDL* 1/41–56)

"Numinous striation" seems a good translation for *shenli* 神理 here because the passage asserts that the "Yellow River Diagram" delineated [河圖] on the back of a dragon-horse 龍馬 and "Luo River Writing" inscribed [洛書] on the back of a spirit-tortoise 神龜 are "natural" markings, just like the striation (textures, inclusions, and so on) naturally occurring in jade and other stones. These markings were read by the sages of remote antiquity as manifestations of the natural order of the cosmos and of mankind. Similar manifestations occur in the manipulation of yarrow stalks and the heat cracking of tortoise shells. Since they were perfectly in tune with such natural manifestations, the sages, including Confucius, were able to expand upon their understanding of these communications of the Tao of heaven, earth, and man and compose texts used to teach the rest of mankind the great truths involved. *Li* 理 are the underlying principles of behavior of heaven, earth, and man (how they work). Why they are so and how they operate are numinous mysteries. The manifestation of *li* (principle) is *wen* 文 (pattern), and the interpretation or communication of *wen* in language is *yan* 言 (words). *Xiang* 象 (images) are particular configurations of *wen*: As the *wen* of *Tian* (heaven) consists of many different *xiang* (sun, moon, stars and planets, constellations), so the *wen* of *Ren* (man) can be differentiated among the eight trigrams and, doubled, the sixty-four hexagrams, each with its own particular configuration or *xiang*.

> So, from the time of man of the surname Feng [Fu Xi] to that of Master Kong [Confucius], the Mysterious Sage creating the *Canon* [*of Changes*] and the Uncrowned King transmitting its teachings, none but sought its source in the mind of the Tao, in order to set forth its written texts, and grind away at it to reach its numinous texture [or striation], in order to establish its teachings. They took the images from the "Yellow River Diagram" and the "Luo River Writing" and fixed the calculations by using yarrow stalks and tortoise shells. They observed the pattern of Heaven in order to examine fully the flux [of the seasons] and investigated the pattern of man in order to perfect the transformation [of the world].[15] For only then could they determine what the warp and woof of the cosmos were and amend and complete its great ordinances. They expressed all this in their deeds and magnificently articulated it in the meaning of their words. Thus we know that the Tao relied on the sages to suspend Its pattern (*wen*),[16] and the sages clarified the Tao through pattern/writing (*wen*), so that It prevailed everywhere without hindrance and was used daily but never used up. The *Changes* say: "To drum people into action all over the world is dependent on the *Phrases*."[17] The reason why the *Phrases* can drum up people all over the world is that they are the pattern/writing of the Tao. (*WXDL* 1/95–117)

The terms "concept" (*yi* 義), "idea" (*yi* 意), "image" (*xiang* 象), and "word" (*yan* 言) also occur with important frequency in *Wenxin diaolong*. A survey of their occurrence should clarify the similarities and differences between their use there and in the writings of Wang Bi.

Chapter 26, "Shensi" 神思 (Thinking with the spirit, or intuitive thinking) contains a compound term, *yixiang* 意象 (idea-image), which combines two of the single terms whose meanings we have been exploring above.

> Therefore, in shaping and turning literary thought one places great importance on emptiness and stillness. Purge the five viscera and purify the spirit;

amass learning so as to collect a treasure; ponder principles so as to enrich ability; use intense observation so as to provide a complete sense of familiarity; be compliant to the utmost[18] so as to make words pleasing. For only then can one engage the butcher who mysteriously cuts things apart and so plot writing according to the rules of sound or employ the carpenter of unique discernment and so wield the ax according to insight into the idea-image.[19] These are the foremost means to handle writing and the great principles for designing a piece. (*WXDL* 26/25–63)

From the context, idea-image seems close to "artistic concept"—the mental image constructed by the operation of thought, which can serve as model, guide, or template for the production of a literary work. Literary thought (*wensi* 文思), as described here, is that operation, a necessary preliminary stage before intuitive control over the medium of language can occur. *Xiang* in the compound *yixiang* is a mental image. There is nothing in *Wenxin diaolong* to indicate if it means anything more than the image of a literary work that a writer holds in his mind before it actually takes form in words. It does, however, appear to represent a preverbal state of the work. The citation of Butcher Ding and Carpenter Shi suggests that Liu Xie believes that there can be a perfect correspondence between idea-image and verbal articulation. Liu ends the "Shensi" chapter with the following.

> Spirit expresses itself through images,
> Which are begot by change inherent in the innate tendency of things.
> Things for images are chosen by their appearance,
> The mind responding to them according to the common principles
>   involved.
> Carved and engraved in words governed by the rules of sound,
> Images sprout forth as similes and evocative associations.
> So gathering your thoughts together, control this tally [the image],
> And with tent-flaps hanging down, devise your victories.
>
> (*WXDL* 26/125–33)

Here, "control the tally" means being in control of the process whereby an idea through an image becomes articulate in words. Idea and words should fit together as perfectly as the two halves of a tally—and the image is that tally. This alludes to the story of General Zhang Liang 張良 (d. 189 B.C.) in the next line. General Zhang won great victories hundreds of miles away from the battleground just by plotting strategy in his tent. However, he had to communicate his ideas to his commanders in the field to make these victories happen, and military communications were always verified by tally halves. The commanding general had a set of halves that fit halves kept by field commanders. It is obvious that *qi* 契 is the general field commander tally. Liu suggests that the writer should use images in the same way General Zhang used tallies: *yi* 意 (ideas)—*xiang* 象 (images)—*yan* 言 (words); and *yi* 意 (ideas)—*qi* 契 (tally)—*ling* 令 (correct orders that lead to victory). The first paradigm expresses the same relationship among *yi* 意, *xiang* 象, and *yan* 言 that Wang Bi describes at the beginning of *Ming xiang*, so it seems likely that Liu had Wang's work in mind here.

If we turn to Wang Bi's *Laozi zhilue* 老子指略 (Outline introduction to *Laozi*), a few passages in it seem to be echoed in *Wenxin diaolong*.

> The term *Tao* 道 [the Way] is derived from the fact that It is that on which the myriad things make their way. The term "mysterious" [*xuan* 玄] is derived from the fact that it is that which emerges from the secret and the dark. The term "deep" [*shen* 深] is derived from the fact that you might try to plumb to the bottom of it but can never reach that far. . . .[20]
>
> Thus, as far as the text of the *Laozi* is concerned, those who try to explicate it though rational argument do violence to its intent, and those who blame it for misuse of names do violence to the concepts involved.[21] This is because its great aim is to discuss the source of the primordial beginning, thereby clarifying the nature of the Natural, and to elaborate on the ultimate reaches of the secret and the dark, thereby putting an end to confusion arising from doubt and bewilderment. It [the text of *Laozi*] responds [to the Tao] and does not act [initiate anything of its own], effaces itself and does not assert, venerates the root and forgoes the branch tips, and holds fast to the mother in order to preserve the child.[22] It disparages cleverness and craft, for action should occur before the need arises. It would have no blame placed on others, but insists that it be found in oneself.[23] These are its essential features.[24]

Several assertions in these parts of Wang Bi's *Outline Introduction to Laozi* are echoed later in Liu Xie's *Wenxin diaolong*. Consider the following passage from chapter 18, "Lunshuo" 論説 (On discourse and discussion).

> In the first place, as a genre the function of the discourse is to distinguish truth from falsehood. It fully explores everything tangible and pursues the formless, it delves so into what is hard [the tangible] that it would find out everything about it and hooks so into the Deep that it would lay hold of

Its ultimate reaches. It is actually both the fish trap or rabbit snare for all thought as well as the scales in which all worldly matters are weighed. Therefore, it is most estimable if its concepts be comprehensive and lucid and most reprehensible if its wording be incoherent and fragmented. It must bring the mind and the principles of things together so tightly that the seam between them is invisible to all and effect such a close fit between mind and words that the enemy would be utterly at a loss for what to do. These are its essential features. (*WXDL* 18/100–114)

Note how Liu's "hooks so into the Deep that it would lay hold of Its ultimate reaches" [鉤深取極。] resembles Wang's "[e]laborate on the ultimate reaches of the Secret and the Dark, thereby putting an end to confusion arising from doubt and bewilderment" [演幽冥之極以定惑罔之迷], and "[t]he term 'deep' [*shen*] is derived from the fact that you might try to plumb to the bottom of It but can never reach that far" [深也者，取乎探賾而不可究也]. Note also Liu's remark that "[i]t [the discourse] is . . . the fish trap or rabbit snare for all thought . . ." [乃百慮之筌蹄 [碲]], which, while alluding directly to the *Zhuangzi*, might also echo Wang's *Ming xiang*: "words are snares for the images, and the images are traps for the ideas" [言者，象之碲也。象者，意之筌也].

However, these passages from Wang's *Outline Introduction to Laozi* also exemplify positions that Liu Xie seems out to refute—at least as far as the classics 經 are concerned. Wang's assertions that names (*ming* 名) cannot go beyond the phenomenal and that human perception, the rational mind, and language in general are all incapable of grasping and communicating true aspects of the Tao are confronted in the passage from *Wenxin diaolong* just quoted and also in the longer passage from the "Yuan Tao" (The Tao as source) quoted earlier. Although most of Liu's claims concerning the powers of the mind and the potential of language refer to the phenomenal world of sensual experience, emotional reaction, and referential and expressive verbal communication, we have seen other passages make larger claims concerning the capacity for writing to communicate aspects of ultimate reality, the very pattern of heaven, earth, and man—the Tao. This is just what Wang Bi, following the teachings of the *Laozi*, thought writing could not do. At one point in *Wenxin diaolong*, Liu even chides the *Laozi* for its negative view of language. "Lao Zi disliked artificiality and therefore declared that 'beautiful words are not true'; yet his own 'Five Thousand Words' are refined and subtle, which shows that he did not reject beauty" (*WXDL* 31/32–35).[25]

We also saw above that Liu believed that the sages, from Fu Xi to Confucius, expressed the Tao in their writings. But is it only the sages who could "express the Tao"? Liu never answers this question directly, but he does suggest at various places in *Wenxin diaolong* that certain kinds of writing have the potential, in effect, to escape the confines of words and, at least indirectly, communicate the ineffable. In the following passage, from chapter 40, "Yinxiu" 隱秀 (The recondite and the prominent), Liu makes the claim that, in the "recondite" mode of writing, words can mean more than they say, concepts can exist through the skillful use of connotative language in an accessible realm "beyond words," and it is possible to communicate multiple meanings simultaneously, just as a single hexagram, depending on how one looks at the lines, can simultaneously contain four different trigram images.

> The action that the arts of the mind can perform is far-reaching; and the change that feelings in literature can undergo is profound. When a source is deep, branching waters start to flow; when the root prospers, the head of grain towers above the others. Since this is so, the most beautiful literary blossoms include both recondite and prominent modes. The recondite becomes an accomplished mode through the compounding of ideas; the prominent becomes a skillful mode by creating unprecedented effects. It is due to these modes that old works achieve their admirable success, for in them occur the most happy marriages of ability and feeling. The recondite is realized when concepts rule [come to life] beyond words, secret sounds resonate everywhere, and hidden splendors emerge from the depths. It is just like when hexagram line images become interchangeable in the "Overlapping Trigrams" [method of interpreting the *Changes*][26] or when rivers contain pearl and jade. Thus, when "trigrams overlap," it interchanges the lines, and this forms four different images [trigrams]. When pearls and jade lie hidden under water, this makes the shape of the waves above them either square or round.[27] (*WXDL* 40/1–23)

The most influential statement in all of Chinese letters about words not exhausting meaning is, of course, the first section of the *Laozi*. I provide here a translation of the first part together with Wang Bi's commentary.

道可道，非常道。名可名，非常名。

The Tao that can be described in language is not the constant Tao; the name that can be given it is not its constant name.

可道之道，可名之名，指事造形，非其常也。故不可道，不可
名也。

The Tao that can be rendered in language and the name [*ming*] that can
be given it point to a thing/matter [*shi*] or reproduce a form [*xing*],[28] neither of which is It in Its constancy. This is why It can neither be rendered
in language nor given a name.

無名天地之始；有名萬物之母。

Nameless, It is the origin of the myriad things; named, it is the mother of
the myriad things.

凡有皆始於無，故未形無名之時，則為萬物之始。及其有形有
名之時則長之，育之，亭之，毒之，為其母也。言道以無形無
名始成萬物，萬物以始以成而不知其所以然，玄之又玄也。

Anything that exists originates in nothingness [*wu*], thus, before it has
forms and still nameless, it serves as the origin of the myriad things, and,
once it has forms and is named, it grows them, rears them, ensures them
their proper shapes, and matures them as their mother. In other words, the
Tao, by being itself formless and nameless, originates and brings the myriad
things to completion. They are originated and completed in this way, yet
we do not know how it happens. This is the mystery [*xuan*] beyond mystery.[29]

Wang asserts that language can only "point to things and reproduce forms"
and so cannot express, describe, or communicate the Tao. The phrase he
uses to identify what language can do, "point to things and reproduce forms"
[*zhi shi zao xing* 指事造形], occurs in several places in *Wenxin diaolong* in
slightly varied forms. Two such passages are presented here.

By the beginning of the Jian'an era [196–220], five-syllabic poetry was
dashing ahead with full speed. Emperor Wen [Cao Pi 曹丕 (187–226)]
and Chen Si 陳思 galloped ahead at free reign, while Wang [Wang Can
王粲 (177–217)], Xu Gan 徐幹, Ying [Ying Yang 瑒 (d. 217)], and Liu
[Liu Zhen 劉楨 (d. ca. 216)], their gaze fixed far down the road, held
their own horse race. They all loved the wind and the moon, outings to
ponds and gardens, telling of grace and honor, and describing drinking
parties and feasts. They gave vent to their great energies with poignant
magnanimity, employed their abilities with candor and artlessness, and,

in reproducing what was in their hearts [expressing feeling] and in pointing to things [describing and narrating], never tried to achieve delicate,
meticulous craft. (*WXDL* 6/93–105)

Lord Cao [Cao Cao 曹操 (155–220)] declared that in writing memorials
[concerning appointment] it was unnecessary to decline three times and
that memorials should not be superficially ornate. Therefore, memorials at
the beginning of the Wei just point to things and reproduce the facts, so,
if one tries to find beauty in them, he will certainly be disappointed.
(*WXDL* 22/79–84)

However, the term *zao xing* 造形 does not appear in the *Wenxin diaolong*,
either together with *zhi shi* 指事 or on its own. Instead, we have *zao huai* 造
情 and *zao shi* 造實, as in the above two passages. The term *zao qing* 造情
(reproduce feelings), which seems to mean about the same thing as *zao huai*
造懷, appears twice in chapter 31, "Qingcai" 情采 (Aspiration and embellishment), along with a contrasting term, *zao wen* 造文 (reproduce pattern
or make literary works).

A long time ago, when the poets of the *Classic of Poetry* composed their
poems, they reproduced pattern [made literary works] for the sake of feeling 為情而造文, but when [later] writers composed prose-poems and
hymns, they reproduced [made up] feeling for the sake of pattern [為文
而造情]. How can we know this is so? The impetus behind the *Airs* and
the *Elegentiae* was the pent-up aspirations and thoughts of the poets, who
expressed their feelings and individual natures in song in order to criticize
their superiors. This is what reproducing pattern [making literary works]
for the sake of feeling means. For such as those later masters, it was not
the case that their hearts were filled with frustration; instead, they dis-
honestly indulged in exaggerated show in order to sell themselves for fame
and fish for worldly glory. This is what reproducing [made up] feeling for
the sake of reproducing pattern [making literary works] means. Therefore,
whereas writing done for the sake of feeling is essential and concise and so
describes the truth, writing done for the sake of writing may be seductively
attractive but also is confusing and verbose. (*WXDL* 31/60–76)

Apparently, *zao* 造 (reproduce) can also mean "produce" (i.e., make up,
fabricate, counterfeit), which echoes the sense of *zao* as it appears in the
passage from *Zhuangzi* noted above.

The entire expression *zhi shi zao xing* 指事造形 (pointing to things and
reproducing forms) may not appear in the *Wenxin diaolong*, but it does

appear in a roughly contemporary work, Zhong Rong's 鍾嶸 *Shipin xu* 詩 品序 ([First] preface to *Classes of Poetry*). There, it seems to refer to the same kinds of things that it does in *Wenxin diaolong*—the expression of sensibilities and emotions and a description of the objective world.

> Five-syllabic verse occupies the most important place in literary expression, for all works in this form have flavor. As such, this explains why it tends to be appropriated by the commonplace and vulgar. But is it not also true that it is the most detailed and precise vehicle for "pointing to things and reproducing forms" [指事造形], that is, giving full expression to feelings and describing things [窮情寫物]?[30]

Whatever interests Liu Xie might have had in the potential for writing to explore and express the ineffable nature of ultimate reality (the Tao) are eclipsed by his greater concern with the power of writing on the phenomenological level. Certain kinds of writing, the *Laozi* and Wang Bi's commentaries and essays on the *Changes* and *Laozi*, for example, writing which Liu praises and obviously knows well, might have realized, at least in part, the potential for knowing and communicating the Tao. However, the only great body of writing that Liu Xie admits can do this, without reservation, is the collection of classics (*Jing* 經) of the Confucian tradition. Liu notes the *Yijing* 易 經 in particular. However, I have not discovered, in any part of *Wenxin diaolong*, any evidence that Liu Xie believed that the tradition of *wen* since the sages allowed writers to do what the sages once did: to suspend their *wen* in the realm of human culture as the Tao itself suspends images in heaven. In other words, Liu does not seem to think that writers can create works of literature as "natural objects" in the same way that the Tao creates and continually recreates heaven, earth, and man. Whereas the sages were one with the Tao and their writings were its "natural" manifestations, later writers always exhibit some degree of separation between nature and their writing. Although the best and most praiseworthy of writers succeed at lessening this degree of separation and close the gaps between self and nature or the Tao on the one hand, and the self and linguistic expression or depiction on the other, no writer succeeds completely. Only the sages were able to accomplish this.

Liu Xie would have us believe that this is true even of writers who set out to achieve unity with the Tao and express perfect truth, as, for example, the *xuanxue* 玄學 writers of the fourth century. In critiquing such writers, Liu refers to *prajñā*, the only overt reference to Buddhism in the entire *Wenxin diaolong*. "It is indeed true that to set the fountainhead of ultimate spirituality in motion one must dwell in the absolute realm of *prajñā*!" (*WXDL* 18/ 86–87). However, Liu does not elaborate on how *prajñā* is achieved, on what it is, how it works, or whether it can be communicated. This silence is attributable to the fact that *prajñā* is the vehicle for understanding ultimate reality or the Tao, and therefore any discussion of it would have to take place outside this secular work on literary theory and criticism. Nevertheless, Liu's reference to *prajñā* is tantalizing. We may wish that Liu had discussed, if briefly, how it compares to the search for and articulation of ultimate reality in the Confucian classics. This would be particularly interesting in the *Yijing*, as well as in the *Laozi*, which succeeded at expressing a vision of ultimate reality that, except for the commentary of Wang Bi, Liu thought *xuanxue* thinkers had failed to reach. Liu does not discuss this because, again, it is not a subject appropriately discussed in a work whose interests are focused elsewhere. Instead, Liu focuses on the literary mind as it encounters phenomenal reality and as it carves the impressions, images, moods, feelings, thoughts, and concepts that result from such an encounter in language—literary language as it constituted all the genres, forms, and styles of literature known to him and his world.

Although Liu does not accord sagehood to any later writer, he credits some writers with getting close to sagehood, implying that such achievement is always possible for the truly talented and dedicated. The embodiment of ontological reality in language might be the most elusive of enterprises, but, for Liu, it is an ideal to which every serious writer should aspire. *Wen* in *Wenxin diaolong* is thus accorded much higher standing than *yan* (words) in the writings of Wang Bi, where words only dimly approximate what they signify and which, at best, can but circuitously hint at ultimate truths. However, Wang never really addresses himself to the potential of writing, to what it *could* do. Instead he focuses on what writing *could not* do, so we shall never know what he might have said if he had had the opportunity to discuss the nature and function of language with the likes of Liu Xie. The dialogue between Liu and Wang described in this paper is necessarily one-sided—only Liu could respond to Wang—but it would be fascinating to know what Wang might have said in response.

PART THREE

The Creative Process

CHAPTER FIVE

Poet, Mind, and World: A Reconsideration of the "Shensi" Chapter of *Wenxin diaolong*

RONALD EGAN

It is difficult to think of a more complex and enduring issue in Chinese literary history than that of the relationship of author to world. A cluster of fruitful and problematic questions clings to this central issue, questions about the historicity of literature, fictionality, the ability of language to reflect "reality," and the relation of real-life authorial experience to representations of the same in writing. Somewhere in this cluster of questions lies one that may not have received the attention it deserves in recent scholarship: namely, the question of the role of the imagination in literary creativity. The reasons for this relative neglect deserve their own study. One likely cause, however, may be mentioned here: The nature of literary imagination—identified explicitly as such and in the way *we* now tend to conceptualize it—is not a primary topic in the literary criticism of the Tang, Song, and later periods. This criticism usually focused on other aspects of the author/world problem. Yet this issue was addressed from time to time and certainly deserves to be a recognized part of the critical tradition.

One major treatment of the issue of literary imagination is found in the "Shensi" 神思 chapter of *Wenxin diaolong*. The issue and its ramifications surface in other chapters of Liu Xie's work, but the "Shensi" chapter is devoted entirely to an exploration of literary imagination, as Liu Xie conceives of it.

This chapter, however, is also filled with obscure and difficult language (more than its share, even when allowances are made for the general difficulty of *Wenxin diaolong*). A look at the many available commentaries and translations (into modern Chinese, Japanese, and English) shows that key passages of the chapter have been read in radically different ways, yielding widely varied impressions of the chapter's general meaning and intent. One suspects that a large amount of this "difficulty" stems from something other than the usual adversities in Liu Xie's diction and style. Many of the particular topics that Liu Xie takes up in this chapter are so unusual, and what he says about them is so novel, that the very unexpectedness of the content has surely added to the linguistic and stylistic challenges we find elsewhere in *Wenxin diaolong*. It has even been suggested that the language of the chapter is in some fundamental sense "indeterminate," in other words, that it is open at key points to variant interpretations, all equally valid but also falling equally short of the open-ended quality of Liu Xie's original.[1]

My own view is that such "indeterminacy" is unlikely to be found in a prose text of Liu Xie's period, and the problems of meaning that the chapter presents should, in theory at least, be resolvable. Believing, moreover, that the chapter's difficulty and originality make it worthy of further examination, in what follows I present my own translation and interpretation, despite the number of treatments that already exist. The general remarks that are appended to my commentary on the chapter all spring from my reading of the chapter and depend upon it.

My translation of the word *shen* 神 as "daimon" follows the lead of A. C. Graham in his work on early Chinese thought. Anciently, the *shen* is of course that element of the human mind or psyche that corresponds to the manifold divinities of the natural world, especially those of mountains and rivers. This human *shen* is essentially beyond human understanding, and therein lies its connection with the impersonal *shen* outside the body. The *shen* are, all of them, "forces wiser than ourselves, throughout the cosmos and in the depths of our own hearts."[2] A cardinal trait of the ancient human *shen* is its ability to travel abroad (*you* 遊), as in the projections of the *shen* outward in shamanistic journeys. "Spirit" is a standard translation of *shen*, but "spirit" has the disadvantages of insipidity (through overuse), diffuse application, and the lack of any acceptable verbal or adjectival form, which are important in Liu Xie's chapter (as they were in *Zhuangzi*). I am aware that "daimon" and "daimonic" have their own drawbacks (oddity, possible confusion with "demon" or "demonic"), but I still prefer it to any term available in modern vocabulary.

There is another knotty terminological problem. In speaking of Liu Xie's treatment of the literary "imagination," we run the risk of distorting his thought by imposing upon it the conceptual implications of the English term. This is, of course, an enormously complicated issue and one that is certainly not limited to this particular topic. (The special difficulties presented by "imagination" are discussed at length by Shuen-fu Lin elsewhere in this volume.) One may defend the use of the term by pointing out that several modern Chinese translations and discussions of Liu's "Shensi" chapter use the modern term for "imagination" (*xiangxiang* 想象) to designate its subject. But this still begs the question of how to be sure that the modern term, in any language, is an appropriate label to apply to Liu's thought. The crux of the problem is that Liu does not use any such abstraction to name his subject, either in the chapter title or the chapter itself. Moreover, his use of "daimonic" is an appropriation of ancient terminology from another field, and so it may arguably be a metaphorical approximation of what he actually means. There is the further complication that even in the Western tradition the meanings and connotations of "imagination" are richly varied, including everything from Plato's illusory images, to St. Augustine's reproductive images, to the Renaissance concept of imagination as the inferior counterpart to imitation, to the Romantic period's idea of imagination as spiritual sensation, to modern notions of intuition, psychic expression, mental sign, and symbol. It is clear at least that the mental process addressed by Liu Xie is strongly visual, involving the calling up or envisioning of worldly images in the mind (see, for example, §1.2 below). There is even a suggestion, to be discussed below, that this envisioning is not limited to images found in the physical world, making it akin to fantasy as often understood in the West. A layman's understanding of "imagination" thus does have a degree of correspondence with Liu Xie's subject in this chapter, and the English term will be used here for want of a more apt alternative. Still, as I shall show, Liu brings his own conceptions and emphases to the subject. One notion that seems to be quite foreign to Liu's understanding is any assumption of an opposition between the mental activity he describes and "reason" or "intellect," a common theme in Western treatments of imagination.

The first (and longest) section of the chapter presents a poetic vision of the flight of the writer's daimon through imagined space, where it encounters images that the mind will eventually fashion into words on the page. It is an inspired and ambitious passage that attempts to describe a stage of "thinking" that precedes ideas and tries to consider the factors that will determine success or failure in this quest.

§1.1 (1–6):[3] 古人云： 形在江海之上，心存魏闕之下。神思之謂也。文之思也，其神遠矣。

§1.1: A man in ancient times said, "My body is here by the river and the sea, but my mind lingers on beneath the gate-towers of Wei."[4] This is known as "daimonic thinking." How distant indeed does the daimon go in the thinking required in literature!

The chapter opens with a bold reinterpretation of a statement found in *Zhuangzi*. Originally, these words are a complaint uttered by Prince Mou of Wei who had been banished to remote rivers and seas. He is counseled there to value the life he still has and to overcome his longing for reinstatement in the capital. Liu Xie transforms Prince Mou's complaint into a tribute to the ability of the daimon to detach itself from the body and to journey distantly away. Later in the chapter, Liu Xie speaks of the capability "daimonic thinking" has to rejuvenate commonplace statements or references by transforming them and investing them with fresh meanings (see §4.1). Consciously or not, what he has done with the *Zhuangzi* statement here, changing its import completely, aptly illustrates and anticipates this literary feat he describes later on.

§1.2 (7–17): 故寂然凝慮，思接千載；悄焉動容，視通萬里。吟詠之間，吐納珠玉之聲；眉睫之前，卷舒風雲之色。其思理之致乎。故思理為妙，神與物遊。

§1.2: When in stillness he concentrates his ruminations, his thinking spans a thousand years. When silently he moves his face, his vision penetrates ten thousand miles. As he recites, his mouth emits the tinkling of pearls and jades. In the space before his eyelashes windblown clouds are unfurled. Is this not the highest achievement of the path of thought? So it is that when the path of thinking is marvelous, the daimon roams about with things.

Commentators rightly point out the many similarities between this passage and several that anticipate it in Lu Ji's 陸機 "Rhapsody on Literature" (文賦). Lu Ji also speaks of the writer's ability to send his mind forth to the corners of the universe and to envision all of space and time in an instant.[5] One difference, of course, is that Liu Xie has a name for this process, "daimonic thinking," whereas Lu Ji describes it but does not name it.

Liu Xie's reference to the writer's "vision" deserves special comment. It is much more difficult than the first sentence in the passage, which refers wholly and unambiguously to the power of the mind to connect to something outside the scope of the individual life. The phrase "move the face" refers, perhaps, to a turning of the head or movement of the eyes to glance in a new direction. Yet we should not be misled by the apparent physicality of this phrase or by the word *vision* (*shi* 視) that follows. This is a special vision that knows no spatial boundary.

The first of the next pair of parallel sentences may be interpreted along the same lines. At first glance, we may suppose that this is nothing more than a conventionally complimentary description of the writer's words: They have the sound of tinkling gems. But it is also possible to turn this around, reading the sentence from the writer's point of view rather than from that of someone listening to him, and to drop the assumption that the words the writer recites are from his own literary composition. This reading allows us to see the connection between this sentence and the succeeding sentence. Just as the writer mentally creates and "sees" swirling clouds before his eyes, so too he mentally produces and "hears" the pleasing sounds of gems. The four sentences describe the creative powers of the mind or imagination with regard to time, space, sound, and sight, respectively. The powers are shown, as Liu Xie aptly concludes, to be "marvelous" in all four categories.

The final statement makes explicit Liu Xie's adaptation of the ancient notion of daimonic roaming. Under the influence of later notions about the "fusion" of self and scene (*qing* 情 and *jing* 景), commentators have identified the concept in an incipient form in this passage. Yet it should be pointed out that the "things" (*wu* 物) mentioned here, while certainly in one sense the objects of the real world, are located in the writer's mind. They are empirical "things" as envisioned in the mind.[6] The whole point so far is that the individual stays put and sends his daimon distantly off. Moreover, the destination of this daimonic flight is not identical with the objective, physical world, since it is a realm in which the boundaries of time and space do not exist.

§1.3 (18–25): 神居胸臆，而志氣統其關鍵。物沿耳目，而辭令管其樞機。樞機方通，則物無隱貌。關鍵將塞，則神有遁心。

§1.3: The daimon dwells inside the breast, and the person's will and breath control the door and latch. Things make contact with the ear and eye, and the power of words governs their pivot and hinge. When the pivot and hinge are open, no aspect of the appearance of things is obscured. But when the door and latch are closed, the daimon hides itself away.

Having described daimonic roaming at its most marvelous, in this passage, Liu Xie begins to consider the factors that permit or prohibit such success. There are two critical operations: the journey of the daimon and its ability to recognize what it encounters. First, the daimon must be able to venture forth. The gatekeeper that governs its ability to do this is the person's will and "breath" (*qi* 氣). Without the right quantity and quality of these, the daimon will find it impossible to leave. Second, once the daimon begins its journey, it will need sharp powers of perception to recognize the things it sees. This must be the same use of "things" (*wu*) that we saw in the preceding section, that is, things envisioned by the daimon, related to but distinguishable from actual things in the empirical world. These are the "things" with which the daimon roams, here said to brush up against the sense perceptions (so that they can be named). Liu Xie understands that recognition is not complete until we name things, and fittingly designates one's mastery of words as the hinge that opens or shuts the eye and ear.

It is unlikely that Liu Xie is thinking here of literary words or, indeed, of literary composition. We are a long way from the point in his account at which he addresses the act of composition. Here, he is only in the initial stages of his description of daimonic roaming, which is a prerequisite for literary inspiration. It may be significant that the phrase Liu uses at this point, *ciling* 辭令, which he does not use later in the chapter when he refers to literary composition, has a history of usage as a designation of outstanding skill in speech—indeed, Liu Xie uses it unambiguously in this sense in a later chapter.[7] It would be appropriate, then, to use it to denote the ability to apprehend and name spontaneously the things that the daimon encounters.

§1.4 (26–33): 是以陶鈞文思，貴在虛靜，疏瀹五藏，澡雪精神。
積學以儲寶，酌理以富才，研閱以窮照，馴致以繹辭。[8]

§1.4: That is why, in the shaping and molding of literary thought, what is
prized is emptiness and quietude, whereby one cleanses the five viscera
and purges the essential daimon. Subsequently, one accumulates learning
to be a storehouse of treasures, steeps oneself in reason to enrich talent,
polishes observation to perfect discernment, and trains the responses to
arrange words.

In this passage Liu Xie analyzes in greater detail the factors that prepare and
qualify the controlling factors he has named above (the "will and breath" and
"power of words") to function as they should. He begins with the stilling and
purging of the body and daimon as a prerequisite to activity. This is a familiar
motif, ultimately derived from numerous descriptions in early philosophical
works of sagely insight. It had already been extended to apply to preparation
for artistic creativity: Lu Ji used it for literary composition and Xi Kang 嵇
康 for musical performance.[9] But Liu Xie has added something to this usage:
In his text a lengthy process of mental cultivation is required in advance of
this settling of the mind. Liu Xie specifies four aspects of this preparation.
Fittingly, because this is an elaboration of the preceding section, each of
these aspects may be doubly linked to the two factors, the will and breath
and the power of words. For example, book learning contributes, presumably,
both to verbal mastery and to the cultivation of the will or character. Liu
Xie's attention to such prior training is a recurrent theme in this chapter.

§1.5 (34–39): 然後使玄解之宰，尋聲律而定墨。獨照之匠，闚意
象而運斤。此蓋馭文之首術，謀篇之大端。

§1.5: Thereafter, one is able to cause the craftsman who is freed from all
bonds to affix the measurements by searching out the rules of sounds,
and the uniquely discerning carpenter to wield his ax while looking at
the image in his mind. This is the first technique used to steer writing,
the major point in planning a piece.

Having given due attention to the prior training required, Liu Xie returns
to the achievements of daimonic thinking, emphasizing its marvelousness.

Several commentators and translators understand this passage to refer simply to the act of composition, taking, for example, the phrases *shenglü* 聲律 and *dingmo* 定墨 to refer to selecting the prosody and words of the piece. But this interpretation is not easily reconciled with the closing sentence. Liu Xie is still describing the actions of daimonic thinking as it develops a general plan for the piece that has not yet begun to be written. He here seems to be addressing the germination of the general idea that shapes or, as he says, "steers" the writing. To read this as describing composition is also at odds with the three-part hierarchy presented later on in the chapter: Daimonic thinking precedes ideas, and ideas precede words on the page. Here, we are at the stage in which thinking is just starting to yield up a general idea or notion for the entire piece.

The measurements (*mo* 墨, literally, ink marks) must be the craftsman's measuring line and marker (*shengmo* 繩墨), which are often paired, in *Wenxin diaolong* and elsewhere, with the ax (*fujin* 斧斤) to invoke the initial stages of building something. First measurements are marked off, and then the ax is swung.[10] There is disagreement over the meaning of the difficult phrase *xuanjie zhi zai* 玄解之宰.[11] We know from §1.2 that all of the sense perceptions are operative when the daimon ventures forth on its journey; that is, sights and sounds are perceived during its roaming with things. On one level, then, the parallel construction in §1.5 speaks of developing a general plan for the piece to be written from these sense perceptions and interaction. On another level, the passage acknowledges that the piece to be written will consist of two essential elements: patterns of sounds and visual images. Naturally, when the writer is ready to compose, he will mimic what his daimon has encountered, investing like sounds and images in his literary piece.

The carpenter (*jiang* 匠) wields his ax while looking at the "image in his mind" (*yi xiang* 意象, literally, idea image). This recalls at least two *Zhuangzi* passages. One is about Carpenter Shi, who whirled his ax to remove a dab of plaster from his friend's nose (without scraping the skin). The other is about Cook Ding, who developed his skill to the point that he no longer saw the ox he was butchering; instead, he "met" it with his daimon.[12] The crucial point in Liu Xie's adaptation of these stories is that the image is in the mind and not an object that can be physically manipulated.

The preceding statement about the craftsman (*zai* 宰) should have a similar import if the prosodic and grammatical parallelism is to be meaningful.

The measuring and marking precedes and is analogous to the slicing and hacking. If the carpenter, surprisingly enough, "looks" elsewhere as he works, it would be appropriate that the measuring is also done according to some unexpected and unseen standard or pattern. Appropriately, the authority for the linear measurements is "the rules of sounds." The craftsman uses the unseen as a guide to the seen, finding synesthetically in sound the spatial dimensions for his plan. Both sentences feature a disjunction between the nature of the guidelines and the work itself. This is because Liu Xie is describing the how the mind converts daimonic thinking to a plan for literary composition.

§1.6 (40–47): 夫神思方運，萬塗競萌。規矩虛位，刻鏤無形。登山則情滿於山，觀海則意溢於海。我才之多少，將與風雲而並驅矣。

§1.6: Once daimonic thinking is set in motion, ten thousand paths vie to open up. The shape and dimensions are still vacant positions, and the engraving and carving are yet without form. If he thinks of climbing mountains, his emotions are filled with mountains. If he thinks of gazing at the sea, his ideas overflow with the sea. His daimon races forth with the wind-blown clouds, as far as his quantity of talent allows.

In this passage Liu Xie describes the formation of ideas (and emotions) that is made possible by the activity of daimonic thinking. The general plan for the piece of writing has already been determined. Liu Xie now addresses the many particular ideas that underlie sentence after sentence of the piece. As the author's thinking is set in motion or begins to turn, countless pathways open up; each pathway beckons him. "Shape and dimensions" (*guiju* 規矩, literally, compass and square) and "engraving and carving" (*kelou* 刻鏤) might refer to the scope and texture of the piece that has yet to be written. They might also refer to the shape of the ideas that will be formed from the thinking that has been set in motion. In either case, everything is still undetermined and formless at this moment. Everything depends upon which path the author chooses. Naturally, whatever path or subject his thinking chooses fills his ideas and emotions. Depending on the amount of talent he possesses, his daimonic thinking and the ideas that result from it may at this point race as far into the distance as the windblown clouds.

Commentators and translators are sharply divided in their reading of Liu Xie's description of "climbing mountains" and "gazing at the sea," and nothing in this chapter better reveals their preferences and larger assumptions about Liu Xie and his thought. Most commentators read the lines literally. When the writer actually climbs mountains, and when he actually looks out over a sea, this is what happens.[13] Of course, Liu Xie explicitly says only this much, and therein lies the justification of this reading. Equally important in encouraging this reading, however, is the unacknowledged but considerable influence of ideas that dominate the later Chinese poetic tradition, including the assumption of first-hand authorial experience, the assumption of sincerity, a distrust for artifice, and the ideal of the poet-historian. The cumulative weight of these concepts, coupled with Liu Xie's somewhat elliptical phrasing, has led most scholars to overlook the immediate context of these sentences or to fail to acknowledge that a narrow and explicit reading does not match what is said in the surrounding lines.[14]

After he has described the activity of the daimonic thinking that precedes the act of literary composition, Liu Xie devotes the second section of the chapter to the act of writing itself, addressing first the difficulty of turning this far-flung thinking into coherent words on the page.

§2.1 (48–54): 方其搦翰，氣倍辭前；暨乎篇成，半折心始。何則？意翻空而易奇，言徵實而難巧也。

§2.1: When the brush is first grasped, there is double the energy before there are words. But once the piece is finished, the mind is half of what it had been before. Why? When ideas soar in emptiness they are readily made marvelous, but when words are verified against reality it is hard to make them artful.

Here Liu Xie confronts the frustration experienced by the writer when he seeks to transform exuberance and indistinct vision into words. The writer regularly feels, as Lu Ji observed, that his composition falls short of the vision he experienced before he began to write. Liu Xie's explanation of this falling short features a contrast between the "emptiness" (*kong* 空) in which ideas are developed and the empirical realities (*shi* 實) referenced by words. Emptiness here effectively recapitulates several earlier statements about daimonic thinking—it creates images that transcend spatial and temporal boundaries, its dimensions are "empty positions," its texture is "formless," and it rushes forward with the windblown clouds. The use of emptiness here lends further support to the reading of the lines on mountains and seas suggested above.

Words are measured against the realities they name, and a degree of veracity or correspondence is required. Daimonic thinking, however, is liberated from the constraints of the empirical world, as we have seen. Consequently, the writer's recourse to words catches him in this gap between the envisioned and the real world. An inherent conflict is acknowledged between the need for words to be credible and the expectation that poetic language be artful.

§2.2 (55–60): 是以意授於思，言授於意。密則無際，疏則千里；或理在方寸而求之域表，或義在咫尺而思隔山河。

§2.2: So it is that ideas derive from thinking, and words derive from ideas. When these are close together there is no margin between them, but when they are apart they may be separated a thousand miles. The reasoning may be contained in the tiny space of the mind, but one goes to the borderlands in search of it. Or the meaning may be a foot away, but the thinking lies across mountains and rivers.

Here Liu Xie elaborates on the problem addressed earlier in the section by presenting the notion of a tripartite hierarchy. He has just mentioned *yi* 意 (ideas), and now he returns to the concept, specifying his views on the relationship of thinking, ideas, and words.

The distinction between "thinking" and "idea" is the most novel and interesting aspect of this scheme. Lu Ji and others wrote eloquently about the gulf between ideas and words and the difficulty of converting thought into writing. Lu Ji uses "thought" (*si* 思) and "idea" (*yi* 意 together with *li* 理 [reasoning]) synonymously, juxtaposing them with "words" (*yan* 言) or "writing" (*wen* 文). Lu Ji tends to use "thought" when he is describing the correspondence between the mental activity of the writer and the words used to express it.[15] He tends to use "idea" when he addresses the problematic issue of the imperfect match between the writer's intended meaning and his words.[16] Lu Ji does not, however, take the bold step of distinguishing "thought" from "idea"—that is, of differentiating stages within the mental process that precede the act of writing. By doing so and by assigning primacy to thinking as he does, Liu Xie divorces "thinking" from its ordinary sense, in which it might be equated with "idea" or "reasoning."

Liu Xie's observations here contrast pointedly with the conviction articulated not long before him by Fan Ye (d. 446) that "idea is what should be primary" in writing [當以意為主].[17] Fan Ye's declaration was motivated by dissatisfaction with contemporary writers who were preoccupied with euphony and stylistic ornamentation at the expense of intellectual substance. Liu Xie's analysis is also noteworthy for the conspicuous absence of emotions (*qing* 情) from his scheme. We might account for this in part by understanding that Liu Xie intends emotions to be subsumed under ideas. (See the earlier matching of emotions with ideas in the lines about mountains and seas in §1.6.) But certainly emotions are not in the forefront of Liu Xie's thinking here.

After introducing the three-part scheme, Liu Xie addresses the issue of the distance between thinking, idea, and words. They may be so closely aligned, he says, that there is virtually no space between them, or they may be far from one another. But he does not give equal treatment to these two possibilities. In the next two sentences he elaborates only on the second situation, abandoning the first altogether, even though the parallel style would have seemed to encourage one sentence given to each. (I take *li* 理 and *yi* 義 in these lines to refer synonymously to the meaning of the completed writing, that is, subsuming both *yi* 意 and *yan* 言, mentioned above.) Liu Xie dwells on the separation of this final meaning that the writing conveys from the thinking that ferrets it out and puts it into words. A distant mental journey is apt to be necessary, even when the reasoning and meaning sought by the writer are close at hand.

Liu Xie's discussion of the distance or separation between thinking, idea, and words in this passage is in some sense analogous to his emphasis in the opening of the chapter on the dislocation of the writer's daimonic thinking from his physical presence. This, of course, is a different order of separation, having to do with the act of writing rather than the act of thinking in the first place. What is consistent is Liu Xie's preference for stressing distinctions between the writer's daimonic thinking and other aspects of his identity and craft. By doing so, he calls attention to the marvelousness of literary thinking, that is, its transcendence of the ordinary world and the senses through which we perceive it.

The section ends with remarks that are at first surprisingly reassuring, considering what has just been said.

§2.3 (61–64): 是以秉心養術，無務苦慮。含章司契，不必勞情也。

§2.3: This is why if the mind is properly managed and technique nurtured, there is no need to ruminate painstakingly. If the pattern and tally are contained inside, it is not necessary to belabor the emotions.

What grounds do we have for this confidence that great mental effort is not necessary, given what has just been asserted about the great distances that daimonic thinking must travel to capture even a meaning that is close at hand? Ji Yun's 紀昀 criticism of this passage, widely quoted by the later commentators, attacks it for giving the impression that assiduous mental effort and searching are not necessary to good writing. Furthermore, he notes that the sense of this is inconsistent with what had been said earlier about carefully preparing the mind, by cleansing and emptying it, for the task ahead.[18] Part of the explanation of these apparent contradictions must be that daimonic thinking is not thinking in any usual sense. This distinction becomes the justification for the claim that there is no need for the writer to "ruminate painstakingly."

More importantly, the key to success is in the proper training and preparation of the daimon and the mind. Section §2.3 must, as those who do not accept Ji Yun's criticism point out, refer back to the earlier discussion in §1.4 (and, more indirectly, that in §1.3 as well) of the cleansing, learning, and discipline required in the shaping of literary thought. I take *hanzhang siqi* 含章司契 to describe nothing other than the mind that has been properly managed and nurtured, which maintains within it the tally or template that will lend control and coherence to wide-ranging daimonic thinking. Compare a statement from a later chapter: "Thinking has no fixed tally, but reason has a consistent presence" [思無定契，理有恆存；] (*WXDL* 44/123–24). The pattern and tally that the trained mind holds within it is "reason." Daimonic thinking in its dynamic aspect is apt to lack this constancy, which must be supplied by the nurtured mind.

In the section that follows, Liu Xie turns to a consideration of the effort and speed with which writers engage in this thinking and the literary composition that flows from it. Liu focuses on a contrast between apparently facile and effortless thought and composition, on the one hand, and a painstaking and drawn-out process, on the other, describing the two through historical examples. What is the logic of this change in subject? In §2 he addresses the difficulty in converting thinking to idea and, finally, to words. Now, he reflects further upon that process of conversion as it is experienced by particular types of writers. His goal is evidently to be pragmatic and inclusive. He wants his description of daimonic thinking to be flexible enough to accommodate a variety of practices and methods commonly observed in the way people write. Despite the contrast in methods Liu Xie now describes, he ends by asserting that all writers face the same challenges. His treatment of these, at the conclusion of the section, provides further clarification of what daimonic thinking entails if it is to be successful.

§3.1 (65–84): 人之稟才，遲速異分，文之制體，大小殊功。相如含筆而腐毫，揚雄輟翰而驚夢，桓譚疾感於苦思，王充氣竭於思慮，張衡研京以十年，左思練都以一紀。雖有巨文，亦思之緩也。淮南崇朝而賦騷，枚皋應詔而成賦，子建援牘如口誦，仲宣舉筆似宿構，阮瑀據案而制書，禰衡當食而草奏。雖有短篇，亦思之速也。

§3.1: A person's innate talent may work quickly or slowly, just as the forms of writing vary from the grand to the small. Sima Xiangru held his writing brush in his mouth until the bristles were ruined, and when Yang Xiong finally finished writing he had a nightmare.[19] Huan Tan became ill from his tortured thinking, while Wang Chong spent his vital energy in brooding.[20] Zhang Heng polished his metropolis rhapsodies for ten years, and Zuo Si refined his capital rhapsodies for a dozen years.[21] These may include some massive compositions, but they all count as instances of slow thinking.

The Prince of Huainan wrote his rhapsody on "Encountering Sorrow" in one morning, and Mei Gao composed his rhapsodies on imperial command.[22] Zijian [Cao Zhi] handled the page as if he were reciting from memory, and Zhongxuan [Wang Can] wielded the brush as if the piece had been previously composed.[23] Ruan Yu wrote a letter while sitting in

the saddle, and Mi Heng drafted his composition at a banquet table.[24]
There may be some short pieces among these, but they all must be considered examples of quick thinking.

Having identified the two approaches, Liu Xie analyzes the reasons for the difference.

§3.2 (85–100): 若夫駿發之士，心總要術，敏在慮前，應機立斷。覃思之人，情饒歧路，鑒在疑後，研慮方定。機敏故造次而成功，慮疑故愈久而致績。難易雖殊，並資博練。若學淺而空遲，才疏而徒速，以斯成器，未之前聞。

§3.2: There are gentlemen who race out ahead and whose minds already grasp all the essentials. Their adroit wit operates before rumination, so that they make their choices in immediate response to each stimulus. Deep thinking persons, however, let their preferences encircle every crossroads. Their insight is achieved only after questioning, and their ruminations must be polished before they are finalized. The former react adroitly to stimulus, so their work is accomplished speedily. The latter ruminate and question, so it is only after a long while that they complete their task. Although the ease and difficulty with which they work may be different, both types of writers rely upon breadth and refinement. But if the writer is slow to no purpose, his learning shallow, or if he is fast to no avail, his talent sparse, under such circumstances he will never, so far as we have heard, produce compositions of any value or utility.

Liu Xie takes pains to represent both methods of writing favorably in this passage, implicitly giving approval to a broad range of approaches to the craft. At the same time, he points out that there is also such a thing as slowness that is not useful and speed that is not clever.

Readers may reasonably ask if Liu Xie has not contradicted himself on the issue of the effort involved in writing. In §2.3, he asserts that if the mind is properly nurtured, there is no need to "ruminate painstakingly" or to "belabor the emotions." Yet, in §3.1 he makes reference to historical figures who have done just that, and in §3.2 he explains this method approvingly. There are various ways to account for the apparent contradiction (apart from the option of simply accepting it as a contradiction, which would make it an example similar to those adduced by Stephen Owen in his paper in this volume). First, in §2.3 Liu Xie may be concerned with the way the mind formulates ideas from daimonic thinking more than with how the writer actually composes his words. Second, it is possible to understand §2.3 to mean that the writer need not necessarily agonize over his craft. Liu Xie does not intend to rule out the possibility that a writer may labor. He has chosen to emphasize, however, that the writer may escape such travail, given the powers of daimonic thinking. The last and, I suspect, most plausible explanation is that in §2 and §3 Liu Xie is addressing different levels or orders of the complex activity of literary composition. The former is a consideration in abstract terms of the relationship between thought, idea, and word. These entities may be distantly separated, but the mind may traverse those distances effortlessly. The latter is a reflection upon what we know, pragmatically, about the amount of time and effort different writers exert at their craft. Liu Xie tries to account for the vast discrepancies in practice.

The tone, originality, and thoughtfulness of Liu Xie's remarks on the slow approach to writing changes considerably from §3.1 to §3.2. In the first passage, Liu Xie simply distills anecdotes from earlier sources that emphasize the obsessive character of selected well-known writers. In the second passage, however, he analyzes much more carefully and generously the complexities of "deep thinking." It would be hard to find a passage from earlier or contemporary sources that so aptly and seriously represents the laborious process of writerly cogitation. In fact, the whole of §3.2 is remarkable for its sympathetic depiction of different mental dispositions.

§3.3 (101–108): 是以臨篇綴慮，必有二患。理鬱者苦貧，辭溺者傷亂。然則博見為饋貧之糧，貫一為拯亂之藥。博而能一，亦有助乎心力矣。

§3.3: Consequently, the writer has two worries as he confronts the page and organizes his ruminations. If his reasoning is pent-up and constricted, his writing will suffer from a deficiency of content. If phrases engulf him, his writing will be confused. Breadth of vision is the grain that feeds this deficiency, and unity of purpose is the medicine that treats this confusion. If he is able to achieve unity along with breadth, these will enhance the power of his mind.

Liu Xie expands here upon the duality of breadth and refinement mentioned in §3.2, substituting unity for refinement. As stated earlier, these are the traits that all good writing relies upon, whether executed quickly or slowly.

Writers may compose in vastly different ways, but they must all overcome the same two challenges or difficulties. These two worries or dangers are described as opposites: Reasoning lies constricted within and cannot get out, while language has become an inundation in which the writer is immersed. "Breadth of vision," a turning of the mind to the envisioned external world, serves to free up the reasoning, thus ending the blockage inside. At the same time, maintaining a unity of focus or purpose (literally, binding everything by a single thread) saves one from the deluge of language and the chaos it might otherwise create. But how precisely is the maintenance of unity related to daimonic thinking?

Daimonic thinking may be a flight of the mind to the distant recesses of the envisioned world, but it is not conceived of as being haphazard or lacking in its own discipline. Various statements and inferences earlier in the chapter anticipate the statement made here about unity. Perhaps the most obvious among these is the insistence that there be reason in the writer's mind. Surely, the reason released by breadth of vision is one component of the unity here mentioned. Reason is also a part of the notion of talent. One's quantity of talent determines how far the daimon soars forth with the windblown clouds (§1.6), but talent itself is nurtured on reason (§1.4). There is also an earlier mention (§1.4) of the need to "train the responses" in order to know what words to select, which implies a mental orderliness. In the images of daimonic thinking traversing great distances to discover a certain meaning (§2.2), there is a strong sense of this thinking being guided by purpose and firm intent. The notion of the writer holding a "tally" in his mind (§2.3, to be repeated in §5) also suggests a coherent plan or template for the entire piece before it is written.

Having elaborated upon the nature of daimonic thinking and its relation to different methods of composition and their shared problems, in his closing section Liu Xie addresses the contributions that this thinking makes generally to literary excellence. He stresses the advantages brought by the restive variability of this thinking, which enables it to transform the hackneyed into the fresh and novel. Liu Xie considers two levels of contribution, beginning with the more modest.

§4.1 (109–116): 若情數詭雜，體變遷貿，拙辭或孕於巧義，庸事或萌於新意。視布於麻，雖云未貴，²⁵ 杼軸獻功，煥然乃珍。

§4.1: If the range of emotions is diverse and mixed, and deviations of style shift and change, then even clumsy phrases may bring forth clever meanings and commonplace references sprout fresh ideas. Compare hempen cloth to the fibers from which it is made: although it is said that the fibers are not valuable, when the shuttle and loom present their work, the bright cloth is highly prized.

This passage presents a number of difficulties and has been variously interpreted. Punctuation is the first problem. Many scholars read the first two clauses as a complete sentence, ending with the phrase *qianmao* 遷貿. But it is evident that these two clauses are prosodically and grammatically parallel (*qianmao* matched with *guiza* 詭雜 and *tibian* 體變 with *qingshu* 情數). In Liu Xie's usage, as we would expect in the parallel prose style generally, when the word *ruo* 若 introduces such a parallel construction, it governs both members. Thus the sentence carries on, extending beyond the initial pairing, whether the word *ze* 則 (then) is present at the head of the second half of the sentence as an explicit marker of the continuation. (An example of this, also without *ze*, occurs earlier in the chapter, at the end of §3.2.)²⁶ Thus the sentence should not end until the conditional expressed by *ruo* has been resolved—in this case by the pair of parallel lines that follow.

Many commentators and translators, though not all, think that *qingshu guiza* 情數詭雜 must be negative, describing an unhealthy strangeness and discordance in the writer's emotions. One objection to this interpretation is that the matching clause, *tibian qianmao* 體變遷貿, must describe a favorable circumstance, preparing the way for the happy transformations of the crude and hackneyed into the "clever" and "fresh" in the second part of the sentence. Compare this with the statement in the succeeding chapter: "As the eight styles repeatedly shift, the merit of the writing is determined by the writer's learning" [若夫八體屢遷，功以學成] (*WXDL* 27/63–64). This asserts that different styles give way to one another and implies nothing untoward about this process. The word *gui* 詭, used alone or in compounds, usually has a negative meaning in *Wenxin diaolong*, especially when applied to diction (strange, exaggerated, or devious). But the word may also mean "variant" in a neutral sense, as in the compound *fangui* 繁詭, which is also used in the next chapter: "The talent and nature [of writers] differ, and the styles of writing are many and variant" [才性異區，文體繁詭] (*WXDL* 27/118–19).[27]

Section 4.1 is best understood in concert with §4.2. The latter passage addresses the most subtle and marvelous workings of daimonic thinking— those that lie beyond the power of words to describe. Section 4.1 concerns a lesser order of the same mental activity. It is that which, though not supreme, still suffices to transform ordinary material into something artful and novel. It accomplishes this feat by introducing, through the exercise of the imagination, unexpected deviations in the mood or style of a piece of writing. This lesser activity of the mind *is* within Liu Xie's ability to evoke with words, including one famous analogy.

My understanding of the hemp analogy is based on the explanation by Wang Yuanhua 王元化, who criticizes as inadequate the widespread reading of the analogy as validation of the refinement or "artfulness" necessary in good writing.[28] In this conventional reading, Liu Xie is simply saying that what makes writing valuable is that the author "weaves" skillfully, transforming ordinary language into that which has intricate patterning and color. In the alternative reading proposed here, the essential contrast is not between ordinary and colorful language but between what we might term unimaginative and imaginative thinking (and writing). Liu Xie's choice of words lends support to this reading. He does not say, in §4.1, that clumsy language is transformed into ingenious language or that commonplace references are replaced by exotic and fascinating ones. Rather, the words and the references, he implies, have remained unchanged, but they have been employed in transformative ways to yield new meanings. Understanding, as does Wang, that the *bu* 布 and *ma* 麻 in the analogy consist of the same material (*bu* 布 is *mabu* 麻布, and *ma* 麻 is *masi* 麻絲) adds further support to this reading. Rearranging the material that other writers work with, he who has mastered daimonic thinking discovers latent new meanings in it. In other words, the work done by the loom is not the writer's "weaving" of words (as per Lu Ji) so much as it is the activity of his mind, which invests even the ordinary with novel meaning and idea.[29]

§4.2 (117–125): 至於思表纖旨，文外曲致，言所不追，筆固知
止。至精而後闡其妙，至變而後通其數。伊摯不能言鼎，輪
扁不能語斤，其微矣乎。

§4.2: As for the delicate notions that lie at the perimeter of this thinking and the nuances that are captured beyond the writing itself, words cannot follow to where these lead, and at this point the brush surely knows to stop. Only he who is perfectly refined will comprehend such marvels, only he who has mastered all deviations will range freely through such diversity. Yi Zhi could not describe the flavors in the cooking pots, and Wheelwright Bian could not explain his skill with the ax.[30] Truly, these are subtleties!

Key words from earlier sections are repeated here, including *bian* (deviations) and *shu* (diversity) from §4.1, emphasizing the special connection between this and what immediately precedes it. It is noteworthy that here, when he alludes to these most subtle nuances, Liu Xie does not use such words as "idea" or "meaning," which he uses in §4.1. Such avoidance appears to be consistent with his earlier assertion that daimonic thinking precedes "ideas." In §4.2, unlike §4.1, he describes such thinking at its most elusive. Once again, throughout his terminology is the motif of the immense distance that the mind travels while engaged in this thinking. Liu Xie admits that his own words cannot keep up or explore so distantly. "The brush surely knows to stop," is the critic's frank avowal of defeat in his task, and it anticipates the end of the chapter, soon to come. The closing sentences are, it must be said, less ambitious than the corresponding ones in §1.5, where Liu Xie fashions his own poetic vision of the mysterious working of this craftsman and carpenter. Here, he is content to repeat well-known allusions to the craftsman's own inability to explain his mastery with mere words.

§5: The verse says (贊曰):

神用象通，	The daimon utilizes images to communicate,
情變所孕。	Emotions and deviations are thus brought forth.
物以貌求，	Things are sought for their appearance,
心以理應。	The mind responds according to reason therein.
刻鏤聲律，	The rules of sound are chiseled and carved out,
萌芽比興。	Analogies and evocative figures sprout forth.
結慮司契，	Ruminations are settled by controlling the tally,
垂帳制勝。	Victory is engineered from behind the curtains.

The closing verse recapitulates primary themes of the chapter, repeating many of its key terms. The first two lines address the link between the activity of the writer's daimon and his emotions and literary styles. (I translate *qing-bian* 情變 as shorthand for *qingshu* 情數 and *tibian* 體變 in §4.1. It is also possible that the phrase refers solely to changes in the writer's emotions.) The first line appears to be ambiguous. *Tong* 通 may refer either to the ability of the daimon to "get through," that is, to traverse great distances of envisioned space, or to its capacity to "express" in writing what it encounters on its journey. In either case, the repetition of the crucial word "images" (*xiang* 象) from §1.5 is significant, reminding us that what the daimon sees are images in the mind as distinct from the physical objects of the world. The main point is that it is the daimon, working through envisioned images, that is the writer's inspiration and guide. The daimon is primary and everything else (emotions, ideas, stylistic choices, things) is secondary.

The second couplet takes up the issue of the interdependence of external appearance and internal reason. The things (*wu* 物) mentioned here are analogous to the images of the preceding couplet. Having just explained the role of these images, Liu refers to them now as the things of the world, but he does so with the preceding statement in mind. The emphasis in the first couplet is on the function and consequences of daimonic movement or flight. The emphasis in the second is on the mind's ability to make sense of that activity or flight. These are complementary aspects of daimonic thinking, and both are essential to its success. While the chapter opens with a vivid account of the venturing abroad of the daimon ("racing forth with the wind-blown clouds"), in fact the requirement that the mind be equipped to make sense of whatever the daimon may encounter has been present as a secondary theme throughout the chapter.

In fact, these two opening couplets of the verse correspond nicely to the pair of problems that all writers are said to face in §3.3, as well as to the two solutions to those problems described there. The penetration or free-ranging movement of the daimon here corresponds to the "breadth of vision" in the earlier passage, which solves the problem of constricted reason having no outlet. The reliance of the mind upon reason to respond to the appearances of things here corresponds to the unity of the earlier passage, which solves the problem of confusion caused by immersion in a plethora of disordered words.

The process of writing itself, that is, of selecting words that conform to the "rules of sound" and figures of speech that convey the right meanings, follows from this appropriate balance of daimonic movement and reason. The process, analyzed into its many components, is the proper subject of other chapters, especially those immediately following, and is just dealt with summarily in the verse's third couplet.

The final couplet returns to the motif of physical disjunction or separation with which the chapter began and which has surfaced repeatedly since the opening lines. This time the emphasis is on *control* from a distance. As in §2.3, Liu Xie invokes the image of a tally or template held inside the mind that is used to shape whatever is encountered in the daimon's external wanderings with things. The function of this tally corresponds to that of reason earlier in the section. The closing line boldly appropriates the image of a magically empowered military strategist (in the tradition of Zhang Liang), who is able to send his mind and intelligence off to remote battlefields and develop plans that ensure victory without emerging from his tent.[31] This is exactly the type of transformation of a standard reference that Liu Xie mentions earlier (in §4.1), when he is speaking of the power of daimonic thinking.

We know, of course, that Liu Xie did not create the concept of daimonic thinking, nor was he even the first to apply it to the act of writing. The idea that the daimon or the mind (*xin* 心) is capable of transcending the physical location of the person, liberating itself to traverse great distances and "see" many things, had already been detached from the ancient notion of shamanistic journeys. Examples abound in *Zhuangzi*, and Liu Xie begins his chapter with one of them. This mundane version of the phenomenon likewise figures in remarks about knowledge found in *Xunzi*: "How does the mind understand [the Way]? By being empty, One, and quiet. . . . He who attains to such enlightenment sits in his room yet views all within the four seas, and dwells in the present yet adjudicates what took place long ago. His contemplation penetrates the myriad things and he understands the true nature of each."[32] By the end of the Han, and on into the Wei and Jin, the idea that superior craftsmanship involves this sort of daimonic insight or transcendence became commonplace (echoing *Zhuangzi*) but was extended to real crafts, including the literary craft. In his rhapsody on a precious sword, Cao Zhi 曹植 speaks of the maker having relied on daimonic thinking to fashion the decorative images on the weapon's handle (據神思而造象).³³ Similarly, Xi Kang credits legendary zither craftsmen with having "set loose their daimons" (騁神) to perform their work.³⁴ Sun Chuo 孫綽 refers to "galloping my daimon forth and turning round my thoughts" (馳神運思) to capture the images of Mount Tiantai that he puts into his rhapsody on that place.³⁵ Lu Ji, as we have seen, makes similar statements about sending the thinking abroad, although his terminology is different. Liu Xie's contemporary, Xiao Zixian 蕭子顯, likewise observes that "[t]he Way of literary composition derives from daimonic thinking" [屬文之道，事出神思].³⁶

Yet there is nothing systematic in these precedents and little that has theoretical pretensions, so that Liu Xie's use of the concept is both new and ambitious. By singling out daimonic thinking and focusing on it in a main chapter of his work that deals with the qualities of writing and their origins (as opposed to the traits of specific literary genres), Liu Xie elevates daimonic thinking to a new level. To us, this may seem natural, since his decision has close affinities with the importance we regularly assign to the literary imagination. Yet, in the tradition in which Liu Xie wrote, such valuation was anything but conventional. *Yi* 意, in the sense of substantive meaning and content (as opposed to mere *wen*, or ornament) would have been a more predictable choice for this privileged position, and *qing* 情 would also have fit well with one standard explanation of the sources of literary expression. But Liu Xie takes pains explicitly to subordinate *yi* to his special brand of thinking, leaving no room for confusion about their relative importance, and he gives even less attention, in this chapter at least, to the emotions.

Even the selection of *si* 思 in other of its well-known compounds would have been far less daring than the choice that Liu Xie actually made. Numerous earlier writers, including Wang Chong, Huan Tan, Lu Ji, and Fan Ye, had already developed a variety of terms designating types of thinking that were regularly applied to literature and which would be used by Liu Xie himself in the course of his work. These include *jingsi* 精思 (concentrated thought), *miaosi* 妙思 (marvelous thought), *caisi* 才思 (talented thought), *zaosi* 藻思 (elegant thought), and *yansi* 研思 (polished thought). These terms remind us of the distinctiveness of the term Liu Xie did select, *shensi* 神思. As used by Liu Xie, *shensi* necessarily involves a disjunction between the author's physical presence and the roamings of his mind.³⁷ It is the only type of literary thinking that does so.

Time and again in his chapter, Liu Xie reminds us of this disjunction. He bolsters his assertions about physical separation with statements that stress the envisioned or imaginary nature of the world through which the daimon journeys. We read, at first, that the daimon "roams about with things" (*yu wu you* 與物遊). But then the word "things" is replaced by the term "images" (*xiang* 象), which is further specified as "idea images" (*yi xiang* 意象), that is, the images that exist in the mind. These are the patterns by which the writer determines the form and shape of his literary piece (§1.5). With his eye affixed inwardly on these, the writer works, without looking out to the real world around him.

The theme of transcendent freedom surfaces as one of the advantages of working in this way. Because his world is an envisioned one, its possibilities are many times what they would be in what we think of as the real world. Once daimonic thinking becomes active, "ten thousand paths vie to open up" before the writer. He can imagine himself now on the top of mountains and now at the edge of the sea. In fact, there is virtually no limit to the flight his thinking may take; his talent is the only limiting factor (§1.6). This theme of freedom returns in a different guise toward the end of the chapter. There the capacity that daimonic thinking has to effect sudden changes and deviations is credited with the ability to refresh the stale and transform the ordinary into something valuable (§4.1).

Nevertheless, are there not limitations to this imaginative power described by Liu Xie? Granted that the writer works from the images in his mind, are these not simply imagined replicas of things in the real world? Much that Liu Xie says implies that this is, indeed, the case. The poet imagines himself in places where he is not, but these are still actual places, places he might have been. Yet there are occasionally suggestions that go beyond this. The very freedom with which daimonic thinking works means that the writer engaged in it can be everywhere at once. Physical and temporal boundaries fade away. The line in §2.1 about the marvelousness of ideas soaring through emptiness (意翻空而易奇) is also richly suggestive of images and ideas that are not of this world. Yet Liu Xie does not elaborate on or explore this point.

His stress upon this imaginary aspect of daimonic thinking does, however, lead Liu Xie to recast the complaint voiced so emphatically by Lu Ji about the difficulty of literary composition and, specifically, the inadequacies of words to convey fully one's meaning. In Liu Xie's reformulation it is not just that words are imperfect and inspiration unreliable—there is an inherent difficulty in bridging the gap between the emptiness in which ideas take shape and the realities that words denote (§2.1). Marvelous ideas are easy to come by precisely because, in Liu Xie's account of them, they are not constrained by reality. This is a new understanding of idea, one that follows from the traits of daimonic thinking that gives rise to it.

While the "Shensi" chapter features Liu Xie's understanding of these issues, support for the claims he makes here may certainly be found in other chapters of *Wenxin diaolong*. The chapters "Kuashi" 夸飾 (Amplification and ornamentation) and "Wuse" 物色 (The appearances of things) are particularly interesting in this regard.

夫形而上者謂之道，形而下者謂之器。神道難摹，精言不能
追其極。形器易寫，壯辭可得喻其真

That which is above and beyond physical form is called the Way, whereas that which is beneath and within it is called an implement. The daimonic Way is hard to replicate, and even refined words cannot trace its extremes. Implements with physical forms are easy to describe, and able phrases can capture their true nature by way of analogy. (*WXDL* 37/1–6)

So begins "Kuashi." Obviously, it is the "daimonic Way" of things that the best writing aspires to convey or intimate. This is the first of many noteworthy assertions in the chapter. Others include a defense of "exaggerated writing" (writing that is not empirically "correct"), of "extreme phrasing," of lines in *The Book of Songs* that are at odds with geographical facts (but remain "right" in a literary sense), and of the doctrine that distortion through ornamentation need not be considered specious or untrue. All such statements complement the various positions discussed in the "Shensi" chapter on the centrality of an envisioned world to the writer's method.

The "Wuse" chapter deals primarily with the lower order described above—the physical forms of the world's "implements." It is evident that, even with this focus, the chapter shows the influence of the predilections found in Liu's thoughts on daimonic thinking. It turns out, for example, that the "appearance" (*se* 色) of things is consistently represented as a synthesis of objective form and subjective perception. In other words, there is no appearance that is unaffected by the workings of the viewer's mind. "Just as the eye goes forth and comes back, so too does the mind suck in and spew forth" [目既往還，心亦吐納] (*WXDL* 46/118–19). The eye traces forms and the mind ruminates on them. "[The poet] lingers in the space of the ten thousand images and croons in the domain of sight and hearing. Tracing the 'breath' and sketching the face, he turns round in accordance with things. Applying color and adding sounds, he likewise paces back and forth with the mind" [流連萬象之際，沈吟視聽之區。寫氣圖貌，既隨物以宛轉。屬采附聲，亦與心而徘徊] (*WXDL* 46/31–36). The "domain of sight and hearing" is the objective world, but the "space of the ten thousand images" is the realm of the poet's "idea images." Similarly, as the poet outlines the forms of things, he circulates around their actual shapes, observing closely. But when it comes time for him to endow these things with *qualities*, here of color and sound, he finds the source in his own mind. This also conforms to and builds upon ideas presented in the "Shensi" chapter.

One of the lasting impressions given by the "Shensi" chapter is that of the balance it strives for between imagination and various types of training or control. In this chapter, Liu Xie writes about the importance and the workings of the literary imagination. Yet, it is clear that, for all his interest in describing the "marvels" of his subject, Liu Xie is committed to an understanding of the literary imagination in which the freedom he is so eager to ascribe to it does not give way to anarchy (his word is *luan* 亂). Consequently, although his primary subject is the flight of daimonic thinking, he ends up giving nearly as much attention to the countertheme of control, which is variously represented as the requirements of prior training of the impulses, mastery of language, a healthy store of reason, and unity of purpose. In this sense, as daring as the chapter may be, it also displays a heightened sense of responsibility toward the subject it treats so boldly.

CHAPTER SIX

Liu Xie on Imagination

SHUEN-FU LIN

> And as imagination bodies forth
> The forms of things unknown, the poet's pen
> Turns them to shapes, and gives to airy nothing
> A local habitation and a name.
>
> —SHAKESPEARE, *A Midsummer Night's Dream*

Modern scholars of *Wenxin diaolong* have generally interpreted the term *shensi* 神思, the title of chapter 26, as essentially referring to the mental faculty of imagination or *xiangxiang* 想像, the modern Chinese equivalent of the word *imagination*.[1] Chapter 26 is not devoted solely to an exploration of the idea of *shensi* itself. Rather, it discusses the entire literary creative process from the stage before the conception of a literary work to its execution, a process in which *shensi* plays a key role. The chapter also touches upon the cultivation of the mental faculty involved in literary creation.

Liu Xie is by no means a complete innovator in his treatment of this creative process. Lu Ji 陸機 was the first scholar in Chinese history to discuss the mental activities in literary creation in his "Wenfu" 文賦 (Rhapsody on literature). The term *shensi* was also used in the works of Cao Zhi 曹植 and several other early writers to designate a similar mental activity.[2] Neverthe-less, Liu Xie is generally credited with having built upon Lu Ji's reflections on the literary creative process. There are in fact modern scholars of Chinese aesthetics who regard Liu Xie's "Shensi" chapter as the most systematic treat-ment of "artistic imagination" (藝術想像) that can be found among tradi-tional Chinese critical and aesthetic texts.[3] In this chapter I attempt to provide a close examination of the concept of *shensi*, its relation to the Western notion of imagination, and its place in Liu Xie's conception of the process of literary creation, with an eye toward revealing the salient characteristics of Liu Xie's discourse on literary imagination.

XIANGXIANG AND IMAGINATION

I should like to begin with a look at the two terms, *xiangxiang* in Chinese and imagination in English, which are generally regarded as equivalent by twentieth-century scholars.

Xiangxiang is a very old compound term that goes at least as far back as the ancient text *Chuci* 楚辭 (The songs of Chu). But before the twentieth century, *xiangxiang* seems to have been used only in the restrictive sense of "visualizing an image of someone or something." For instance, in the "Yuan-you" 遠遊 (Distant roaming) chapter of *Chuci*, we find the lines: "Thinking of my beloved, I visualized an image of her; / Heaving long sighs, I brushed my tears away" [思故舊以想像兮，長太息而掩涕].[4] *Xiangxiang* also appears in these lines from the "Luoshen fu" 洛神賦 (The rhapsody on the goddess of the River Luo) by Cao Zhi: "With lingering affection, I visualized an image of her; / I looked back, with a heart full of sorrow" [遺情想像，顧望懷愁].[5] Again, it means essentially the same thing in this couplet from a poem by Xie Lingyun 謝靈運 (385–433): "Visualizing the beauty of the Kunlun Mountains / I feel far removed from affairs of the world" [想像崑山姿，緬邈區中緣].[6] In all three instances, the meaning of *xiangxiang* is identical to the literal sense of the English word *imagine*, the verbal form of the word imagination. Despite the close parallel between *xiangxiang* and *imagine* or *imagination*, however, *xiangxiang* has never been used as a principal term in premodern Chinese criticism and aesthetics, while its counterpart, imagination, has occupied an important place in Western philosophy, aesthetics, and literary criticism.

The topic of imagination constitutes a vast and well-trodden field in Western civilization. Ever since the time of Plato, philosophers and poets have reflected upon the relations between imagination and reason, fiction and truth, and sense experience and thought, as well as the whole issue of artistic creation. It is beyond the scope of this essay for me to make even a brief excursion into this incredibly rich territory. Instead, I shall limit myself to a few dominant ideas about imagination in the Western tradition, which will serve as a comparison with Liu Xie's reflections on the subject.

The contemporary British philosopher Mary Warnock, who has published two books on imagination, defines the term simply as "that which creates mental images."[7] This definition is valid and useful because the production of vivid, usually visual, images is the commonest sense implied by the word.[8] The creation or production of images can entail two aspects: the occurrence of mental images accompanying sense perceptions, and the creation of images in the absence of objects or in various combinations.[9] Indeed, as Mary Warnock has suggested, the simple, literal definition of imagination enables us to see the connection between our "commonplace perceptual experience" and "our most outlandish interpretations" of this experience.[10] These connotations can be seen in the etymology of the word itself. Imagination is derived from the Latin *imaginatio*, which was in turn a late substitute for the Greek word *phantasia* from which the English words fancy and fantasy are derived.[11] As noted by A. S. P. Woodhouse, the two terms *imaginatio* and *phantasia*, "with their derivatives, long appeared as synonyms designating the image-receiving or image-forming faculty or process."[12] Imagination is thus fundamentally the faculty or process for having or making mental images.

It has been observed that although reflections on imagination go as far back as Plato, there was no fully worked-out theory of what we now think of as imagination until the Enlightenment.[13] Before then, discussions of imagination are found only in brief passages or random remarks made by philosophers and writers. Nonetheless, according to the contemporary American philosopher Mark Johnson, two different approaches to imagination can be distinguished among the most influential discussions of the subject in the Western tradition: "One that associates it with art, fantasy, and creativity, and another that treats it as a faculty that connects perception with reason."[14] Johnson ascribes the former approach to the Platonic tradition, developed from interpretations of Plato's writings, and the latter to the Aristotelian tradition, derived from Aristotle's brief remarks on imagination.[15] The Platonic tradition embraces a prejudice against imagination. It claims that no true knowledge can be based on either sense experience or images of things. Thus the poet's imagination is not a rational process but an act of possession by the daimon (divine power).[16] By contrast, the Aristotelian tradition "sees imagination as an indispensable and pervasive operation by which sense perceptions are recalled as images and are made available to discursive thought as the contents of our knowledge of the physical world."[17] While downplaying the Platonic notion of the wild and unruly, albeit creative, aspect of imagination, the Aristotelian tradition regards imagination as "the faculty that mediates between sensation and thought."[18] Johnson argues that the Platonic and the Aristotelian traditions "might be construed as two dominant themes that have more or less defined the issues discussed in standard treatments of imagination to the present day."[19]

At the end of the eighteenth century, the Romantic movement effected a radical transformation in Western literary criticism. M. H. Abrams has provided a remarkable account of this transformation in his book *The Mirror and the Lamp*. The most important feature of the Romantic transformation was its theory of the mind and imagination. During the Romantic period, Abrams argues, the prevailing metaphor of the mind changed from that of "a reflector of external objects" to that of "a radiant projector which makes a contribution to the objects it perceives."[20] According to Abrams, the reflector (or mirror) metaphor "was characteristic of much of the thinking from Plato to the eighteenth century," while the projector (or lamp) metaphor "typifies the prevailing romantic conception of the poetic mind."[21] The Romantic conception of the mind can be seen as an attempt to overcome man's alienation from the world by healing the rigid separation of mind from body, subject from object, intellect from emotion, as well as rationality from imagination, which is deeply rooted in Western cultural and philosophical traditions.[22]

I shall focus mainly on the ideas of Samuel Taylor Coleridge (1772–1834) to illustrate the Romantic conception of imagination. Coleridge's "Dejection: An Ode," written in 1802, epitomizes the early-nineteenth-century view of imagination. The poet laments his sense of loss of imaginative power or genius, which he calls "my shaping spirit of imagination."[23] In this poem, imagination is identified with joy, an inner condition that enables a poet not only to see and hear but also to feel. Because of this loss, "I see them [the sky, the clouds, the stars, and the moon] all so excellently fair / I see, not feel, how beautiful they are."[24] As M. H. Abrams points out, Coleridge here mourns the loss of "the reciprocating power of the mind, leaving it a death-in-life as a passive receptor of the inanimate visible scene."[25] In "Dejection," Coleridge uses a series of five metaphors for the mind equipped with the "shaping spirit of imagination": a fountain, a light, "a sweet and potent voice" that is the life of "all sweet sounds," "a luminous cloud/Enveloping the earth," and the suggestion of "a marriage with nature." The "marriage with nature" resonates with William Wordsworth's (1770–1850) notion of "a marriage of mind and nature," expressed in the conclusion to the first book of *The Recluse*.[26] These metaphors represent the mind as capable of projecting life and passion into the external world, rather than as a purely receptive or reflective device. With the loss of the power of imagination, Coleridge can no longer shape what his mind has received into an idea or impression of his own.[27]

In a notebook entry of May 10, 1804, Coleridge makes reference to this same experience of loss.

> Whither have my animal spirits departed? . . . I have many thoughts, many images; large stores of the unwrought materials; scarcely a day passes but something new in fact or in illustration, rises up in me like Herbs and Flowers in a garden in early Spring. But the combining power, the power to do, the manly effective Will, that is dead or slumbers most diseasedly.[28]

Coleridge bemoans the loss of his imaginative power in language that suggests sexual impotence. It is clear that, in addition to being a power that transforms what is passively seen to what is actively felt, imagination is also a "combining power" that creates forms out of things by bringing together thoughts and images.

In his critical writings, Coleridge discusses the "shaping" or "combining" function of imagination in more straightforward language. In chapter XIV of *Biographia Literaria,* we find the following remarks about

> that synthetic and magical power, to which we have exclusively appropriated the name of imagination. This power, first put in action by the will and understanding, and retained under their irremissive, though gentle and unnoticed, controul . . . reveals itself in the balance or reconciliation of opposite or discordant qualities; of sameness, with difference; of the general, with the concrete; the idea, with the image; the individual, with the representative; the sense of novelty and freshness, with old and familiar objects; a more than usual state of emotion, with more than usual order; judgement ever awake and steady self-possession, with enthusiasm and feeling profound or vehement; and while it blends and harmonizes the natural and artificial, still subordinates art to nature; the manner to the matter; and our admiration of the poet to our sympathy with the poetry.[29]

For Coleridge, imagination is a capacity that organizes, intensifies, and idealizes what is received or grasped by, and what emerges in, the mind in an act
of artistic creation.

Has Coleridge, then, completely removed imagination from its original
meaning of an "image-producing" faculty? Not exactly. At the close of chapter
XIII of *Biographia Literaria*, he delineates two kinds of imagination.

> The primary Imagination I hold to be the living Power and prime Agent
> of all human Perception, and as a repetition in the finite mind of the eter-
> nal act of creation in the infinite I Am. The secondary Imagination I con-
> sider as an echo of the former, coexisting with the conscious will, yet still
> as identical with the primary in the kind of its agency, and differing only
> in *degree*, and in the *mode* of its operation. It dissolves, diffuses, dissipates,
> in order to recreate; or where this process is rendered impossible, yet still
> at all events it struggles to idealize and to unify. It is essentially *vital*, even
> as all objects (as objects) are essentially fixed and dead.[30]

Coleridge's division of imagination into two types is believed to have been
derived from the philosophy of Kant. According to Mary Warnock's interpretation, Coleridge's primary imagination is derived from Kant's a priori
imagination, a capacity shared by all human beings, which enables us to
know and make sense of the world.[31] Kant holds that we, as rational creatures,
are in possession of certain laws or categories with which we order our sense
data and interpret the world.[32] "Schematism" is considered by Kant as "a
function of the imagination."[33] He further introduces the notion of an obser-
ver, the "I" who perceives, the "I" who "is fitted out a priori with the imagination."[34] Coleridge's secondary imagination is reminiscent of Kant's idea
of a man of genius who possesses an imaginative power "for creating as it
were a second nature out of the materials supplied to it by the first nature."[35]
Coleridge seems to describe this creation of a second nature as an act of
"recreation" of the first. Secondary imagination "coexists with the conscious
will" and "dissolves, diffuses, dissipates, in order to recreate" something out
of the materials which we acquired from perception with our primary imagination. Coleridge argues that secondary imagination differs from primary
imagination only in degree and in mode of operation, not in kind. Thus
Coleridge's two types of imagination, as Mary Warnock aptly observes,
"operate in fundamentally the same way, the one 'making' the world in which
we normally lead our lives, the other 'making' new worlds."[36] In "Dejection:

An Ode," Coleridge laments the loss of this latter power to make new worlds, the power of the creative imagination.

Both Kant and Coleridge downplay the older understanding of imagination as merely an "image-making" faculty, stressing instead its role in the production of unified images in our perceptions. Kant and Coleridge do not share Plato's prejudice against imagination, his view of artistic creativity as possession by the daimon; they recognize the imaginative power of the poet and the artist in a rational way. According to Mark Johnson, Kant argues that "the schematizing activity of the imagination . . . mediates between images or objects of sensation, on the one hand, and abstract concepts, on the other."[37] In a previously quoted passage, Coleridge holds that imagination reconciles the idea with the image. It seems clear that both viewpoints are steeped in the Aristotelian tradition, which regards imagination as a faculty that mediates between sensation and thought. In conclusion, therefore, we can say that Kant's and Coleridge's theories of the imagination are serious attempts to combine and refine both the Platonic and the Aristotelian approaches to the subject.

SHENSI, OR DAIMONIC THINKING

As noted earlier, the premodern Chinese usage of *xiangxiang* is never broad enough to include all of the connotations of the Western concept of imagination, especially in its post-Romantic usage. When twentieth-century Chinese scholars had to come up with a Chinese equivalent for the Western notion of imagination, they chose *xiangxiang* for the obvious reason that its literal meaning is identical. The fact that the enriched usage of *xiangxiang* was the result of importation of ideas from the West does not mean that earlier Chinese had no conception of a faculty comparable to that of the Western imagination. In actual fact, during the Six Dynasties (220–589), the formative period in Chinese literary thought and criticism, some scholars—notably Lu Ji and Liu Xie—devoted considerable energy to discussions of a mental activity very similar to what we now call imagination. The terms used are: *jing* 精 (quintessence, spirit) and *xin* 心 (mind-heart) by Lu Ji and *shensi* 神思 by Liu Xie. I shall concentrate on Liu Xie's *shensi* because it is the concept in the Chinese tradition that comes closest to the Western notion of imagination.

In classical Chinese usage, the character *si* 思 in *shensi* means not only *siwei* 思維 (thought) and *sisuo* 思索 (thinking), but also *huainian* 懷念 (to cherish the memories of) and *xiangnian* 想念 (to remember with longing, to miss.)[38] A good example of the former usage can be found in this statement by Confucius: "To learn without thinking is deceiving; to think without learning is dangerous" [學而不思則罔，思而不學則殆].[39] Examples of the latter usage can readily be found in early Chinese texts. For instance, in *Shijing* 詩經 or *The Book of Songs*: "Not to think about the old relations by marriage, / To seek your new fine man instead" [不思舊姻，求爾新特], and "If you love me and think about me, / Lift your garment and cross the Zhen River" [子惠思我，褰裳涉溱].[40] In the "Rhapsody on Filial Thought" (*Xiaosifu* 孝思賦) by Xiao Yan 蕭衍 (464–508), King Wu of Liang (梁武帝), *si* 思 and *xiang* 想 are used as synonyms. Xiao Yan writes, "想緣情生，情緣想起" in the preface to the rhapsody, and "思因情生，情因思起" in the text of the rhapsody itself.[41] These two couplets are clearly meant to be identical statements, to wit, "Remembrance emerges from emotion; emotion arises from remembrance." In this second set of examples, then, *si* implies that one is thinking about things, people, or events which are no longer in front of one's eyes.[42] Absent things, people, and events are seen again in images stored in one's memory. We can say that the early usage of the Chinese word *si* in this sense of *huainian* and *xiangnian* possesses a nuance comparable to one of the basic semantic values of the English word *imagination*, namely, that this image-making faculty "enables us to think about things that are not present to us now."[43] In spite of this interesting parallel, a closer look at *si* reveals some interesting, unique Chinese characteristics.

When *si* is used to mean "to cherish the memories of" or "to remember with longing," it carries a strong emotional content. This is evident from all three examples cited above. When it is used to mean "thought" or "pondering," as in the example from the *Analects* of Confucius cited earlier, it carries an essentially intellectual content. *Si*, then, designates the activity of "thinking" or "thinking about," which can involve intellectual aspects, emotional aspects, or both. This is very different from imagination, which is conceived as a distinct function of the mind, separate from the faculty for reasoning. As is commonly known, the Chinese word *xin* 心, used to refer to that in charge of *si*, can mean either "mind" or "heart," or both at once, depending on the context. The use of *xin* to refer to the mind-heart, rather than just the mind or the heart, is a good example of the Chinese predilection for seeing close connections between mind and body and between reason and emotion.

The word *shen* in *shensi* carries a double meaning, too.[44] On the one hand, it qualifies *si* or thinking as an activity of a person's *jingshen* 精神 (spirit) that resides in his mind-heart. On the other hand, it also connotes that this *si* has a marvelous, unfathomable, or daimonic quality.

In ancient Chinese religion, *shen* originally refers to the "heavenly spirits or deities," in contrast to the "earthly ghosts." However, from early on *shen* acquired the verbal or adjectival senses of "to be unfathomable" or "miraculous" (as the deities, obviously). In the "Appended words" section ("Xici" 繫辭, which is also called the "Great Treatise" or *Dazhuan* 大傳) of the *Book of Changes* (*Yijing* 易經), we find the following definition: "*Shen* is that which cannot be fathomed in terms of the interaction of yin and yang cosmic forces" [陰陽不測之謂神].[45] A commentary to this text reads: "The so-called *shen* is an expression for something that reaches the limit of changeableness and is miraculous in all things. It is something that cannot be investigated in terms of shape" [神也者，變化之極，妙萬物而為言，不可形詰者也].[46] In the Taoist text *Zhuangzi* 莊子, the term *shenren* 神人 is used to name the person who has attained absolute spiritual freedom and thus can roam freely (*you* 遊) in the boundless realm. A. C. Graham has borrowed the term "daemonic" from Johann Wolfgang von Goethe (1749–1832) to translate *shenren* as the "daemonic man."[47] Goethe muses about this extraordinary power: "The Daemonic is that which cannot be accounted for by understanding or reason. . . . In Poetry there is from first to last something daemonic, and especially in its unconscious appeal, for which all intellect and reason is insufficient, and which therefore has an efficacy beyond all concepts."[48] In borrowing the term from Goethe, Graham adds a cautionary note: "'Daemonic' seems to me to be the modern word closest to *shen*, but I use it with the warning that its restless, anguished quality is foreign to the Chinese word, not to mention the malign associations which it tends to collect by confusion with 'demoniac.'"[49] I believe Graham's application of Goethe's word "daemonic" to render *shen* in the *Zhuangzi*, with appropriate qualification, illustrates his tremendous care in selecting the precise word in translating Chinese texts. To be consistent with Ronald Egan's essay, I shall render *shensi* as "daimonic thinking," rather than "daemonic thinking." In the *Zhuangzi*, as Graham correctly observes, *shen* alludes to "the inscrutable forces wiser than ourselves, throughout the cosmos and in the depths of our own hearts."[50] The "Daimonic Man" (*shenren*) is conceived by Zhuangzi (ca. 369–286 B.C.) as the highest kind of human being who has "lifted above himself by infusion of the daemonic from outside when the heart is cleared of all accretions of past knowledge."[51]

There is no question that in using the word *shen*, Liu Xie preserved its old connotation of a miraculous and unfathomable power, as found in "Xici zhuan" and *Zhuangzi*. But in Liu Xie's theory, "daimonic thinking" is not a unique capacity of the "daimonic man," as portrayed in the *Zhuangzi* text, who has been infused with the daimonic from outside. Nor is it comparable to the kind of thinking that is at work when a poet or artist creates a work of art in an act of possession by the daimon, as argued in the Platonic tradition. In "Yangqi" 養氣 (The nourishing of pneuma), Liu Xie says, "Ears, eyes, nose, and mouth are organs that serve our life; thinking and speech are functions of our daimon" [夫耳目口鼻，生之役也；心慮言辭，神之用也].[52] Clearly he believes that every human being possesses the daimon, enabling him to think and to use language. Let us get a clearer understanding of Liu's concept of daimonic thinking. The beginning of the "Shensi" chapter reads as follows:

古人云：形在江海之上，心在魏闕之下。神思之謂也。

Somebody in ancient times said, "My body is here by the river and the sea, but my mind-heart remains beneath the lofty gate-towers of the palace." This is what is called "daimonic thinking." (*WXDL* 26/1–4)

This opening passage contains an allusion to the "Yielding the Throne" (讓王) chapter of *Zhuangzi*. "Someone in ancient times" (*guren* 古人) refers to the Zhongshan Prince Mou (*Zhongshan gongzi Mou* 中山公子牟) of Wei, and his remark is directly quoted from *Zhuangzi*.[53] Liu Xie ignores the original context of the allusion in which Prince Mou of Wei, now living as a recluse, still thinks of his life of wealth, prestige, and status in the palace. He uses Prince Mou's remark to write about the power of the mind-heart to transport a person to places far away from his body. Prince Mou of Wei is not described as an ideal personality in *Zhuangzi*. Liu Xie's phrase "someone in ancient times" certainly does not suggest that this is somebody out of the ordinary. The remark suggests not so much that life and happiness are more important than possession of wealth and status but rather that the experience of seeing in one's mind's eye allows one to be beneath the palace gate-towers without being physically there. In this respect, then, daimonic thinking corresponds to the Western notion of imagination, which, as we recall from Mary Warnock's comment, "enables us to think about things that are not present to us now."

"My body is here by the river and the sea" describes an actual event here and now; my body is confined within the temporal and spatial boundaries of the present moment and the actual location of the river and the sea.[54] "My mind-heart remains beneath the lofty gate-towers of the palace" constitutes a reminiscence of past experiences. In an act of daimonic thinking, images ("lofty gate-towers of the palace") from past experiences are brought back to life. Thus, daimonic thinking can be defined as an activity of the mind-heart that reactivates remembered images of past experiences, transcending the restrictions of actual time and space.[55] Earlier, in his "Rhapsody on literature," Lu Ji wrote about the journeys of a writer's *jing* and *xin* to the remote reaches of the cosmos and about the writer's transcendence of all temporal and spatial limitations.[56] Nevertheless, Liu Xie makes an important contribution to Chinese aesthetic thought by giving the capacity of the imagination the name of "daimonic thinking," and providing some vivid descriptions of its operation. It should be noted, however, that Liu Xie's real focus in the "Shensi" chapter is not imagination in general but literary imagination as a specific kind of daimonic thinking.

WEN ZHI SI, OR LITERARY THINKING

After briefly defining daimonic thinking, Liu Xie immediately goes on to talk about *wen zhi si* 文之思 (literary thinking).

> 文之思也，其神遠矣！故寂然凝慮，思接千載；悄焉動容，視通萬里；吟詠之間，吐納珠玉之聲；眉睫之前，卷舒風雲之色：其思理之致乎！

The daimon goes far indeed in literary thinking. When one is tranquilly absorbed in contemplation, his thinking reaches back one thousand years.

When his countenance quietly stirs, his vision penetrates ten thousand leagues. In chanting and reciting, he issues forth the sounds of pearls and jade. Right before his eyebrows, there unfurls the colors of windblown clouds. Are these not accomplished by ordered and reasoned thinking? (*WXDL* 26/5–15)

As Zhang Shuxiang 張淑香 convincingly argues, in this passage Liu Xie establishes literary thinking as a special category of daimonic thinking.[57] Literary thinking is daimonic thinking that occurs in the creation of literature. Apart from the opening passage that defines daimonic thinking, the entire "Shensi" chapter is about the process of literary creation. The term *shensi* appears in another section, but the phrase that begins this section—夫神思方運 (When daimonic thinking is first set in motion)[58]—makes it clear that here Liu Xie is talking about the beginning of the creative process when the writer's daimon is set in motion. Since literary thinking is daimonic thinking, it must possess the characteristics of this magical power. But because it is a special kind of daimonic thinking, it has some particular characteristics of its own.

Like the larger category of daimonic thinking, literary thinking is an activity of the mind-heart that transcends spatial and temporal restrictions. Literary thinking can bring forth images (both aural and visual) of things and events that are not necessarily confined to experiences here and now.

What are the special features of literary thinking? First, it involves a long process, one that begins with "absorbing oneself in contemplation" and leads to the expression of ideas in language. Ordinary daimonic thinking does not involve this complex process; it is simply an activity of the mind-heart. Literary thinking leads to the creation of a work of literature, while ordinary daimonic thinking produces only imaginings, fantasies, or daydreams.

Second, literary thinking can only take place when the mind-heart is in a condition of tranquility. Even in the sentence in which the stirring of a writer's countenance is described (suggesting obviously the effect of a feeling or emotion that becomes observable on his face), Liu Xie adds the adverb "quietly" to parallel the condition of "tranquility" noted in the preceding sentence. I shall discuss the necessity of this "tranquil absorption in contemplation" in greater detail below.

Third, literary thinking is reasoned and ordered in a way that ordinary daimonic thinking is not. In the above quoted passage from the "Shensi" chapter, I translate Liu Xie's term *sili* 思理 as "ordered and reasoned think-ing," taking *li* essentially as a stative verb for the noun *si*. *Sili* has been a difficult term for most scholars of *Wenxin diaolong*. It is usually given short shrift by scholars who interpret the "Shensi" chapter or translate it into modern Chinese or English. Vincent Shih simply renders *sili* as "imagina-tion."[59] Zhou Zhenfu 周振甫 equates *sili* with the modern Chinese term *gousi* 構思, which means "conception" or "working out the plot of a literary work."[60] Stephen Owen renders *sili* as "the basic principle of thought" and Ronald Egan as "the path of thinking," but neither of them has provided any explication of the literal meaning of the term.[61] While these readings and translations are by no means wrong, they do not help us understand the importance of the idea of *sili* in Liu Xie's literary theory.

To my knowledge, Zhang Shuxiang has provided perhaps the best, and certainly the most provocative, reading of this interesting term. She suggests that *sili* means "a kind of thinking that is orderly or rational" [一種有條理的或理性的思].[62] I consider Zhang's suggestion to be a significant insight into Liu Xie's theory of literary thinking. *Li* 理 is a word that appears frequently in *Wenxin diaolong*. In the vast majority of occurrences, *li* is used by Liu Xie as a noun to mean "inherent principle," "reason," "argument," "truth," or "rule." In several places, it is used as a verb meaning "to arrange," "to put in order," and "to give pattern and texture to something," as in "The rhapsodies arranged by Chu poets" [楚人理賦], "to put in order the head and the tail" [條理首尾], "to spread out the forms that give the earth pattern and texture" [以鋪理地之形].[63] In at least one case, *li* is used in the expres-sion of *youtiaoliyan* 有條理焉, literally meaning "having order within it."[64] It seems to me that the interpretion of *sili* as "thinking that is based on reason and sense of order" is supported by evidence within *Wenxin diaolong*. This interpretation certainly makes it easier for us to differentiate literary thinking from ordinary daimonic thinking, which may sometimes be no more than wild flights of fancy. It also makes it easier for us to recognize the importance of "tranquil absorption in contemplation" in producing well-ordered and reasoned thought. The term *sili*, thus interpreted, indicates that reason and imagination (daimonic thinking) are integral parts of liter-ary thinking. Unlike in the Western tradition, there is no rigid separation between the two capacities of reason and imagination in the Chinese context.

Having clarified the distinction between ordinary daimonic thinking and literary thinking, we can now proceed to examine the process in literary thinking in greater detail.

THE DAIMON ROAMS WITH THINGS

Liu Xie outlines the beginning of the process of literary thinking in the following section of the "Shensi" chapter.

> 故思理為妙，神與物遊。神居胸臆，而志氣統其關鍵；物沿耳目，而辭令管其樞機。樞機方通，則物無隱貌；關鍵將塞，則神有遁心。

> Thus ordered and reasoned thinking is marvelous, [allowing] the daimon to roam with things. The daimon dwells in the chest, and intent-pneuma controls the bolt to the gate. Things coast along the ear and eye, and language governs the pivot and sill of the door [to their perception by the daimon]. When the pivot and sill allow passage, things do not conceal any aspect of their appearance. When the bolt to the gate is obstructed, the daimon vanishes from the mind-heart. (*WXDL* 26/16–25)

The section begins with the idea that ordered and reasoned thinking is a marvelous activity of the mind-heart, in which the daimon "roams with things." Liu Xie does not elaborate on the meaning of "the daimon roams with things" in this chapter. To understand this statement fully, we must not only explicate the rest of the passage but also piece together related remarks from other chapters of *Wenxin diaolong* in order to illuminate some fundamental issues in Liu Xie's theory of literary creation.

As we have seen, Liu Xie claims that "[e]ars, eyes, nose, and mouth are organs that serve our life; thinking and speech are functions of our daimon." In the passage quoted above, only "the ear and eye" are mentioned, but it is clear that Liu Xie means to evoke all the other sense organs. The argument set forth here seems to be that sense organs serve our life because they are receptors of external stimuli when we come into contact with things (*wu* 物) outside ourselves. The daimon is the power within us that processes and stores up the sensation data for the purposes of thinking, understanding, and communication. These sensation data are essentially "images." The daimon is said to reside in the "chest," where the heart is housed. But in traditional Chinese usage, the chest is where the *xin* 心 (mind-heart) is located. Here Liu Xie actually uses the chest as a substitute for the mind-heart. The daimon, then, is the miraculous power that dwells in our mind-heart, a power uniquely possessed by human beings. Liu Xie goes on to say that "intent and pneuma control the bolt to the gate [that lets the daimon in and out]." In other words, a person's intent-pneuma (*zhiqi* 志氣) controls the activity of his daimon and therefore also the whole process of his daimon roaming with things. What is intent-pneuma, and how is it related to external things? To answer these questions, let us take a closer look at three relevant remarks from other chapters.

人稟七情，應物斯感，感物吟志，莫非自然。

Human beings are endowed with seven emotions,[65] which are stimulated in response to things. It is only natural for them to be stimulated by things and to sing about their intents. (*WXDL* 6/16–19)

春秋代序，陰陽慘舒，物色之動，心亦搖焉。‧‧‧‧歲有其物，物有其容；情以物遷，辭以情發。

Spring and autumn succeed one another, alternating with the gloom of Yin and the ease of Yang. When the colors of things are stirred into motion, the mind-heart is swayed along with them. . . . Different things appear in the course of the year, and they all have different appearances. Human emotions change in accordance with the [changing appearances of] things, and the language used depends on the emotions [which emerge in response to things]. (*WXDL* 46/1–4, 21–24)

若夫八體屢遷，功以學成。才力居中，肇自血氣；氣以實志，志以定言，吐納英華，莫非情性。

The eight styles [of composition] are constantly changing, and success in them is accomplished through learning. The force of talent dwells within and emanates from blood and pneuma. Pneuma gives substance to intent, and intent determines what is said. The utterance of the [verbal] flower is all due to [a person's] emotion and nature. (*WXDL* 27/66–70)[66]

By focusing on these three passages we can investigate Liu Xie's views on inspiration and on the manifestation of the world and of the experience and personality of a writer in his literary expression. Every human being is born with feelings and emotions that are continuously stimulated by external things. Continuous stimulation provokes continuous responses, some of which may result in the writing of literature. This lyrical view is reminiscent of William Wordsworth's statement that "poetry is the spontaneous over-flow of powerful feelings."[67]

In the third passage above, Liu Xie says that the force of a person's talent (i.e., a person's expressive power) emanates from his blood and breath (*xueqi* 血氣). As a compound term, *xueqi* can be found in such ancient Chinese philosophical and historical texts as *Zuozhuan* 左傳, *Lunyu* 論語, *Zhongyong* 中庸, *Liji* 禮記, and *Yueji* 樂記.[68] *Xueqi* refers to the matter-energy or physical vigor of an animal or a human being.[69] From early on, the character *qi* is used to mean the same thing as *xueqi*. The Greek word *pneuma* (liter-ally, "the breath of life") seems to be a perfect equivalent of the Chinese concept of *qi*.[70] The inclusion of blood in the compound term certainly makes it more explicit that Chinese philosophy and literary theory pay significant attention to the human body or physiology.

Traditionally, Chinese scholars spoke of nourishing a person's pneuma with culture, moral sense, and reason. For instance, Mencius says that he is good at cultivating within himself a *haoranzhiqi* 浩然之氣 or "floodlike pneuma" that unites righteousness with Tao, fills the space between heaven and earth, and is vast and unyielding.[71] This floodlike pneuma is the result of Mencius's elevation of his physical vitality endowed by nature to a spiri-tual level that includes knowledge, reason, and moral principles. Similarly, the pneuma for traditional Chinese critics is an artist's physiological nature and his cultivation of cultural values. In the end, the *qi* observable in a literary or artistic work is no longer simply a product of its creator's physical vigor; it is a manifestation of his personality. Also, exemplified in the third passage above, the Chinese believed traditionally that there is a continuum from an artist's or writer's personality to the work he creates.

The blending of nature and culture is also relevant to the concept of *zhi*. Liu Xie says, "Pneuma gives substance to intent (*zhi*), and intent determines what is said." *Zhi* is one of the cardinal concepts in Chinese literary theory. As James J. Y. Liu has observed, *zhi* is traditionally "interpreted as 'where the heart goes' (i.e., heart's wish, or emotional purport) or 'where the mind goes' (i.e., mind's intent, will, or moral purpose)."[72] It should be recalled, of course, that the Chinese concept of *xin* includes both the heart and the mind. Thus, *zhi* can perhaps be rendered as "that which preoccupies the mind-heart," because it involves both the emotional and the intellectual aspects of a person. Further, as Liu Xie says, "Pneuma gives substance to intent [*zhi*]," and what preoccupies a person's mind-heart cannot be completely unconnected to his physiological nature, even in a context in which the intellectual aspect of *zhi* is dominant. Liu Xie's use of the term *zhiqi* (intent-pneuma) in the "Shensi" chapter therefore suggests some bodily basis in literary thinking. The third passage quoted above ends with the remark, "The utterance of the [verbal] flower is all due to a person's emotion and nature [*qingxing* 情性]." "Flower" is a metaphor for literary expression. Thus, the creation of a literary work is due to a person's emotion and nature. Xu Fuguan notes that *qingxing* here consists of "talent" (*cai* 才), *qi*, and *zhi* three interrelated elements.[73] *Xing* refers to the "individuating nature" possessed by an artist.[74] The stirring into motion of one's pneuma (and hence one's creative talent) can be caused by either intent or emotion. The addition of *qing* (emotion) to *xing* (nature) to create a term is clearly intended to emphasize the importance of feelings and emotions in literary inspiration and creation. What Liu Xie calls *qingxing* is often called *qingzhi* 情志 (emotion and intent) by many other ancient Chinese scholars.[75] Liu Xie himself only uses *qingzhi* once in the entire *Wenxin diaolong*.[76] The tendency of Chinese critics to use words and terms with overlapping implications is indicative of the Chinese preference for not using analytically precise and abstract concepts. For the purposes of this essay, I want to stress that the critical terms discussed here do not reveal a rigid dichotomy between body and mind or between nature and culture. I shall have more to say about the issue of the body, but now I want to return to the passage that gives expression to the idea of "the daimon roaming with things."

As noted earlier, Liu Xie considers *ganwu yinzhi* 感物吟志 or "the stimulation of feelings and emotions in response to external things and the singing of intents," to be a natural process. Every human being is endowed by nature with various feelings and emotions which enable him to be continuously stimulated by things in the external world. This interaction between the feelings and emotions (*qing*) and external things (*wu*) naturally generates an intent in the mind-heart, and an artistic expression (or "singing") of this intent becomes poetry and literature. *Ganwu*, or "the stimulation of feelings and emotions in response to things," signifies real experience, and *yinzhi*, or "the singing of intents," denotes the resulting poetic or literary expression. *Ganwu yinzhi* may be called a naturalistic,[77] lyrical conception of the origin of literature. "The daimon roaming with things," however, describes literary thinking that leads to the actual creation of a literary work. This process of thinking begins with whatever is preoccupying an author's mind-heart (*zhi, qingzhi*, or *qingxing*) and ends with its expression in appropriate and effective language. Between *zhi* and *yan*, a writer must relive the experience of the interaction between his inner emotions and external things and search for the right language and form to depict the experience.

The daimon plays a key role in this creative process, but as Liu Xie has stated, its activity is controlled by a writer's intent-pneuma at the beginning and his command of language in the end. If there is any obstruction to the writer's intent-pneuma (for example, if he cannot concentrate on what pre-occupies his mind-heart), the daimon within him will not be able to exercise its magical power. Unless one has a good command of language, one's daimon cannot capture all aspects of the appearances of things that have stimulated one's emotions. Because the process of literary creation involves the reenactment of an experience, the *wu* (things) mentioned in such phrases as "[t]he daimon roams with things" and "[t]hings coast along the ear and eye" do not refer to real things in the external world. It has been argued that the *wu* in these instances stand for *wuxiang* 物象 (thing-images), which are impressions of external things as first perceived by one's mind-heart and stored as sensation data or images in memory.[78] Indeed, Liu Xie distinguishes between *wuxiang* (thing-images) and *yixiang* 意象 (idea-images), even though sometimes he only uses the words *wu* (things) and *xiang* (images). This implicit distinction is discernible in the two more or less parallel phrases that designate two stages in the process of literary creation: *shen yu wu you* 神與物遊 [the daimon roams with things] and *shen yong xiang tong* 神用象通 [when the daimon is applied, (idea-)images are accomplished].[79] The latter appears in the "Zan" 贊, or "supporting verse," at the end of the "Shensi" chapter. It should be noted that when it is roaming with things, the daimon is being applied and being put to work already. In fact, Liu Xie's claim that "[w]hen the daimon is applied, images are accomplished" is to be grasped in the context provided by the subsequent line in the "supporting verse": *qingbian suoyun* 情變所孕 [brought forth by the mutations in emotion] (*WXDL* 26/ 128). As discussed earlier, *qing* (emotion) here can stand for *qingzhi* (emotion-intent). If the initial stage of literary thinking can be characterized as harmonious and free but dispassionate, the emergence of "idea-images" can be said to be caused by mutations in one's emotion and intent.

For simplicity's sake, I shall render *yixiang* as "idea-images." I should point out, however, that *yi* can also mean "desire," "feeling," "intention," "meaning," "thought," or "wish." Thing-images and idea-images are thus rather different: The former emphasize the representation of external things, while the latter integrate the subject's ideas, feelings, and wishes. Thing-images first appear when one comes into contact with things and reappear at the beginning of the process of literary thinking. Both kinds of images should ideally be close representations of the real things themselves. But in addition to allowing no aspect of the appearances of things to be hidden, one must also allow images to be infused with ideas and feelings. Thus, idea-images are no longer impressions of things passively or objectively received: They embody a person's intents. One can say that the first aspect of the daimon's roaming with things is to sort out which thing-images can best express, or embody, intent, thereby permitting idea-images to emerge.

At this juncture, we should ask why Liu Xie uses the word *you* 遊 (roaming, wandering) to describe the activity of the daimon prior to the creation of a literary work. It is obvious that Liu Xie has borrowed the word from the *Zhuangzi* text. The first Inner Chapter in *Zhuangzi* is entitled "Xiaoyaoyou" 逍遙遊 (Wandering without any restriction). In the *Zhuangzi* text, and especially in its first seven Inner Chapters, the image of *you* is used as a metaphor for the idea of absolute spiritual freedom that does not depend on anything and transcends all restrictions, boundaries, and limitations. It is very fitting for Liu Xie to use the word *you* to describe the marvelous unbridled activity of daimonic thinking. The expression "roaming with" (*yu . . . you*) echoes its usage in *Zhuangzi*. In "Dechongfu" 德充符 (The signs of fullness of power): "I have been roaming about with the Master for nineteen years now" [吾與夫子遊十九年矣].[80] Here "roaming about with" describes a relationship that involves harmony, equality, freedom, and non-attachment.

In "Wuse" 物色 (The colors of things), Liu Xie makes another important allusion to the *Zhuangzi* which conveys his view of the relationship between the daimon and things. Liu Xie writes:

是以詩人感物，聯類不窮，流連萬象之際，沈吟視聽之區；寫氣圖貌，既隨物以宛轉；屬采附聲，亦與心而徘徊。

> Thus when poets are stimulated by things, the categorical associations are endless. They linger about the myriad images, even to their edges, and ponder over every area of what they have seen and heard. In writing about the pneuma and appearances of things in nature, they roll smoothly along with them. In applying coloration and attaching sounds, they whirl about in accordance with [the wishes of] their mind-hearts. (WXDL 46/29–36)

The expression "rolling smoothly along with things" (隨物以宛轉) is borrowed with a slight change from "Tianxia" 天下 (Below in the empire) in *Zhuangzi*. In "Below in the empire" the phrase is given as "rolling smoothly along with things" [*yu wu wan zhuan* 與物宛轉] in a section on the philosophy of the Warring States thinker Shen Dao 慎到.[81] In adapting this textual allusion from Zhuangzi, Liu Xie repeats the idea of following along with things in their natural transformations without imposing any subjective feelings upon them.[82] This approach to nature is juxtaposed with the approach that is conveyed at the end of the passage: "to whirl about in accordance with one's mind-heart's wishes" [與心而徘徊]. In contrast with the former approach, the latter gives the writer's mind-heart the power to mold or change nature. Liu Xie is not a thoroughgoing Taoist who regards nature (rather than human beings) as the ultimate touchstone of values. Nonetheless, by proposing that "the daimon roaming with things" is the beginning of literary thinking, Liu advocates a Taoist approach. For it is only when things are approached in this nonpurposive manner that they reveal their true appearances to human beings through thing-images. This approach is related to the "tranquil absorption in contemplation" mentioned earlier and the "emptiness and tranquility" (*xujing* 虛靜) Liu Xie mentions in the "Shensi" chapter. I shall discuss this "tranquil absorption" (as an aspect of the cultivation of literary thinking) in my conclusion. Let us now move on to discuss the second stage of literary thinking, which comes after the emergence of idea-images.

CARVING SOMETHING OUT OF
THAT WHICH IS WITHOUT FORM

The next excerpt from the "Shensi" chapter follows a passage on the cultivation of literary thinking, but deals with the second stage in literary creation.

然後使玄解之宰，尋聲律而定墨；獨照之匠，窺意象而運斤：
此蓋馭文之首術，謀篇之大端。夫神思方運，萬塗競萌，規矩
虛位，刻鏤無形，登山則情滿於山，觀海則意溢於海，我才之
多少，將與風雲而並驅矣。

Thereafter, one can cause the one in command who is freed from bonds to fix up the words in accordance with rules of sound, and the matchlessly discerning carpenter to wield his ax while eyeing idea-images. This is the first technique in steering writing, the key point in planning a piece. When daimonic thinking is first set in motion, ten thousand paths compete with each other in budding forth. [It then] shapes and regulates empty positions, as well as cuts and carves [something] out of the formless. If one climbs a mountain, the mountain is filled with one's emotions; if one views the sea, the sea overflows with one's ideas. According to the measure of one's talent, one can run neck and neck with the wind and clouds. (*WXDL* 26/34–47)

The first line in this passage is ambiguous and difficult. Some scholars see it as an allusion to the Cook Ding 庖丁 story in the chapter entitled "Yangshengzhu" 養生主 (What matters in the nurture of life) in *Zhuangzi*. Vincent Shih, for instance, renders *xuanjiezhizai* 玄解之宰 simply as the "mysterious butcher," presumably interpreting *xuan* as "mysterious" and *jiezhizai* as "butcher."[83] There are problems with this interpretation. First, in classical Chinese, although *zai* can mean "cook" in such compounds as *zaifu* 宰夫 (the man who butchers) and *zaiyin* 宰尹 (the "official" who butchers), it usually means "the one in command" when used as a noun, and "to slaughter or carve up" when used as a verb, as in *tuzai* 屠宰 and *zaige* 宰割, for example. I wonder why Liu Xie did not use the word *pao* 庖 if he indeed intended to allude to Cook Ding. Second, Cook Ding's supreme skill in cutting up oxen has never been referred to as *xuanjie* in the *Zhuangzi* text, in commentaries on *Zhuangzi*, or in other texts, to my knowledge. Thus it seems very problematic to read the line literally as "the cook with the mysterious skill of butchering."

Zhou Zhenfu takes the line as "the one in command who understands mysterious theories." He also cites the line, "of old this was called 'the releasing from Di's bonds'" [古者謂是帝之縣〔懸〕解] from the ending section to "What matters in the nurture of life" as a possible source for the compound word *xuanjie* 玄解.[84] Zhou Zhenfu interprets "the one in command" as referring to one's mind-heart. But the citation of the phrase "the releasing from Di's bonds" does not in any way support his reading of the line as "the mind-heart which understands mysterious theories," because the character *jie* has different meanings in the two contexts.

My own, tentative, interpretation takes *zai* as "the one in command" and *xuanjie* 玄解 as an allusion to the idea of "the releasing of bonds" toward the end of "What matters in the nurture of life." However, there is a problem with this interpretation as well. 玄 and 縣〔懸〕, though both pronounced *xuan*, do not mean the same thing. In *Jingdian shiwen* 經典釋文 (The explication of words in classical works), the Tang dynasty scholar Lu Deming 陸德明 says, "縣 is pronounced *xuan* 玄 and 解 is pronounced *xie* 蟹 . . . ."[85] Perhaps Liu Xie has taken the liberty of substituting the word 縣, meaning "bonds," with the word 玄, originally meaning "mysterious," because it is pronounced the same way.

If this is indeed the case, and if Lu Deming is also correct about the shared pronunciation, the phrase in the "Shensi" chapter should be read as *xuanxiezhizai*, not *xuanjiezhizai*. Furthermore, the "bonds" in the *Zhuangzi* chapter refer to the bondages inflicted upon the human spirit by life and death, while the "bonds" in the "Shensi" chapter refer more generally to limitations and restrictions. I think both *zai* (the one in command) here and *jiang* 匠 (carpenter, alluding to Carpenter Shi in the *Zhuangzi*)[86] in the third line are Liu Xie's metaphors for the daimon (residing within one's mind-heart) which is freed of all bondages and limitations. *Zai* and *jiang*, as Ronald Egan notes in Chapter 5, make up the term *zaijiang* 宰匠, referring either to the one who actually governs such as in the case of a prime minister (*zaixiang* 宰相), or to a master artisan or craftsman (*zongjiang* 宗匠). The daimon exhibited in literary thinking is the power in command of the entire creative process. It also selects the right path from many, and it shapes, regulates, and carves something out of what is without form. Other elements vital to literary creation such as rules of prosody, images, emotions, ideas, experience, and nature are also mentioned in Liu Xie's passage. The most important point to be observed during this second stage in literary thinking is that daimonic thinking now emerges as something comparable to what Coleridge named secondary imagination, or the "shaping spirit of imagination," the power to create.

In Liu Xie's theory, daimonic thinking is essential to literary creation. It selects from one's sense data of lived experiences (or thing-images) and combines them with ideas and feelings to produce idea-images. Then daimonic thinking uses language and literary convention to create a unified, coherent, and artistic work of literature. In both stages, Liu Xie's daimonic thinking is indeed comparable to the notion of imagination in the Western tradition.

THE BODILY BASIS OF IMAGINATION

Zhang Shuxiang has observed that one important difference between Liu Xie's daimonic thinking and the Western concept of imagination is that Liu Xie recognizes the influence of physiology on the writer's daimonic thinking.[87] In my earlier discussion of the issue of intent-pneuma (*zhiqi*), I noted Liu Xie's recognition of the presence of the physiological nature and personality of a writer in his literary creation. Cao Pi was the first Chinese critic to talk about this issue. However, Liu Xie is regarded as having improved upon Cao Pi's conception of the relation between a writer's personality and his work. In a famous passage from "Lunwen" 論文 (A discourse on literature), Cao Pi writes: "Pneuma is the main factor in literature. Pneuma has forms—clear and murky—which cannot be brought by force" [文以氣為主，氣之清濁有體，不可力強而致].[88] Although Cao Pi probably means to apply the categories of "clear and murky" as they are used in music appreciation to discuss literature, Xu Fuguan thinks that Cao Pi's distinction is not sound because ordinarily people tend to regard "murkiness" as negative.[89] Liu Xie substitutes Cao Pi's "clear and murky" with "the firm and the yielding" in describing pneuma: "Pneuma varies between the firm and the yielding" [氣有剛柔] (*WXDL* 27/6). Although pneuma can be encouraged with cultural values, its qualities, as distinguished by Cao Pi and Liu Xie, are largely endowed by nature in one's physical body. Since intent-pneuma affects daimonic thinking, the physiological characteristic and condition of a writer must have a bearing on his creative imagination. Liu Xie is clearly aware of the issue, even though he has not provided elaborate discussion of it in his *Wenxin diaolong*.

There is another area in which the body plays an important part in the working of the imagination. Here I want to draw on the work of Mark Johnson, who explores the ways that meaning, understanding, and reason arise from and are conditioned by the patterns of our bodily experience. In an attempt to counter the rigid separation of mind from body, cognition from emotion, and reason from imagination in Western philosophy and culture, Johnson attempts to put the body back into the mind. He uses the word *body* "as a generic term for the embodied origins of imaginative structures of understanding, such as image schemata and their metaphorical elaborations."[90] He defines image schema as follows:

> [I]n order for us to have meaningful, connected experiences that we can comprehend and reason about, there must be pattern and order to our actions, perceptions, and conceptions. *A schema is a recurrent pattern, shape, and regularity in, or of, these ongoing ordering activities.* These patterns emerge as meaningful structures for us chiefly at the level of our bodily movements through space, our manipulation of objects, and our perceptual interactions.[91]

Image schemas, also called "imaginative structures," emerge from our experience of bodily interaction with the environment. Johnson gives the example of the verticality or up-down schema.

> We grasp this structure of verticality repeatedly in thousands of perceptions and activities we experience every day, such as perceiving a tree, our felt sense of standing upright, the activity of climbing stairs, forming a mental image of a flagpole, measuring our children's heights, and experiencing the level of water rising in the bathtub. The VERTICALITY schema is the abstract structure of these VERTICALITY experiences, images, and perceptions.[92]

We can project this up-down schema, this embodied imaginative structure from the domain of vertical experience, metaphorically to another domain. We often speak of quantity in terms of the verticality schema: "prices keep going up"; "his gross income fell last year"; "turn down the heat."[93] Johnson's purpose is to rectify the rigid Western dichotomy between mind and body, as well as reason and imagination, by showing that abstract patterns usually originate in bodily experience. One of Johnson's most important contributions is his persuasive argument that "creativity is possible, in part, because imagination gives us image-schematic structures and metaphoric and metonymic patterns by which we can extend and elaborate those schemata."[94] Johnson also directs the reader's attention to the bodily basis of imagination, which is not often treated in the Western cultural tradition.

In the Chinese tradition, we find that bodily experience usually constitutes a significant part of critical discussions of imagination and literary creation. In addition to being keenly concerned with the physiological nature and personality of a writer, traditional Chinese critics also pay much attention to an artist's bodily experience in creative imagination. In other words, the body was never driven out of the mind in early Chinese philosophy. This is illustrated by the following passage from the "Appended words" section of the *Book of Changes*, one of the earliest classics in the Chinese tradition.

古者包犧氏之王天下也，仰則觀象於天，俯則觀法於地，觀鳥獸之文，與地之宜。近取諸身，遠取諸物。於是始作八卦，以通神明之德，以類萬物之情。

When in early antiquity Baoxi ruled the world, he looked upward and contemplated the images in heaven; he looked downward and contemplated the orders on earth. He contemplated the patterns of birds and beasts and the adaptations to the regions. He proceeded from his own person [*shen*, literally, "body"] nearby and from things afar. Thus he invented the eight signs in order to enter into connection with the power of the daimonic-and-illumined and to serve as the categorizing correspondences for the true conditions of all things.[95]

This passage is an interesting account of the invention of abstract signs by the mythical founder of Chinese civilization, Baoxi. The *bagua*, first rendered as "eight signs" by the German scholar Richard Wilhelm, are better known as "eight trigrams" in English scholarship on the *Book of Changes*. The trigrams are collections of linear signs, each consisting of three lines (either the solid line for yang, or the divided line for yin: ☰, ☱, ☲, ☳, ☴, ☵, ☶, ☷), and they were used as oracles in divination. Of the *bagua* in the *Yijing*, Richard Wilhelm writes:

These eight signs were conceived as images of all that happens in heaven and on earth. At the same time, they were held to be in a state of continual transition, one changing into another, just as transition from one phenomenon to another is continually taking place in the physical world. Here we have the fundamental concept of the *Book of Changes*. The eight signs are symbols standing for changing transitional states; they are images that are constantly undergoing change. Attention centers not on things in their state of being—as is chiefly the case in the Occident—but upon their movements in change. The eight signs therefore are not representations of things as such but of their tendencies in movement.[96]

Very early in the history of the evolution of the *Book of Changes*, these eight signs (trigrams) were combined with one another to form a total of sixty-four signs (hexagrams). To borrow a term from Mark Johnson, we can consider the trigrams and hexagrams as image schematas which represent primordial patterns of continual change in the cosmos. Baoxi's invention of the eight trigrams is described in the passage from the "Appended words" as based on observation of patterns in nature. In the passage, only visual observation is noted. But the eight trigrams are said to yield a set of basic images of heaven, earth, thunder, water, mountain, wind, fire, and lake.[97]

There is no reason to question whether Baoxi used all of his senses in grasping the primordial patterns of nature before he invented the eight signs. Not only was Baoxi's invention of his set of eight image schematas based on bodily experience, but his own person or body was also the immediate subject of his observation and investigation. The importance of the body and bodily experience cannot be denied.

Returning now to *Wenxin diaolong*, I would like to look at some examples from "Wuse" (Colors of things) to further illustrate Liu Xie's concern with bodily experience. Earlier I noted two brief passages from this chapter: one in the context of the mind-heart being stirred by things, and the other of the daimon roaming about with things. The idea of *you*, or roaming, suggests the involvement of one's entire being. The title of the chapter also deserves special attention. Stephen Owen has translated "Wuse" as "The sensuous colors of physical things" with the intention of making the reader aware of the rich implications of the term.[98] *Wu* refers to things in the physical world. *Se* implies more than surface appearances, because it is the Chinese translation of the Sanskrit term *rupa*, the outward appearances and forms "that cause delusion and desire."[99] Although Liu Xie's emphasis is on the sense of sight, he refers to the other senses as well. The central concern of the "Wuse" chapter is undoubtedly the role of sensuous, bodily impressions in literary creation.[100] The chapter ends with a "supporting verse."

山沓水匝，	Mountains pile up, waters meander,
樹雜雲合。	Trees intermix, and clouds merge.
目既往還，	When the eyes have interacted with them,
心亦吐納。	The mind-heart expresses what's received.
春日遲遲，	The sun in spring moves so slowly,
秋風颯颯。	The winds of autumn sough and sough.
情往似贈，	Our emotions go forth as if to give a gift,
興來如答。	And inspiration comes back like a reply.

(*WXDL* 46/116–23)[101]

The verse begins with visual images of things in nature. The compound phrase *wanghuan* can mean both "to move back and forth" and "to hold intercourse with." The whole line *mujiwanghuan* thus implies "the eyes move back and forth, interacting with [things in nature]," echoing "rolling smoothly along with things." The phrase *tuna* means literally "to emit and take in." But I think it makes better sense not to take *tu* and *na* as two equivalent verbs, but instead to take the latter as subordinate to the former. The first half of the "supporting verse" describes the intimate relation between verbal expression generated from the mind-heart and visual (and by extension, bodily) perception. If the first half of the verse dwells upon what can be perceived by the eye, the second half is not limited to perception by one sense.

The verse concludes with the notion that our emotions respond to and interact with things in the external world, resulting in literary inspiration. Liu Xie mentions two sets of images as examples of things in the external world. The line *chunri chichi* is directly taken from song 154 in *Shijing* 詩經 (The book of songs). In the original context, it means "[t]he days of spring pass so slowly."[102] In the context of "The colors of things" it should mean "[t]he sun in spring moves so slowly" in order to make a closer parallel with the next line "The winds of autumn sough and sough." It seems self-evident that the statement "[t]he days of spring pass so slowly" is a metonymic projection of the perception that "[t]he sun in spring moves so slowly." In any case, both readings are derived originally from visual experience. The line, "[t]he winds of autumn sough and sough" contains an appeal to the sense of hearing. The "supporting verse" that ends "The colors of things" is a poem about literary thinking or imagination at work. Clearly, Liu Xie believes that daimonic thinking is deeply rooted in bodily experience.

CULTIVATING LITERARY THINKING

Let us return to a passages we examined earlier, which concerns the "cultivation of literary thinking."

> 是以陶鈞文思，貴在虛靜，疏瀹五藏，澡雪精神，積學以儲寶，酌理以富才，研閱以窮照，馴致以懌辭。

> Thus in shaping and molding literary thinking, what is highly valued is emptiness and tranquility, whereby one dredges clear the five viscera and cleanses the quintessential daimon. One must accumulate learning to build a storehouse of treasures, immerse oneself in reason to enrich talent, investigate experience to exhaust observation, and tame one's inner state to spin out words. (*WXDL* 26/26–33)

As Li Zehou and Liu Gangji have pointed out, "emptiness and tranquility" (*xujing*), "accumulation of learning" (*jixue*), "immersion in reason" (*zhuoli*), "investigating experience" (*yanyue*), and "taming the inner state" (*xunzhi*) are five things that can affect the free and unhindered activity of the daimon in its "roaming with things."[103] The five factors are also important in enabling one's daimonic thinking to create a unified literary work out of a dazzling array of images and ideas. I think this is why Liu Xie has inserted this passage between the sections in which he discusses the two stages in the creative process.

Liu Xie does not comment on the interrelations among the five factors. By placing "emptiness and tranquility" first, however, he seems to indicate that this condition of the mind-heart is a prerequisite for the other four factors.[104] The linguistic features of the terms Liu Xie has used for the five factors also seem to support this interpretation. While *xujing* is made up of two nouns, the other four terms, *jixue, zhuoli, yanyue,* and *xunzhi*, are all structured in the form of a verb followed by a noun. Further, Liu Xie mentions a method to attain *xujing* in the two subsequent lines: "dredging clear the five viscera," and "cleansing the quintessential daimon." He does not do this with the other four factors. There is one other peculiar point to this whole passage in the chapter. While *xujing* and *xunzhi* can be said to refer to the desired condition under which daimonic thinking is at work, *jixue, zhuoli*, and *yanyue* refer to the long process of preparation and cultivation prior to the moment of literary creation. Of course, *xujing* is to be viewed as a condition of the mind-heart that applies to the process of preparation and cultivation as well.

Some scholars have noted the connection between Liu Xie's notion of "emptiness and tranquility or stillness" and Taoist philosophy.[105] The two words *xujing* appear in the following lines in chapter 16 of the *Daodejing*.

致 虛 極 ，	I do my utmost to attain emptiness;
守 靜 篤 。	I hold firmly to stillness.
萬 物 並 作 ，	The myriad creatures all rise together
吾 以 觀 復 。	And I watch their return.
夫 物 芸 芸 ，	The teeming creatures
各 復 歸 其 根 。	All return to their separate roots.
歸 根 曰 靜 。	Returning to one's roots is known as stillness.[106]

There is good reason to believe that this is the primary source for Liu Xie's term *xujing*. Laozi is here talking about a mode of perception that does not involve the imposition of human interests and values. If one remains absolutely empty and still, one will be able to see things in their pristine state. This approach is obviously what Liu Xie intends when he writes about being "quietly absorbed in contemplation" and in "the daimon roaming freely with things."

Liu Xie's two qualifying statements about *xujing* allude to one parable in "Knowledge roams north" of the *Zhuangzi*. Laozi says to Confucius, "You must fast, dredge clear your mind-heart, cleanse your quintessential daimon, and smash your knowledge" [汝 齋 戒 ， 疏 瀹 而 心 ， 澡 雪 而 精 神 ， 掊 擊 而 知].[107] Liu Xie substitutes "the mind-heart" with "the five viscera." This passage in "Knowledge roams north" echoes several passages in the Inner Chapters—the core portions of the *Zhuangzi*—in which the ideas of *xinzhai* 心 齋 (the fasting of the mind-heart) and *zuowang* 坐 忘 (sitting down and forgetting everything) are set forth.[108] *Xinzhai* appears in a parable involving Confucius and Yan Hui 顏回 in "In the world of men." Confucius advises his favorite disciple to do a "fasting of the mind-heart" before he goes to serve the Lord of Wei.

> 若一志，無聽之以耳，而聽之以心；無聽之以心，而聽之以
> 氣。聽止於耳，心止於符。氣也者，虛而待物者也。唯道集
> 虛。虛者，心齋也。

Make your will one! Rather than listen with your ears, listen with your mind-heart. Rather than listen with your mind-heart, listen with your pneuma. Listening stops with the ears, and the mind-heart stops with what tallies with thought. As for pneuma, it is that which is empty and waits for things. Only the Tao accumulates emptiness. Emptiness is the fasting of the mind-heart.[109]

The term *zuowang* comes from another parable involving Confucius and Yan Hui that appears in "The great and venerable teacher." In this story, Yan Hui, who has reached the state of "just sit and forget," says to his teacher:

> 墮枝體，黜聰明，離形去知，同於大通，此之謂坐忘。

I let organs and members drop away, dismiss eyesight and hearing, part from the body and expel knowledge, and go along with the universal thoroughfare. This is what I mean by "just sit and forget."[110]

In the passage from "In the world of men," the word *qi* (pneuma) is described as being "empty." Thus it must not be equated with the physiological matter-energy, discussed at some length previously, that has substance. Chen Gu-ying 陳鼓應 suggests that it refers to the activity of the mind-heart in a state of purity and emptiness.[111] Wang Shumin suggests that *qi* here can be considered as equivalent to the daimon.[112] *Xinzhai* and *zuowang* are metaphors employed by Zhuangzi to describe the mind-heart in a pure state that transcends the senses and intellect, as well as the knowledge, distinctions, and values acquired by them. As Zhuangzi argues, in this spiritual state an enlightened Taoist is one with Tao. This is not what Liu Xie means when he alludes to the *Daodejing* and *Zhuangzi*. He is not concerned with a person's mystical oneness with Tao but with the release of his daimon for free and unlimited wandering. This is what Cook Ding says to Lord Wenhui about his great skill in butchering oxen: "Nowadays, I meet [an ox] with my daimon and don't look with my eyes. Both my sense organs and intellect have come to a stop and my daimon moves where it desires" [方今之時，臣以神遇 而不以目視，官知止而神欲行].[113] Before Liu Xie, Lu Ji has already adopted this Taoist method in describing the beginning of the literary creative process. In his "Rhapsody on literature," he writes:

其始也，	Thus as one begins,
皆收視反聽，	One retracts vision, reverts hearing,
耽思傍訊，	Indulges in thinking, seeks all around,
精騖八極，	And lets the essence gallop to the eight directions,
心遊萬仞。	The mind-heart roam up-and-down ten thousand leagues.[114]

Liu Xie follows this view in setting forth his argument for the first stage in literary thinking, the daimon's free and unrestricted roaming with things. What Lu Ji and Liu Xie are talking about here is, of course, not the same as Zhuangzi's mystical experience of *xinzhai* and *zuowang*. They are concerned with spiritual concentration that is essential to the activity of creative imagination. It is necessary for one to cut off all sensual influences, concerns, and worries in the mind-heart. The retraction of vision and the reversion of hearing, resulting in a state of emptiness and tranquility for the mind-heart, do not run counter to the recognition of bodily experience discussed earlier. As mentioned, the word "things" in Liu Xie's remark "the daimon roaming with things" refers to "thing-images," which are sense-impressions of things in the external world that are stored in memory. Liu Xie argues that concentrating the mind-heart till it is free from external influences and internal disturbances will allow the daimon to roam freely with thing-images. We should not ignore that the word *jing* (tranquility, stillness) does not appear in the contexts in which *xinzhai* and *zuowang* are described. *Jing* does not even appear in the Inner Chapters of *Zhuangzi*. It does not belong to the same category of importance as *you* (roaming) or *xu* (emptiness) in the core portions of *Zhuangzi*.[115] Apart from Laozi, the Confucian thinker Xunzi 荀 子 (ca. 298–238 B.C.) also highly values "emptiness and tranquility." In an essay entitled "Dispelling Obsession" Xunzi says, "How does a man understand the Way? Through the mind[-heart]. How can the mind[-heart] understand it? Because it is empty, unified, and still" [人 何 以 知 道 ？ 曰： 心。 心 何 以 知 道 ？ 曰： 虛 壹 而 靜].[116] Here *xu* refers to the capacity of the mind-heart not to let the ideas and sense data it already possesses to inter fere with new data it will receive. *Yi* refers to the capacity of the mind-heart to remain unified, preventing fragmentation and chaos from occurring. *Jing* refers to the mind-heart's state of tranquility, which prevents daydreams and wayward thoughts from affecting its ability to know truth.[117] Liu Xie purposefully chooses to use Laozi's term *xujing*, qualifies it with textual allusions to Zhuangzi's ideas about "the fasting of the mind-heart," and then allows the context of his passage to bring out Xunzi's rationalist theory that the mindheart is empty, unified, and still. Thus the Taoist mystical sense of "emptiness and tranquility" is relevant to the first stage of literary thinking, during which the daimon must be allowed total freedom of activity, and Xunzi's rational sense of "emptiness and stillness" is essential to the second stage of literary thinking and to the long process of self-cultivation.

The four subsequent factors in cultivating literary thinking all involve self-conscious or intellectual efforts that the philosophical Taoist must avoid or transcend in his attempt to attain "emptiness and tranquility." Taoism idealizes nature, rejects artificial devices of civilization, and highly values intuition and spontaneity. Zhuangzi depicts the mode of action of his ideal personality as follows: "The utmost man uses the (mind-)heart like a mirror; he does not escort things as they go or welcome them as they come, he responds and does not store. Therefore he is able to conquer other things without suffering a wound" [至 人 之 用 心 若 鏡， 不 將 不 迎， 應 而 不 藏， 故 能 勝 物 而 不 傷].[118] Such an accomplished Taoist certainly does not engage in "accumulating learning" or acquiring other knowledge. As A. C. Graham puts it, the Taoist attitude is to have "the experience of achieving without knowing how."[119] Indeed, "accumulation of learning to build a storehouse of treasures," "immersion in reason to enrich talent," "investigating experience to exhaust observation," and "taming the inner state to spin out words" are more in line with Xunzi's mode of thinking than with Taoist philosophy. These processes require one to have an "empty, unified, and still" mind-heart.

"Accumulation of learning" and "immersion in reason" refer largely to studying the classics and other ancient texts. In his supporting verse to "Allusion and reference," Liu Xie writes:

經籍深富，	The classics and ancient texts are profound and rich,
辭理遐亙。	Their language and reasoning are far-reaching;
皛如江海，	They are pure as if cleansed in rivers and seas,
鬱若崑鄧。	And luxuriant as the peach forest on Mount Kunlun.
文梓共採，	They are like fine-grained catalpa woods for people to lumber,
瓊珠交贈。	And jade and pearls for them to give as gifts to each other.
用人若己，	To use the words of others as if they are their own
古來無懵。	Is what people know well about since ancient times.

(WXDL 38/161–68)

Although the chapter is titled "Allusion and reference," Liu Xie obviously regards the classics and ancient texts as more than just sources from which a writer draws materials. From the rich classical tradition, an aspiring writer can learn the various skills of writing, ranging from the use of language to reasoning that is relevant to literary creation. As discussed earlier, reason constitutes an important aspect of Liu Xie's concept of literary imagination. It is therefore not surprising for us to see him refer to it frequently in *Wenxin diaolong*, even in this chapter on the use of allusion and textual reference.

In addition to learning from canonical works, Liu Xie recommends two other items for inclusion in a writer's self-cultivation. He thinks it is important for a writer to examine his own lived experience in order to exhaust his observation. When one has acquired learning, cultivated the ability to reason, and examined one's experiences, one still needs to nurture an inner state that is most conducive to the entire process of literary creation. "The nourishing of pneuma" focuses on this issue, although there are comments on it in other chapters, as well. Again the "supporting verse" in "The nourishing of pneuma" presents a succinct statement of Liu Xie's ideas.

紛哉萬象，	So chaotic are the myriad images,
勞矣千想。	So wearing are the thousand thoughts.
玄神宜寶，	The mysterious daimon should be treasured,
素氣資養。	The native pneuma should be nourished.
水停以鑒，	When water stops moving, it reflects like a mirror,
火靜而朗。	When fire does not flicker, it glows.
無擾文慮，	Don't disturb your literary thinking,
鬱此精爽。	And let this radiant essence flourish.

(WXDL 42/93–101)

The beginning of this verse echoes the passage in "Daimonic thinking," which says that when daimonic thinking is first set in motion, myriad paths compete with each other in budding forth. At this moment, one's mind-heart is filled with an abundance of images and thoughts. One needs to have a calm inner state for the power of the imagination to bring shapes to the dazzlingly chaotic images and ideas. The third couplet clearly reiterates the idea of "emptiness and stillness" and "tranquilly absorbed in contemplation." Taming one's inner state, keeping it empty and still, is one way to treasure one's daimon and to nourish one's pneuma. Only in a calm inner state can one's daimon be alert, undisturbed, discerning, and creative.

Liu Xie's insistence on the cultivation of daimonic thinking, or artistic imagination, in the entire creative process from the preparatory stage to the execution of a work of art is one of his important contributions to Chinese aesthetic and literary theory. Coleridge and Wordsworth regard the poet's "shaping spirit of imagination" as genius or natural talent that, once lost, cannot be regained. In their conception of the poet's creative imagination, they both perhaps still unconsciously come under the influence of the Platonic idea of the poet's possession by the daimon. Toward the end of "Daimonic thinking," Liu Xie acknowledges that when daimonic thinking reaches the highest order as demonstrated by the great artists, it defies adequate explanation and description. Nevertheless, in his emphasis on the importance of continuous cultivation, Liu Xie offers his reader the optimistic notion that a writer's power of the imagination is not something with which he alone is endowed, but something he shares with other fellow human beings and that requires continuous effort to bring to fruition.

PART FOUR

The Art of Rhetoric

CHAPTER SEVEN

The Bones of Parallel Rhetoric in *Wenxin diaolong*

ANDREW H. PLAKS

In this essay, I will turn aside from the sublime and breezy abstractions about verbal art that provide some of the more profound moments in *Wenxin diaolong*, and focus instead on a more solid aspect of practical criticism taken up in its pages. Here is one case in which the intangible "wind" of aesthetic theory may be more weighty and substantial than the actual flesh and bones that give shape and strength to a given composition. To put it in quantitative terms, of the fifty chapters that make up this compendium— forty-nine brief treatises on specific topics, plus the final appended "Xuzhi" 序志 (Exposition of intentions)—fully sixteen or seventeen deal with aesthetic variables and aspects of the creative process that can properly be called "theoretical."[1] Even in the twenty-four chapters devoted to each of the particular genres of prose and poetry current in the corpus and curriculum of Liu Xie's time, primary attention is paid more to the historical development and subject matter of each form, and to the subjective evaluation of individual authors and pieces, than to the technical aspects of composition.[2] This leaves only about nine chapters, plus occasional passages in other contexts, that actually get down to the nuts and bolts of literary construction.[3] If, as has been suggested, the title of the overall collection should be taken to indicate an intention of restoring a counterpoise between the underlying conceptions of literary art (*wenxin*) and the more external aspects of the writer's craft (*diaolong*), then the final balance between wind and bone here remains a rather disproportionate one.[4]

The specific bones of literary practice I wish to discuss here are those of rhetorical parallelism. This is a topic that has already been examined and belabored in general terms by a number of recent writers, including myself.[5] Now I would like to go back to *Wenxin diaolong* and reconsider the treatment of this critical concept here in what is a primary locus classicus for this notion among the various texts of early Chinese literary theory, with the aim of reassessing its formulation of the rhetorical significance of parallelism both as a compositional element and as a conceptual principle governing the generation of meaning.

In my earlier writing on the broader subject, I argued, first, that the marked incidence of parallelism in all the high classical literary traditions (Chinese, Sanskrit, Arabic, Hebrew, and less so in Latin and Greek) represents not just a decorative feature of style, but rather an essential underpinning of verbal art. Second, I argued that in the classical Chinese literary system, with its grounding in a linguistic structure highly conducive to the formation of equal line lengths and thus numerically balanced patterns of recurrent periods, this principle is developed to a degree of subtlety and complexity unequalled in the other classical literatures.

Revisiting *Wenxin diaolong* as one of the primary sources for investigating this subject, I attempt to demonstrate that Liu Xie must have grasped the significance of parallelism as a master variable at the heart of his literary system have been less conclusive than I might have hoped. True, the opening lines of the "Yuan Dao" chapter, with their famous celebration of the mimesis of structural patterns inherent in the natural universe in literary form, would seem to point promisingly to such an understanding. For what, after all, are these patterns in question if not a variety of forms growing out of the core concept of paired opposites conceived on the yin-yang model?. This is the sort of thing I once glibly referred to as "complementary bipolarity," but which may perhaps be described more meaningfully in terms of Joseph Needham's notion of "correlative thinking."[6]

Unfortunately, the remainder of Liu Xie's text—both the sections on aesthetic theory and the exercises in practical criticism—does not make much of what I still believe represents the essence and glory of Chinese literary art.

Aside from the explicit discussion of this principle in chapter 35, "Lici" 麗辭 (Parallel phrasing), to be analyzed in detail here, we have to dig rather deep in other sections to find occasional, oblique references to other kinds of dual patterning. Notably, we find these under the heading of metrical balancing in the chapter on prosody ("Shenglü") and with respect to the articulation of topical divisions and rhetorical periods in the essay on compositional units, "Zhangjü" 章句. One might also perceive a looser sense of aesthetic balance in parallel phrasing in various contexts. This may be praised as a sign of poetic virtuosity, as in the "Mingshi" 明詩 chapter—儷采百字之偶，爭价一句之奇—or it is faulted as a piling up of redundancies, as for example in the "Rongcai" 鎔裁 chapter: 二意兩出，義之駢枝也，同辭重句，文之疵贅也. Failing that, we might point to the more abstract use of a range of dual conceptualizations in such chapters as "Tixing," "Qingcai," "Fuhui," "Wuse," "Zongshu," and others. Finally, we could resort to citing Liu Xie's own highly parallelistic style as an oblique demonstration of the importance of this compositional pattern in his own literary system.[7] I argue below that the marked emphasis throughout the text on various aesthetic criteria having to do with originality of conception or singularity of presentation (*qi* 奇, *yi* 異, *xin* 新, *zhi* 質, and so on) is itself clearly set against the assumption of a basic literary grid built upon parallel constructions.[8] But in stretching the idea of parallelism to these lengths, we must be wary of falling into our own rhetorical trap and confusing these various notions of dual patterning with the specific set of compositional devices properly termed "parallelism" in rhetorical theory. Otherwise, we risk rendering the term fairly meaningless as a conceptual tool in the critical system of *Wenxin diaolong*. After all, the entire book—or at least its major portion—is ostensibly about "patterned writing" (*wen* 文 or *ci* 辭), pointedly distinguished from "plain writing" (*bi* 筆) by recurrent metrical and rhyming patterns in verse and parallel periods in prose.[9]

Bearing these pitfalls in mind, I now propose to lower my sights and take a closer look at exactly what Liu Xie has to say about parallel rhetoric in the "Lici" chapter of *Wenxin diaolong*. The specific insights found there are not dazzlingly original or unique—they can be seen in poetic guise in the *Wen fu* 文賦 and are later worked out with far greater precision in, for example, the *Wenjing mifu lun* 文鏡秘府論 (Discussions from the secret repository of the mirror of literature). But I believe we should give Liu Xie credit for making some significant observations on the subject that are more interesting than what Stephen Owen has called "crude classifications."[10]

Before proceeding, let us take a look at the terms of discourse in which this subject is presented in the book. We notice immediately that the primary expression for parallelism in the *Wenxin diaolong* is *li* 麗, while the word most frequently associated with this phenomenon in later critical writings, *dui* 對, is reserved for more neutral usage in the central analytic scheme of the chapter. As applied by Liu Xie here, *dui* should be understood as conveying a basic semantic value of "matching" textual elements (not to be confused, of course, with the matching of response to query in the formal genre of court debate known by the same name—*yidui* 議對).[11] In Liu Xie's time, *dui* was apparently not yet compounded with various secondary terms (*zhang* 仗, *cheng* 稱, *zhao* 照, *zhi* 峙, *shu/zhu* 屬, and so on) as a general designation for parallel constructions, and even the descriptive expression *duijü* 對句 does not yet seem to have become part of the critical vocabulary. In its simple meaning, *dui* is often interchangeable with a variety of nearly synonymous terms for pairing and doubling, including *pei* 配, *shuang* 雙, and even *xian* 銜, in the sense of the "interlocking" of complementary elements.[12] When reduced to the semantic minimum of sheer "duplication" (*zhong* 中), the idea always carries negative connotations.[13]

Looking more closely at the term *li* itself, we can identify its basic meaning of balanced pairing, a usage possibly derived etymologically from the original sense of a conjugal pair. This can be observed in the compound *kangli* 伉儷, the latter graph possibly associated with the archaic betrothal ritual of presenting a pair of deerskin pelts (*lipi* 儷皮) as a kind of bride price. (Note the appearance of this character with the addition of the "man-radical" in modern editions of *Wenxin diaolong*, functioning as a verb in this chapter to mean something like "set in pairs.") In some contexts, the word *li* is correctly glossed and translated in the sense of its later common usage, "beautiful," although here, too, it may be argued that its fundamental meaning is the particular beauty of symmetrical balance. A similar sense is expressed by the character *ou* 偶, also related to the metaphor of conjugal pairing. As we shall see, this term takes on deeper significance when it is viewed in an antithetical relation to the term for asymmetrical singularity, *qi* 奇. This semantic value will lead us to consider the complex relation of likeness and contrast among parallel and nonparallel elements in Chinese literary aesthetics.[14]

造化賦形，支體必雙；神理為用，事不孤立。夫心生文辭，運裁百慮，高下相須，自然成對。

Chapter 35 opens with a reformulation of the initial message of the "Yuan Tao" chapter, taking it one step farther by describing the spontaneous patterning of the natural universe in terms of a pairing of elements, either on the analogy of symmetrical limbs in the forms of living creatures, or in terms of the appearance of objective phenomena governed by "the workings of unseen principles," in the form of dual correspondence rather than as "isolated occurrences" (神理為用，事不孤立). Thus, it is only natural for the creative impulse of the human mind, in forging verbal patterns through exercise of mental effort, to fall into a similar kind of hierarchical ordering of interdependent elements, as manifested in the pairing of textual units (⋯高下相須).[15] This introductory generalization seems at first to set the tone for the entire piece, but in the remainder of this chapter Liu Xie proceeds to back away from the idea of spontaneous doubling and to qualify it with an emphasis on the self-conscious crafting of parallel forms.

唐虞之世，辭未極文，而皋陶贊云：罪疑惟輕，巧疑惟重。益陳謨云：滿招損，謙受益。豈營麗辭？率然對爾。易之文繁，聖人之妙思也：序乾四德，則句句相銜；龍虎類感，則字字相儷；乾坤易簡，則宛轉相承；日月往來，則隔行懸合：雖句字或殊，而偶意一也。至於詩人偶章，大夫聯辭，奇偶適變，不勞經營。自揚馬張蔡，崇盛麗辭，如宋畫吳冶，刻形鏤法，麗句與深采並流，偶意共逸韻俱發。至魏晉群才，析句彌密，聯字合趣，剖毫析釐。然契機者入巧，浮假者無巧。

The second section of the chapter traces the development of parallel conceptions from the earliest stages of written civilization. The author cites two passages from the *Shang shu* as illustrations of an original and apparently "effortless flow of matched utterances" (豈營⋯率然對爾).[16] However, by the time Liu gets to his second example from the *Yijing* classic—taken, significantly enough, from the later prose layers of the *Wenyan* commentary and the "Xici zhuan" treatise[17]—his interest turns to a "tight verbal structure of matching words and lines" (句句相銜⋯字字相儷). Most important for our purposes, Liu Xie introduces here for the first time a crucial distinction between two kinds of textual pairing, one on the level of verbal patterns and one on the level of ideas—what I propose to call "lexical" and "semantic" parallelism, respectively.

Moving ahead in the received chronology of canonical texts (but actually backwards in time to the two "classics" of early literary art that by all accounts predate the "Xici zhuan" [Commentary on the appended phrases]), Liu Xie now focuses on the manner in which the medium of expression in both texts tends to fall into double units. The verse of the "Odes" does so by virtue of the basic couplet form, and the prose rhythms of the discourse of the "great officers" exemplified by the *Zuozhuan* are shaped by the rhetorical give and take of courtly repartee.[18] Here he astutely observes another aesthetic variable, distinguishing between the use of paired and unpaired expressions, varying less by careful manipulation than "in response to inner flow of the texts themselves" [···奇偶適變].[19] Coming to more recent times, Liu praises the ability of leading Han stylists to "forge strictly paired constructions without impeding the free flow" of inspiration [麗句與深采並流] and to bring the matching of ideas into harmony with the musical effect of verbal rhythms. He concludes, with reference to the Wei and Jin poets, that the successful manipulation of these variables depends on the skill of the writer to fine-tune his craft without allowing it to become an empty show of pointless formalism.[20]

> 故麗辭之體，凡有四對：言對為易，事對為難，反對為優，正對為劣。言對者，雙比空辭者也；事對者，並舉人驗者也；反對者，理殊趣合者也；正對者，事異義同者也。

At this point, Liu Xie turns to his primary analytical scheme. At first glance, the four-part scheme of paired elements in parallel composition, with its two baldly stated distinctions between the matching of "words" (言對) and of "phenomena" (事對) and between the "direct" (正對) and "antithetical" (反對) modes of parallelism seems a bit simplistic. So too does his unhesitating valorization of the level of "things" over that of words (assuming that what is more "difficult" is necessarily better) and of contrastive over correlative pairing. This observation of distinct levels of application may seem particularly redundant, since he had already distinguished between lexical or syntactic parallelism versus semantic parallelism earlier in this chapter, as well as in a number of different contexts in other chapters in the book. But he adds a new dimension to the discussion, a substantive definition of the matching of words and "things," respectively. This allows him to contrast the "mechanical setting of verbal elements side-by-side" [⋯ 雙 比 空 辭 者 ⋯] with what he describes as the correlated citation of "evidence," that is, the "instantiation" of the writer's meaning through "coordinated examples drawn from parallel frames of reference" [⋯ 並 舉 人 驗 者].[21]

Similarly, the contrast between "direct" and "antithetical" parallelism that follows is such a staple of Chinese literary art as to virtually go without saying. But, at the very least, we should pause to give Liu Xie credit for what appears to be the first explicit formulation of this idea as a principle of classical literary theory (as opposed to philosophy of language, where this idea can be found much earlier—for example, in the *Gongsunlongzi* 公 孫 龍 子).[22] Of course, the logic of similarity and antithesis in paired expressions is not an exclusive discovery of the ancient Chinese literary thinkers. Aristotle, for one, discusses the matching of parallel elements (*parisôsis* or *paromoiôsis*) under the general heading of "antithesis" in his *Rhetoric*.[23] But just as, at their best, the plotting of antithetical couplets in *lüshi* or the double periods in various genres of parallel prose go beyond the clumsy matching of equivalent utterances to explore the subtle interface of likeness and difference, so too the identification of this principle in Chinese literary theory carries more far-reaching implications than does its counterpart in classical Western poetics. I should note that simply labeling antithetical parallelism as "superior" and straight matching as "inferior" [⋯ 為 優 ⋯ 為 劣] does not settle the question, since the author is clearly not rejecting the latter mode of parallelism out of hand, as we shall see.[24] Instead, Liu Xue draws out the deeper implications of this distinction, identifying rhetorical antithesis in cases of "divergence of ground of argument and convergence of import" [⋯ 理 殊 趣 合 者 ⋯], as opposed to cases of "different examples with a common meaning" [⋯ 事 異 義 同 者]. In the second case, this formulation directs our attention to the essential logic of semantic categories and analogical thinking, to be picked up and developed a bit further on in the chapter.

長 卿 上 林 賦 云： 修 容 乎 禮 園， 翱 翔 乎 書 圃。 此 言 對 之 類 也。 宋 玉 神 女 賦 云： 毛 嬙 鄣 袂， 不 足 程 式； 西 施 掩 面， 比 之 無 色。 此 事 對 之 類 也。 仲 宣 登 樓 賦 云： 鍾 儀 幽 而 楚 奏， 莊 舃 顯 而 越 吟。

此反對之類也。孟陽七哀云：漢祖想枌榆，光武思白水。此正
對之類也。

Having set out his basic grid of variables and attached to it an apparently
unequivocal set of value judgments, Liu Xie now provides a small number
of judiciously selected examples to substantiate his points. While it is true
that one man's antithesis is another man's equivalence, still a quick glance at
these citations serves to illustrate Liu's four basic categories. First, a couplet
from Sima Xiangru's 司馬相如 "Shanglin fu" 上林賦 (Rhapsody on the
Shanglin Park), true to the spirit and conventions of the *fu* 賦 (rhapsody)
genre, demonstrates the strict matching of syntactic unit to syntactic unit
by which "verbal parallelism" (言對) is defined. By contrast, the lines that
follow from Song Yu's 宋玉 (ca. 290–223 B.C.) "Shennü fu" 神女賦 (The
goddess rhapsody) are quoted ostensibly to show the yoking of the separate
examples with their closely parallel images of two proverbial beauties—one
hiding behind her sleeve and the other covering her face with her hands—in
order to bring out a single sense of the incomparable beauty of the goddess
in the poet's vision.[25] Note that the category of parallel coordination of
"things" is illustrated here with an example in which the import is one of
equivalence rather than antithesis. Immediately after this, Liu Xie adduces
two other couplets by "recent" poets. First, he draws our attention to the
multiple layers of antithetical significance that emerge when a reference to a
piece of music performed by an obscure man is matched with another case
in which a sigh of inner feeling is uttered by a figure in full public view.
Then he gives us a pair of lines in which one Han emperor's thoughts of his
old hometown are precisely matched, both in form and in meaning, to those
of his dynastic successor.[26]

凡偶辭胸臆，言對所以為易也；徵人之學，事對所以為難也；
幽顯同志，反對所以為優也；並貴共心，正對所以為劣也。又
以事對，各有反正，指類而求，萬條自昭然矣。張華詩稱遊雁
比翼翔，歸鴻知接翮；劉琨詩言宣尼悲獲麟，西狩泣孔丘：若
斯重出，即對句之駢枝也。

At this point, Liu Xie returns to his earlier definitions to explain that
verbal matching is relatively "easy" precisely because formally parallel expressions can be virtually invented at will. The poet intent on matching "phenom-

ena," however, must draw upon his store of learning to come up with an appropriate allusion, which is necessarily more difficult. By the same token, Liu argues, the way in which the contrasting situations in the Wang Can (177–217) couplet are used to convey common aspirations demonstrates the superiority of antithetical matching over the synonymous expression of an identical sentiment by interchangeable figures in the second example. Having restated these rather obvious points with only minor elucidation, Lu Xie now makes an interesting observation. Whereas he explicitly points out that the matching of phenomena lends itself to either straight or antithetical parallelism, he implies by his silence that verbal matching, by contrast, does not. In his rather cryptic explanation of why this should be, Liu returns to the logic of analogical reasoning. He argues that when a writer applies one or the other form of "matching" in conformance with the specific category of phenomena in question (literally, "seeks it with reference to the category"), the result is a clear exposition of meaning.[27] Citing as negative evidence two couplets by the Six Dynasties masters Zhang Hua 張華 (232–300) and Liu Kun 劉琨 (271–318), he apparently ignores the syntactic slippage in the first case [比翼 … 知接翮], and the instance of chiasmus in the second [宣尼 … 孔丘]. He concludes that such examples of the simple duplication of equivalent utterances represent a use of matching lines as superfluous as Zhuangzi's proverbial webbed toes and extra fingers.[28]

是以言對為美，貴在精巧；事對所先，務在允當。若兩事相配，而優劣不均，是驥在左驂，駑為右服也。若夫事或孤立，莫與相偶，是夔之一足，踸踔而行也。

Next, Liu Xie refines some of his preliminary conclusions about verbal and semantic parallelism, now allowing that the "easy" matching of lexical units may still be a vehicle of aesthetic beauty, as long as a premium is placed on consummate skill, this latter criterion left undefined. In like manner, the preference for the matching of phenomena lies in finding just the right images to set up a meaningful contrast or correspondence. Inability to maintain a proper balance in the pairing of elements, or the most extreme case of complete "abandonment of parallel structure in favor of solitary presentation," results in an aesthetic failure expressed in familiar metaphors of an unequally harnessed team of horses or the mythical hobbling of a one-legged creature.

若氣無奇類，文乏異采，碌碌麗辭，則昏睡耳目。必使理圓事
密，聯璧其章；迭用奇偶，節以雜佩，乃其貴耳。類此而思，
理自見也。

The suggestive insertion of the words *youlie* 優劣 (superior and inferior)
above is probably not intended to be a direct allusion to the two contrasted
modes of parallelism presented earlier. But, in the final substantive section
of the chapter, Liu Xie turns the argument in this direction precisely.[29] He
first states that if "the creative spirit is not manifested in fresh and singular
analogies" [氣無奇類] or if the "patterning of a text lacks originality" [文
乏異采], this results in a tediously mechanical repetition of parallel phrasing.
The most highly prized literary quality, he concludes, can only be achieved
through the "seamless matching of parallel textual units" based on a full
understanding of the underlying relationship between logical categories and
concrete imagery.[30] All this must be couched in a carefully modulated "alternating use of paired and unpaired [奇偶] constructions." We may recall
that this same notion of the complementary use of parallel and nonparallel
styles [奇偶適變] was already cited earlier in praise of the *Shijing* and *Zuozhuan*, the two classic texts that stand at the fountainhead of the traditions
of classical poetry and narrative, respectively.[31]

赞曰：體植必兩，辭動有配。左提右挈，精味兼載。炳爍聯
華，鏡靜含態。玉潤雙流，如彼珩珮。

In the conventional verse reprise at the end of the chapter, Liu Xie restates
his opening observation that parallel structure in a literary text, like the
symmetry of the natural world, is virtually inescapable. By this point, however, this principle has been redefined as a variable quality, one which, to be
applied successfully, must be adjusted and modulated, applied or withheld,
in conformance with the inner logic of the subject at hand. Thus, Liu ends
with a series of metaphors (themselves arranged in two balanced pairs) drawn
from both the world of natural imagery and objects of human artifice.

We have seen that in covering, perhaps for the first time, what with hind-
sight seems to be familiar territory, Liu Xie expresses some interesting insights
into the particular workings of the aesthetics of parallel rhetoric in the classical
Chinese literary medium. But still we must ask why the subject of parallelism is not presented as a more central focus of the critical apparatus of
Wenxin diaolong as a whole? The easiest answer that comes to mind would

be to explain Liu Xie's treatment as a direct reflection of his fifth- and sixth-century literary milieu, in which, we are often led to believe, the parallelistic excesses of *piantiwen* [駢體文] were running rampant. Though this common observation may well be overstated—and, certainly, the prominence of parallel genres is in no way exclusive to this period—this may at the very least reinforce the sense that all references to nonparallel style must be weighed against the inevitable presence of parallelism as the major grounding of Chinese literary aesthetics. This would mean that in a compendium of treatises on literary theory such as this, the workings of parallelism become almost too obvious and too basic to require extensive analysis and comment.[32] Perhaps more to the point, we should recall that Liu Xie, writing at the turn of the sixth century, was just a bit too early to see the fruition of the parallelistic tendencies long incubating in classical poetry—practiced in all verse forms from the *Shijing* on down, raised to a high degree of sophistication in the Han and Six Dynasties, and codified in metrical terms by the likes of Shen Yue—that had not yet blossomed into what Kao Yu-Kung has called the "perfect form" of Tang "regulated verse." Even in *lüshi*, after all, the seamless parallelism of the inner couplets can only be appreciated when set within the refreshing singularity of their nonparallel outer frame. Liu Xie, standing on the cusp of this development, can thus be forgiven for putting parallel rhetoric into a more relative, even marginal, light.[33]

CHAPTER EIGHT

Liu Xie and the Discourse Machine

STEPHEN OWEN

In this essay I would like to consider Liu Xie's arguments not as the "expression" of ideas already fully formed and fixed, but rather as a *process* of exposition. This process is not unitary: In many cases we can identify two "players" contending for control of the exposition. One of these players we will call "Liu Xie," a human character with beliefs, an education of received ideas, and common sense. The other main player is the rhetoric of parallel exposition, what I call the "discourse machine," which produces utterances by its own rules and requirements. Although Liu Xie would like to believe that these two players are a perfect unity and although modern criticism treats them as such, much in *Wenxin diaolong* becomes clearer if we understand the text as dialogic. We often see the productive rhetoric of the discourse machine processing an initial statement and amplifying it according to predictable rules. No less often we see Liu Xie following in the traces of the discourse machine, ingeniously correcting unwanted utterances and attempting to make the argument conform to beliefs, received ideas, and common sense.

THE DANGER OF THE TOO SHARP AX

Toward the middle of his chapter on the "discourse" (*lunshuo* 論説), which is the "form" (*ti* 體) of his own writing, Liu Xie sets forth clearly the values to be sought in the practice of the form.

> 原夫論之為體，所以辨正然否；窮於有數，究於無形，鑽堅求通，鉤深取極；乃百慮之筌蹄，萬事之權衡也。故其義貴圓通，辭忌枝碎，必使心與理合，彌縫莫見其隙；辭共心密，敵人不知所乘；斯其要也。是以論如析薪，貴能破理。斤利者，越理而橫斷；辭辨者，反義而取通。覽文雖巧，而檢跡知妄。唯君子能通天下之志，安可以曲論哉。

Essentially the discourse as a form is the means to correctly distinguish what is so and what is not so. It is exhaustive regarding what is determinate and thorough regarding what is formless.[1] It bores into the intractable and seeks passage through [comprehensiveness/complete comprehensibility]; it draws out what is deep and grasps the ultimate.[2] It is indeed the "fish-trap and snare" for all concerns and the balance on which to weigh every factual matter.[3] Thus perfection and comprehensiveness are valued as its principles, while digression and fragmentation are prohibited in its verbal expression. One must make mind and natural process match, tightly darned so that one does not see any holes; one must make the verbal expression and mind so close together than an enemy does not know from where to mount an attack.

   Thus, the discourse is like chopping wood: what is important is to be able to break it along the grain [following the natural process]. If the ax is too sharp, it cuts across the grain; when the verbal expression is too "sharp" in making distinctions, it goes counter to principle in achieving comprehension. In examining a work, though it be clever, one knows it is false when examining the traces left. Only the superior man is able to comprehend [make comprehensible] universal aims—how can he [merely] make intricate arguments [discourses]! (*WXDL* 18/99–123)

When writing a *lun* on Liu Xie's *lun* on the *lun*, the modern interpreter is always in danger of wielding too sharp an ax and cutting across the grain of Liu's exposition and his beatific vision of natural process, words, and mind, all fused into a perfect unity that forestalls assault. But Liu Xie himself reminds us that there may be places in the discourse where holes have been darned [*mifeng* 彌縫—the common figure for "fixing mistakes"]. When he shifts craft metaphors from the textile to carving, it is he who worries about the too sharp ax that will leave traces of cutting across the grain. In the preface to *Wen fu* 文賦 (The poetic exposition on literature), Liu Xie's predecessor Lu Ji invoked the *Shijing* figure of taking an ax in hand to chop an ax handle, suggesting that in critical discourse the lesson may be in the means of imparting the lesson. Thus in considering *Wenxin diaolong*, we would do well to examine Liu Xie's procedures and the tools *he* uses to weave and cut his text.

Immediately following the passage cited above, in which Liu celebrates discourse's dense integrity and natural cut, we find a striking example of a gaping hole that needed to be darned. The case of commentary comes to Liu's mind, a discursive form whose inherent characteristics directly contradict the tightness of linear argument that he has just described as essential to the "discourse." "Now when it comes to the phrasing of commentary, it dissolves the form of the discourse" [若夫注釋為詞，解散論體] (*WXDL* 18/126–27)—this represents the very fragmentation (specifically of phrasing, [*ci* 辭]) that Liu had just declared was prohibited in the form [辭忌枝碎]. Liu Xie, however, approves of commentary and recognizes that it is a highly successful discursive form; all he can do is combine it with other, unnamed variations as "diverse writings" [*zawen* 雜文] and declare that they share some higher unity with the *lun*: "though these diverse writings differ, on a general level they are the same" [雜文雖異，總會是同] (*WXDL* 18/128–29).

This brief segment is characteristic of a process that occurs throughout *Wenxin diaolong*. There is a discourse machine that can be seen at work in the first passage quoted: It tries to cut along the grain, producing symmetrical divisions of the topic, sustained by an ideology in which the natural order, the linguistic order of exposition, and mind are supposed to be a perfect unity in which everything [*tong* 通] both "gets through" and "is comprehensible." Had Liu Xie simply let the machine do its work, few would have been the wiser; but Liu knew on some level that, in fact, the machine was flawed and perhaps mindless. Perhaps it was itself the too sharp ax whose cut Liu recognized to be false [*wang* 妄]. The machine produced text that left important things out, that generated incorrect or misleading terms, and that continually grew polydactyls [*pianmu* 駢拇]. Frequently in *Wenxin diaolong*, Liu Xie had to set to work to repair the products of the machine, and, as in the opening passage quoted, he was constantly aware of what could go wrong.

To find an emblem of this double process of producing discourse and correcting it, one needs look no farther than his own explanation of his book's title at the beginning of the final chapter.

> 夫文心者，言為文之用心也。昔涓子琴心，王孫巧心，心哉美矣，故用之焉。古來文章，以雕縟成體，豈取騶奭之群言雕龍也。

> *Wen xin* means the use of mind [hard effort] in making *wen*. Long ago there was Juanzi's "Zither Mind" and Wangsun's "Artful Mind"—is not "mind" a fine thing indeed—thus I have used it here. Since ancient times literary works have completed their forms by carving and embellishment—of course I am not using "carving dragons" in the sense meant by Zou Shi and that lot! (*WXDL* 50/1–9)

The discourse machine takes the title apart into two terms, one representing the "inner" term, "mind," and the other representing the "outer" term, "craft." But even before he can name "carving dragons" as craft in a positive sense, he must immediately cancel a potential misunderstanding—taking the term as used by others, apparently implying frivolous ornament.[4] The traces of broken parallelism are immediately apparent:

夫文心者，言為文之用心也。	Significance of term A (文心)
昔涓子琴心，王孫巧心，心哉美矣，	Precedents for use
故用之焉。	Thus I used it
古來文章，以雕縟成體，	Significance of term B (雕龍)
豈取騶奭之群言雕龍也。	Precedent has bad associations
	That's *not* why I used it

Liu Xie would certainly not approve of my figure of a discourse machine for certain of his expository procedures. In the discussion of *lun* and elsewhere, Liu Xie would like to believe not only that language is adequate to communicate (*tong*) the order of things (*li* 理), but that language's compounds and their components correspond to natural categories. Authoritative past texts supply verbal fragments that can be deployed in this orderly structure, which seems to map nature rather than refer to it through a system of conventional signs. To rename this a discourse machine is to stress the generative nature of these discursive procedures and to suggest that they are governed by an unreflective automatism, internal rules that Liu Xie can operate but not fully control. We discover Liu Xie as a critic distinct from his discourse machine precisely in such moves of correction and compensation.

We can see such moves everywhere and on every level of *Wenxin diaolong*. On the smallest scale, we can see the generation of incorrect terms and the need to correct them. In chapter 49, "Chenqi" 程器 (Measuring capacity), Liu Xie discusses "literary men" (*wenshi* 文士) offering a dazzling set of examples of their vices and shortcomings. He sums up: "since this happens in regard to *wen* . . ." [文既有之]. This discourse machine mindlessly supplies the apodosis: "it is also to be expected in *wu* [the military]" [武亦宜然] (*WXDL* 49/33–34). *Wu* 武 is the proper antithesis of *wen* 文; it is a linkage of historical accident in language that has become mechanical. But Liu Xie does *not* want to talk about militarists per se, much less the common soldier. The comparison that he wants to draw is between literary men and those prominent in public life. To get his argument back on track, Liu ingeniously continues by conjoining militarists with the upper echelons of the civil bureaucracy in the common compound *jiangxiang* 將相 (generals and ministers): "truly many were the flaws and failings of ancient generals and ministers" [古之將相，疵咎實多] (*WXDL* 49/35–36). To smooth the turn, he includes a few examples of military figures, but it is clear that the successful civil officials are his primary terms of comparison.

On the largest scale the discourse machine can generate a chapter where none is wanted. Chapter 4, "Zhengwei" 正緯 (Correcting apocrypha), justly ignored, is a case in point. Liu Xie has little to say about the apocrypha and less to say that is favorable. The chapter exists purely for the sake of parallelism, so as not to leave chapter 3, "Zongjing" 宗經 (Revering the classics), without the corresponding term *wei* 緯. The discourse machine demands the obvious literalization of the central terms, balancing "warp" (*jing*) and "woof" (*wei*) and making the woof (apocrypha) the necessary complement of the warp (classics).

Nowhere else do we see Liu Xie taking such a clear stand against the machine. He declares what the "woof" *should* be and then declares the apocrypha to be "false" (偽) for failing to be a proper woof. "The way the woof completes the warp is as in weaving; when the fibers of silk or hemp do not mix, only then is fabric completed. But in this case the warp [classics] is straight [normative], while the woof [apocrypha] is strange; they go one thousand leagues in opposite directions. This is the first instance of its falseness" [蓋緯之成經，其猶織綜，絲麻不雜，布帛乃成；今經正緯奇，倍摘千里，其偽一也] (*WXDL* 4/19–25). Liu continues with a series of instances of the falseness of the apocrypha, sometimes appealing to the literalization of the textile metaphor. For example, the antiquity claimed for some works of apocrypha is erroneous because the warp must precede the woof. "A form in which the woof precedes the warp runs counter to the weaving process" [先緯後經，體乖織綜] (*WXDL* 4/46–47). His conclusion is: "The Classics are sufficient unto themselves for teaching, and the apocrypha supply them nothing" [經足訓矣，緯何豫焉] (*WXDL* 4/51–52). This leaves us, however, with a woofless warp, undermining the principle of complementarity that produced the chapter in the first place. Liu Xie continues his chapter with further animadversions against the apocrypha (grudgingly conceding that some aspects of it might be useful for literary writing). At last he is left to lamely explain why he wrote the chapter: "Former ages paired it with the Classics so I discussed it in detail here" [前代配經，故詳論焉] (*WXDL* 4/107–8).

BEWARE THE HOPPING KUI!

> "If some matter should happen to stand alone and
> nothing form a pair with it, it is the single-footed *Kui*,
> who goes hopping"
> 若夫事或孤立，莫與相偶，是夔之一足，踸踔而
> 行也[5]
> —"LICI" 麗辭 (Parallel phrasing), *WXDL* 35/105–8

Liu Xie's imaginary universe tends to be populated by deformities of excess: weird shapes and rank growth, a proliferation of detail. But the Kui is a monster of insufficiency. Although Liu Xie blames ancient habit for persuading him to include a chapter on the apocrypha, the discourse machine commonly generates unwanted symmetries quite on its own. If we remove a proposition from its paired context, we not infrequently find statements that are indeed hopping Kui monsters, apparently affirming what no Chinese literary theorist would normally say. That is, if cited as distinct propositions ("As Liu Xie wrote . . ."), they would be shocking in their contravention of the shared "truths" that sustain *Wenxin diaolong*.

Toward the beginning of chapter 31, "Qing Cai" 情采 (The affections and colors), we find a striking statement: "Substance is contingent on patterning" [質待文也] (*WXDL* 31/11). Even if we restore an element of context ("Under some circumstances substance is contingent on patterning"), this is still a hopping monster. Like Liu Xie's claim of the self-sufficiency of the Classics [經足訓矣], the inverse of the problematic statement ("pattern is contingent on substance") can, in fact, stand alone; it is unsurprising and often affirmed. Here is how Liu Xie comes to declare the opposite, that substance may be contingent on pattern.

聖賢書辭，總稱文章，非采而何。夫水性虛而淪漪結，木體實而花萼振，文附質也。虎豹無文，則鞹同犬羊，犀兕有皮，而色資丹漆，質待文也。

The writings of sages and worthy men are collectively known as "literary works." Why would this be if they did not have colors? Water is by nature plastic, and ripples form in it; the normative form of wood is solid, and flowers bloom from it. The [external] pattern is subordinate to the substance. If the tiger and leopard had no patterns, their pelts would be the same as those of dogs or sheep; the rhino has a hide, and color is supplied by red lacquer [for armor]. The substance is contingent on the patterning. (*WXDL* 31/1–11)

It is not that the cases of tiger and rhino-hide armor compelled Liu Xie to affirm that in some cases substance is contingent on patterning: it is rather a tribute to his ingenious learning that he could come up with these examples, however forced and different. The problematic proposition is clearly generated out of the commonplace proposition for the sake of balancing the paragraph.[6]

We might be troubled less by the assertion of the circumstantial priority of pattern if the rest of the chapter were not devoted to amplifying and restating the commonplace proposition—the "inner" term ("the affections" [*qing* 情] or "substance" [*zhi* 質]) should be primary and the "outer" term ("colors" [*cai* 采, or *wen* 文]) should follow from it. Later in the chapter, Liu Xie again pairs the priority of the inner term with its inversion. "In the works of the Poets [of the *Classic of Poetry*] they fashioned patterned expression for the sake of feeling; but in the poetic expositions and encomia of the rhetoricians, they fashioned feeling for the sake of patterned expression" [昔詩人什篇，為情而造文；辭人賦頌，為文而造情] (*WXDL* 31/61–64). This antithetical statement is formally the same as the opening pair:

In Case A,	outer follows from inner
夫水性虛而淪漪結，木體實而花萼振，	文附質也
昔詩人什篇，	為情而造文

In Case B,	inner follows from outer
虎豹無文，則鞹同犬羊，犀兕有皮，	質待文也
而色資丹漆，	
辭人賦頌，	為文而造情

Formal identity, of course, here covers a profound difference in meaning: The earlier pair is complementary, encompassing a complete range of variation, and the later pair is historical and hierarchical, with the proper relationship and sequence between *qing* and *wen* having been perverted by the rhetoricians.

When I speak of "formal identity" in the examples above, I refer to the level of relative indeterminacy in the syntax and taxis of rhetorical exposition. There is nothing in the explicit terms of the exposition to distinguish the opposition of wood-tree versus tiger-rhino hide on the one hand and of the poems of the *Shijing* versus the poetic expositions of the rhetoricians on the other hand. The discourse machine operates on this formal level of relative indeterminacy. For a passage to have full meaning, however, additional determinations must be supplied by context. Thus every reader knows that the earlier pair is complementary, while the later pair describes historical change, passing from an ideal state to its perversion.

At the heart of the discourse machine in *Wenxin diaolong* is "division," an old term of Western rhetorical exposition that is, I think, the best translation for *bian* 辨. Whatever *bian* may have come to mean in later Chinese rhetoric,

in Liu Xie's time it is a "division of the topic" under discussion into its constituent parts (the ax cutting along the grain) so that one can understand the
constituents more clearly. The modern term "analysis" has the same etymological basis, though its operational claims are epistemological rather than
rhetorical.[7] *Bian* moves between the epistemological and the rhetorical: It is
an epistemological activity always in danger of becoming merely rhetorical
(if the ax is too sharp). Since the presumed order of the world and the
language that claims to account for it are constituted of privileged pairings,
the task of the discourse machine is to take the constituents apart. In this
way, it is quite similar to Aristotelian discourse, likewise grounded in natural logic, in which the procedures *are* a thought's *form* rather than the mere
expression of thought. That is, one is not trying to prove a prior point but
rather analyzing the matter at hand to see what it yields.

"Division," however, works at that formal level of relative indeterminacy.
Although division has more semantic content than Aristotelian logic, it prom-
ises only that a set of propositions is correctly formed and not that it makes
full sense.[8] Thus the discourse machine produces divisions of both the complementary variety and of the hierarchical variety. That is, in some pairs the
terms are to be taken as of equal value, together constituting "completeness"
(*yuan* 圓), while in other cases they constitute some version of a hierarchy
(prior/posterior; norm/deviation or inversion; good/bad; better/inferior).
Liu never directly addresses this question of the complementary versus the
hierarchical, but it is an important force shaping the movement of many of
the chapters as he maneuvers the discourse machine to balance complementarity with hierarchy or hierarchy with complementarity.

The case of "The affections and colors" discussed above is an excellent
example. The complementary pair (external pattern contingent on substance,
substance contingent on external pattern) is obviously unstable, with the
second member of the pair being a proposition that is unacceptable in the
context of received opinions. In the course of the chapter, Liu Xie changes
the terms of division, asserting the correctness of the first commonplace
proposition of the initial pair—the inner term has priority and the outer
term is contingent upon it. After the wonderful series of analogies in which
the affections themselves are declared to be the medium of a literary work—
"[t]he five affections emerge and become literary texts" [五情發而為辭
章] (*WXDL* 31/28)—on the analogy of sounds in music and color in visual

pattern, Liu turns to the danger of decorative ornamentation getting out of hand and declares such cases to be "deviation in rhetoric" (文辭之變). The term *bian* 變, here demanding translation as "deviation," is a loaded term, setting up a historical model—it is difference that does not produce complementary "wholeness" (*yuan* 圓).

CONTINUITY AND VARIATION

In chapter 29, "Tongbian" 通變 (Continuity and variation), the tensions between complementarity and hierarchy come to the fore. In part these tensions arise from the way in which the "Appended comments" ("Xici zhuan" 繫辭傳) of the *Yi* attempt to reconcile the opposed terms (using *tong* 通 as the verb for "carrying through changes" [通其變] and saying that "continuity" is achieved through "changes" [變則通]). An even greater reason for the tensions follows from the complex semantics of the term *bian* 變, which we have just seen as "deviation" in "The affections and colors": "In this the deviation in rhetoric reached its extreme" [文辭之變，於斯極矣] (*WXDL* 31/43–44). In a literary frame of reference, Liu Xie cannot escape the meaning of *bian* 變 in *Mao Shi* studies: *zhengbian* 正變 (norm and deviation). In this sense *bian* is the term for literary historical change as something negative.

Liu Xie begins his chapter using *bian* in its *Yijing* sense of *tongbian*, but once he comes to the operation of change in literary history, a remarkable set of rhetorical reformulations brings him to the *bian* of *zhengbian* (norm and deviation). Liu opens by returning to the idea of "normative form" [*ti* 體] as a constant, existing prior to and encompassing many possible particular realizations. The variability of particular realizations is conceptualized as *bian*: "There are constants in the normative forms in which a work may be posed, but the possibilities of varying those works is limitless" [夫設文之體有常，變文之數無方] (*WXDL* 29/1–2).[9]

"Constants" like normative forms are essentially timeless. However, citing the "Appended comments" of the *Yi*, Liu finds in *bian* a different kind of duration appropriate to historical time, nicely phrased as "long-lasting" [*jiu* 久]. "The force of *qi* in writing becomes long-lasting by carrying through a continuity of variations" [文辭氣力，通變則久] (*WXDL* 29/7–8). Overcoming limits to duration is precisely what is at stake in "continuity and variation," as can be seen in the subsequent metaphors of galloping along a road without blockage or drawing from an inexhaustible well. "Continuity" [*tong*] is clearly secondary to the term "variation" here. The following botanical figure of trees and plants is essential: The *ti* 體 is the norm of the species, but any particular plant varies according to local circumstances. "Root and trunk cleave to the soil and share a common nature, but smell and taste are of different types according to their exposure to sunlight" [根幹麗土而同性，臭味晞陽而異品矣] (*WXDL* 29/22–23). This happy vision of organic diachrony, of developmental variation sharing a common ground, however, runs afoul of human history.

Liu's opening thesis on variation in literary history is complicated by one of those textual problems that seem to crop up at points where they are most unwanted.[10] The original text reads: "Thus in the songs on the nine dynasties [from antiquity to recently], the aims matched the wealth of *wen*" [是以九代詠歌，志合文財] (*WXDL* 29/24–25). *Wenxin diaolong* critics were quick to recognize that something was wrong with the *cai* 財, which makes little sense in the context. (I might also add that it is a word not used elsewhere in *Wenxin diaolong*.) Xu Yanzu (Xu Wunian) proposed the standard emendation *ze* 則, thus producing something like "aims matched the norms of *wen*." We should recognize that such emendations are purely conjectural, no matter how many editions they are printed in. If, however, Xu is correct, then Liu is here affirming the continuing correctness of literature from Chu through the Jin dynasty, something he subsequently denies. Liu Yongji suggested *bie* 別 instead: "[T]heir aims matched but the textual expression differed."[11] Although this version does not call into question the legitimacy of literature from Chu through the Jin, it leaves open the possibility. But since we are dealing here with an irresolvable textual problem, we must leave blank the proposition illustrated by following examples.

黃歌斷竹，質之至也。唐歌在昔，則廣於黃世；虞歌卿雲，則文於唐時。夏歌雕墻，縟於虞代；商周篇什，麗於夏年。至於序志述時，其揆一也。

The Yellow [Emperor's time] sang of "Broken Bamboo"; it was the ultimate in plainness. When Tang [Yao] sang "The Zha," it was broader than [the song of] the Yellow [Emperor's] age. When Yu [Shun] sang "Blessed Clouds," it was more literary than the times of Tang. Xia's age sang of the

"Graven Wall"; it was more ornamental than the generation of Yu. The compositions of the Shang and Zhou were more lovely than those of the generations of Xia. But when it comes to giving account of their aims and their ages, their measure is the same. (*WXDL* 29/26–37)

The first set of examples brings us from the Yellow Emperor down to the Zhou, with each age exceeding the preceding age in some quality. The song from the age of the Yellow Emperor is "the ultimate in plainness" [質之至]. Following that, we have a set of four qualities by which each age surpassed the preceding age: Tang [Yao] excelled in "breadth" [廣], Yu [虞] [Shun] in "literariness" [文], Xia in "ornamentation" [縟], and Shang and Zhou in "loveliness" [麗]. Such a development from simplicity to ornamentation follows Liu Xie's standard literary historical account and is an implicit vector towards decadence. Thus at the end of that series, Liu stresses the continuity that keeps this set of [linear] variations positive and not passing over into decadence: "When it comes to giving account of their aims and their ages, their measure is the same."

暨楚之騷文，矩式周人；漢之賦頌，影寫楚世；魏之篇制，
顧慕漢風；晉之辭章，瞻望魏采。

The Sao writing of Chu took norm and statute from the Zhou people. The poetic expositions and encomia of the Han drew a silhouette of the age of Chu. The compositions of the Wei look back with admiration to the influence of Han. The rhetorical texts of the Jin had their eyes on the colors of the Wei. (*WXDL* 29/38–45)

This next set are four examples from later, more historical ages: Chu, Han, Wei, and Jin. In this case each age models itself on the preceding age: Chu on Zhou, Han on Chu, and so on (though at this point none of these ages is characterized further). The stress is on continuity. If we were to look for some failing here, the phrasing would permit only the critique of a failure to change and vary.

On one level these two sets, comprising nine "ages" in all, are a rhetorical illustration of "continuity and variation." The first set described "variations" from age to age, with a summation stressing their continuity; the second set described how each age looked to the preceding age as a model, thus affirming "continuity," but only serially between adjacent terms. A similar serial continuity was also implicit in the comparative formulation of the first set, with each age being "more" characterized by a certain quality than the preceding age (唐歌在昔，則廣於黃世, and so on). Moreover, the variable terms in the first set constituted a clear linear sequence toward decadence, an outcome prevented only by the affirmation of unity and continuity in the summation.

Thus far we have a literary historical account of *tongbian* (continuity and variation) in two sets—but with broken chiasmatic parallelism. In this series the evaluative summation is missing; it would be expected to formally parallel the evaluative summation of the first series. As when Liu Xie explains the title of his book, an omitted parallel term is the sign of a problem. In series A, each age varied from the preceding, but there was unity and continuity; in series B, each age emulated the preceding, but there was variation (*bian* 變). The omitted parallel term, that the period from Chu to the Jin dynasty was characterized by *bian*, does appear, but with a different meaning: It is not that the ages from the Chu Kingdom through the Jin "varied" [*bian*] from one another, but in the aggregate they represent a "deviation" [*bian*] from antiquity—what Liu Xie earlier called "the deviation in rhetoric" [文辭之變] (*WXDL* 31/43).

This new version calls for a retelling of the literary historical story, which Liu Xie offers in a long parallel series. In place of limitless variation, here we find a linear account of a long downhill slide, from good to bad, from antiquity to "novelty" (*xin* 新). The passage from the positive to the negative occurs at the juncture between the two sets in the first series. Shang and Zhou may still weigh positive in the balance, but their qualities pave the way for the negative developments in the following age (Chu and Han). In short, Liu has passed from a *tongbian* (continuity and variation) view of literary history to a *zhengbian* (norm and deviation) view of literary history.

推而論之，則黃唐淳而質，虞夏質而辨，商周麗而雅，楚漢
侈而豔，魏晉淺而綺，宋初訛而新。從質及訛，彌近彌澹。
何則。競今疏古，風末氣衰也。

If we investigate and discuss this, then [we find that] the Yellow Emperor and Tang were pure and plain; Yu and Xia were plain and [yet] made distinctions; Shang and Zhou were lovely and [yet] possessed of classical grace;

Chu and Han were excessive and voluptuous; Wei and Jin were shallow and frilly; the beginning of the [Liu-] Song was false and crazy for novelty. Passing from the plain to the false, the nearer we come to the present, the more insipid things have become. Why is this? It is from trying to outdo one another in being contemporary and estrangement from antiquity, the last gasp of *feng*, the decay of vital energy. (*WXDL* 29/46–57)

No one familiar with *Wenxin diaolong* will be much surprised by this account. Yet, it follows not from the theoretical discussion of *tongbian* in the opening but from Liu Xie's "opinion," which overrides the account of endless positive "variation" and substitutes another story.

The formal identity of the phrase patterns formally imply a steady linear gradualism (each phase is formally equivalent to other phases). Embedded, however, in that formal identity is a period of crisis and substantial change. A key term by which difference is disguised in the rhythms of identity is the innocent conjunction *er* 而, which may join like things (as "and"), but often conjoins things that are different (as "and yet"). The style of composition in the ages of the Yellow Emperor and Yao is "pure" [*chun* 淳] and "plain" [*zhi* 質]. These terms may not be precisely synonymous, but they are, at the least, semantically overlapping: There is no hint of tension between them. A similar affinity can be seen in the terms that characterize the ages of decadence: "excessive" [*chi* 侈] is close to "voluptuous" [*yan* 豔]; "shallow" [*qian* 淺] is close to "frivolous" [*qi* 綺]. At the beginning and end of literary history, the *er* 而 is simply "and."

The transformation from the "pure plainness" of origin to decadence occurs, in fact, in the second two of the three ages of virtuous antiquity. In the ages of Shun and the Xia, style is "plain *yet* making distinctions" [*zhi er bian* 質而辨]. The term "plain," carried over from the age of the Yellow Emperor and Yao, affirms an essential continuity. "Making distinctions" or "analytical" [*bian* 辨] has associations very different from "plain" and is virtually antithetical to "pure" [*chun*] (which implies something undifferentiated). *Bian* (differentiating) is a term that easily becomes pejorative in Liu Xie's system of values; the "plain" stabilizes such change. *Er* 而 here is clearly "and yet."

If the style of Shun and the Xia has a positive base that moves toward a problematic characteristic, the stylistic qualities of Shang and Zhou are the mirror image, a potentially problematic quality that is restrained or held in check by the second term: "lovely yet possessing classical grace" [*li er ya* 麗 而 雅]. "Loveliness" [*li* 麗] is the problematic term that can easily become pejorative; it also implies parallelism, which follows from the *bian* tendency of the preceding age.[12] Such a term must be qualified and restricted, which is the function of *ya* 雅 (possessing classical grace). This term of restraint fails and unleashes the excess of succeeding eras.[13]

In this second version, Liu Xie adds a new age, the Liu-Song, which is *e er xin* 訛 而 新 (false and crazy for novelty). 訛, translated as "false," is a term often used by Liu. One of the primary contexts is *yin e* 音 訛, a "mis-pronunciation," in which the original sound has been garbled with the passage of time. Thus, in its falling away from the proper, ancient standard, *e* is closely related to *xin* 新 ([crazy after] novelty). This is the final stage of attenuation, in which origins are lost and novelty reigns.

The phrasing here is suggestive: "the last gasp of *feng*, the decay of vital energy" [風 末 氣 衰]. Here Liu Xie might say: "In this the deviation in rhetoric reached its extreme" [文 辭 之 變 ， 於 斯 極 矣]. Yet we might recall the phrase from the opening of the chapter, which promised precisely the endurance of the "force of *qi*" through *bian* 變: "The force of *qi* in writing becomes long-lasting by carrying through a continuity of variations" [文 辭 氣 力 ， 通 變 則 久].

Although this model of linear attenuation through history is, as I said, not surprising in Liu Xie, it is a very different model from the concept of time and change in *tongbian*, the compound that gives the chapter its title. *Tongbian* belongs to the world of the hexagrams of the *Yi*, describing not only the internal dynamic of a hexagram but also the process by which one hexagram changes into the following hexagram.[14] The *Yi* meaning of *tongbian* is a linear variation on the microlevel that is cyclical on the macrolevel. In the *Yi* change is not a falling away from origins. Such a model of *tongbian* is consonant with the first two sets of literary historical accounts, in which each age is described in relation to the preceding age. It is not consonant with the model of attenuation in the final account.

Liu Xie's reaction to linear devolution and his injunction to "go back" is formal rather than historically grounded. By this I mean that a sense of devolution can attach itself to any period after origins, and the model to which one should go back can be any earlier period. This is nicely illustrated in the passage that follows the one quoted above, in which, we may recall, the Han was characterized as "excessive and voluptuous" [侈而艷]—not qualities that Liu Xie would espouse. Liu continues: "Exceptional talents of the present hone their concepts and study *wen*; they usually overlook the Han pieces and model themselves on the collections of the [Liu-]Song. Even though they have comprehensively examined both past and present writings, still the recent is adhered to and the remote is estranged" [今才穎之士，刻意學文，多略漢篇，師範宋集，雖古今備閱，然近附而遠疏矣] (*WXDL* 29/58–63). There are no stable judgments of any literary historical period except the most ancient and most recent. The former is unattainable, and the latter is undesirable.

In place of the vision of infinite variation with which Liu Xie begins and ends this chapter, at this point, having just provided an account of extreme devolution, Liu envisions a world in which one is perpetually taking only one step away from origins. Here Liu offers one of his wonderfully problematic metaphors. Liu Xie's analogies and metaphors often produce more complications than they resolve. They are intended to be illustrative examples and are usually drawn from conventional sets of analogies (for example, carriage driving, weaving, carving, adornment, botanical lore) that command assent. But often the attractive metaphor on which everyone agrees sends the author galloping down the wrong path and makes him finally have to force his way back to the main road.

夫青生於藍，絳生於蒨，雖踰本色，不能復化。

The blue is born of indigo; the red is born of madder. Although these [dye colors] go apart from the original color, they cannot be further transformed. (*WXDL* 29/64–67)

At this point I must confess that in *Readings in Chinese Literary Thought* I gave the most generous possible reading to this metaphor of dyeing: I suggested that Liu was replacing a model of serial linear change with a model of infinitely variable change that always returns to and begins at origins. The interpretation was too generous.

The metaphor follows from the need to provide a new model for *bian* as "variation" or "change," but one that escapes the meaning of "devolution." There is an "original color" [*bense* 本色] in the material of a dye that is transformed in the process of dyeing, but this "secondary color" does not permit further transformation [不能復化]. The metaphor reduces the original model in the past (associated specifically with the Classics) to rather pale material (Vincent Shih even translates the *yu* 踰, that blue and red "go beyond" the original color, as "better colors than their sources"). Moreover, the transformation produced is both determined and itself invariable. This timid, normative version of *bian* is anything but the limitless variation envisioned in the opening [通變無方], and to which Liu Xie returns at the end. Through this metaphor Liu sacrifices variability to the imperative to stay proximate to origins.

Liu Xie's expository procedures of division and amplification—the discourse machine—constitute a relatively impersonal means of explanation. Although the discourse machine is ideologically grounded in cosmological binarism and the faith that concepts have determinate constituent "numbers" [*shu* 數], this ideological basis is essentially formal and not determined by any particular content. That is, the discourse machine can easily produce statements that are wrong or go against generally held beliefs. It is a form eminently well suited for descriptive prose, but often has difficulties in making "arguments." (Liu Xie does not make true "arguments"; instead, he describes forms and concepts.)

In a number of the cases we examined, Liu Xie as critic goes along, trying to correct or redirect the problematic products of the machine. Our lengthy examination of "Continuity and variation" represents a rather different case, in which the discourse machine is producing a fine, almost flawless elaboration of the *Yi* concept of *tongbian* applied to literature. But while Liu Xie is content with the concept on a general level, he discovers that the elaboration conflicts with his own opinions or habits of thought. Here the critic intervenes ("If we investigate and discuss this" [推而論之]) and essentially rewrites the account of history to conform to his opinions.

In comparison to contemporary masters of parallel prose, Liu Xie's chapters have an unmistakable awkwardness. He rarely achieves the illusion of perfect union of thought and words that he holds as a value. In part this is due to the difficulty of the concepts with which he is working; but in part it seems due to the fact that there are two writers competing for control of the text.

Between "Literary Mind" and "Carving Dragons": Order and Excess in *Wenxin diaolong*

WAI-YEE LI

In *Wenxin diaolong*, Liu Xie tries to build a comprehensive system of literary creation, signification, and communication. In the process, the word *wen* 文 is used in various contexts to mean pattern, words, language, writing, literature, refinement, aesthetic surface, culture, or civilization, with the idea of pattern as the apparent common denominator facilitating logical transitions. But even as patterning can be both sedate balance and arabesque effervescence, *wen* embodies immanent order as well as excesses that undermine order in *Wenxin diaolong*.

THE AMBIGUITIES OF *WEN*

In chapter 1, "Yuan Dao" 原道 (Its sources in the Way), Liu Xie elevates *wen* as the unifying, formative principle behind myriad phenomena.[1] It is coeval with heaven and earth: planetary, meteorological, and topographical variations are patterns of the Way (*Tao zhi wen* 道之文). Animal and vegetative realms all display patterns of colors and sounds (*dongzhi jie wen* 動植皆文). *Wen* is the manifestation of the Way in the world of appearances; it is thus not external decoration (*waishi* 外飾) but the externalization of an internal necessity.[2] Indeed, the beginning proclamation implicitly refutes relegation of *wen* to the status of being outer correlative of an inner meaning or essence: "As an inner power [*de*], pattern [*wen*] is very great indeed, born together with heaven and earth" [文之為德也大矣，與天地並生者何哉] (Owen, *Readings* 187; *WXDL* 1/1–2). In pre-Qin texts the compound *wende* 文德 often means "the virtue or power of civil instruction," especially in connection with government.[3] *Wen* and *de* are sometimes designated as outer and inner correlates in Han texts. Thus, Yang Xiong writes, "[H]is words form patterns, his movements form virtue" [言則成文，動則成德]; and in a similar vein, Wang Chong writes, "Empty writing creates patterns, concrete actions create virtue" [空書為文，實行為德].[4] By speaking of "pattern as inner power" or "the inner power of pattern," Liu Xie effectively collapses the distinction between inside and outside.

Instead of the model of inward and outward correspondence, Liu Xie turns to metaphors of becoming and of the generative power of "mind" (*xin* 心). Humans are declared "the mind of Heaven and Earth" (*tiandi zhi xin* 天地之心). "When mind came into being, language was established; and with the establishment of language, pattern became manifest. This is the natural course of things, the Way" [心生而言立，言立而文明，自然之道也] (*Readings* 189; *WXDL* 1/18–20). There is no boundary between nature and culture in this scheme. The most primary of human pattern, the hexagrams, are derived from the "Yellow River Diagram" (*Hetu* 河圖) and the "Luo River Writing" (*Luoshu* 洛書), which are mysterious gifts from heaven and earth with no known human provenance. The "pattern in words" (*yan zhi wen* 言之文) is "the mind of Heaven and Earth" (Owen, *Readings* 191; *WXDL* 1/49–50). The realization here implies a natural, necessary, and inevitable process. It follows that the Classics and the words of the sage, as the highest expressions of "human pattern" (*renwen* 人文), represent the inevitable external aspect of the Way and the fulfillment of a symmetry that has "heavenly pattern" (*tianwen* 天文) and "earthly pattern" (*diwen* 地文) as counterparts. "Thus we know that the Way sent down its pattern through the sages, and that the sages made the Way manifest in their patterns" [故之道延聖以垂文，聖因文而明道] (Owen, *Readings* 193; *WXDL* 1/109–10).

But human patterning from its inception (with the exception of the point of mysterious origins when texts appear through divine intervention) involves the act of making which departs from the model of spontaneous manifestation defining heavenly and earthly patterns. Hence Liu Xie's rather startling suggestion that "when it reached the dynasties of Shang and Zhou, pattern-ing predominated over substance" [逮及商周，文勝其質] (based on Owen, *Readings* 190–91; *WXDL* 1/73–74). Confucius's moral mission is to "carve and sculpt human nature, ply and weave words" [雕琢情性，組織辭令] (*WXDL* 1/89–90). The metaphor of sculptural fashioning (*diaozuo* 雕琢) enjoys a long and varied life in the book. Here it is used positively, but Liu Xie feels the need to defend Confucius against the charge that he "decorates his feathers and paints them, merely engaging in beautiful rheto-ric" [飾羽而畫，徒事華辭] (*WXDL* 2/79–80),[5] maintaining that the sage "holds beauty that matches reality" [*xianhua er peishi* 銜華而佩實]. He also quotes Yang Xiong who compares the *wen* of the Five Classics to "carv-ing jade to form a vessel" [*diaoyu yi zuoqi* 雕玉以作器] (Owen, *Readings* 200; *WXDL* 3/110). It seems artifice and mediation are inevitable in human patterns.

However, the sages and the Classics transcend the opposition between artifice and naturalness and hence, their privileged position in Liu Xie's system of *wen*. Chapters 2 and 3, "Seeking criteria from the sages" and "Honoring the Classics," demonstrate unity through diversity, the continuity between intentions, affective states, and their expression, and the importance of *wen* in various spheres of experience, such as moral self-cultivation, diplomacy, and political culture (*WXDL* 2/12–28). As the highest embodiment of *wen*, the words of the sages and the Classics are morally superior and prior to later writings.[6] In theory the Classics also encompass all polarities of expres-sion, including brief words (*jianyan* 簡言) and elaborate pattern (*buowen* 博文), illumined principles (*mingli* 明理) and concealed meanings (*yinyi* 隱義) (*WXDL* 2/37–40). For this reason Liu Xie traces the genealogies of various genres to the Classics (*WXDL* 3/84–97). To honor the Classics is to also abide by their normative constraints.

一則清深而不詭，二則風清而不雜，三則事信而不誕，四則義直而不回，五則體約而不蕪，六則文麗而不淫。(*WXDL* 3/104–9)

A depth in feelings [*qing*] without deceptiveness; the affective force [*feng*] clear and unadulterated; the events [*shi*] trustworthy and not false; the principles [*yi*] upright and unswerving; the normative form [*ti*] terse and not overgrown [with weeds]; the literary quality [*wen*] beautiful and not excessive. (Based on Owen, *Readings* 200)[7]

In building a hierarchical system with the Way as the basis of *wen* and the Classics as its epitome, Liu Xie departs from earlier and contemporary delineations of *wen* as literature or, more broadly, as what is finely expressed through language. Lu Ji and the scions of the Liang royal house provide interesting comparisons. Liu Xie's famous precursor, Lu Ji, writes about the act of poetic creation in "Wen fu" (A poetic exposition on literature). The starting point is literary communication; by considering "what is made by persons of talent" (*caishi zhi zuo* 才士之作),[8] Lu Ji tries to grasp "the way they use their mind" (*yongxin* 用心). He then refers to his own struggle with the discontinuities between "things of the world" (*wu* 物), and "conceptions" (*yi* 意), and between "conceptions" and "writing" (*wen*). "Thus I write 'A Poetic Exposition on Literature': first to transmit the splendid intricacy of craft [*shengzao*] of previous writers, and second, thereby to discuss the origins of success and failure in their act of writing" (Owen, *Readings* 84) [故作文賦以述先士之盛藻，因論作文之利害所由] (Guo and Wang 1:170). Whereas Liu Xie tries to objectify and systematize *wen*, Lu Ji makes grand claims for *wen* in terms of the act of poetic creation: The Way and the Classics are sources of literary inspiration, and the poet encompasses all temporal and spatial dimensions as he writes.

佇中區以玄覽，	He stands in the very center, observes in the darkness,
頤情志於典墳…	Nourishes feeling and intent in the ancient canons. . . .
觀古今於須臾，	He observes all past and present in a single moment,
撫四海於一瞬…	Touches all the world in the blink of an eye. . . .
籠天地於形內，	He cages Heaven and Earth in fixed shape,
挫萬物於筆端。	Crushes all things beneath the brush's tip.

(Owen, *Readings* 87–110; Guo and Wang 1:170–71)

In Liu Xie's system, the ideal *wen* of the sages is objectified in the Classics, which the latter-day (after the *Classic of Poetry*) poet may aspire to internalize as normative forms, but the process is rarely couched in terms of the preternatural power of the poet as in "A poetic exposition on literature," except in chapter 26, "Spirit thought."

Xiao Tong's preface to his *Wen xuan* (Selections of literature) is roughly contemporaneous with, or more probably somewhat later than, *Wenxin diaolong*.[9] Xiao Tong makes similar rhetorical moves in appealing to the philosophical and cosmological underpinnings of the idea of *wen*, constructing parallels between heavenly pattern and human pattern, as he cites the *Changes*: "Observing heavenly patterns to discern changes of the times, observing human patterns to transform all under heaven" [觀乎天文，以察時變，觀乎人文，以化成天下].[10] However, the quotation serves an argument on the protean and changeable nature of *wen*.

文之時義，遠矣哉，若夫椎輪為大輅之始，大輅寧有椎輪之質，增冰為積水所成，積水曾微增冰之凜，何哉，蓋踵其事而曾華，變其本而加屬，物既有之，文亦宜然，隨時變改，難可悉詳。 (Guo and Wang 1:329)

The time-bound meanings of *wen*, how far-reaching! For the hubless wheel is the beginning of the royal carriage, yet does the royal carriage retain the substance of the hubless wheel? Layered ice is made from accumulated water, yet accumulated water does not have the coldness of layered ice, why is it so? To follow a precedent and increase its beauty, to change its basis and heightens its intensity: it is so with the things of the world, and it is fitting that literature should be likewise. Such changes that follow the times are difficult to comprehend fully.

By focusing on the meanings of *wen* that change with the times (*shiyi* 時義), Xiao Tong implicitly negates the idea of *wen*'s immutable essence. The changing meanings of *wen* justify principles of selection whereby works with predominantly discursive, philosophical, or historical concerns are excluded. In the case of the canonical classics, exclusion is piously presented as fear of violating the integrity of those texts. Also excluded are the works of various thinkers such as Laozi, Zhuangzi, Guanzi, and Mengzi, because they "aim at establishing [schools of] thought [*liyi*], [and hence] their basic concern is not literary competence [*nengwen*]" [蓋以立意為宗，不以能文為本] (Guo and Wang 1:330). Historical writings are excluded because their prime concerns are judgments and distinctions. In compiling his anthology, Xiao Tong thus articulates a conception of *wen* as literature, a category distinct from the Classics, philosophy, and historical writings, which are all included in Liu Xie's conception of *wen*.[11]

In "Li yan pian" (Establishing words), a chapter in *Jin Louzi*, Xiao Yi offers even finer distinctions. "Confucians" (*ru*) transmit the Classics; latter-day "scholars" (*xue*) have technical mastery of the tradition but not real understanding; "practical scribes" (*bi*) engage in "useful" compositions, such as decrees and memorials. As a category apart, literary persons "entone and chant airs and rhymes, lingering over deep longings"[12] [吟詠風謠，流連哀思].[13] "As for literature, it only needs to be covered by phrases like the finest silks, delicate and intoxicating musical tones; as [moving] lips gather and close, feelings and spirit sway" [至如文者，惟須綺縠紛披，宮徵靡曼，唇吻猶會，情靈搖蕩]. Movements and intoxication suggest the loss of control, as author and reader yield to the lush beauty of aesthetic surface. In his letter to Xiao Yi ("Yu Xiangdong wang shu"), Xiao Gang singles out for approbation and emphasis that most ambiguous portion of the Classics, the licentious (*yin*) poetry of Zheng. He chides contemporary writers for their shallowness and deviations from principles of comparison and affective image (*bixing*) as they turn against the Airs (of the *Classic of Poetry*) and "Lisao". But he also disparages imitation of the Classics.

> 未聞吟詠性情，反擬內則之篇，操筆寫志，更摹酒誥之作，遲遲春日，翻學歸藏，湛湛江水，遂同大傳。(Guo and Wang 1:327)

I have not heard that singing of feelings, one would go against the grain and imitate "Inner Rules" ["Neize" from the *Book of Rites*]; or that holding the brush to express intent, one would use as model "Proclamation Against Wine" ["Jiugao" from *Documents*]; or that "spring days slowly passing"[14] [would inspire] one to turn around and learn from *Return to Containment* [*Guizang*, one of the three *Changes*[15]]; or that "river water deep and clear"[16] [would produce] similarities with the "Great Commentary" [of *Changes*].

Imperatives of restraint and order are presented as inimical to literary expression. For both Xiao Yi and Xiao Gang, intensity, excess, and beauty of surface justify the categorization of literature as a separate domain.

Liu Xie builds a system of *wen* in which the latterday poet occupies an ambiguous position,[17] in contradistinction to Lu Ji or the Liang princes and emperors,[18] who grant that figure preeminence in their reflections on literature. This ambivalence is in turn rooted in Liu Xie's conception of *wen*. On the one hand, *wen* is natural order and an all-encompassing system whose basis is the Way and whose highest realization is the moral perfection of the

Classics. On the other hand, *wen* is elaborateness, intensity, excess, and aesthetic surface. Liu Xie is fascinated by this latter conception of *wen* but he also feels uneasy about its implications for the integrity of *wen* as a moral-cosmological system. This is evident in his discussion of the *Chuci* (楚辭) tradition, which is presented as a nodal point both of the rise and decline of *wen*.

Liu Xie's discussion of the *Chuci* tradition is one of five chapters defining "the pivotal point of literature" (*wen zhi xuniu* 文之樞紐).[19] In the final chapter, "Telling of my intent," he writes:

蓋文心之作也，本乎道，師乎聖，體乎經，酌乎緯，變乎騷，文之樞紐，亦云極矣。(*WXDL* 50/98–105)

This work of mine on the literary mind [*wenxin*] has its base in the Way [chapter 1], takes the Sage as its teacher [chapter 2], finds the normative form [*ti*] [of literature] in the Classics [chapter 3], consults the classical apocrypha [chapter 4], and shows the [initial] mutation in the *Sao* [i.e., the *Chuci* tradition, chapter 5]. Here the pivotal point of literature has been followed through to its limit. (Owen, *Readings* 296)

The first five chapters thus constitute temporal and logical progression: from origins to later developments, from essence to transformations, from grand philosophical scheme to a great literary achievement. Chapter 4, "Rectifying the Classical apocrypha," might well have been included for the sake of symmetry with chapter 3. The classical apocrypha "does not add anything to the Classics but provide assistance to literature" [無益經典而有助文章] (*WXDL* 4/108–9). The implicit opposition between the Classics (*jingdian* 經典) and literature (*wenzhang* 文章) here rebels against the conception of *wen* as a system based on unity and continuity. The rich lore of the apocrypha does not illuminate the Classics but feeds the literary imagination. With much greater ramifications for literary history, the *Chuci* tradition also challenges the moral-metaphysical dimension of *wen* as normatively defined in the first three chapters.

In "Judging the *Sao*," Liu Xie begins by sorting out the conflicting judgments of the *Chuci* tradition. Liu An (King of Huainan), Wang Yi, Emperor Xuan of Han, and Yang Xiong claim that *Chuci* expresses the values of the

Classics (as understood by the Han); while Ban Gu attacks Qu Yuan for his excessive pride and rancor against his ruler, and for fabrications deviating from the Classics. Liu Xie claims that both praise and blame are too extreme and proceeds to analyze the case for and against the filiation of *Chuci* from the Classics.

故其陳堯舜之耿介，稱禹湯之祇敬，典誥之體也；譏桀、紂之猖披，傷羿、澆之顛隕，規諷之旨也；虯龍以喻君子，雲蜺以譬讒邪，比興之義也；每一顧而掩涕，歎君門之九重，忠怨之辭也；觀茲四事，同於風、雅者也。至於託雲龍，說迂怪，駕豐隆，求宓妃，憑鴆鳥，媒娀女，詭異之辭也；康回傾地，夷羿彈日，木夫九首，土伯三目，譎怪之談也；依彭咸之遺則，從子胥以自適，狷狹之志也；士女雜坐，亂而不分，指以為樂，娛酒不廢，沉湎日夜，舉以為懽，荒淫之意也；摘此四事，異乎經典者也。 (*WXDL* 5/52–87)

Thus it sets forth the great uprightness of Yao and Shun, and praises the reverence of Yu and Tang: This is the normative form of official decrees. It criticizes Jie and Zhou for their transgressions, and mourns the demise of Yi and Zhao: this is the goal of remonstrance. It uses the young dragon as analogy for the superior man, and dim rainbow clouds as metaphor for slanderous, evil beings: This is the principle of comparison and affective image. With each glance he wipes his tears, sighing that the ruler's gates are nine-layered: These are words of loyalty and plaint. Observing these four aspects, one can see similarities with the "Airs" and "Odes" [sections of the *Classic of Poetry*]. As for expressing intent through clouds and dragons, and speaking of the extravagant and the bizarre, as when the cloud god Fenglong seeks the goddess Fufei, and the magpie makes matches with the Song daughter: These are paradoxical and strange words. Kang-hui overturns the earth, Yiyi kills the suns, wooden men with nine heads, earthen lords with three eyes: these are devious and bizarre excursus. To abide by the example Pengxian left behind, and follow Zixu's way of ful-filling his will: This is the intent of narrow defiance. To point to and take pleasure in men and women sitting together, in confusion and not sepa-rated, to uphold as joy ceaseless drinking and intoxication through days and nights: This is the will to indulge and transgress. Picking out these four aspects, one can see how it diverges from the Classics.

One may note that the perceived divergences from the Classics are but logical extensions or variations of the traits Liu Xie approves of. "The principle of comparison and affective image" (*bixing zhi yi* 比興之義) sustains an allegorical scheme that can potentially assimilate the paradoxical, strange, devious, and bizarre (*guiyi* 詭異, *jueguai* 譎怪). Indeed, starting from Wang Yi, criticism of "Lisao" is devoted to precisely that end. Similarly, Qu Yuan's "narrow defiance" (*juanxia* 狷狹) is but the result of "words of loyalty and plaint" (*zhongyuan zhi ci* 忠怨之辭) unheeded, and accounts of indulgence and excesses (*huangyin* 荒淫) may yet serve "the goal of remonstrance" (*kuifeng zhi zhi* 規諷之旨).

The ambiguities in Liu Xie's appraisal of *Chuci* are provisionally resolved in his final praise of the genre.

雖取鎔經意，亦自鑄偉辭。故騷經、九章，朗麗以哀志；九歌、九辯，綺靡以傷情，遠遊、天問，瑰詭而慧巧，招魂、大招，豔耀而深華；卜居標放言之致，漁父寄獨往之才。故能氣往轢古，辭來切今，驚采絕豔，難與並能矣。(*WXDL* 5/97–112)

The *Chuci* tradition takes up and assimilates the meanings of the Classics, yet it also forges its own impressive phrases. Thus *The Classic of Encountering Sorrow*[20] and *Nine Works* are expansive and beautiful in their intent of lament. The *Nine Songs* and *Nine Arguments* are intricate and sensuous in their elegiac sentiments. *Distant Wandering* and *Questions to Heaven* are wondrous and paradoxical, yet gracious and clever. *Summoning the Soul* and *The Great Summon* are dazzling yet profound. *Divining the Abode* emphasizes the mood of unrestrained verbal expression. *The Fisherman* allegorizes the talent of he who proceeds alone. That is why the spirit of these works can go back and defy the ancients, while their words can come down with special pertinence for the present. Such astounding coloration and quintessential beauty are indeed difficult to rival.

In this summary the surface brilliance of *Chuci* is redeemed by profound meanings, and expansiveness and intricacies are justified by the intensity of emotions. However, Liu Xie does not elaborate on "the intent of lament" (*aizhi* 哀志) and "elegiac sentiments" (*shangqing* 傷情) that easily overstep boundaries of balance and restraint believed to be embodied by the *Classic of Poetry*. In the value system of *Wenxin diaolong*, *Chuci* is deemed inferior to the *Classic of Poetry* (*Ya Song zhi buotu* 雅頌之博徒), yet Liu Xie recognizes its definitive influence on Han and later literature. He concludes by urging reflective and selective assimilation.

若能憑軾以倚雅、頌，懸轡以馭楚篇，酌奇而不失其貞，翫華而不墜其實；則顧盼可以驅辭力，欬唾可以窮文致。(*WXDL* 5/ 134–38)

If one can lean against the chariot beam and abide by "Odes" and "Hymns" [of the *Classic of Poetry*], and hold on to the reins to have mastery over Chu writings, taking in with due deliberation its strangeness without losing its truth, savoring its beautiful surface without letting go of facts, then with confident glances one can spur on the strength of words, between coughing and spitting one can plumb the depths of literary expression.

According to Liu Xie, the legacy of *Chuci* should be received with moderation and restraint, although this seems to be a paradoxical injunction that goes against the spirit of *Chuci*.

The *Chuci* tradition marks a point of departure from the Classics as well as the beginning of a new kind of imaginative literature. Thus toward the end of "Honoring the Classics," Liu Xie maintains that the principles of sincerity (a continuum between affective states and expression, between intention and execution) and order embodied in the Classics are flouted in the poems of Chu and Han. "Thus the pitfalls of Chu sensuousness and Han excesses flowed to later periods and there was no turning back. Wouldn't it be wonderful if we could correct the later phases and return to the root?" [是以楚艷漢侈，流弊不還，正末歸本，不其懿歟] (Owen, *Readings* 200, *WXDL* 3/120–24). As noted earlier, Liu Xie's ambivalence toward the *Chuci* tradition is symptomatic of deeper contradictions in his conception of *wen*. On the one hand, it is the outward manifestation of a moral-cosmological system based on order, unity, and continuity. On the other hand, it tends toward excess, intensity, and imbalance, especially as realized in literature. This results in a dialectic of excess and restraint in Liu Xie's discussion of his system of *wen*, in its diachronic aspect as literary history and synchronic aspect as a set of relations, and its bearing on the act of literary creation and communication.

LITERARY HISTORY

There are two versions of literary history in *Wenxin diaolong*. One rehearses a familiar formulation: Initial simplicity prevails at the beginning of the tradition, and then the proliferation and elaboration of *wen* sets in. The precarious balance of surface and meaning is upset, as excessive *wen* and its degenerative import become more evident the closer one gets to the fifth and sixth centuries. Liu Xie asserts in chapter 29, "Continuity and mutation":

則黃、唐淳而質，虞、夏質而辨，商、周麗而雅，楚、漢侈而豔，魏、晉淺而綺，宋初訛而新。從質及訛，彌近彌澹。(*WXDL* 29/46–53)

The ages of the Yellow Emperor and Yao were pure and plain, the ages of Shun and Yu were plain but more articulated, the Shang and Zhou had a dignified loveliness, the Chu and Han works were excessive and sensuous, the Wei and Jin were shallow and decorative. At the beginning of the Liu-Song dynasty, indifference to facts and rules fed a hunger for novelty. From substantive plainness on to falseness—the nearer we come to our own times, the more insipid literature becomes. (Based on Owen, *Readings* 226)

Characterized by plainness and substance (*zhi* 質), the era of the legendary sage kings maintains its purity (*chun* 淳) and sincerity. Perfect balance of *wen* and *zhi* is achieved in Shang and Zhou times, presumably as realized in the Confucian classics.[21] The critical moment of change, when *wen* supercedes *zhi*, comes with the works of Chu and Han, whose excess (*chi* 侈) and sensuous beauty (*yan* 艷) both fascinate and disconcert Liu Xie. Excess is compounded by mediation. In chapter 47, "Talent and judgment," Liu Xie locates "the great divide" in Han when learning and allusions prevail over unencumbered expression of native talent (*WXDL* 47/136–41).[22] Han works show signs of decline when compared to the optimal balance and restraint in the Classics, yet Liu Xie upholds them as models of emulation for his contemporaries, whom he chides for neglecting Han writings in favor of more recent Song creations.

There are thus strange shifts in "Continuity and mutation." Liu Xie tries to define core concerns that persist, or should persist, through changes. He maintains that until the Shang and Zhou dynasties, literary works "tell of [the authors'] intent and describe their times" [*xuzhi shushi* 序志述時], (*WXDL* 29/35). This core is often lost in later periods, which look only to the immediately preceding era for inspiration. To recover it and combat false- ness and shallowness, one must "return to a reverence for the Classics" [*huan zong jinggao* 還宗經誥] (Owen, *Readings* 227; *WXDL* 29/76). Critics such as Huang Kan and the Qing scholar Ji Yun thus emphasize a "return to the ancients" (*fugu* 復古) and rectification of contemporary trends of ornate- ness and frivolity as the indirectly stated thrust of Liu Xie's argument.[23] However, to illustrate constancy and changes, Liu Xie adduces as examples Han poetic expositions describing extremes of perceptual horizons.

夫誇張聲貌,則漢初已極,自茲厥後,循環相因,雖軒翥出 轍,而終入籠內。(*WXDL* 29/81–85)

The expansive description of sounds and the appearances of things reached an extreme early in the Han; thereafter writers followed along as if on a ring: though they might soar above the wheel tracks [of their pre- decessors], in the final analysis they remained within the same scope. (Owen, *Readings* 228)

How can one surpass what is already excessive and extravagant? This question engages Liu Xie more than the "return to the Classics" (which he emphasizes on a more abstract level). In the examples he cites, words that capture the limits of the imaginable produce their own genealogies. Since this is already achieved in Mei Sheng's "Qifa" (Seven stimuli), later examples are not pro- gressions but variations of the same theme.[24] In other words, although Liu Xie valorizes continuities with moral implications (such as reverence for the classics or the sincerity in "telling of intent"), he is drawn to literary geneal- ogies premised on rhetorical excess, technical mastery, extremes of perception and experience.

In chapter 45, "Times and changes," Liu Xie traces developments in liter- ary history in relation to cultural and sociopolitical contexts. He declares at the outset that "the cycles of the times meet and move, eras of substance and plainness alternate with eras of patterns and elaborateness in transforma- tions" [時運交移,質文代變] (*WXDL* 45/1–2). Here literary history is not a simple descent into increasingly ornate surfaces and impoverished content. Even the beginning proposition of alternating periods of substance and pattern does not quite apply, as Liu Xie delineates the particularities of each literary epoch. What emerges is a more sympathetic and judicious account than that obtained in "Continuity and mutation." While recent developments are disparaged in the latter, they are presented as glorious high points in "Times and changes." Thus Song writers are praised for their "dragon patterns" (*longzhang* 龍章) and "phoenix colors" (*fengcai* 鳳采), and contemporary writings are said to "surpass Zhou and crush Han" (*kua Zhou li Han* 跨周轢漢). Decorum probably dictates such eulogies for one's times. In any case, what emerges here is a picture of progress, the reverse of the account of decline in "Continuity and mutation."[25] The evaluation of *wen* also changes subtly: if there is surreptitious attention to excessive *wen* in "Continuity and mutation," the celebration of that category is open and defiant in "Times and changes."

One especially interesting moment is realized in the works of Chu and Han. Characterized as "excessive and sensuous" (*chi er yan* 侈而艷) and therefore as harbingers of decline in "Continuity and mutation," they are celebrated in "Times and changes" for their exuberance and freedom in conjuring new realms of experience.

> 春秋以後，角戰英雄，六經泥蟠，百家飆駭…唯齊、楚兩國，頗有文學…鄒子以談天飛譽，騶奭以雕龍馳響，屈平聯藻於日月，宋玉交彩於風雲。觀其艷說，則籠罩雅頌，故知暐燁之奇意，出乎縱橫之詭俗也。(*WXDL* 45/28–53)

Following the Spring and Autumn era, heroes fought for ascendancy. The Six Classics were like dragons coiled in mud, the hundred schools rose like whirlwind. . . . Only in Qi and Chu did literature flourish. . . . Zouzi [Zou Yan] sent his reputation soaring by his "discourse on heaven," Zou Shi gained galloping renown with his "carving of dragons." Qu Ping [Qu Yuan] linked fine phrases that rival the sun and the moon, Song Yu wove with the colors of the wind and the clouds.[26] Judging by their beautiful, sensuous words, the principles of the "Odes" and "Hymns" are covered up. Thus does one know that the dazzling brilliance of the sublime thoughts [of *Chuci*] comes from the daring extravagance of the itinerant politician-diplomats.

With great insight Liu Xie draws analogies between literary, philosophical, and political developments in the late Warring States period. Zou Yan's cosmographic imagination encompasses new spatial and temporal dimensions,[27] which are further elaborated by Zou Shi's intricate verbal skills "carving patterns of dragon" (*diaolou longwen* 雕鏤龍文). Both were associated with the group of erudites and rhetoricians who gathered at Jixia in Qi and, "instead of participating in government engaged in discussion and disputation."[28] These Qi thinkers are juxtaposed with the Chu poets, Qu Yuan and Song Yu, who describe journeys to other worlds, extreme emotions, and palpable illusions. Such radical expansiveness is in turn linked to the Warring States itinerant persuaders who seek acceptance of their ideas on power and politics through extravagant rhetoric. In all these spheres, self-conscious word magic conjures realms of experience cut from the moorings of mundane facts and references as it flaunts transgressions and new orders. This is a moment in Chinese literary history that Liu Xie describes with obvious gusto, as if he tacitly recognizes the emergence of a conception of *wen* with vital reverberations for his own times. In chapter 2 of *Wenxin diaolong*, Liu Xie writes of "honoring the Classics" as the origins of literature. But here the abeyance of the Classics seems to be the precondition for opening up new rhetorical and imaginative realms.

LITERARY SYSTEM

Liu Xie's conflicting perspectives on *wen* and literary history may also be examined in the light of the dynamics of system building. *System* implies wholeness and comprehensiveness, and Liu sets out to incorporate literature into models of well-being of the person and of the polity. In chapter 42, "Nourishing energy," Liu Xie discusses the importance of nourishing energy (*yangqi* 養氣) in literary creation. Again, ancient simplicity is contrasted with modern artifice and the obsession with novelty and glamour. Such modern tendencies are decried not only for creating inferior literature but also for undermining an author's physical and psychological well-being. Nourishing energy is thus the obverse side of nourishing life (*yangsheng* 養生). As such, it is the art of accepting limitations, a cautionary note for those whose "vessels and allotments are limited, yet whose uses of the mind know no bounds" [器分有限，智用無涯] (*WXDL* 42/39–40). Whereas learning is more a matter of acquisition and indefatigable application, writing is the release and letting flow of what is blocked up (*shenxie yuzhi* 申寫鬱滯).

是以吐納文藝，務在節宣，清和其心，調暢其氣，煩而即捨，勿使壅滯，意得則舒懷以命筆，理伏則投筆以卷懷，逍遙以針勞，談笑以藥倦，常弄閑於才鋒，賈餘於文勇，使刃發如新，湊理無滯，雖非胎息之萬術，斯亦衛氣之一方也。(*WXDL* 42/76–91)

Thus for the expression and containment [*tuna*, literally, spitting out and taking in] of literary art, the important thing is regulation and release [*jie-xuan*]. Purify and harmonize the mind, regulate and facilitate the flow of energy. If overburdened, immediately put it aside and do not allow blockage. When the meaning is obtained, free the mind to order the brush; when the principle is in abeyance, throw aside the brush to enfold the mind. Use ease and freedom to cure overexertion, use conversation and laughter as medicine for fatigue. Always play with leisure on the sharp point of talent, and have excess for sale when it comes to the valor of writing, so that the blade, as if newly polished, meets with no obstacles among the tissues and tendons [of composition]. Even if this is not the all powerful technique of embryonic breath [*taisi*], it would still be one way to guard the energy [*weiqi*].

The Taoist vocabulary (*tuna* 吐納, *taisi* 胎息, *weiqi* 衛氣) describing the mental balance and inward ordering, which is the prerequisite for literary composition, merges life and literature. The exercise of literary talent is compared to the newly polished blade moving easily among the tissues and tendons of composition, an obvious allusion to Cook Ding's art of cutting up the ox in *Zhuangzi* (chapter 3, "The secret of caring for life"). Literary activity as conceived here becomes one way of "nourishing life." In "Nourishing energy," literature is both play and moral self-cultivation.

The continuum between life and literature parallels that between politics and literature. Here Liu Xie implicitly addresses Cao Pi's assertion that "literary personalities past and present are as a rule not mindful of details of their conduct" [古今人文之類不護細行] ("Letter to Wu Zhi," cited in *WXDL* 49/7). The idea that life and literature can follow different rules is also articulated somewhat later by Xiao Gang in his letter to Lord Dangyang: "The way to establish oneself is quite different from that of writing. To establish oneself one has to be prudent, but to write one needs wanton abandonment" [立身之道，與文章異，立身先須謹慎，文章且須放蕩].[29] By contrast, Liu Xie asserts that literary talent has its proper place in the moral-socio-political order. In chapter 49, "Measuring vessels," Liu Xie cites the example of Jingjiang of Lu, a (mere) woman who applied her talents to government. "How can there be men who learn about literature and culture, and not attain understanding of government!" [安有丈夫學文，而不達於政事哉] (*WXDL* 49/77–78). The older meanings of *wen* and *zhi* come to the fore. The opposition no longer refers only to the form and content of a literary work, but "substance" also defines the character, aspirations, and achievements of the author as a moral and sociopolitical being. For a writer to "concentrate on surface splendor and abandon substance" (*wuhua qishi* 務華棄實) is thus a moral blemish. Great poets such as Yang Xiong and Sima Xiangru did not rise above a lowly position in government because they "possess pattern but not substance" (*youwen wuzhi* 有文無質).

These formulations are in direct contrast to the idea that poetic perfection is achieved at the expense of worldly advancement and both physical and psychological well-being. The alternative view that literature is against life, or that the unfulfilled life provides the impetus for literature, has deep roots. Thus Sima Qian enumerates examples of how suffering, anguish, and frustration produce great writing in the last chapter of the *Shiji* and in his letter to Ren An. In this vision, it is precisely the fact of being dispossessed of power and position that endows writing with special urgency and significance. This idea finds expression in Zhong Rong's *Shipin* (Categories of poetry). Zhong Rong gives special prominence to "rancor" (*yuan* 怨) as the impetus of poetry as he enumerates situations eliciting poetic response.[30] Suffering and consequent rancor as the raison d'être of poetry are mentioned in his judgments of the authors of the "ancient poems" (*gushi*), Li Ling, Ban Jieyu, all from the highest category (*shangpin* 上品), and of Qin Jia, Xu Shu, Lu Chen from the middle category (*zhongpin* 中品). Quoting the *Analects*, Zhong Rong also refers to the function of poetry in "forging ties in a group" (*qun* 群), but in his discussion *qun* is more the extension of the poet's feelings to his world than the realization of "group cohesion."

In chapter 47, "Talent and judgment," Liu Xie gives one example that fits Sima Qian's model. The Han *fu* poet Feng Yan is said to have written "Xian-zhi" 顯志 (Manifestation of intent) and "Zixu" 自序 (Preface to my writings) despite, or because of, adversities, just as "the sickness of the oyster produces the pearl" (*bangbing chengzhu* 蚌病成珠).³¹ But Feng Yan is just one of ninety-eight writers mentioned and discussed in this chapter. His example is not presented as dominant or typical but is included in the spirit of comprehensiveness as Liu Xie tries to build an all-encompassing system. In a similar vein, Liu Xie tries to rectify the common misunderstanding that Cao Pi, Emperor Wen of Wei, is as a poet vastly inferior to his brother Cao Zhi. "Thus Emperor Wen's talent appears diminished because of his exalted position, and Chen Si's [Cao Zhi] reputation rises because of his distressing situation" [遂令文帝以位尊減才。陳思以勢窘益價] (*WXDL* 47/156–57). Liu Xie's defense of Cao Pi is part of his more general concern with the continuity of worldly accomplishments and literary pursuits.

We now move from the relationship between literature and other facets of existence to internal distinctions and classifications in the literary system. Congruence of literature with life and polity in a broad system implies a view of literature as built on principles of order and balance. It does not thereby eschew intensity and excess, which are included as aspects of *wen*. Thus, in chapter 27, "Nature and form," Liu Xie outlines eight "normative forms," which are then paired off in symmetrical opposites, and then presented as variations of an underlying unity. There is implicit hierarchy among these eight "normative forms," yet Liu Xie chooses to emphasize complementarity rather than struggle or opposition. The eight normative forms are given as follows: "*dianya*, decorous [or 'having the qualities of canonical writing'] and dignified; *yuanao*, obscure and far-reaching; *jingyue*, terse and essential; *xianfu*, obvious and consecutive; *fanru*, lush and profuse; *zhuangli*, vigorous and lovely; *xinqi*, novel and unusual; *qingmi*, light and delicate" [一曰典雅，二曰遠奧，三曰精約，四曰顯附，五曰繁縟，六曰壯麗，七曰新奇，八曰輕靡] (Owen, *Readings* 214; *WXDL* 27/24–31). "Decorous and dignified" is a distinctively Confucian form. The "obscure and far-reaching" form invokes mysterious doctrines. As such, they may claim philosophical seriousness beyond the other categories. Conversely, the "novel and unusual" form risks shortsightedness and erroneous judgments, while the "light and delicate" form borders on the trivial and superficial.

The "lush and profuse" form is problematic, and dazzling brilliance suggests incommensurability of surface and meaning. Notwithstanding the implied hierarchy, Liu Xie turns these categories into four pairs of complementary opposites, putting them on the same level as the components of his system.

Liu Xie concludes by dwelling on unity beyond diversity.

八體雖殊，會通合數，得其環中，則輻輳相成。故宜摹體以定習，因性以練才。(*WXDL* 27/108–13)

> Though the eight forms differ, there is a way of merging them that comprehends all. If you attain the center of the ring, all the spokes meet there to make the wheel. Thus it is fitting that one imitates normative forms in order to fix practice; then according to individuating nature, he refines his talent. (Owen, *Readings* 217)

The metaphor of "attaining the center of the ring" (*de qi huanzhong*) is used in *Zhuangzi* to describe the transcendence of contradictions, the perspective that holds all perspectives provisional and contingent.[32] According to *Zhuangzi*, this mental state overcoming either-or, sometimes designated as quietude (*xujing* 虛靜) or forgetfulness (*wang* 忘), has the greatest creative potential. In the context of Liu Xie's argument, such mental disposition would indeed allow imitation of various normative forms, but it also implicitly negates the idea of "individuating nature" (*xing* 性). In other words, Liu Xie tries to have it both ways: the aspiring child may imitate and master all forms if he begins with "proper and dignified construction" (*yazhi* 雅製), yet he also has to follow his individuating nature (*yinxing* 因性) and refine his talent accordingly. The symmetry of parallel prose thus masks a logical inconsistency: normative form is here both determined and acquired by choice, both one and many.

Underlying unity and structural balance sustain the integrity of a system. Liu Xie tries to accommodate divergences and excesses in his system by showing how they are determined, by examining the logic that produced them. He proposes two major determinants of style: personality and literary models. Many scholars have noted how the appreciation and appraisal of a person's appearance, speech, actions, and talent (*renlun jianshi* 人倫鑒識) influence Six Dynasties literary thought.[33] There is thus a vital link between styles of personality and literary expression. In "Nature and form," normative forms are presented as the realizations of different temperaments. They all obey the logic of the movement from inside to outside, from being hidden to being manifest. For example, "Sima Xiangru was proud and brash, thus in natural principle he was extravagant and in diction excessive" [長卿傲誕，故理侈而辭溢] (Owen, *Readings* 216, *WXDL* 27/72–73). Extravagance and excess are not traits Liu Xie usually approves of, but here they fulfill the necessary correspondence between inside and outside (*biaoli xiangfu* 表裏相符).

In chapter 30, "Determination of development," Liu Xie also discusses the formation of style through imitation of literary models. "Whoever takes the Classics as his model will naturally come into the excellence of the decorous and dignified mode. Whoever decides that his work should imitate the "Lisao" will always come to the splendor of a sensuous and unrestrained mode" [是以模經為式者，自入典雅之懿，效騷命篇者，必歸艷逸之華] (*Readings* 233, *WXDL* 30/15–18). The inevitable logic to such developments are presented as analogous to the developments in Nature: "just as swift waters form no ripples or a barren tree gives no shade" [譬激水不漪，槁木無陰] (*Readings* 233, *WXDL* 30/6–8). By the same logic, different genres are supposed to embody different normative styles.[34] For example, petitions to the throne strive to be "decorous and dignified" (*dianya* 典雅). *Fu* and *shi* poetry should be "limpid and beautiful" (*qingli* 清麗). A "clever and sensuous" (*chiaoyan* 巧艷) style is not prized, yet Liu Xie regards it as proper for rhetorical genres such as "linked pearls" (*lianzhu* 連珠) and "seven arguments" (*qici* 七辭)—thus it has a place in his system. The one style that Liu Xie is not willing to accommodate in his system is the tendency toward "the bizarre and artful" (*guichiao* 詭巧). It is derived from the "unfolding of deception" (*eshi* 訛勢), the desire for novelty and contrivance. "What seems difficult is, in fact, nothing but an inversion of the proper. When literature [*wen*] inverts the proper, it is wanting; when language inverts the proper, it is strange" (Based on Owen, *Readings* 237–38; *WXDL* 30/108–11). The quality of strange or unusual (*qi* 奇)[35] may be a necessary counterpoint to what is proper (*zheng* 正), but it threatens to undermine the whole system of "natural order" when pursued to the exclusion of other styles.

Differences among genres and literary models are thus external counterparts to the writer's individuating nature. Again, one is faced with the paradox of the one and the many. Liu Xie suggests that a writer has to encompass a range of sensibility as he writes in different genres and imitates various models.

然淵乎文者，並總群勢；奇正雖反，必兼解以俱通；剛柔雖殊，必隨時而適用。(*WXDL* 30/34–39)

The attainment of depth in literature means that one has comprehended all the different kinds of developments: the unusual may stand in opposition to the proper, but one must understand both and be able to carry both through; firm and yielding may differ, but one must be able to apply each according to the demands of the moment. (Based on Owen, *Readings* 234)

Yet Liu Xie also insists that a writer should fulfill the contours of his individuating nature. Indeed, all the emphasis on the "naturalness" of literature—the necessary correspondence of inside and outside, surface and meaning, a person's essence and verbal expression—is derived from that position. The inward and outward foci of the classificatory impulse in *Wenxin diaolong* (the inward directed toward individuating nature, the outward toward different genres and styles) are thus related to conceptions of *wen* as natural manifestation and as fashioning and artifice. The logic of natural manifestation accounts for existing divergences and accommodates them in a comprehensive system. Writing according to his temperament and character, an author comes to different normative forms and genres. Theoretically, even the expression of "unworthy emotions," so long as it is sincere, should have a place in this scheme. Opposed to this is the ideal of unity, which stipulates that an author should achieve the archimedean point that allows him to fashion different normative styles and summon requisite inner resources to write in different genres. The emphasis on control is linked to an implied hierarchy of normative forms and genres. For only through mastery of the highest category, "proper and dignified construction," and seeking inspiration from the Classics, can one "attain the center of the ring."

LITERARY ACT

The dialectic of excess and restraint is evident in Liu Xie's account of literary creation. Chapter 26, "Spirit thought," the first of the theoretical chapters, develops the metaphor of literary creation as a "spirit journey" derived from *Zhuangzi* and "The poetic exposition on literature" by Lu Ji. It begins with a rather strange allusion to *Zhuangzi*: "Long ago someone spoke of 'the physical form's being by the rivers and lakes, but the mind's remaining at the foot of the palace towers of Wei.' This is what is meant by spirit thought" [古人云「形在江海之上，心存魏闕之下」；神思之謂也] (Owen, *Readings* 202; *WXDL* 26/1–3). On one level this merely refers to the mind's independence from physical location. But in its original context, the allusion defines a state of dependence, the inability to unburden oneself of the desire for power and profit.[36] It is tempting to read this beginning "definition" as the imperative of control and volition built into the idea of "spirit wandering" (*shenyou* 神遊).

Liu Xie elaborates on the movement of the mind in literary creation.

故思理為妙，神與物游。神居胸臆，而志氣統其關鍵；物沿耳目，而辭令管其樞機。樞機方通，則物無隱貌；關鍵將塞，則神有遁心。 (*WXDL* 26/15–24)

When the basic principle of thought is at its most subtle, the spirit wanders with things. The spirit dwells in the breast; intent [*zhi*] and energy [*qi*] control the bolt to its gate [to let it out]. Things come in through the ear and eye; in this, language controls the hinge and trigger. When hinge and trigger permit passage, no things have hidden appearance; when the bolt to the gate is closed, then spirit is concealed. (Owen, *Readings* 202)

"The spirit wandering with things" (*shen yu wu you* 神與物遊) is resonant with echoes from *Zhuangzi*, where the word *you* (wander, roam, play) is frequently used to described freedom of the spirit in its supreme disinterestedness and creative potential.[37] Stephen Owen notes that the relationship between self and world here is "not so much a fusion (in which the autonomous identity of each disappears) as a tentative association, poised between unity and difference" (Owen, *Readings* 203). Even if "spirit thought" stops short of fusion, the boundaries between the mind and things of the world are blurred in the contingent association of "spirit wandering." However, intention and articulation reimpose order. Spirit, as a more primary and amorphous entity, is governed by intent and energy, volitional acts with a shade of moral and rational emphasis.[38] Things impinge on the senses, but sensuous impressions can only be articulated through language, which is always already the medium for system and cultural memory. In other words, both spirit and things border on the ineffable, and it is the mediatory and determining categories, intent and language, that Liu Xie chooses to emphasize.

"Spirit thought" is presented as the conjunction of a kind of Taoist empty-ing of the self with meticulous preparation and technical mastery.

是以陶鈞文思，貴在虛靜，疏瀹五藏，澡雪精神；積學以儲寶，酌理以富才，研閱以窮照，馴致以繹辭。 (*WXDL* 26/25–33)

Thus in shaping and turning [as on a potter's wheel] literary thought [*wensi*], the most important thing is emptiness and stillness within. Dredge clear the inner organs and wash the spirit pure. Amass learning to build a treasure house; consult principle [*li*] to enrich talent; investigate observations to illumine all things; master conceptions to draw the words out. (Based on Owen, *Readings* 204)

The aspiration for "emptiness and stillness within" (*xujing* 虛靜) is reminiscent of "the fasting of the mind" (*xinzhai* 心齋) proposed in *Zhuangzi* as the precondition for heightened perception and consciousness.[39] It also rings with echoes of Lu Ji's lines on "observing in darkness" (*xuanlan* 玄覽) and "retraction of vision, reversion of listening" (*shoushi fanting* 收視反聽). Here inner purification is couched in terms of emptiness, fluidity, and open-ness, but this apparent negation of conscious effort is immediately followed by injunctions regarding the accumulation of learning (*jixue* 積學), the deliberation of principles (*zhuoli* 酌理), meticulous observation (*yanyue* 研閱), and rhetorical control (*xunzhi yi yici* 馴致以繹辭). Thus schooled, the actual execution is spontaneous and final.

The movement of spirit thought is expansive and creative: It "regulates empty positions" (*kuiju xuwei* 規矩虛位) and "carves the formless" (*kelou wuxing* 刻鏤無形).[40] Again, boundaries are apparently effaced: "Climbing a mountain, one's affections (*qing*) fill the mountain; contemplating the sea, one's thoughts (*yi*) brim over the sea. And, according to the measure of talent in the self, one may speed off together with the wind and clouds" [登山則情滿於山，觀海則意溢於海，我才之多少，將與風雲而並驅矣] (based on Owen, *Readings* 205; *WXDL* 26/41–46). Physical or perceptual motion is matched by the movement of "spirit thought," whereby one's feelings and thoughts infuse, or are infused by, things of the world. The mountain and the sea are properly immense entities for imagining expansiveness. Thus conditioned, one's creative power soars with the wind and the clouds. Yet, from this point on, Liu Xie turns to the constraints on the apparently boundless freedom of "spirit thought." He dwells on the shadow between conception and articulation. "When concepts soar across the empty sky, they easily become wondrous; but it is hard to be artful by giving them substantial expression in words" [意翻空而易奇，言徵實而難巧也。] (Owen, *Readings* 206; *WXDL* 26/52–53).[41] There is no real solution to this problem, and Liu Xie cautions against overexertion, proposing instead mental poise and technical mastery (*bingxin yangshu* 秉心養術) as preparation for literary creativity. These themes are taken up even more emphatically in chapter 42, "Nourishing energy."

More generally, spirit thought has to be situated in a system of literary temperament. Between the boundless freedom of "spirit thought" and the ineffable meanings beyond words is the more tangible struggle with articulation, which devolves on the writer's engagement with generic and stylistic imperatives. Hence Liu Xie concludes his reflections on "spirit thought" with manners of expression (quick or slow, tortuous or effortless) and turns to "nature and form" (*tixing*) in the next chapter. There is thus a dual focus in "Spirit thought." Ideas on expansiveness and freedom are juxtaposed with injunctions on order and restraint.

The obverse side of "the spirit wandering with things" is the beckoning of things of the world. In chapter 46, "The sensuous color of physical things," Liu Xie proceeds from the traditional stimulus-response paradigm in poetic creation to warnings against the seduction of the world of things, which invites an increasingly ornate and elaborate language that tries to match the multifariousness of phenomenal existence. He asserts that "Lisao" begins the trend of creating a dense aesthetic surface that lingers over (*liulian* 流連) sensuous existence as well as intense emotions, but his real target is contemporary tendencies to strive for "(mere) resemblance" (*xingsi* 形似) and "close adherence (to the original)" (*mifu* 密附). Poetic response to the world of things is described in two ways here. On the one hand, Liu Xie celebrates the stimulus-response model as he evokes a beautiful picture of universal beckoning, stirring, attraction, and participation, using words that describe nondirectional and nonvolitional movements.

物色之動，心亦搖焉⋯是以詩人感物，聯類不窮。流連萬象之際，沉吟視聽之區，寫氣圖貌，既隨物以宛轉；屬采附聲，亦與心而徘徊。(*WXDL* 46/3–4, 28–35)

And as the sensuous colors of physical things are stirred into movement, so the mind, too, is shaken. . . . That is why when the poet is moved by things, his categorical associations are endless. He lingers over the boundaries of myriad images, ponders in the realm of sights and sounds. Delineating the spirit and portraying appearances, he follows things in their circumlocutions; applying colors and matching sounds, he lets things move back and forth with his mind.

On the other hand, Liu Xie advocates calmness and inward distance in mood (*xian* 閑) and simplicity of language (*jian* 簡) in order to resist the world of things. "The four seasons revolve in profusion, for the writer to enter into the stirrings of the affective image, calm is important. Though the sensuous colors of physical things are lush and dense, their exposition in language demands succinctness" [是以四序紛迴，而入興貴閑；物色雖繁，而析辭尚簡] (based on Owen, *Readings* 284; *WXDL* 46/96–99).

This dialectic between freedom and restraint is also expressed as the relationship between immediacy and mediation through tradition. Liu Xie postulates a moment of plenitude at the origins of Chinese literature, when there is seamless continuity between surface and meaning, an effortless commensurability of expression and intent. However, since the Han dynasty, the aesthetic surface has become increasingly elaborate, to the detriment of sincerity and order ideally embodied in literature. To regain that original balance, the writer has to internalize a whole range of emotions and literary forms from the past. In other words, second innocence can be attained only through mastery of history. Thus in chapter 28, "Wind and bone," the human body provides the key metaphors for the affective basis and verbal structure of writing. Words depend on "bones," just as the human body is based on a skeletal structure. Affections or feelings contain "wind," just as breath or energy (*qi* 氣) infuses the human form.[42] Such metaphors based on the elements and human physiology suggest something basic and unmediated.

However, the author striving for originality and unusual effect within the framework of "wind and bone" must do so through internalization of the tradition ("models of the Classics" [*jingdian zhi fan* 經典之範] and "techniques of the thinkers and historians" [*zishi zhi shu* 子史之術]) which allows him to fully grasp "the mutations of the affections" (*qingbian* 情變) and "forms of literature" (*wenti* 文體). "Only then can one cause fresh concepts to sprout; only then can one carve out and paint wondrous phrasing. Having the forms revealed means that concepts will be fresh but not in disarray; comprehending the mutations means that phrasing will be wondrous without becoming too extravagant" [然後能孚甲新意，雕畫奇辭。昭體故意新而不亂，曉變故辭奇而不黷] (based on Owen, *Readings* 222–23; *WXDL* 28/84–87).

Such mediation arrests the excessive proliferation and elaboration of aesthetic surface. Elsewhere in *Wenxin diaolong*, this is achieved through the full expression of substance. In making the argument for the mutual dependence and ideal balance between substance and surface, Liu Xie imposes normative constraints on potential excess in both categories. For example, note the treatment of the word *qing* 情 in chapter 31, "Affections and coloration." When Lu Ji writes that "the poem follows from the affections and is sensuously intricate" [詩緣情而綺靡] (Owen, *Readings* 130), *qing* as a range of emotions is not delimited, literary creation is almost abdication of control in the act of "following from" (*yuan* 緣) the affections, and the result is a sensuous and intricate aesthetic surface (*qimi* 綺靡). In the classification of poetic exposition (*fu*) in *Selections of Literature*, Xiao Tong associates *qing* with desire (under its rubric are "*Fu* on Gaotang" [*Gaotang fu*], "*Fu* on the goddess" [*Shengnü fu*], "*Fu* on Master Dengtu enamored of beauty" [*Dengtuzi haose fu*] by Song Yu, and "*Fu* on goddess of River Luo" [*Luoshen fu*] by Cao Zhi) and distinguishes it from *zhi* 志, intent and aspirations with moral and political dimensions (examples include "*Fu* on thoughts of profound mysteries" [*Sixuan fu*] and "*Fu* on returning to the fields" [*Guitian fu*] by Zhang Heng and "*Fu* on leisure living" [*Xianju fu*] by Pan Yue). By contrast, in "Affections and coloration," *qing* has an implied moral content and is almost synonymous with intent (*zhi*).

> 蓋風、雅之興，志思蓄憤，而吟詠情性，以諷其上，此為情而造文也…［故為情者要約而寫真，為文者淫麗而煩濫…］況乎文章，述志為本。(*WXDL* 31/65–69, 95–96)

What stirred the "Airs" and "Odes" was a repressed intensity in their thoughts and what they were intent upon: and "they sang forth their affections and their natures" to criticize those in power. This is producing *wen* for the sake of feeling. . . . The very basis (of literature) is the transmission of that upon which mind is intent. (Owen, *Readings* 243)

In this sense, the *Classic of Poetry* validates Liu Xie's beginning assertion that substance depends on pattern (*zhi dai wen* 質待文), since the raison d'être of this ideal poetry lies in the fact of expression as well as its purpose of moral and political critique. If the affections and intent remain latent, then the poem cannot have any effect on the world.

The parallel argument that pattern depends on substance (*wen dai zhi* 文待質) is directed against excessive *wen*, which is pure artifice and cleverness, and insincerity in "producing feeling for the sake of *wen*" (為文而造情) (Owen, *Readings* 243, *WXDL* 31/74). This argument is based in part on the idea that *wen* should be a natural manifestion. Just as the fluid (*xu* 虛) nature of water gives rise to ripples, and the solid (*shi* 實) nature of wood produces blossoms, so the various affective natures (*xing* 性)—the five *xing* here are designated as joy, anger, desire, fear, and anxiety in *Da Dai liji*, "Wen wang guanren"—are manifested (*fa* 發) as patterned words and phrases (*cizhang* 辭章). The affective states are the "stuff" of literature, analogous to the relationship between sounds and music, colored threads and embroidery. Beautiful and patterned words may adorn language as cosmetics adorn a woman's face,[43] but the analogy becomes problematic when pursued: "The allure of glance and smile are borne of lovely charm" [而盼倩生於淑姿] and "The beauty of an argument is rooted in affections and nature" [而辯麗本於情性] (*WXDL* 31/52, 54). Glance and smile particularize charm—they are of the same substance. But between a beautiful argument and its corresponding affections and nature lies linguistic mediation. The deliberate conflation of medium and impetus allows Liu Xie to speak of the pattern of the affections (*qingwen* 情文). The elision emphasizes the natural and unmediated continuity between *qing* and *wen*.

The pruning of excessive rhetoric is thus the same project as the control of emotions.

研味孝、老，則知文質附乎性情；詳覽莊、韓，則見華實過乎淫侈。(*WXDL* 31/44–47)

If we reflect studiously on the flavor of what was said in the *Book of Filial Piety* and by Laozi, we realize that pattern and plainness are contingent upon one's nature and the state of the affections; on the other hand, if we look carefully over what was said by Zhuangzi and Hanfeizi, we see that flower and fruit [floweriness and substance] have gone past the mark into excess and dissoluteness. (Owen, *Readings* 242)

Both the *Book of Filial Piety* and *Laozi* contain injunctions against adorned language, but both circuitously affirm linguistic expression as a vehicle for moral and philosophical truths. Liu Xie seems to be suggesting that their sobriety urges restraint and order, thereby showing how "nature and affections" determine the substance and surface of verbal expression. Zhuangzi praises how eloquent language (*bian* 辯) "carves the myriad things,"[44] although he is skeptical about language in other places. Hanfeizi criticizes the rhetoricians,[45] but also indulges in his rhetorical ploys. Such extravagant and paradoxical language leads Liu Xie to lament that both "flower and fruit" have deteriorated into "excess and dissoluteness." The use of the compounds *wenzhi* 文質 and *huashi* 華實 shows how Liu Xie collapses the distinction between surface and substance in his discussion.

Following the logic that producing *wen* for the sake of feelings is good and producing feelings for the sake of *wen* is bad, the culprit should be excessive *wen* that conceals inadequate feelings (*guaqing* 寡情) or insincere feelings (*xuqing* 虛情). Theoretically "too much *qing*" may justify extravagant *wen*. However, the only example of "producing *wen* for the sake of feelings" cited here is the *Classic of Poetry*, which shows a natural restraint and whose purpose is moral criticism of those in power. When Liu Xie writes about regulating excesses in chapter 32, "Casting and paring," control of emotions parallels the modulation of rhetoric: "[To have] the affections complete yet not overly abundant, the language coursing yet not excessive" [情周而不繁，辭運而不濫] (*WXDL* 32/101–2). Similarly, in chapter 44, "General technique," technique (*shu*) is valorized as the higher principle of regulation and is opposed to (mere) refinement of verbal surface (*lianci* 練辭). The author who understands technique can thereby "control and regulate the source of affections" (控引情源). The control of excessive *wen* is thus a moral choice between proper and deviant feelings. "If we choose between the sources of the [clear river] Jing and the [muddy river] Wei, if we guide the halter at the juncture of deviant and proper paths, then we can control the coloration of pattern" [若擇源於涇渭之流，按轡於邪正之路，亦可以馭文采矣] (based on Owen, *Readings* 242; *WXDL* 31/48–50).

The conception of the transparency of *wen* is juxtaposed with images of artifice. "When it comes to the overall transmission of our spirit nature or the ample delineation of images of things [literally, "vessels"], we inscribe our minds in the 'tracks of birds' [the written word] and weave phrases on fishnet [paper]. And the brilliant glitter of this is given the name of 'lush coloration'" [若乃綜述性靈，敷寫器象，鏤心鳥跡之中，織辭魚綱之上其為彪炳，縟采名矣] (based on Owen, *Readings* 240; *WXDL* 31/11–16). Nature and culture fuse in the kennings for the written word and for paper. Whereas "overall transmission" carries Confucian echoes and implies moral seriousness, and "ample delineation" suggests attention to "things as they are," notions of carving or inscribing (*lou* 鏤) and weaving (*zhi* 織) convey the sense of artifice and of meticulous craftsmanship. All of the chapters in *Wenxin diaolong* devoted to the formal, technical, rhetorical aspects of composition (roughly chapters 32–40) explore the implications of the idea of *wen* as artifice.

The mechanics of control is built into the notion of artifice. Excesses and shapelessness ensue when "the techniques are not established from the beginning, and the mind is allowed to chase fine phrases" [若術不素定，而委心遂辭] (*WXDL* 32/44–45). Artifice thus mediates between affective state and objectified norms. "Thus to lay hold of these techniques and control a piece of writing is much like a master chess-player's full understanding of the odds. To abandon these techniques and follow one's heart is like rolling the dice and hoping for good luck" [是以執術馭篇，似善弈之窮數；棄術任心，如博塞之邀遇] (based on Owen, *Readings* 275; *WXDL* 44/73–76). A good example is the art of phonal rules nascent in the fifth century. They are supposed to be rooted in human sounds, yet "the sounds sprouting from my heart may yet lose harmonious rhythms. Why is it so? It is probably because listening inwardly, it is difficult to hear well" [聲萌我心，更失和律，其故何哉？（良由外聽易為巧，而）內聽難為聰也] (*WXDL* 33/28–31).[46] Paradoxically, artifice is also the perceived villain in Liu Xie's polemic against the latter-day poet manipulating excessive *wen*. More precisely, there is good artifice and bad artifice in *Wenxin diaolong*. The former is the overarching principle of form and structure, and the latter is extravagant attention to aesthetic surface. In "Casting and paring" and "General technique," the concept of technique exercises an ordering function vis-à-vis both rhetorical and emotional excesses (*WXDL* 32/10–47, 102–5, 44/67–72, 85–94).

The rhetorical techniques Liu Xie discusses are all presented as being based on natural order, but the moment of inevitable loss of innocence sets in (usually with the later Chu court poets, and certainly by the Han). The result is sometimes too much artifice. There is thus a dual foci: to impose order through artifice and to control artifice that threatens natural order. Take, for example, chapter 35, "Parallel phrasing." Liu Xie begins with a familiar move, asserting the continuity between nature and verbal construct. "When Creation unfurled the shape [of things], the limbs of all bodies [*ti* 體] were in pairs. In the functioning of the spirit's principle [*shenli* 神理], no event occurs alone" [造化賦形，支體必雙，神理為用，事不孤 立 (Owen, *Readings* 255; *WXDL* 35/1–4). Analogously, human mind and language are anchored in parallel constructions. In the Classics, parallel phrasings come together unconsciously and effortlessly (*shuairan* 率然); "they do not require cultivation and maneuvering" [*bulao jingying* 不勞經營] (*WXDL* 35/34). From the Han on, parallelism becomes ever more elaborate and subtle, but the danger of shallowness and deception (*fujia* 浮假) also sets in. Despite the implicit valorization of "natural parallelism," however, Liu Xie praises the aesthetics of surprise expressed through qualities of wonder (*qi* 奇) and strangeness (*yi* 異) in his classification of parallelism. By the same token, he ranks opposite parallelism (*fandui* 反對), based on apparently opposed situations, higher than direct parallelism (*zhengdui* 正 對), because the latter is more straightforward.

The making of ideal verbal expression, precisely because it borders on the ineffable, cannot sustain much discussion. Such is the burden of Liu Xie's praise of the principle of latency (*yin* 隱), whereby concealment and subtlety point to "deep meanings beyond words" (*wenwai zhi chongzhi* 文外之重 旨) in chapter 40, "Latent and outstanding." Unfortunately, we no longer have the complete chapter, and the present version has little to say about the functioning of the principle of latency. In chapter 36, "Comparison and affective image," 起興), Liu Xie considers the affective image, with its indirectness and mysterious power to rouse the affections (*qixing* 起興), as being much more significant than comparison (*bi* 比). However, like natural parallelism, the affective image can be examined for its moral import but not in terms of its making. Much of the chapter is thus devoted to modes of comparison that are more tangible. Liu Xie laments that the principle of affective image is lost with the advent of the Han poet's exaggerated rhetoric, whose favored mode is comparison. Yet he seems to reveal his own affinity with comparison, whose different types appeal to his classificatory instinct and whose interplay of sameness and difference very much characterize the progression of his own prose.

In some ways chapter 37, "Ornamentation by overstatement," best exemplifies Liu Xie's attraction to both excess and order, artifice and naturalness. He begins by appealing to the *Xici*: "For what is above forms is called the Tao, what is beneath [governed by] forms is called the vessels. The way of the spirit is difficult to describe, even fine words cannot pursue its extremes; forms and vessels are easy to delineate, bold phrases can capture their truth" [夫形而上者謂之道，形而下者謂之器。神道難摹，精言不能追其極；形器易寫，壯辭可得喻其真] (*WXDL* 37/1–5). In other words, the world of phenomenal appearance invites bold phrases, and from the very beginning ornamentation by overstatement has always existed. Since the Classics purport to encompass all human events, its verbal surface must also have elements of excess. "Although the phrases are excessive, the meaning is not thereby impaired" [辭雖已甚，其義無害也] (*WXDL* 37/22–23).

The profound intention of praising the virtuous produces distortion and ornamentation (*jiaoshi* 矯飾) regarding meaning. Verbal excesses are excused by the moral purpose of praise and blame, and the reader is cautioned not to, as Mencius says, "let the pattern harm the phrase, not to let the phrase harm the meaning" [不以文害辭，不以辭害意] (*WXDL* 37/32–33). The reader is to get to the kernel of meaning, going beyond patterns and phrases. But from the time of Chu and Han, "ornamentation by overstatement" becomes ever more paradoxical, excessive (*guilan* 詭濫), and disconnected from moral purpose. Again Liu Xie looks for the point of optimal balance: "If one can consult the broad meanings of the *Poetry* and the *Documents*, and prune the excesses of Yang Xiong and Sima Xiangru, so that overstatements are regulated, and excesses nondeceptive, then [the result] may be called virtue" [若能酌詩書之曠旨，翦揚馬之甚泰，使夸而有節，飾而不誣，亦可謂之懿也] (*WXDL* 37/87–91). In fact, the examples taken from the Classics and those from Han *fu* are structurally no different. Obviously interested in, and party to, rhetorical display, Liu Xie tries to set boundaries of reason and moral purpose to a trope that, by definition, defies constraints.

AFTERTHOUGHTS

In chapter 6, "Illuminating poetry," Liu Xie juxtaposes the view of poetry as (involuntary) expression—"What lies in the heart is intent, expressed as words it becomes poetry" [在心為志，發言為詩]—with the idea of control: "Poetry means 'to hold,' holding or regulating people's nature and emotions. The meaning of the three hundred poems is summed up as 'no deviation.' The gloss of poetry as 'holding' is thus verified" [詩者，持也，持人情性；三百之蔽，義歸無邪，持之為訓，有符焉爾。] (*WXDL* 6/9–15). The apocrypha to the *Classic of Poetry, Containing Divine Mist* (*Han shenwu* 含神霧) glosses poetry (*shi*) as *chi* 持, whose range of meanings include hold, control, or regulate.[47] The phonetic similarity probably accounts for the association. Liu Xizai notes: "As for the meanings of 'holding' with respect to poetry, there is none more important than to hold on to one's intent inside, following that is the idea of regulating mores and morals outside" [詩之言持，莫先于內持其志，而外持風化從之].[48] The tension between opposite forces—expressive and affective dimensions on the one hand and regulation and moral education on the other—obviously echoes the Great Preface to the *Classic of Poetry*. This duality arguably persists throughout the history of Chinese poetics.[49]

In the context of the exegetical traditions of the *Classic of Poetry*, emphasis on the idea of involuntary creation, vaguely folkish origins, and the expressive and affective process often informs the nostalgia for untrammeled communication with the ancients—the desire to reach the pristine core of the text unencumbered by exegetical authorities. For this is what makes the past present, and brings the canonical text to here and now (a longing as vibrant in Song or Ming or the twentieth century.)[50] It seems to me that this is a self-reflexive impulse that periodically takes over Chinese culture. Liu Xie is not interested in exegetical concerns per se (his passing nod to the classical apocrypha being meant to reveal how they fail to be exegetical). But in his scheme ideal literary communication is transmission from mind to mind (*yi xin chuan xin* 以心傳心): "In the case of composing literature, the affections are stirred and words come forth; but in the case of reading a work of literature, one opens the text and enters the affections [of the writer], goes against the current to find the source, and though it may [at first] be hidden, it will certainly become manifest" [夫綴文者情動而辭發，觀文者披文以入情，沿波討源，雖幽必顯] (Owen, *Readings* 290; *WXDL* 48/95–99). Characteristically, Liu Xie also enumerates the technical and deliberative aspects of literary appreciation and judgment: "First, observe [*guan*] the normative form; second, observe the arrangement of words; third, observe continuity and mutation; fourth, observe extremes and propriety; fifth, observe the events and principles; sixth, observe the musical properties. When these techniques are practiced, the relative values will be obvious" [一觀位體，二觀置辭，三觀通變，四觀奇正，五觀事義，六觀宮商，斯術既行，則優劣見矣] (based on Owen, *Readings* 290; *WXDL* 48/87–94). One may argue that the technical preparation facilitates intuitive communion. Nevertheless, significant differences remain between these two sets of concerns, which have general ramifications throughout the book.

In the final chapter, "Telling of my intent," Liu Xie dwells on the reverberations of the title of his book. "Literary mind" refers to "the use of the mind in writing" (為文之用心). Echoing Lu Ji, the line evokes the mystery of literary creation. The conjunction of *wen* with mind emphasizes that *wen* is not the external correlate of an inner meaning, it is itself the manifestation of an inward necessity. The phrase "literary mind" is also reminiscent of assertions in the first chapter that humans and the pattern of words (*yan zhi wen* 言之文) are the mind of heaven and earth (*tiandi zhi xin* 天地之心). Liu Xie's recurrent emphasis on the natural order unfolding at the dawn of literature (with the Classics) and to a certain extent reproduced in the literary act brings further associations with essence, immanent order, original balance, spontaneous function, unity, and continuity. A kind of essentialism and nostalgia for the pristine core underlie the rise of aesthetic self-consciousness in this period. "Literary mind" suggests the mysterious convergence of expressive and affective immediacy and spontaneity with moral-cosmological order. There is no perceived contradiction between the two in *Wenxin diaolong*. Perhaps this is why Liu Xie needs to recount two dreams in chapter 50—the dream of aesthetic longing followed by the dream of moral purpose. "It was at the age of six that I dreamed of brocade-like clouds of many colors, of climbing up to them and culling them. When I had passed the age of thirty, one night I dreamed that I was holding ritual vessels of red lacquer, going off southward with Confucius" (based on Owen, *Readings* 294) [予生七齡，乃夢彩雲若錦，則攀而採之。齒在踰立，則嘗夜夢執丹漆之禮器，隨仲尼而南行] (*WXDL* 50/29–34).

The counterpoint here is of another kind. It is set up between "literary mind" and "carving dragons," between the attributes and associations enumerated above and the *techne* of literary craft, the realization of *wen* as artifice and aesthetic surface. (In some ways "literary mind" and "carving dragons" correspond to the recurrent inside-outside metaphors of process, becoming, and manifestation in the book.) Liu Xie glosses "carving dragons" (*diaolong* 雕龍) with some unease and a proleptic protestation: "Literary works have since ancient times achieved their form by carving and rich ornamentation. Yet how can I be said to have taken after Zou Shi carving dragons with his myriad words." [古來文章，以雕縟成體，豈取騶奭之群言雕龍也] (*WXDL* 50/6–8).[51] Carving and rich ornamentation is natural to *wen* in two senses. It is an inevitable attribute and should ideally manifest a natural order. Yet all too often it becomes, as with Zou Shi, a dense verbal surface cut from the moorings of reference and Confucian moral order. Under the rubric of "literary mind," nature and artifice unite to bring forth an immanent order. With the idea of carving dragons the initial proposition is always that artifice is a form-giving force regulating emotions and expression, and yet the development of wanton abandonment and willful elaboration arouses both interest and unease in Liu Xie. He devotes more attention to *wen* as artifice and aesthetic surface, which also seems to have deeper affinities with the style of his argumentation. The substance of his propositions, however, often purports to articulate the original order of the "literary mind" as bulwark against the always latent, and sometimes manifest, excesses and dangers of "carving dragons."

CHAPTER TEN

A Survey of Studies on *Wenxin diaolong* in China and Other Parts of East Asia

ZHANG SHAOKANG

Contemporary research on *Wenxin diaolong* started at the beginning of this century with the lectures given by Liu Shipei 劉師培 and Huang Kan 黃侃 at Beijing University. Huang's *Notes on WXDL* (文心雕龍札記) remains a major reference book to this day. In the 1930s, his student Fan Wenlan brought out the standard edition of *WXDL* under the title 文心雕龍註 (*Annotated Edition of WXDL*). Later, two other important editions were published: Liu Yongji's 劉永濟文心雕龍校釋 (Collation and explanations of *WXDL*) and Wang Liqi's 王利器文心雕龍校證 (Collation and verification of *WXDL*). This century has witnessed an explosion of scholarly works about *WXDL*. More than 140 books and 2,400 articles have been published. About two-thirds of these publications appeared in the last two decades. Due to the limitations of space, I shall focus on the most noteworthy achievements in recent *WXDL* scholarship.

The Chinese *WXDL* Association (中國文心雕龍學會), established in Mainland China in 1983, has played a key role in promoting *WXDL* scholarship. It has organized five national conferences and three international conferences. Select papers delivered at these conferences subsequently appeared in the association's serial publication, 文心雕龍學刊 (The *WXDL* journal), renamed 文心雕龍研究 (Studies on *WXDL*) in 1993, after its seventh issue. Under this new name, three issues have been published. In addition to producing its serial publication, the association has sponsored the publication of 文心雕龍研究薈萃 (Collected studies on *WXDL*) and 文心雕龍綜覽 (A comprehensive survey of studies on *WXDL*), the most comprehensive reference book for *WXDL* scholars.

Scholarship on *WXDL* has also been quite active in Taiwan. While *WXDL* studies came to a halt in the Mainland during the 1960s and 1970s, Taiwanese scholars published many important books and articles. The most noteworthy contributions have come from Pan Zhonggui, Xu Fuguan, Wang Meng'ou, Huang Jinhong, Zhang Lizhai, Zhang Yan, Li Jingrong, Wang Gengsheng, and Wang Shumin. In 1987, a conference on *WXDL* was convened in Taiwan and a volume subsequently came out under the title 文心雕龍綜論 (Comprehensive discussions on *WXDL*). Since 1987, Wang Gengsheng has published three more books on *WXDL*: 文心雕龍研究 (Studies on *WXDL*), 文心雕龍新論 (Discussions on *WXDL*), and 文心雕龍導讀 (Guided readings in *WXDL*).

In Japan, three major translations of *WXDL*—by Kōzen Hiroshi, Mekada Makoto, and Toda Kogyo—have appeared in recent years. Among major theoretical studies of *WXDL* by Japanese scholars are Mekada Makoto's 劉勰的風骨論 (Studies on the "Wind and the bone") and two essays by Kōzen Hiroshi: 文心雕龍的自然觀 (The concepts of *Ziran* view in *WXDL*) and 文心雕龍與出三藏記集 (*WXDL* and collected notes on the production of the tripiṭaka). A collection of Chinese translations of Kōzen Hiroshi's articles on *WXDL* was published in China in 1984.

There are also two Korean translations of *WXDL*, both based on Kōzen's Japanese translation. Neither of these Korean translations was made in consultation with any important annotated editions of *WXDL* in the original language. In recent years, young Korean scholars have produced a number of theoretical studies on *WXDL*, of which Min-na Kim's 文心雕龍的美學 (The aesthetics of *WXDL*) is the most noteworthy.

Asian scholarship on *WXDL* covers four broad areas: the investigation of Liu Xie's life, the discussion of his intellectual orientation, the annotation and translation of *WXDL*, and theoretical studies of *WXDL*.

LIU XIE'S LIFE

More than twenty substantive articles have been published on Liu Xie's life. The most detailed study of this issue is Yang Mingzhao's 梁書劉勰傳箋注

(Annotations on the biography of Liu Xie in the *History of Liang*), first published in 1941 and later substantially revised and included in his book 文心雕龍校注拾遺 (Supplements to the collation and commentary on *WXDL*). The chronological table, family tree, and life experiences of Liu Xie are also well documented in the works of Zhang Yan, Wang Gengsheng, Li Yuegang, Kōzen Hiroshi, and Li Qingjia. Mou Shijin's 劉勰年譜匯考 (A study of collected chronological tables of Liu Xie) puts all the major studies on Liu Xie's life into one volume and greatly facilitates further research on the subject. With regard to Liu's family tree, scholars do not have any significant difference of opinion. They agree that Liu's family line was already in decline during his grandfather's time. However, they could not reach an agreement as to whether Liu Xie came from a family of officials or commoners. In the preface to his *Collation and Commentary on WXDL*, Wang Liqi argues that that Liu was born into an official's family. Wang Yuanhua 文心雕龍講疏 (Lectures and notes on *WXDL*) presents the opposite view that Liu Xie came from a family of poor commoners. There is also a divergence of views regarding the year of Liu's birth, even though most scholars date it on the basis of Liu's account of his own life in the last chapter ("Xuzhi" 序志) of *WXDL*. "When I had passed the age of thirty," wrote Liu, "one night I dreamed that I was holding ritual vessels of red lacquer, going off southward with Confucius. . . . Thus I took my brush in hand and mixed my ink, beginning my discourse on literature" (*WXDL* 50/30–35, 70–71; trans. Owen, *Readings*, 294–95). Most scholars seek to figure out the year of Liu's birth by subtracting thirty years from the date of the composition of *WXDL* given by Liu Yusong of the Qing dynasty. Another frequently debated issue concerns the reason for Liu's entry into the Dinglin Buddhist Temple. It has been variously attributed to his dire need to escape poverty (Wang Yuanhua), to his Buddhist conviction (Yang Mingzhao), and to his attempt to find political opportunities by befriending the influential Buddhist master Sengyou. The year of Liu Xie's death is also debated. It has been identified to be 521 by Fan Wenlan, 532 by Li Qingjia, and 538 by Yang Mingzhao. These divergent views in turn affect our understanding of the political conditions of Liu Xie's later life and his decision to become a Buddhist monk.

Liu Xie's later life has recently become a topic of intense interest. Su Zhaoqing 蘇兆慶 puts forward an argument that Liu Xie returned to his native place, Ju County of Shandong Province, in his final years and presided over the construction of a Dinglin Temple there. This view, however, is rejected by most scholars. A recent related development is the attempt by some scholars to challenge the widely accepted dating of *WXDL* by Liu Yusong as a work produced toward the end of the Qi dynasty (479–502). Jia Shuxin, for instance, argues that Liu wrote *WXDL* late in his life during the early years of the Liang dynasty (502–557).

LIU XIE'S INTELLECTUAL ORIENTATION

Liu Xie's intellectual orientation is a topic of continual debate in *WXDL* studies of this century. Some (Fan Wenlan, Wang Yuanhua, and others) emphasize Liu's commitment to Confucian values and ideals. They focus on Liu's endorsement of the Confucian Tao, his eulogy of Confucian sages, and his adoption of Confucian classics as the model of literature in the first three chapters of *WXDL*. They also call attention to Liu's account of his dream to join the company of Confucius and his desire for political accomplishment explicitly expressed in chapter 49 ("Chengqi" 程器). Some (Zhang Qicheng and others) underscore Liu's embrace of Taoist ideas in *WXDL*, especially in chapter 1 ("Yuan Dao" 原道) and chapter 26 ("Shensi" 神思). Identifying the Tao described in chapter 1 to be the Taoist Tao, they contend that Liu regards the Taoist Tao as the ultimate aesthetic principle and all literary works as its outer manifestations (*wen* 文). In discussing Liu's Taoist orientation, they also give close attention to his extensive references to *Laozi* and *Zhuangzi*, the two most important Taoist texts, in his description of the creative process in chapter 26.

Others (Rao Zongyi and Ma Hongshan) regard Buddhism as the mainstay of Liu's thought. To demonstrate Liu's Buddhist orientation, they discuss his lifelong involvement with various Buddhist institutions and personages, his writing of two Buddhist treatises, his free borrowing of Buddhist terminology, his transcendence of fixed positions in the Mādhyamika Buddhist mode, and above all his construction of a rigorous critical system on the model of the Buddhist science of logic (*yinming xue* 因明學). In recent years, however, the divergence of these three views has become less conspicuous. Now, the majority of scholars believe that Liu did not draw from a single philosophical tradition but blended Confucian, Taoist (including neo-Taoist), and Buddhist ideas in *WXDL*. Liu's syncretic tendency attests to the influence of the Qi and Liang literary cultures characterized by a convergence of the three traditions. Of late, some scholars have closely examined the relationship between *WXDL* and the Qi and Liang literary cultures and reevaluated Liu's debt to neo-Taoist and Buddhist developments in Qi and Liang times. Representative of this new research direction are Wang Chunhong's and Qiu Shiyou's recent articles on the Buddhist influence in *WXDL*.

THE ANNOTATION AND TRANSLATION OF *WENXIN DIAOLONG*

The editing and annotation of *WXDL* have occupied the attention of most leading *WXDL* specialists. Fan Wenlan's edition marks the transition from the premodern exegesis pursued by Qing scholars Mei Qingsheng 梅慶生, Wang Weijian 王惟儉, and Huang Shulin 黃叔琳, to the modern analytical annotation. The most important achievements of Fan's edition are its exposition of the theoretical significance of the entire book, its clarification of the meanings of key concepts and terms, and its collection of a huge amount of textual references that shed light on the sources of Liu's thought. However, some of the commentaries given in this edition are inaccurate or insufficient. Although Liu Yongji's edition cannot claim much achievement in textual collation, it does provide many concise and thought-provoking observations. Many new editions of *WXDL* have appeared since the 1950s. Wang Liqi's and Yang Mingzhao's editions have remarkable collations of various texts and copious textual notes. Yang's edition contains a section of citations of *WXDL* through the ages. However, these two editions have not done much to expound the theoretical meanings of *WXDL* on the basis of their textual analyses. Completed in the early 1980s, Lu Kanru and Mou Shijin's edition, 文心雕龍譯注 (Translation and annotation of *WXDL*), is known for its careful and concise annotations and its translation of *WXDL* into lucid modern prose. It has a high academic value and yet is accessible to the general reader. The strength of Zhou Zhenfu's edition, 文心雕龍注釋 (Commentaries on and explanations of *WXDL*), lies in its detailed semantic explanations and its examination of allusions used in *WXDL*. This book is very useful for our grasp of literal meanings of words and phrases, but it does not render much help in understanding the theoretical system of *WXDL*. It does not give a thorough elucidation of aesthetic terms and categories. Li

Yuegang's edition, 文心雕龍斟詮 (Comprehensive collation and commentary on *WXDL*), represents a comprehensive collection of earlier commentaries and annotations. This book helps make up some of the insufficiencies in Fan's edition and offers some insightful views of its editor. But it is a bit too lengthy. Drawing from the strong points of earlier editions, Wang Gengsheng produced 文心雕龍讀本 (*WXDL*: a reader), an edition that is not only up to high academic standards but is also easy to read. It is noted for its direct commentaries, lucid prose style, and penetrating arguments. Zhan Ying's edition, 文心雕龍義証 (Investigation of the meanings of *WXDL*), is a colossal piece of scholarship. Completed in 1989, it consists of three volumes with a total of more than 1.3 million characters. It is the result of an exhaustive study of earlier editions and other major scholarly works on *WXDL*. The editor extensively collected other scholars' textual commentaries and analyses and offered his own discerning critiques. One regret about this variorum edition is that its selection of materials is sometimes too broad and lacks a clear focus.

To sum up, there is still much room for improvement in the editing and annotation of *WXDL*. In particular, we need to address the lack of theoretical depth in the existing annotations of *WXDL*. This shortcoming may be attributed to the fact that most of the editors and annotators are well trained in traditional textual criticism but rather unfamiliar with modern literary and aesthetic theories. Evidently, without a thorough grasp of the theoretical system of *WXDL*, no major breakthroughs can be made in the area of textual criticism.

THEORETICAL STUDIES OF *WENXIN DIAOLONG*

Theoretical studies of *WXDL* may be traced back to Huang Kan's *Notes on WXDL*. In addition to copious textual notes, Huang expounds the theme of each chapter of *WXDL* and thus sets the stage for the rise of theoretical studies of *WXDL* in the second half of this century. In exploring the theoretical significance of *WXDL*, scholars tend to focus on four closely related subjects of investigation. The first subject is the theoretical system of *WXDL*. Many recent publications on *WXDL* are devoted to the reconstruction of a comprehensive theoretical system in this masterwork. The most important works in this area are two books that bear the same title, 文 心 雕 龍 研 究 (Studies on *WXDL*), one by Wang Gengsheng and one by Mou Shijin. To shed light on the theoretical system of *WXDL*, Wang pursues an in-depth discussion of Liu's views on the origins of literature, literary styles, compositional rules, and the principles of practical criticism. He addresses issues ranging from the fields of aesthetics, historiography, and philosophy. Mu's book is an investigation of the theoretical system of *WXDL* on an equally impressive scale. On this subject, I myself wrote a book entitled 文 心 雕 龍 新 探 (New explorations of *WXDL*). All in all, the results of research on this subject are none too satisfactory and certainly cannot compare with the achievements of textual scholarship. A definitive work on the theoretical system of *WXDL* is yet to be produced.

The second subject of study is Liu's specific theories. A number of substantial books have been written on Liu's theories on literary creation, genres, stylistics, practical criticism, the qualities of the author, and literary history. Wang Yuanhua's 文 心 雕 龍 創 作 論 (The theory of literary creation in *WXDL*) is the foremost study on the topic to date. It not only gives an illuminating account of Liu's theory but also draws extensive comparisons with Western views of literary creation. The most outstanding study on stylistics is Zhan Ying's 文 心 雕 龍 的 風 格 學 (The theory of styles in *WXDL*). In this book, Zhan focuses on Liu's views on the relationships between style and the author's talents, between style and generic conventions, and between style and the spirit of the times. Shen Qian's 文 心 雕 龍 批 評 論 發 微 (On the subtle meanings of the theory of criticism in *WXDL*) is a representative work that discusses Liu's principles and methods of criticism in the light of modern literary and aesthetic theories. Zhang Wenxun's 劉 勰 的 文 學 史 論 (Liu Xie's theory of literary history) is a comprehensive discussion of Liu's views on the historical development of literature.

The third subject concerns the conceptual categories employed in *WXDL*. A large number of works have been published on conceptual categories such as spirit and thought (*shensi*), the wind and the bone (*fenggu* 風 骨), the hidden beauty (*yinxiu* 隱 秀), and continuity and variation (*tongbian* 通 變). Of these works, Wang Jinling's 文 心 雕 龍 文 論 術 語 析 論 (An analysis of critical terminologies in *WXDL*) and the late Kou Xiaoxin's 文 心 雕 龍 美 學 範 疇 研 究 (Studies on aesthetic categories in *WXDL*) are particularly worthy of attention.

The fourth subject of study is the evaluation of the importance of *WXDL* in the history of Chinese literary criticism. In the appendix to his 文心雕龍校注拾遺 (Supplements to the collation and commentary on *WXDL*), Yang Mingzhao presents a large collection of notes and comments on *WXDL* by Chinese scholars through the ages. Wang Gengsheng also treats this subject at considerable length in some chapters of his *Studies on WXDL*. Many other articles have been written on this subject. However, few of these contain truly original ideas or shed new light on the significance of *WXDL* in the history of Chinese literary criticism. We are still waiting for the emergence of groundbreaking works on this subject.

Tremendous progress has been made in the *WXDL* scholarship over the past few decades, but much remains to be done. First, we must do everything possible to enlarge the rank of scholars devoted to studies of *WXDL*. In China, the older generation of scholars has retired and is no longer active in *WXDL* scholarship. To attract and train more young scholars for advanced research on *WXDL* is now a matter of paramount importance. While some young Korean scholars have recently joined the community of *WXDL* specialists, only a small number of Japanese scholars are currently engaged in *WXDL* studies. In Europe and America, the number of scholars working on *WXDL* is even smaller. Second, we must strive to improve the quality of our publications on *WXDL*. Although the quantities of publications over the recent decades are truly impressive, the same cannot be said about their qualities. There are not many works that break new ground in either theoretical or textual studies. How to achieve new breakthroughs in the *WXDL* scholarship is an issue for our serious consideration. Third, we must seek to transform our *WXDL* studies into an international scholarly enterprise. As a masterpiece of literary theory, *WXDL* has already been translated in its entirety into English, Japanese, Korean, Italian, and Spanish. There are also German, French, and Russian translations of its major chapters. On the basis of these accomplishments, we should exert our utmost to promote international exchange and collaboration. It is my hope that the international conference held at the University of Illinois and the publication of the present volume will help usher in more international collaborative endeavors in *WXDL* studies in the years to come.

Translated by Jing Liao

Notes

The following abbrevations are used throughout:

SBBY   *Sibu beiyao* 四部備要

SBCK *Sibu Congkan* 四部叢刊

SSJZ   Ruan Yuan 阮元 (1764–1849), comp. *Shisanjing zhushu* 十三經注疏. 2 vols. Beijing: 1977.

WXDL Zhu Yingping 朱迎平, ed. *Wenxin diaolong suoyin* 文心雕龍索引. Shanghai: Shanghai guji chubanshe, 1987.

Introduction

I am grateful to Kang-i Sun Chang, Victor H. Mair, Stephen Owen, and Andrew H. Plaks for their valuable comments on earlier versions of this introductory essay.

    1. Unless indicated otherwise, all citations of *Wenxin diaolong* are from Zhu Yingping 朱迎平, ed., *Wenxin diaolong suoyin* 文心雕龍索引 (Indexes to *Wenxin diaolong*) (Shanghai: Shanghai guji chubanshe, 1987); hereafter *WXDL*. *WXDL* 50/105 stands for chapter 50, sentence 105 of *Wenxin diaolong*. This book consists of four different indexes: one of individual sentences, one of personal names, one of books and essays cited, and one of key literary terms. All four indexes are keyed to Fan Wenlan 范文瀾, ed., *Wenxin diaolong zhu* 文心雕龍注 (Annotated edition of *Wenxin diaolong*) (Beijing: Renmin wenxue chubanshe, 1958).

    2. Mary Warnock, *Imagination* (London: Faber and Faber, 1976), 10.

Chapter 1

I am grateful to Zong-qi Cai, Zhengguo Kang, Charles Laughlin, Richard

John Lynn, and Longxi Zhang for extremely helpful comments on an earlier draft of this paper.

1. Translation taken from Stephen Owen, *Readings in Chinese Literary Thought* (Cambridge, Mass.: Harvard University Press, 1992), 294.

2. See Vincent Yu-chung Shih's introduction to *The Literary Mind and the Carving of Dragons*, rev. ed. (Hong Kong: The Chinese University Press, 1983), xxxix.

3. See also translation in Owen, *Readings*, 200.

4. See the opening statement in "Zhengsheng": "The creative author is called a sage" (*WXDL* 2/1).

5. For an English translation, see Shih, *The Literary Mind and the Carving of Dragons*, 45.

6. See T. S. Eliot, "What Is a Classic?" in *On Poetry and Poets* (New York: Noonday Press, 1961), 62.

7. See David Hawkes's introduction to *The Songs of the South*, rev. ed. (New York: Penguin Books, 1985), 27.

8. The modern scholar Wang Yuanhua argues that "Bian sao" is an important part of Liu Xie's general introduction ("Zonglun" 總論) to the book. See Wang Yuanhua, *Wenxin diaolong jiangshu* 文心雕龍講疏 (Lectures and notes on *Wenxin diaolong*) (Taipei: Shulin, 1993), 188–94.

9. Shih, *The Literary Mind and the Carving of Dragons*, 51–53, with modifications.

10. Ibid., 53, with modifications.

11. Ibid., 55, with modifications.

12. Ibid., 55.

13. Some editions have it as *zhuang zhi* 壯志 (great ambition) rather than *zhuang cai* 壯采 (beautiful diction). But most modern scholars, including most Japanese, prefer *zhuang cai* because that is how the Tang manuscript edition reads. See Zhan Ying 詹瑛, ed., *Wenxin diaolong yizheng* 文心雕龍義證 (Investigation of the meanings of *Wenxin diaolong*), 3 vols. (Beijing: Renmin wenxue chubanshe, 1989), vol. 1, 168, note 3.

14. See Wang Dajin 王達津, "Lun *Wenxin diaolong* de wenti lun" 論文心雕龍的文體論 (On the theory of genres in *Wenxin diaolong*) and Zhang Zhiyue 張志岳, "*Wenxin diaolong* 'Biansao pian' fawei" 文心雕龍辨騷篇發微 (On the subtle meanings of the "Biansao" chapter of *Wenxin diaolong*) in *Wenxin diaolong yanjiu lunwenji* 文心雕龍研究論文集 (Collected essays on *Wenxin diaolong*), edited by Zhongguo *Wenxin diaolong* Xuehui (Beijing: Renmin wenxue chubanshe, 1990), 447, 394–97. See also Wang

Dajin, "Yetan 'cong Handai guanyu Qu Yuan de lunzheng dao Liu Xie de Biansao'" 也談從漢代關於屈原的論爭到劉勰的辨騷 (Another discussion on the development from the debate on Qu Yuan to Liu Xie's "Biansao") in *Zhongguo wenxue piping yanjiu lunwen ji: Wenxin diaolong yanjiu zhuanji* 中國文學批評研究論文集: 文心雕龍研究專集 (Collected essays on Chinese literary criticism: a special volume in the studies of *Wenxin diaolong*), edited by Zhongguo yuwen xueshe (Beijing: Zhongguo yuwen xueshe, 1969), 22–26.

15. Harold Bloom, *The Western Canon* (New York: Harcourt, Brace & Co., 1994), 4.

16. For the controversy concerning the compiler of "Lisao jing," see Hawkes's introduction to his *The Songs of the South*, 32. For Wang Yi's canonization of Qu Yuan, see Pauline Yu, *The Reading of Imagery in the Chinese Poetic Tradition* (Princeton, N.J.: Princeton University Press, 1987), 104–5.

17. See Bloom, *Western Canon*, 29.

18. T. S. Eliot writes: "No poet, no artist of any art, has complete meaning alone. His significance, his appreciation is the appreciation of his relation to the dead poets and artists. You cannot value him alone; you must set him, for contrast and comparison, among the dead. I mean this as a principle of aesthetic, not merely historical criticism. The necessity that he shall conform, that he shall cohere, is not one sided; what happens when a new work of art is created is something that happens simultaneously to all the works of art which preceded it. The existing monuments form an ideal order among themselves, which is modified by the introduction of the new (the really new) work of art among them." See T. S. Eliot, "Tradition and the Individual Talent," *Selected Essays, 1917–1932* (New York: Harcourt Brace Jovanovich, 1932), 5.

19. Wendell V. Harris, "Canonicity," *PMLA* (January 1991): 110.

20. In distinguishing between biblical canons and literary canons in the Western tradition, Wendell V. Harris says: "the very entelechy of the process of biblical canonizing was toward closure, whereas literary canons have always implicitly allowed for at least the possibility of adding new or revalued work." See Harris, "Canonicity," 111.

21. See "Biansao," where Liu Xie advises readers not to overlook all these qualities in *Chuci* (*WXDL* 5/136–37).

22. Such an "innovative mixture" of proper content and exotic style cannot always be seen without problems. For example, Wai-yee Li sees a prevailing sense of ambivalence rooted in Liu Xie's conception of *wen*: On the one hand, Liu Xie promotes the style of simplicity typical of the ancients; on the

other hand, he is fascinated by *wen* for its elaborateness, proliferation, and colorful surface. See Chapter 9.

23. See Shih, *The Literary Mind and the Carving of Dragons*, 55, with minor modifications.

24. Eliot, "Milton, Part I," in *On Poetry and Poets*, 156.

25. Translation taken from Owen, *Readings*, 226, with minor modifications in romanization.

26. See "Qingcai" 情采 (*WXDL* 31/62, 64).

27. See Shih, *The Literary Mind and the Carving of Dragons*, 333. See David R. Knechtges, "Introduction" in *Wen Xuan, or Selections of Refined Literature*, vol. 1 (Princeton, N.J.: Princeton University Press, 1982), 14–15, on how Liu Xie and some of his contemporaries tried to strike a balance between classical norms and stylistic innovation.

28. See "Dingshi," in Zhan Ying, ed., *Wenxin diaolong yizheng*, vol. 2, 1140.

29. See "Mingshi," in Zhan Ying, ed., *Wenxin diaolong yizheng*, vol. 1, 208.

30. Charles Altieri, "An Idea and Ideal of a Literary Canon" in Robert Von Hallberg, ed., *Canons* (Chicago: University of Chicago Press, 1984), 52.

31. Longinus, "On the Sublime," trans. W. R. Roberts, in Hazard Adams, ed., *Critical Theory Since Plato* (New York: Harcourt Brace Jovanovich, 1971), 86. I am indebted to Charles Altieri for this reference. See Altieri, "An Idea and Ideal," 53.

32. Translation taken from Owen, *Readings*, 295.

33. For commentaries on this idea, see Zhan Ying, ed., *Wenxin diaolong yizheng*, vol. 2, p. 1937, note 5.

34. Translation taken from Owen, *Readings*, 29.

35. Ibid., 291.

36. I am indebted to Tao Ouyang for these references to Keats and Tennyson. See Tao Ouyang, "The Language of Loss" (course paper, Yale, 1996), 1.

37. Translation taken from Owen, *Readings*, 298.

38. See also Hazard Adams, "Canons: Literary Criteria/Power Criteria," *Critical Inquiry* 14 (1988): 748–64.

Chapter 2

I am grateful to Patricia Ebrey and Victor H. Mair for their valuable comments on earlier versions of this paper.

1. For a summary of extensive scholarship in this area, see Li Miao 李淼, "Xingzhe, jiegou, lilun tixi" 性質、結構、理論體系 (Essential qualities,

structure, and theoretical system) in *Wenxin diaolong xue zonglan* 文心雕龍
學綜覽 (A comprehensive survey of studies on *Wenxin diaolong*), edited by
Wenxin diaolong xue zonglan bianweihui (Shanghai: Shanghai shudian chubanshe, 1995), 86–90. *Wenxin diaolong xue zonglan* is the fruit of many years
of collaboration among scholars from all over the world and is an indispensable tool for research on *Wenxin diaolong*.

2. Liu Xie also assimilates other concepts of literature into his organismic
scheme. For instance, he draws liberally from Cao Pi's and Lu Ji's concepts of
literature (focusing on *qi* 氣 and *qing* 情, respectively) when formulating his
views on the poet's character and the creative process.

3. The "Canon of Yao" is divided into two chapters, the "Canon of Yao"
and the "Canon of Shun" ("Shun dian" 舜典), in *Shang shu zhengyi* 尚書正
義 (Correct meanings of *Shang shu*), commentary by Kong Yingda 孔穎達,
collected in *Shisanjing zhushu* 十三經注疏 (Commentary and subcommentary to the thirteen classics), compiled by Ruan Yuan 阮元, 2 vols. (Beijing:
Zhonghua shuju, 1977). Hereafter cited as *SSJZ*. The "Shi yan zhi" statement
appears in the latter chapter in this edition of the *Book of Documents*.

The dating of this chapter, along with some others, is a matter of long-
standing debate. Gu Jiegang 顧頡剛 traces it to the transitional period
between the Western Zhou (1111–771 B.C.) and the Eastern Zhou (770–256
B.C.) in his "Lun jinwen *Shang shu* zhuzuo shidai shu" 論今文尚書著作時
代書 (A letter on the date of the composition of *Shang shu*), in *Gushi bian*
古史辨 (An analysis of ancient histories) (Hong Kong: Taiping shuju, 1962),
vol. 1, 200–206. Gu's date is accepted by Zhu Ziqing 朱自清, *Shi yan zhi
bian* 詩言志辨 (An analysis of "Poetry expresses the heart's intent") (Beijing: Guji chubanshe, 1956), 9, and by Lo Genze 羅根澤, *Zhongguo wenxue
piping shi* 中國文學批評史 (A history of Chinese literary criticism), vol. 1
(Shanghai: Gudian wenxue chubanshe, 1957), 36. However, Qu Wanli 屈萬
里, "*Shang shu* bu ke jin xin di cailiao" 尚書不可盡信的材料 (Material in
Shang shu that is not fully trustworthy), *Xin shidai* 新時代 (New era) 1.3
(1964): 23–25, chooses to date this chapter to the end of the Warring States
period.

4. The word *zhi* has been translated as "earnest thought" in James Legge,
The Shoo King or the Book of Historical Documents: The Chinese Classics, vol. 3.
(Taipei: Wenxin, 1971), 48, and as "the heart's intent" in James J. Y. Liu,
Chinese Theories of Literature (Chicago: University of Chicago Press, 1975), 75.
Liu's translation seems to be more appropriate because it avoids the rational-
istic connotation of "earnest thought" and yet subtly implies moral inclination.
However, *zhi*'s meaning depends upon the historical periods and particular
contexts in which it is used. For this reason, Liu finds it necessary to render it

as "emotional purport," "moral purpose," or "heart's wish" in other contexts (*Chinese Theories of Literature*, 184). Liu's translation has been adopted with slight modification ("heart/mind") in Pauline Yu, *The Reading of Imagery*, 31. For a discussion on the translation of *zhi*, see Owen, *Readings*, 26–29.

5. See *Shang shu zhengyi*, in *SSJZ*, vol. 1, 131.

6. This sequence of activities seems to correspond with what Mihail Spariosu calls the "archaic mythopoeic unity of poetry reciting, music making, and dancing, as well as ritualistic and dramatic performance" in ancient Greece. See Spariosu, *The God of Many Names: Play, Poetry, and Power in Hellenic Thought from Homer to Aristotle* (Durham, N.C.: Duke University Press, 1991), 141.

7. See Guo Shaoyu 郭紹虞 and Wang Wensheng 王文生, eds., *Zhongguo lidai wenlun xuan* 中國歷代文論選 (An anthology of writings on literature through the ages) (Shanghai: Shanghai guji chubanshe, 1979), vol. 1, 2.

8. These remarks of Kong Yingda appear in *Shang shu zhengyi*, in *SSJZ*, vol. 1, 132.

9. Eliot Deutsch, *On Truth: An Ontological Theory* (Honululu: University of Hawaii Press, 1979), 14.

10. On this religious function of ancient Chinese dances, see Ye Shuxian 葉舒憲, *Shi jing di wenhua chanshi: Zhongguo shige di fasheng yanjiu* 詩經的文化闡釋——中國詩歌的發生研究 (A cultural exegesis of *Shi jing*: studies on the genesis of Chinese poetry) (Wuhan: Hubei renmin chubashe, 1994), 9–17, 273–87.

11. Wang Yi, ed., *Chuci buzhu* 楚辭補注 (Supplementary commentary to *Chuci*), *SBBY* ed., 2.1b–2a.

12. "Shi song" 釋頌 (An explanation of *Song*) in *Yanjingshi yiji* 揅經室一集 (A collection from the Yanjing Studio), *SBCK* ed., 1.13.

13. Liang Qichao, "Shi sishi mingyi" 釋四詩名義 (An explanation of the meanings of the four poetic genres) in *Yinbingshi heji: Zhuanji* 飲冰室合集·專集 (A combined edition of collected writings from the Yinbing Studio. Part II: Specialized writings) (Shanghai: Zhonghua shuju, 1936), vol. 10, 74.92–97.

14. *Gu wuyi yu liushi kao* 古巫醫與六詩攷 (Study of ancient shaman-doctors and the six poetic genres and modes) (Taipei: Jinglian chubanshe, 1986), 265–68. *Weng* 甕 is an ancient container used for measurement.

15. See Ye Shuxian, *Shijing di wenhua chanshi*, 439–530.

16. See Zhang Binglin, *Wenshi* 文始 (Genesis of *Wen*) (Taipei: Taiwan Zhonghua shuju, 1970), 5.19a, 104; Chen Mengjia, 陳夢家, "Shangdai shenhua yu wushu" 商代神話與巫術 (Myths and shamanistic arts in the Shang

dynasty), *Yanjing xuebao* 燕京學報 (Journal of the Yenching University) 20 (1936): 572–74; Wang Guowei, *Song Yuan xiju kao* 宋元戲劇攷 (Study of Song and Yuan drama) (Taipei: Yiwen yinshuguan, 1964), 3–6; and Liu Shipei, "Wenxue chuyu wuzhu zhi guan shuo" 文學出於巫祝之官說 (An explanation: literature came from the officials in charge of shamanistic incantations) in *Zuo An waiji* 左盦外集 (Supplementary collection of Zuo An) juan 8, collected in *Liu Shenshu yishu* 劉申叔遺書 (Posthumous writings of Liu Shenshu), 4 vols. (Taipei: Huashi, 1975), vol. 3, 1519.

17. Zhu, *Shi yan zhi bian*, 4.

18. The belief that literature is a process has been noted by many scholars of Chinese poetics. For instance, Stephen Owen, *Traditional Chinese Poetry and Poetics: Omen of the World* (Madison, Wisc.: University of Wisconsin Press, 1985), 59, observes that in traditional Chinese poetics, "[t]he movement from the condition of the world or of the age, through the poet, into the poem, and finally to the reader was conceived not as a series of causes and effects but as an organic process of manifestation." Aware that M. H. Abrams's diagram of four coordinates cannot accommodate this cyclical process, James J. Y. Liu reconceptualizes the four coordinates "as the four phases that constitute the whole artistic process," rearranging them into a cyclical diagram. See his *Chinese Theories of Literature*, 10.

19. The neglect of dance is particularly conspicuous in the passages from *Zuo Commentary* and *Speeches of the States* to be discussed below. In these passages, music is seen to occupy the center of courtly ceremonies in lieu of dance.

20. Zhu, *Shi yan zhi bian*, 8.

21. See *Zhou li zhushu*, juan 22, in *SSJZ*, vol. 1, 787.

22. Zhu, *Shi yan zhi bian*, 6.

23. For a study of these two types of poetry, see Xia Chengtao 夏承濤, "'Caishi' yu 'fushi'" 采詩與賦詩 (On collected poetry and presented poetry), in *Zhonghua wenshi luncong* 中華文史論叢 (Forum on Chinese literature and history), 1 (1962), 171–82. Dong Zhi'an 董治安, *Xian Qin wenxuan yu xian Qin wenxue* 先秦文獻與先秦文學 (Pre-Qin texts and pre-Qin literature) (Jinan: Qi Lu shushe, 1994) provides four useful comparative charts on *yinshi* 引詩, *fushi* 賦詩, and *geshi* 歌詩 in the *Zuo Commentary* and *Speeches of the States*. The last two charts (35–45) identify the time, speaker, and title of the cited work for every single occurrence of *yinshi*, *fushi*, and *geshi* in the *Zuo Commentary* and in *Speeches of the States*.

24. For examples of the expression of these two types of moral-political *zhi* (intent), see *Chunqiu Zuo zhuan zhengyi* 春秋左傳正義 (Correct meaning

of *The Zuo Commentary to Spring and Autumn Annals*), Wengong 13, in *SSJZ*, vol. 2, 1853, and Xianggong 27, in *SSJZ*, vol. 2, 1997.

25. In "Zhou yu" 周語 (Speeches of the Zhou) of *Speeches of the States*, Duke Shao 邵公 urges King Li 厲王 (r. 878–842 B.C.) to examine the admonitions and remonstrations submitted by his subjects in the forms of poetry, music, and pithy sayings; see Wei Zhao 韋昭 (204–73), annot., *Guo yu*, 2 vols. (Shanghai: Shanghai guji chubanshe, 1978), juan 1, vol. 1, 9–10. This seems to be the first known explicit mention of music and poetry as means of observing popular sentiment and the state of governance, even though the practice of collecting admonitions and remonstrations from the populace can be traced to earlier times. The *Book of Documents*, for instance, notes: "Every year in the first month of spring, the herald with his wooden-tongued bell goes along the roads, proclaiming 'Ye officers able to direct, be prepared with your admonitions.'" See *Shangshu zhengyi*, juan 7, in *SSJZ*, vol. 1, 157; trans. James Legge, *The Shoo King*, in *The Chinese Classics*, vol. 3, 164.

26. Kenneth DeWoskin, *A Song for One or Two: Music and the Concepts of Art in Early China* (Ann Arbor, Mich.: Center for Chinese Studies, University of Michigan, 1982), 23, note 7, rightly points out that "the 'eight winds' may be either a reference to the eight 'timbres,' or instrumental voices . . . or a reference to the influence of the 'airs' of surrounding areas." I am inclined to accept the latter interpretation because it fits well with the context and conveys the idea of the spheres under particular ethico-socio-political influence, or *feng*. The phrase "eight winds" has no fixed referent, and its meaning must be contextualized. In another passage from *Speeches of the States*, "eight winds" occurs in a different context and takes on the meaning of a generalized reference to natural processes and forces.

27. Yan Zi is Grand Minister of the Qi state, to whom *Spring and Autumn Annals of Master Yan* (*Yan Zi Chunqiu* 晏子春秋) is attributed.

28. *Chunqiu Zuo zshuan zhengyi*, Zhaogong 22, in *SSJZ*, vol. 2, 2093–94. For a previous translation, see James Legge, trans., The *Ch'un Ts'ew with the Tso Chuen* in *The Chinese Classics*, vol. 5, 684.

29. Ibid. For similar discussions of this function of music and poetry, see *Chunqiu Zuo zhuan zhengyi*, Zhaogong 1, in *SSJZ*, vol. 2, 2024–25; "Chu yu" 楚語, in *Guo yu*, juan 17, vol. 2, 528.

30. *Guo yu*, juan 4, vol. 1, 128–30.

31. In this context, the term "eight winds" is a generalized reference to natural processes and forces. For a similar account of music's impact on the "winds" or natural processes and forces, see the remarks by Shi Kuang 師曠, the great music master, in "Jin yu" 晉語, 4, in *Guo yu*, juan 14, vol. 2, 460–61.

32. *Guo yu*, juan 4, vol. 1, 128–30.

33. Ibid. In addition to this passage, in "Speeches of Zhou" is another excellent example of the overriding concern with natural processes and forces during the Spring and Autumn period. It is the long speech made by Prince Jin 晉公子 to his father King Ling 靈王 in 549 B.C., about twenty-seven years earlier. In this speech, Prince Jin explains the systematic correlation of human society and natural processes and forces, and he urges his father not to disrupt the order of nature (*Guo yu*, juan 3, vol. 1, 101–12). For a discussion of the cosmological significance of this passage, see James A. Hart, "The Speech of Prince Chin: A Study of Early Chinese Cosmology" in Henry Rosemont, ed., *Explorations in Early Chinese Cosmology*, (Chico, Calif.: Scholar Press, 1984), 35–65.

34. This preface to the entire body of 305 poems is often called the "Great Preface" ("Da xu" 大序) as opposed to the "Lesser Prefaces" ("Xiao xu" 小序) that introduce individual poems. The authorship of the "Great Preface" is a matter of speculation among traditional Chinese scholars. Some consider it the work of Confucius's disciple Zi Xia 子夏, while others attribute it to Wei Hung 衛宏, a scholar living in the first century A.D. See Yong Rong 永瑢 et al., ed., *Siku quanshu zongmu* 四庫全書總目 (General catalog of the Imperial Library) (Beijing: Zhonghua shuju, 1965), juan 15, vol. 1, 119.

35. Owen, *Readings*, 37. For studies of this preface, see Steven Van Zoeren, *Poetry and Personality: Reading, Exegesis, and Hermeneutics in Traditional China* (Stanford, Calif.: Stanford University Press, 1991), 80–115; Owen, *Readings*, 37–49; and Haun Saussy, *The Problem of a Chinese Aesthetic* (Stanford, Calif.: Stanford University Press, 1993), 74–105.

36. *Mao shi zhengyi*, annot. Kong Yingda, juan 1, in *SSJZ*, vol. 1, 269–70.

37. See *Liji zhengyi*, annot. Kong Yingda, juan 39, in *SSJZ*, vol. 2, 1545.

38. The key to understanding this order of decreasing importance is the phrase *buzu* 不足 (not adequate), used here to introduce various lesser activities as supplements to the core activity of poetic verbalization. Interestingly, *buzu* has the same function of indicating a graduated order as its antonym *zu* 足 (adequate) does in Confucius's remarks on *yan* (speech) and *wen* (embellishment) quoted in the *Zuo Commentary*. "Confucius said, 'The record contains this: Words [*yan*] are to make one's intent [*zhi*] adequate [*zu*], and embellishment [*wen*] is to make one's words adequate [*zu*].' If one does not employ words, who can know his intent? If one employs words without embellishment, he will not go far" (*Chunqiu Zuo zhuan zhengyi*, Xianggong 25, in *SSJZ*, vol. 2, 1985). Apparently, what embellishment is to words is analogous to what dance, songs, or chanting are to poetic verbalization in the "Great Preface."

39. *Mao shi zhengyi*, juan 1, in *SSJZ*, vol. 1, 270.

40. It is ironic that his elevation of poetry over music is modeled on the argument for the elevation of music in the "Record of Music." There, the author seeks to align music with cultural processes rather than natural processes. He demonstrates the paramount importance of music by elucidating its harmonizing effects on individuals, families, clans, and states. The author of the "Great Preface" makes a corresponding shift of emphasis to cultural processes and justifies his elevation of poetry on the ground of its unparalleled efficacy in harmonizing these processes.

41. See a chart of these references in Dong, *Xian Qin wenxuan yu xian Qin wenxue*, 64–65.

42. *Lunyu yinde* 論語引得 (Concordance to the *Analects*), Harvard-Yenching Institute Sinological Index Series, supp. 16, (Beijing: Harvard-Yenching Institute, 1940), 8/8 (i.e., book 8, chapter 8). For a different translation, see Waley, trans., *Analects*, VIII, 8, 134.

43. *Lunyu yinde*, 17/8. Compare with Waley, trans. *Analects*, XVII, 9, 212.

44. See the charts on the citation of the *Poetry* in *Mencius* and *Strategies of the States* in Dong, *Xian Qin wenxuan yu xian Qin wenxue*, 65–66, 88.

45. *Mao shi zhengyi*, juan 1, in *SSJZ*, vol. 1, p. 272.

46. Ibid., 271.

47. Ibid.

48. Ibid., 270.

49. Ibid., 272.

50. Ibid.

51. Ibid.

52. For instance, Zhu Ziqing leaves out any discussion of *Wenxin diaolong* in his *Shi yan zhi bian*.

53. Unless otherwise indicated, the translations of *Wenxin diaolong* are mine. For other English translations of *Wenxin diaolong*, see Shih, *The Literary Mind and the Carving of Dragons*, and Owen, *Readings*, 183–298. In the course of translating this and other passages from *Wenxin diaolong*, I have consulted Shih's and Owen's translations and benefited from their insights into the original work as well as their choices of words and expressions.

54. Compare this passage with the opposite view held by Plato: "I cannot help feeling, Phaedrus, that writing is unfortunately like painting; for the creations of the painter have the attitude of life, and yet if you ask them a question they preserve a solemn silence. And the same may be said of speeches. You would imagine that they had intelligence, but if you want to know anything and put a question to one of them, the speaker always gives one unvarying answer. And when they have been once written down they are

tumbled about anywhere among those who may or may not understand them, and know not to whom they should reply, to whom not; and, if, they are maltreated or abused, they have no parent to protect them; and they cannot protect or defend themselves." *Phaedrus*, 275; trans. Benjamin Jowett, *The Dialogues of Plato* (New York: Random House, 1937), vol. 1, 278–79.

55. Liu Xie's view on the creative process is a subject that has attracted much critical attention in the studies of *Wenxin diaolong*. For a summary of research in this area, see Xiong Lihui 熊黎輝, "Chuangzuo lun" 創作論 (Theory of literary creation), in *Wenxin diaolong xue zonglan*, 98–105.

56. For a discussion of the use of these important terms in *Wenxin diaolong* and Wang Bi's 王弼 (226–249) writings, see Richard John Lynn's essay in this volume.

57. For a critique of Liu Xie's own failure to achieve such a perfect fusion of authorial intent and language, see Stephen Owen's essay in this volume.

58. See, for instance, *WXDL* 5/58, 64; 6/48–49; 8/133–34; 15/40–41, 93–94; 16/38–41.

59. It is important to stress that my following stratum-by-stratum analysis is meant only to distinguish Liu Xie's treatment of various external and internal processes, not to suggest that those processes are clear-cut, unrelated entities. On the contrary, they are interactive and interdependent within his organismic scheme.

60. To see this transformation clearly, one may compare Liu's account of the religious invocation to *shen*, the numinous spirits, by the earliest people in chapter 10, "Zhu Meng" 祝盟 (Sacrificial prayer and oath of agreement), and his own description of the *shen*, the subtlest of the mind's operations, in chapter 26, "Shensi."

61. To grasp this difference, one may compare Liu's account of the comments on music's effects on the "Seven Beginnings" (*qishi* 七始, namely, heaven, earth, man, and the four seasons) and the "Eight Winds" by Ji Zha and Shi Kuang 師曠 in chapter 7, "Yuefu" 樂府 (Yuefu poetry), and his own discussion of the relevance of those natural processes to artistic creation in chapter 46, "Wuse" (The colors of nature).

62. See chapter 42, "Yangqi" 養氣 (The nourishing of vital breath).

63. For a succinct summary of the ongoing debates on the Tao in *Wenxin diaolong*, see He Yi 何懿, "Yuan Tao" 原道, in *Wenxin diaolong xue zonglan*, 137–47.

64. For an interpretation of the Tao in *Wenxin diaolong* as a Buddhist Tao, see Victor H. Mair's essay in this volume.

65. See *Zhou yi zhengyi* 周易正義 (Correct meaning of the *Book of*

Changes), commentary by Wang Bi and subcommentary by Kong Yingda, juan 8, in *SSJZ*, vol. 1, 90. For other translations, see Richard Wilhelm, trans., *The I Ching or Book of Changes*, translated from German into English by Cary F. Baynes (Princeton, N.J.: Princeton University Press, 1950), 351–52, and Richard John Lynn, trans., *The Classics of Changes: A New Translation of the I Ching as Interpreted by Wang Bi* (New York: Columbia University Press, 1994), 92.

66. The term "organismic" is used and popularized by Joseph Needham for reference to the all-embracing systems of correspondence and resonance among natural and human processes and phenomena developed during the Warring States period and the Han. Of these systems, the most sophisticated and dynamic is that developed in the "Commentary on the Appended Phrases," the most important of the *Commentaries to the Book of Changes* (*Yi zhuang* 易 傳), on which *Wenxin diaolong* is modeled. While this term aptly conveys the idea of intricate, interactive relationships among all ongoing processes, it carries the alien association of Western biological science.

67. These remarks are applied, respectively, to Cao Pi's "Lun wen" 論 文 (Discourse on literature), Ying Chang's 應場 "Wen lun" 文 論 (Discourse on literature), and Li Chong's 李 充 "Hanlin" 翰 林 (The grove of writing brushes). See *WXDL* 50/72–97.

68. As Victor H. Mair has convincingly shown in Chapter 3 of this book, Liu Xie is most likely to have also used Buddhist texts as an organizational model even though he does not openly acknowledge them as he does the *Book of Changes*.

69. See *Zhou yi zhengyi*, juan 7, in *SSJZ*, vol. 1, 80.

70. This belief of literature as a cyclical process in Chinese poetics has long been noted by various scholars. Stephen Owen, *Traditional Chinese Poetry and Poetics*, 59, observes that in traditional Chinese poetics, "The movement from the condition of the world or of the age, through the poet, into the poem, and finally to the reader was conceived not as a series of causes and effects but as an organic process of manifestation." Aware that M. H. Abrams's diagram of four coordinates cannot accommodate this cyclical process, James J. Y. Liu reconceptualizes the four coordinates "as the four phases that constitute the whole artistic process," rearranging them into a cyclical diagram. See his *Chinese Theories of Literature*, 10.

71. Elliot Deutsch, *On Truth: An Ontological Theory*, 37, sketches a three-stage pattern of development in Western literature and arts. "In sum, art emerges from religion, first from its identification with religion by way of its centering in magical or holy power, and second from its subservient role in communicating an independently formulated meaning. It then becomes

autonomous by virtue of its own quality and strives, when autonomous, to be at once aesthetically forceful, meaningful, and beautiful." We can perceive a similar pattern in the evolution from the dance-centered or music-centered to the verbalization-centered and finally to the text-centered concepts of literature in early China.

72. For a discussion of these critical tenets, see Guo Shaoyu, "Zhongguo wenxue piping lilun zhong 'Tao' di wenti" 中國文學批評理論中道的問題 (The issue of "the Tao" in Chinese theories of literary criticism), in his *Zhaoyushi gudian wenxue lunji* 照隅室古典文學論集 (Collected writings on classical Chinese literature from the Zhaoyu Studio) (Shanghai: Shanghai guji chubanshe, 1983), vol. 2, 34–65. See also Chow Tse-tsung, "Ancient Chinese Views of Literature, the Tao, and Their Relationship" in *Chinese Literature: Essays, Articles, Reviews*, 1, no. 1 (1979): 3–29.

73. Qian Zhonglian 錢仲聯, "Shi qi" 釋氣 (An explanation of *Qi*), *Gudai wenxue lilun yanjiu* 古代文學理論研究 (Research on classical Chinese literary theory) 5 (1981): 129–150, lists and discusses twenty-three *qi*-centered terms. Peng Huizi 彭會資, *Zhongguo wenlun da cidian* 中國文論大辭典 (Comprehensive dictionary of Chinese literary criticism) (Guangxi: Baihua wenyi chubanshe, 1990), 286–334, lists as many as 103 *qi*-centered terms. The great majority of these fall into the five levels of human interaction with external processes. For instance, we have *xueqi* 血氣, *qili* 氣力, *guqi* 骨氣, and *qizhi* 氣質 on the physiological level; *xiqi* 喜氣, *shuangqi* 爽氣, and *nuqi* 怒氣 on the psychological level; *zhiqi* 志氣, *haoqi* 浩氣, *zhengqi* 正氣, and *gangqi* 剛氣 on the moral level; *shenqi* 神氣, *lingqi* 靈氣, *qiqi* 奇氣, and *zhenqi* 真氣 on the intuitive level; and *caiqi* 才氣, *wenqi* 文氣, and *ciqi* 辭氣 on the intellectual level. It is important to stress that these five categories are interdependent and hence are often used interchangeably. For instance, *guqi* and *xueqi,* while literally belonging to the physiological category, are often used on the moral level. In addition to these five categories, there are terms, such as *qidiao* 氣調, *qiyun* 氣韻, *qixiang* 氣象, and *qihou* 氣候, which may well be taken as descriptions of the generalized conditions arising from the interplay of external and internal processes.

This nomenclature of *qi*-centered terms strikes us as a microcosmic reflection of the "process-centered" we have noted. The word *qi*, a process more concrete than, but sometimes used interchangeably with, the Tao, aptly bears upon the core idea of "process" in traditional Chinese concepts of literature. Meanwhile, its multifarious, often protean, compounds attest to the dynamic interplay of external and internal processes on the five levels. Furthermore, the fact that many *qi*-centered terms are used to describe the writer's creative process, the reader's aesthetic experience, the qualities of a work, and a work's impact on the external world shows that traditional Chinese critics conceptualize all major aspects of literary experience in terms of the interaction and harmonization of external and internal processes. See Hou Naihui's attempt to examine the interaction of internal and external processes during literary creation within the framework of the all-embracing *qi* in her article, "Cong 'qi' de yiyi yu liucheng kan *Wenxin diaolong* de chuangzuo lilun" 由 氣 的 意 義 與 流 程 看 文 心 雕 龍 的 創 作 理 論 (Theory of literary creation in *Wenxin diaolong*: A view from the perspective of the idea of *Qi* as a process), in *Wenxin diaolong zonglun* 文 心 雕 龍 綜 論 (Comprehensive discussions of *Wenxin diaolong*), ed. Zhongguo gudian wenxue yanjiuhui (Taipei: Taiwan xuesheng shuju, 1988), 241–83.

Chapter 3

I am grateful to Seishi Karashima for reading an early draft of this paper and for making several helpful suggestions.

1. Here, *ding* 定 (Skt. *samādhi*) is translated as "rest," and *zheng* 正 (Skt. *samyak*) is translated as "correct." Translation adapted from Shih, *The Literary Mind and the Carving of Dragons*, 343.

2. At the 1997 conference at Illinois on *Wenxin diaolong*, Qiu Shiyou presented an in-depth analysis of the philosophical implications of *prajñā* for *WXDL*. His paper is entitled "Liu Xie lun wenxue de bore juejing" 劉 勰 論 文 學 的 般 若 絕 境 (Liu Xie on the incomparable literary realm of *prajñā*), published in *Wenxin diaolong yanjiu* 文 心 雕 龍 研 究 (Studies on *Wenxin diaolong*), 3 (Beijing: Beijing University Press, 1998).

3. For the Buddhist philosophical background of *jing* (Sanskrit *viṣaya, artha, gocara*) and *jingjie* (both = "realm"), see Sun Changwu, *Fojiao yu Zhongguo wenxue*, 佛 教 與 中 國 文 學 (Buddhism and Chinese literature) in *Zhongguo wenhua shi congshu* 中 國 文 化 史 叢 書 (Chinese cultural history series) (Shanghai: Shanghai renmin chubanshe, 1988), 347–55.

4. See Feng Chuntian, *Wenxin diaolong yuci tongshi* 文 心 雕 龍 語 詞 通 釋 (A comprehensive glossary of terms in *Wenxin diaolong*) (Jinan: Mingtian chubanshe, 1990), 744–47.

5. Among the many papers directed against *WXDL* by Ma Hongshan, see especially "Dui Liu Xie 'jia pin bu hunqu,'" *Wenxin diaolong xuekan* 1 (1983): 434–46; "*Wenxin diaolong* zhi 'Dao' bian—jian lun Liu Xie de zhexue sixiang" *Zhexue yanjiu* 7 (1979): 74–78; "Lun *Wenxin diaolong* de wang," *Zhongguo shehui kexue* 4 (1980): 177–95; and "Liu Xie qianhou qi sixiang 'cunzai yuanze

fenqi' ma?" *Lishi yanjiu* 5 (1980): 117–30. A baker's dozen of Ma's vitriolic attacks against *WXDL* have been collected in his *Wenxin diaolong san lun* (Ürümchi: Xinjiang renmin chubanshe, 1982).

6. Zhang Shaokang, in "*Wenxin diaolong* de yuan dao lun—Liu Xie wenxue sixiang de lishi yuanyuan yanjiu zhi yi" *Wenxin diaolong xuekan* 1 (1983): 156–70, holds a similar view regarding Liu Xie's career objectives, taking the cynical view that Liu Xie acted out of political convenience whether attaching himself to Sengyou or aligning himself with the Buddhistically devoted emperor, Liang Wudi. See also another of Zhang's essays, "Liu Xie weishenme yao 'yi shamen Sengyou'?—Du *Liang shu*, 'Liu Xie zhuan' zhaji," in *Beijing Daxue xuebao* 6 (1981): 91–93.

7. Cheng Tianhu and Meng Erdong ("*Wenxin diaolong* zhi 'shenli' bian—yu Ma Hongshan tongzhi shangque," in *Wenxin diaolong xuekan* 1 (1983): 185–99) reject Ma's interpretations on various grounds (primarily according to their own analysis of the content of these terms as expressed in *WXDL* itself). However, they recognize that the debate over Liu Xie's intellectual and ideological affiliations has been going on for centuries.

8. In Wang Yuanhua, "'Mie huo lun' yu Liu Xie de qianhouqi sixiang bianhua," *Wenxin diaolong jiangshu*, 27–52.

9. "Mie huo lun" is in scroll 8 of *Hong ming ji* 弘明集 (Collection for spreading illumination). For a systematic study of this essential work by Liu Xie, see Huang Jichi, "Liu Xie de 'Mie huo lun,'" Rao Zongyi, ed., *Wenxin diaolong yanjiu zhuanhao* (1962), 8–34. The stele inscription is in scroll 16 of the Song period florilegium entitled *Guiji duo ying zong ji* 會稽掇英總集 (General collection of gathered flowers from Guiji) and in scroll 76 of *Yiwen leiju* 藝文類聚 (Classified collection of artistic writing), where it is partially recorded and referred to as *Shanxian Shicheng si Mile shixiang beiming* 剡縣 石城寺彌勒石像碑銘 (Stele inscription for a stone statue of Maitreya at Shicheng Temple of Shan County).

10. None of the three extant works by Liu Xie has been securely dated, although there is a rough—but far from unanimous—consensus that *WXDL* was written around the end of the Qi dynasty in 502. Rao Zongyi (in "*Wenxin Diaolong* 'Shenglü Pian' yu Jiumoluoshi *tongyun*—lun 'Sisheng Shuo' yu Xitan zhi guanxi jian tan Wang Bin, Liu Shanjing, Shen Yue youguan zhu wenti," *Fanxue ji*, Rao Zongyi, 117–18) makes a strong and closely reasoned case that, even if Liu Xie might have started to write *WXDL* under the Qi, he did not finish it until the Liang and it certainly did not circulate in finished form until then.

11. Kong Fan, "Liu Xie yu Fojiao," *Wenxin diaolong xuekan* 1 (1983): 414–33.

12. Li Qingjia, "*Wenxin diaolong* yu Foxue sixiang," *Wenxue pinglun cong-kan* 13 (1982): 263–94.

13. Wang Chunhong, "Guanyu *Wenxin diaolong* zhi Fojiao yuanyuan de xin sikao," *Wenxin diaolong yanjiu* 2 (1996): 126–54.

14. See Zhang Shaokang, *Wenxin diaolong xin tan*, 42–62.

15. *Tixing* is probably a Sanskriticism. Although this combination of graphs occurred earlier (in *Guoyu* 國語 [Conversations of the states], *Shang Jun shu* 商君書 [Book of Lord Shang], *Zhuang Zi* [Master Zhuang], etc.) with such meanings as "body," "disposition," "temperament," and "experience reality," it did not have the abstract meaning it connotes in *WXDL*, namely, the "body" (i.e., form or style) of a literary work. We shall examine the Indian antecedents of this concept in poetics below.

Another of Liu Xie's favorite expressions, one that is even more bizarre than *tixing*—if we are to accept the author of *WXDL* as a guileless Confucian—is *tuna* 吐納 (literally, "breathing in and out"; compare with Shih, glossary in *Literary Mind*, 540, no. 14, for some extended meanings). This expression is generally considered to be Taoist, since it is found in the *Zhuang Zi*, *Baopu Zi* 抱朴子 (The master who embraces simplicity), and countless other texts thought to be more or less representative of Taoism. See, for example, Ji Kang's 嵇康 (223–262) "Yangsheng lun" 養生論 (Discourse on nourishing life), trans. Kenneth J. Dewoskin, in Mair, *Anthology*, p. 575, line 1. In addition, see Kristofer Schipper, *The Taoist Body*, trans. Karen C. Duval (Berkeley: University of California Press, 1993), 136–39, and Isabelle Robinet, *Taoism: Growth of a Religion*, trans. and adapt. Phyllis Brooks (Stanford, Calif.: Stanford University Press, 1997), 106–7f., and also 6, 74, 216, and 222. Historically, the sources of such Taoist breath control practices may be traced back to Yogic *prāṇāyāma*. See Victor Mair, trans. and annot., *Tao Te Ching: The Classic Book of Integrity and the Way* (New York: Bantam, 1990), 140–48, 155–61. Also see Mair, trans. and annot., *Wandering on the Way: Early Taoist Tales and Parables of Chuang Tzu* (New York: Bantam, 1994), 52, 145, 370–71. Recent discoveries of the so-called Huang-Lao ("Yellow Emperor—Old Master") manuscripts from the ancient southern state of Chu have only served to corroborate in precise ways (e.g., descriptions of how to engage in "anal breathing") that the foundations of Taoist yoga are to be found in Indian traditions of great antiquity. Whether *tuna* can be thought of as Taoist or, at a deeper level, as yogic, it is no wonder that doctrinaire Confucians (and no-nonsense Communists such as Ma Hongshan) are concerned about Liu Xie's rectitude.

16. Wang Chunhong, "Guanyu *Wenxin diaolong*," 151.

17. Rao Zongyi, "Liu Xie wenyi sixiang yu Fojiao" in *Xiangang daxue Zhongwen xuehui* (Journal of the Chinese Society), *Wenxin diaolong yanjiu zhuanhao* 文心雕龍研究專號 (Special issue on the study of *Wenxin diaolong*), edited by Rao Zongyi (December 1962): 17–19.

18. Kōzen Hiroshi cites persuasive evidence from Liu Xie's biography and *Gaoseng zhuan* 高僧傳 (Biographies of eminent monks), which indicates that Liu Xie was intimately involved in the compilation of *Chu Sanzang ji ji* and Sengyou's other major Buddhist works, including *Hong ming ji*, and may even have been the author of some of these works. See the Chinese translation of Kōzen's long article on this subject by Peng Enhua, *Xingshan Hong Wenxin diaolong lunwen ji* 興膳宏《文心雕龍》論文集 (Jinan: Qi-Lu shushe, 1984), 5–6. Kōzen points out a whole series of unusual terms, usages, and phrases that occur both in *WXDL* and in the preface to *Chu Sanzang ji ji*. This powerfully suggests that Liu Xie must have been the author of both. Ibid., 24–30. We may further note that some of these uncommon usages reflect Liu Xie's immersion in the language of Buddhism (e.g., *benyuan* 本源 [original source]). It is broadly accepted that Liu assisted Sengyou in writing not only *Chu Sanzang ji ji* and *Hong ming ji*, but also *Fa yuan ji* 法苑記 (Records of the Dharma garden), *Shijie ji* 世界記 (Records of the world), and *Shijia pu* 釋迦譜 (Śākyamuni genealogy). Collectively, these are some of the most vital works of the formative period of Chinese Buddhism. Liu Xie was thus a notable figure in the history of Chinese Buddhism. To disregard the possibility of significant Buddhist influence upon *WXDL* would seem, at best, to be obtuse and, at worst, perverse.

19. Rao returns to the matter of "spirit" and "mind" in item 2 just below, together with their Buddhist foundations.

20. Richard Mather (in a letter dated August 2, 1997) has rightly pointed out that Liu Xie's chapter-ending *zan* were already anticipated by the *Taishigong yue* 太史公約 (The Grand Historian says) statements at the end of each scroll of the *Shi ji* 史記 (Records of the grand historian, c. 90 B.C.) and the *zan yue* 贊曰 (the eulogy says) statements at the end of each scroll of the *Han shu* 漢書 (Han history, 82 A.D.). A notable distinction, however, is that Liu Xie's *zan* are poetic verses very much like Buddhist *stotras*, whereas the statements at the end of each scroll of the *Shi ji* and the *Han shu* are in prose.

21. Compare with Sun Changwu, *Fojiao yu Zhongguo wenxue*, 232. In another article ("*Wenxin diaolong* 'Shenglü pian'," 119–20), Rao argues that the tightly organized structure of *WXDL* and its systematic reasoning on a grand scale could not possibly have been written by someone who was steeped only in Confucian texts. Rao points out that the author frequently uses numerical

categories and groupings to organize his presentation and to formulate his conception of literature. Although Confucian texts occasionally use this method, they do so neither nearly so often nor to the elaborate extent as the Buddhists with their fondness for "numerical dharmas" in logical exposition. Fan Wenlan likewise notes that "Liu Xie was deeply versed in Buddhist principles. In writing *WXDL*, the clarity of the organization is without parallel in earlier works" [彥和精湛佛理，文心之作，科條分明，往古所無]. See *Wenxin diaolong zhu*, 728, note 2. Wang Liqi expresses similar views in his notes to *WXDL*, 19–21.

22. The *Gyakubiki Bukkyōgo jiten* (665, 265a) lists more than 650 different Buddhist terms ending with *xin* (mind), including even *xinxin* 心心, which is equivalent to Sanskrit *citta-caitta* (mind of mind). Compare with Schwarz, *Rückläufiges Wörterbuch des Altindischen*, 189–90. We shall return below to a fuller discussion of the word *xin* in the title of the *WXDL* and its meaning for the whole book.

23. Pan Chonggui, "Liu Xie wenyi sixiang yi Foxue wei gendi bian," *You shi xuezhi*, 15.3 (1979): 100–111.

24. *Liang shu* 梁書 (Zhonghua shuju ed.), 710.

25. Cai Zhongxiang and Yuan Jixi ("*Wenxin diaolong* yu Wei-Jin xuan-xue," *Wenxin diaolong xuekan* 3 [1986]: 19) claim that, "without the abstruse learning of the Wei-Jin, there would be no *WXDL*" [沒有魏晉玄學就沒有文心雕龍]. Some may object to the hyperbole of such a statement, but it does point to the complexity of Liu Xie's work and to the eclecticism of the age. The implication of this is that any reading of the *WXDL* that claims that it is ideologically monolithic and pure is wrong. Sun Rongrong (*Wenxin diaolong yanjiu* 文心雕龍研究 (Nanjing: Jiangsu jiaoyu chubanshe, 1994), *passim*, but see especially 252–62) rightly insists that a balanced view of *WXDL* recognizes that it embraces elements of Confucianism, Taoism, and Buddhism.

"Mie huo lun" provides a good indication of Liu Xie's attitude toward the religion which he espoused. In it, he pays a great deal of attention to pointing out areas of compatibility between Buddhism and Confucianism, but is caustic in his remarks concerning Taoism. (The Taoists, after all, composed the "San po lun" 三破論 (On the three destructions), a savage denunciation of Buddhism, to which Liu Xie responds in "Mie huo lun." In spite of the fact that "Mie huo lun" is an open defense of Buddhism whereas *WXDL* is a work of literary criticism and theory, the ideological thrust of both is fundamentally the same: the compatibility of Confucianism and Buddhism. See Kimura Kiyota, "Ryū Kyō ni okeru 'Bukkyō' no yakuwari," *Shūkyō kenkyū* 42 (4): 71–73.

26. See, for example, Peng Enhua, trans., *Xingshan Hong Wenxin diaolong lunwenji* (Jinan: Qi-Lu shushe, 1984), 24–30. Rao Zongyi ("Wenxin yu Apitanxin," *Fanxue ji* [Shanghai: Shanghai guji chubanshe, 1993], 179–85) suggests that the notion of mind in *WXDL* may be linked to the idea of mind elaborated in the *Abhidharmahṛdaya-śāstra*, but he does not make a sustained or convincing argument in favor of such a suggestion.

27. See Sun Changwu, *Fojiao yu Zhongguo wenxue*, 333–34, for examples.

28. Ibid., 335.

29. *Hanyu da cidian* 漢語大詞典 (Great dictionary of Sinitic), vol. 7, 369–70a.

30. In Sanskrit, the equivalent compound would be one of the following: *kāvya-hṛdaya, sāhitya-hṛdaya, kāvya-citta,* or *sāhitya-citta*. I have not found any of these compounds attested in extant Sanskrit manuscripts from the period of the *WXDL*, but there was a Sanskrit text, probably from a later period, entitled *Sāhitya-hṛdaya-darpaṇa* (Mirror of the literary mind). See Monier Monier-Williams, *A Sanskrit-English Dictionary*, 1212c.

Wenxin appears in Chinese to consist of two nouns and, hence, should be considered as "literature-mind/essence" or, more felicitously, "the mind/ essence of literature." On the other hand, my English rendering of *wenxin* (following that of Vincent Shih) takes *wen* as an adjective, in which case it would be more proper to think of *wenxin* as a *karmadhārya* compound. The problem is that, since Literary Sinitic does not make overt morphological distinctions between adjectival and noun forms of a word, it is impossible to tell for certain which usage Liu Xie intended.

31. See Feng Chuntian, *Wenxin diaolong yuci tongshi*, 998. There is a difference, however, since in its previous classical occurrences, the expression *diaolong* must almost always be parsed as verb plus object ("carve dragons"), whereas in the title of *WXDL* it is constrained by the *tatpuruṣa* or *karmadhārya* formation of *wenxin* to act in a similarly attributive fashion, hence "carved dragons."

32. Richard B. Mather, *The Poet Shen Yüeh (441–513): The Reticent Marquis* (Princeton, N.J.: Princeton University Press, 1988), 55–56, 60–61.

33. Liu Xie wrote an entire chapter ("Shenglü" 聲律 [Rules for sounds]) on prosody and emphasized the musicality of poetry in other chapters of *WXDL*. This shows his affinity with Shen Yue. Rao Zongyi has written a lengthy article explaining the relationship between Liu Xie's exposition of prosody and Shen Yue's theory of the four tones, together with a discussion of the background of the latter in Siddham script studies and in Kumārajīva's (fl. 405) phonological treatise entitled *Tongyun* 通韻 (Comprehensive rhymes). A fragment of this text was recovered from Dunhuang (S1344), and

it has been preserved in its entirety in a couple of early Japanese sources. Several important findings emerge from the close study of Kumārajīva's *Comprehensive Rhymes*: (1) the phonological analysis of Chinese languages that emerged during the Six Dynasties was clearly derived from Indian models; (2) Kumārajīva played a vital role in the transmission of these Indian concepts to China; and (3) Liu Xie's chapter on prosody was profoundly influenced by this Indian tradition of phonological analysis.

34. For the ultimate Indian models that inspired the rules governing the four tones, see Victor H. Mair and Tsu-Lin Mei, "The Sanskrit Origins of Recent Style Prosody," *Harvard Journal of Asiatic Studies* 51, no. 2 (1991): 375–470.

35. Mather, *Shen Yüeh*, 135–73.

36. Wu, "Self-examination and Confession of Sins in Traditional China" (*Harvard Journal of Asiatic Studies* 39.1 [July 1979]: 5–38), 10–11. Shen Yue probably also considered himself to be something of a Taoist, since he called in a Taoist confessor on his deathbed. See Wu, "Self-examination," 12.

37. *Nan shi* 南史 (History of the southern dynasties) (Zhonghua shuju ed.), scroll 72, 1782.

38. Personal communication, April 11, 1997.

39. The chief sources for this section are M. Winternitz, *History of Indian Literature*. vol. 3, part 1: *Classical Sanskrit Literature;* part 2: *Scientific Literature*, Subhadra Jha, trans. (Delhi: Motilal Banarsidass, 1985), esp. 1–35; S. N. Dasgupta and S. K. De, *A History of Sanskrit Literature: Classical Period*. vol. 1: *History of Alaṃkāra Literature and History of Kāvya Literature* (Calcutta: University of Calcutta, 1947); S. D. De, ed., *History of Sanskrit Poetics*, 2d rev. ed. (Calcutta: K. L. Mukhopadhyaya, 1960); P. V. Kane, *History of Sanskrit Poetics*, 3rd rev. ed. (Delhi, Varanasi, Patna: Motilal Banarsidass, 1961); and Edwin Gerow, *Indian Poetics*, in *A History of Indian Literature*, edited by Jan Gonda, V, Fasc. 3 (Wiesbaden: Otto Harrassowitz, 1977).

40. As Edwin Gerow has justly pointed out (in a letter dated July 31, 1997), the usage of terms such as *alamkāra* and *upamā* by Pāṇini is not necessarily always identical to that of the later writers on prosody. Yet it is fair to say that the latter grew out of the former and they show an intense attentiveness to the fine nuances of poetic language. As an example of the extensive background of Indian poetics, we may note that Yāska (fl. 320 B.C.), author of the standard work on Vedic etymology and exegesis, himself mentions seventeen predecessors and deals with *upamā* (simile) in a rather sophisticated manner.

41. Victor H. Mair, "Ma Jianzhong and the Invention of Chinese Gram-

mar," in Chaofen Sun, ed., *Studies on the History of Chinese Syntax*, Journal of Chinese Linguistics Monograph Series, no. 10 (1997): 8, 20 (note 5).

42. Judging from its rather loose structure, diversity of styles, and abundant echoes in earlier and later texts, it is virtually certain that the *Nātyaśāstra* is not the purely original work of Bharata alone, but is more on the order of a compilation from previous sources.

43. Despite the fact that the *Nātyaśāstra* is intended mainly as an exposition of histrionic art, it also functions as a treatise on poetic literature in general. But note that Aristotle's *Poetics* was also based on the dramatic form. Indeed, the parallels between Aristotle's *Poetics* and Hellenistic dramatic theory on the one hand and Bharata's *Nātyaśāstra* and its commentaries on the other hand are so numerous and so striking that one cannot dismiss the possibility of contact. (These parallels include unity of action; unity of time; dramatic conventions limiting the number of persons on stage and restricting the portrayal of violent or unseemly actions; the doctrines of mimesis and *anukṛti* [imitation]; the classification of characters as ideal/high, real/middle, and inferior/low; division of the play into acts and scenes; use of the prologue; employment of stock characters; use of asides and soliloquies; etc.) This is especially the case since, as early as Pāṇini, reference was made to *yavanānī* (Greek writing).

44. Dasgupta and De, *History*, 532–33 (see esp. note on p. 532); P. V. Naganatha Sastry, ed., trans., and annot., *Kāvyālaṃkāra of Bhāmaha*, 2d ed. (Delhi: Motilal Banarsidass, 1970), ix. Many authorities dispute this date, however, and place Bhāmaha and Daṇḍin as late as the eighth or ninth century. There is also tremendous controversy over whether Bhāmaha or Daṇḍin came first. The most recent "general consensus," as reported by Gerow (in a letter dated July 31, 1997), is that "both Bhāmaha and Daṇḍin should be placed, more or less, in the seventh century—not later than the eighth, not earlier than the sixth."

45. De, *History*, vol. 1, pp. 50, 67–68, 109; vol. 2, 26. It cannot be emphasized too strongly that Bhāmaha and Daṇḍin are considered here as representatives of the Indian tradition of poetics that is clearly evident already in the *Nātyaśāstra*, manifestly embodied in the writing of the great Buddhist poet and dramatist, Aśvaghoṣa (second c. A.D.) (whose works have been found in Central Asia and were translated into Chinese well before Liu Xie's time), and developed by other prosodists before them whose names are known and quoted by them.

46. Tanya Storch, "Chinese Buddhist Historiography and Orality," *Sino-Platonic Papers* 37 (1993): 1–16.

47. For the hoary antiquity of the notion of the "body of poetry" (*kāvya-śarīra*) in India, see De, *History*, vol. 2, pp. 34–37, especially the long footnote number 4 on pp. 35–36.

48. It is noteworthy that an important, premodern commentary on the *Kāvyādarśa* is entitled *Hṛdayaṃgama*. Once again, the notion of "heart/mind" in relation to poetry is brought to the surface.

49. Gerow, *Indian Poetics*, 228.

50. In his essay in this volume.

51. Sun Changwu, *Fojiao yu Zhongguo wenxue*, 329.

52. One of the most characteristic features of Xuanxue was its eclecticism, drawing heavily as it did on the other three major systems of thought.

53. Lu Xun, "Chi jiao."

54. Vincent Shih, like many others, is thus mistaken when he states (*Literary Mind*, 203, note 16) that Liu Xie's use of *prajñā* "is the only occasion on which we find him using a Buddhist term explicitly." *Prajñā* may be the only transcribed Sanskrit term in *WXDL*, but it is far from being the only Buddhistically imbued expression in the book. This is the balanced view adopted by Liu Mengxi in his brilliant article, "Hanyi Fodian yu Zhongguo de wenti liubian," *Chuantong de wudu* (Shijiazhuang: Hebei jiaoyu chubanshe, 1996), 28–45.

55. See selection 19 (138–39) in Mair, *Columbia Anthology*. For more than two decades, I have been collecting materials that demonstrate the intimate relationship between the *liu fa* and the *ṣaḍaṅga*. I hope one day to prepare them for publication.

56. Similarly, we may ask whether Confucianism is a significant component of *WXDL*, to which we would be compelled to answer in the affirmative. The presence of Buddhism in *WXDL* by no means precludes the presence of Confucianism, and vice versa. It is a gross simplification to claim that *WXDL* is either exclusively Buddhist or exclusively Confucian.

57. In his closing remarks to the Illinois *WXDL* conference. Earlier, Richard Bodman made a similarly astute comment with regard to the *Bunkyō hifuron* as a *śāstra* (scholastic commentary). See William H. Nienhauser Jr., ed., *The Indiana Companion to Traditional Chinese Literature* (Bloomington, Ind.: Indiana University Press, 1986), 197a. Considering the history of the tradition in India, it is not at all unexpected that a late-ninth-century or early-tenth-century *śāstra* on poetics by Bhaṭṭanāyaka was entitled *Hṛdaya-darpaṇa* (Mirror of the heart/mind).

58. If we accept the proposition that the *WXDL* is in some sense a *kāvya-hṛdaya-alaṃkāraśāstra*, that is, a treatise on the soul (*ātman*) and the body (*śarīra*) of literature, as the Indian masters of poetics were wont to put it in

other terms (cf. above in the text note 47 and following), then Liu Xie shows himself to be all the more clever in making his polemical points in the Chinese argument over "carved dragons" (i.e., ornate rhetoric) versus the spirit of literature within the framework of an Indian *śāstra*. No mean feat!

Chapter 4

1. All translations from *Wenxin diaolong* are my own unless otherwise indicated.

2. According to the *Jingjizhi* 經籍志 (Treatise on bibliography) in the *Suishu* 隋書 (History of the Sui), under the category *Yijia* 易家 (Writers on the classic of changes), Sung Dai lived during the Jin 晉 dynasty (265–317) and was the author of *Zhouyi lun* 周易論 (Discourse on the *Changes of the Zhou*) in one *juan*. See Wei Zheng et al., eds., *Suishu* (Shanghai, Zhonghua shuju, 1973), 910.

3. "During the Liang [502–57] and Chen [557–89], the two commentaries [on the *Changes of the Zhou*] by Zheng Xuan and Wang Bi were both included in the curriculum of the National University. During the Qi era [479–502], only Zheng's interpretation had been taught, but, by the Sui [590–618], Wang's commentary had become predominant, and Zheng's approach gradually faded away to the point where nowadays it is virtually unknown." See *Jingjizhi* 經籍志 (Treatise on bibliography) in *Suishu*, 913.

4. This is a quotation from the *Zhuangzi* 莊子 (fourth century B.C.) (*Zhuangzi yinde* 莊子引得 ed.), 75/26/48.

5. This refers to the doubling of the trigrams to form the hexagrams; compare with "Xici zhuan" 繫辭傳 (Commentary on the appended phrases), Part 2, 1. See Richard John Lynn, trans., *The Classic of Changes: A New Translation of the I Ching As Interpreted by Wang Bi* (New York: Columbia University Press, 1994), 75. The "strokes" are, of course, the hexagram lines.

6. Lou Yulie, ed., *Wang Bi ji jiaoshi* (Critical edition of the works of Way Bi with explanatory notes), 609.

7. Lynn, *Classic of Changes*, 67.

8. Ibid., 138–39.

9. Ibid., 382.

10. Fung, Yu-lan, *A History of Chinese Philosophy*, Derk Bodde, trans. (Princeton, N.J.: Princeton University Press, 1953), vol. 2, 186.

11. Tang Junyi 唐君毅, *Zhongguo zhexue yuanlun: Yuan Tao pian* 中國哲學原論: 原道篇 (Fundamental discourses on Chinese philosophy: The Tao as source) (Hong Kong: Xinya yanjiusuo, 1973), vol. 2, 885.

12. Fung, *A History of Chinese Philosophy*, vol. 2, 186. Others have had the same trouble with 意 and 義 in Wang Bi's thought. Chung-yue Chang reviews the issue and also concludes that "the meanings are very close." Accordingly, he translates both as "meaning" when translating passages in Wang's works. See Chang-yue Chang, "The Metaphysics of Wang Pi (226–249)," Ph.D. Dissertation, University of Pennsylvania, 1979 (Ann Arbor: University Microfilms International, 1987), 45n45.

13. "Xici zhuan," Part 1, 11: "Therefore, in change there is the great ultimate. This is what generates the two modes [the yin and yang]." Han Kangbo's 韓康伯 (d. ca. 385) commentary states: "Existence necessarily has its origin in nothingness. Thus the great ultimate generates the two modes. Great ultimate is the term for that for which no term is possible. As we cannot lay hold of it and name it, we think of it in terms of the ultimate point to which we can extend existence and regard this as the great ultimate." See Lynn, *Classic of Changes*, 65.

14. Compare with "Shuo gua" 説卦 (Explaining the trigrams), Part 1: "In the distant past, the way the sage [Fu Xi] made the *Changes* is as follows: He was mysteriously assisted by the gods [*shenming*, literally, the numinous and the bright] and so initiated the use of yarrow stalks." See Lynn, *Classic of Changes*, 119.

15. Compare with Hexagram 22: *Bi* 賁 (Elegance), *Tuan* 彖 (Commentary on the judgments): "One looks to the pattern of Heaven in order to examine the flux of the seasons, and one looks to the pattern of man in order to transform and bring the whole world to perfection." See Lynn, *Classic of Changes*, 274.

16. Compare with " . . . the sun and the moon endlessly alternate their disks of jade and so suspend images that cohere to Heaven"—forming the "pattern of Heaven" (*tianwen* 天文).

17. From "Xici zhuan," part 1, 12; Lynn, *The Classic of Changes*, 68.

18. Compare with Hexagram 2, *Kun* 坤 (Pure Yin), First Yin, "Xiang zhuan" 象傳 (Commentary on the images): "The frost one treads on becomes solid ice: This yin thing begins to congeal. Obediently fulfilling its Tao [*xunzhi qi Dao* 馴致其道], it ultimately becomes solid ice." See Lynn, *Classic of Changes*, 146.

19. Reference here is to two parables in the *Zhuangzi*, one concerning Butcher Ding 庖丁 and the other concerning Carpenter Shi 匠石; see *Zhuangzi yinde*, 7/3/2 and 66/24/48.

20. Lynn, *The Classic of the Way and Virtue: A New Translation of the Tao-te ching of Laozi as Interpreted by Wang Bi* (New York: Columbia University Press, 1999), 32.

21. It is likely that Wang refers here to the *ming* 名 (name)–*shi* 實 (actuality) problem that preoccupied many thinkers of the late Han and early Wei eras. Many scholars were attacked for supposedly failing to ensure that the names they used matched the realities to which the names pointed; they were punished for using "false" names. The most important figure concerned with the *ming-shi* problem at this time was Xu Gan 徐幹 (170–217), who died a little less than a decade before Wang Bi was born. For a detailed history and analysis of the name-reality issue and Xu Gan's role, see John Makeham, *Name and Actuality in Early Chinese Thought* (Albany, N.Y.: State University of New York Press, 1994). Wang, of course, says that those who try to fault the *Laozi* on such grounds are missing the point: a name cannot, because of its limited nature and limiting function, ever designate ultimate reality, the Tao, in any of its aspects.

22. Compare with *Laozi*, Section 52: "All under Heaven has a generatrix, which we regard as the mother of all under Heaven. Once we have access to the mother, through it we can know the child. Once one knows the child, if he again holds on to his mother, as long as he lives, no danger shall befall him." See Lynn, *Classic of the Way and Virtue*, 151.

23. Compare with *Laozi*, Section 79.

24. Lynn, *Classic of the Way and Virtue*, 33.

25. Translation by James J. Y. Liu, *Language—Paradox—Poetics: A Chinese View*, Richard John Lynn, ed. (Princeton, N.J.: Princeton University Press, 1988), 8.

26. The "Overlapping Trigrams" (*Huti*) method was a popular way to interpret the *Changes* in early times. Lou Yulie 樓宇烈 provides a succinct description: "The Overlapping Trigrams was a method used by the Han era specialists on the *Changes* to interpret the hexagrams. . . . In all hexagrams, sets of the second, third, and fourth lines and sets of the third, fourth, and fifth lines mingle together but each set separately forms a trigram. This is what is meant by one hexagram contains four trigrams [images]." See *Wang Bi ji jiaoshi*, 612n20. For example, Hexagram 26, *Daxu* 大畜 (Great domestication), consists of the trigrams *Qian* 乾 (Pure Yang) below and *Gen* 艮 (Restraint) above, but, at the same time, it also contains the trigrams *Dui* 兌 (Joy) (lines 2–4) and *Zhen* 震 (Quake) (lines 3–5). The point that Liu makes here is that just as "the images change right before our eyes" in the "overlapping trigrams" method of interpreting the hexagrams (one hexagram contains four trigram/images), so can the "recondite" literary mode simultaneously convey multiple meanings using the same words.

27. The notion that pearls and jadestones on the bottom of bodies of water can give different shapes to waves on the surface may strike one as fanciful.

Yet, as any good fly-fisherman knows when "reading" a trout stream, differently shaped objects (sunken logs, rocks, etc.), even those deep under water, form distinctly different ripples on the surface.

28. *Zhishi* 指事 (Point to the thing) is the first of Xu Shen's 許慎 (fl. ca. 100 A.D.) Six Graphic Principles [of Chinese characters] (*liushu* 六書): the simple ideogram *zaoxing* 造形 (reproduce the form/make a semblance of something) is probably a variant of *xiangxing* 象 [像] 形 (image the form), Xu's second Graphic Principle: the simple pictogram. See Xu Shen, *Shuowen jiezi* 說文解字 (Explanations of simple and compound characters) (Taipei: Yiwen yinshuguan, 1974), 15A:3a–3b. Wang Bi here reminds his reader of the limited way language functions—too limited to capture the ontological reality of the Tao because it always must refer to things on the phenomenological level. *Zaoxing* also occurs in the *Zhuangzi*: "Although your lordship would practice benevolence and righteousness, it almost amounts to counterfeit versions of them! Their forms certainly may be reproduced, but if you were successful, it would unquestionably provoke attack, and, once such abnormality occurred, foreign states would assault you without fail" [君雖為仁義，幾且偽哉。形固造形。成固有伐。變固有外戰。]. See *Zhuangzi yinde*, 65/24/21. Wang Bi also probably had this passage in mind: Not only is language limited to the phenomenological, it is a mere false approximation of the phenomenological at best.

29. Lynn, *Classic of the Way and Virtue*, 51.

30. Zhong Rong, *Shipin* 詩品 (Classes of poetry), Cheng Yanjie, ed. (Beijing: Renmin wenxue chubanshe, 1980), 2.

Chapter 5

1. I am grateful to Stephen Owen for bringing this possibility to my attention in his comments on an earlier version of this essay.

2. A. C. Graham, *Chuang-tzu: The Seven Inner Chapters and Other Writings from the Book Chuang-tzu* (London: George Allen & Unwin, 1981), 18. For Graham's justification of "daimon" (alternatively, "daemon") as a translation for *shen*, see ibid., p. 35, note 72.

3. Throughout this paper, the section and paragraph numbers given for the *Wenxin diaolong* text are my own and reflect divisions I feel to be natural in the chapter. The secondary numbers, given in parentheses, are line numbers as assigned in the standard text, *Wenxin diaolong suoyin*.

4. *Zhuangzi yinde* 莊子引得 (A concordance to *Zhuangzi*), Harvard-Yenching Institute Sinological Index Series, supplement no. 20 (Cambridge,

Mass.: Harvard University Press, 1956 reprint), 79/28/56; trans. Graham, *Chuang-tzu*, 229.

5. Lu Ji, "Wen fu," lines 17–18 and 33–34, Jin Taosheng, ed., *Lu Ji ji* 陸機 集 (Collected works of Lu Ji) (Beijing: Zhonghua shuju, 1982), vol. 1, sections 1 and 2, following the line numbering in Knechtges, *Refined Literature*, vol. 3, 215.

6. This point is made by Sun Rongrong, *Wenxin diaolong yanjiu*, 92.

7. *WXDL* 47/28. Elsewhere in *Wenxin diaolong*, however, this nuance may be absent. See, for example, the usage in *WXDL* 47/3.

8. Reading the textual variant *yi* 繹 in place of *yi* 懌.

9. See Lu Ji, "Wen fu," lines 15–16, *Lu Ji ji*, 1.1 (Knechtges, *Refined Literature*, vol. 3, 215), and Xi Kang, "Qin fu" 琴賦 (A rhapsody on the lute), lines 143–52, in Dai Mingyang, ed., *Xi Kang ji jiaozhu* 嵇康集校注 (Collation and commentary on the works of Xi Kang) (Beijing: Renmin wenxue chu-banshe, 1962), 2.94–95 (following the line numbering in Knechtges, *Refined Literature*, vol. 3, 291).

10. Following the interpretation in Zhan Ying, ed., *Wenxin diaolong yi-zheng*, chapter 26, 984, note 6. For other instances of this pairing of *shengmo* 繩墨 and *fujin* 斧斤, see *WXDL* 32/17–18, and Xi Kang, "Qin fu," lines 85–86, *Xi Kang ji jiaozhu*, 2.90 (Knechtges, *Refined Literature*, vol. 3, 287).

11. *Zai* 宰 here is usually understood as "cook," making the clause an allu-sion to Cook Ding in *Zhuangzi*. But it is difficult to apply the phrase *xuanjie* 玄解 to the famous cook, especially when it is matched with the phrase *du-zhao* 獨照, and the carpenter reference itself seems to be a composite (see below). Also, the parallelism of "ink" and "ax," as explained in note 10 above, makes it awkward to understand *zai* in its obvious sense. Instead, I am treat-ing *zai* as a synonym of *jiang* 匠, as in the phrase *zaijiang* 宰匠, describing he who "gives shape to, fashions, has control of." I am reading *xuanjie* in the sense it has elsewhere in *Zhuangzi*; see *Zhuangzi yinde* 8/3/19 and Graham, *Chuang-tzu*, 65.

12. *Zhuangzi yinde* 66/24/48–49, 7/3/2–6.

13. Those who read the lines this way include Zhou Zhenfu, *Wenxin diao-long jinyi* 文心雕龍今譯 (A modern translation of *Wenxin diaolong*) (Bei-jing: Zhonghua shuju, 1986), 248, and see his paraphrase on 245; Toda Kogyo, *Bunshin choryu* 文心雕龍 (*Wenxin diaolong*) (Tokyo: Meitoku Shuppansha, 1972), vol. 2, 397; Du Lijun, *Wenxin diaolong wenxue lilun yanjiu he yishi* 文 心雕龍文學理論研究和譯釋 (Translation, annotation, and study of the literary theory in *Wenxin diaolong*) (Beijing: Beijing chubanshe, 1981), 132; Guo Jinxi, *Wenxin diaolong zhuyi* 文心雕龍注譯 (Annotation and transla-

tion of *Wenxin diaolong*) (Lanzhou: Kansu renmin chubanshe, 1982), 321; He Suishi, *Wenxin diaolong jindu* 文心雕龍今讀 (A modern reading of *Wenxin diaolong*) (Henan: Wenxin chubanshe, 1987), 139; and Zhao Zhongyi, *Wenxin diaolong yizhu* 文心雕龍譯注 (Translation and annotation of *Wenxin diaolong*) (Taipei: Guanya wenhua shiye youxian gongsi, 1991), 291.

Interestingly, Zhou Zhenfu changed to this "literal" reading after interpreting the same lines more flexibly and contextually in his earlier selective translation; see his *Wenxin diaolong xuanyi* 文心雕龍選譯 (Translated selections from *Wenxin diaolong*) (Beijing: Zhonghua shuju, 1980), 132.

14. Those who read the lines as I do include Lu Kanru and Mou Shijin, eds., *Wenxin diaolong yizhu* 文心雕龍譯注 (Translation and annotation of *Wenxin diaolong*) (Jinan: Qilu shushe, 1981), vol. 2, 88; Sun Rongrong, *Wenxin diaolong yanjiu*, 93; and Wang Gengsheng, *Wenxin diaolong duben* 文心雕龍讀本 (*Wenxin diaolong*: A reader) (Taipei: Wen shi zhe chubanshe, 1985), B.26, 14. Stephen Owen also argues in favor of this reading in an endnote, although it is not reflected in his translation or discussion of the passage; see *Readings*, 611, note 78, 205–6. For Zhou Zhenfu, see note 13 above.

15. For the pairing of *si* and *yan* in "Wen fu," see, for example, lines 47–48, 67–68, *Lu Ji ji*, 1.2 (Knechtges, *Refined Literature*, vol. 3, 217).

16. For the pairing of *yi* and *wen* in "Wen fu," see the preface and lines 125–126, *Lu Ji ji*, 1.1, 1.3 (Knechtges, *Refined Literature*, vol. 3, 211, 217).

17. From Fan Ye's letter to his nephews, quoted in Shen Yue, *Song shu* 宋書 (History of the [Liu] Song) (Beijing: Zhonghua shuju, 1974), 69.1830.

18. Quoted in the commentary by Fan Wenlan in Fan Wenlan, *Wenxin diaolong zhu* 文心雕龍註 (Annotated edition of *Wenxin diaolong*) (Beijing: Renmin wenxue chubanshe, 1978), 6/26:501.

19. On Sima Xiangru's slowness in writing, see Ban Gu, *Han shu* 漢書 (History of the Han) (Beijing: Zhonghua shuju, 1962), 51.2367. On Yang Xiong's nightmare, see Huan Tan, "Qubi," in *Xin lun* 新論 (New treatise), *Quan Hou Han wen* 全後漢文 (Complete prose of the later Han), in Yan Kejun, comp., *Quan shanggu sandai Qin Han sanguo liuchao wen* 全上古三代秦漢三國六朝文 (Complete prose of antiquity, the Three Dynasties, Qin, Han, the three kingdoms, and the Six Dynasties) (Beijing: Zhonghua shuju, 1965), 14.6a.

20. On Huan Tan, see "Qubi," *Xin lun*, in *Quan Hou Han wen*, 14.6a. On Wang Chong and his massive *Lun heng*, see Fan Ye, comp., *Hou Han shu* 後漢書 (History of the later Han) (Beijing: Zhonghua shuju, 1965), 49.1630.

21. On Zhang Heng's ten years, see Fan Ye, *Hou Han shu* 59.1897. On Zuo Si's dozen, see Li Shan's commentary on Zuo's "San du fu xu," in Xiao

Tong, comp., *Wen xuan* 文選 (Selections of refined literature), Hu Kejia, ed. (Taipei: Zhengzhong shuju, 1971), 14.12a, quoting Zang Rongxu, *Jin shu.*

22. Liu An's (Prince of Huainan) rhapsody on the famous "Encountering Sorrow" does not surivive, but his speed in composing it is referred to in Gao You, "Huainanzi xu" 淮南子序 (Preface to *Huainanzi*) in *Quan Hou Han wen* 全後漢文, in Yan Kejun, comp., *Quan Shanggu sandai Qin Han sanguo liuchao wen,* 17.8a. On Mei Gao, see Ban Gu, *Han shu,* 51.2367.

23. On Cao Zhi, see Yang Xiu (Yang Dezu), "Da Linzi hou jian," in Xiao Tong, comp., *Wen Xuan,* 40.14b. On Wang Can, see Chen Shou, comp., *Sanguo zhi* 三國志 (Memoirs of the three kingdoms) (Beijing: Zhonghua shuju, 1959), 21.599.

24. On Ruan Yu, see Pei Songzhi's commentary on *Sanguo zhi,* 21.601, note 2. On Mi Feng, see *Hou Han shu* 80B.2657.

25. Reading the textual variant *gui* 貴 for *fei* 費.

26. Other examples of this construction occur in *WXDL* 24/102–5, 28/17–20, 32/102–5, and 35/105–8.

27. Reading the textual variant *ti* 體 for *ci* 辭.

28. Wang Yuanhua, *Wenxin diaolong chuangzuo lun* 文心雕龍創作論 (The theory of literary creation in *Wenxin diaolong*) (Shanghai: Shanghai guji chubanshe, 1979), 95–99.

29. Lu Ji, "Wen fu," lines 141–42, *Lu Ji ji,* 1.3 (Knechtges, *Refined Literature,* vol. 3, 223).

30. For Yi Yin (Zhi), see D. C. Lau et al., ed., "Ben wei," *Lüshi chunqiu zhuzi suoyin* 呂氏春秋逐字索引 (A concordance to *Spring and Autumn Annals of Master Lü*), The ICS Ancient Chinese Texts Concordance Series, no. 12 (Hong Kong: Commercial Press, 1994), 14.2/71/20; and for Wheelwright Bian, see *Zhuangzi* 36/13/68–74.

31. Sima Qian, *Shiji* 史記 (Records of the Grand Historian) (Beijing: Zhonghua shuju, 1959), 8.381.

32. *Xunzi yinde* 荀子引得 (A concordance to *Xunzi*), Harvard-Yenching Institute Sinological Index Series, Supplement no. 22 (Taipei: Ch'eng-wen Publishing Company, 1966), 80/21/34 and 41–42.

33. Cao Zhi, "BaoTao fu," *Cao Zhi ji jiaozhu* 曹植集校注 (Collation and annotation on the works of Cao Zhi) (Beijing: Renmin wenxue chubanshe, 1984), 1.160. There is, however, a textual variant *shengong* 神功 for *shensi.*

34. Xi Kang, "Qin fu," *Xi Kang Ji Jiaozhu,* 2.90; trans. Knechtges, *Refined Literature,* vol. 3, 287.

35. Sun Zhuo, "You Tiantai shan fu," in Xiao Tong, comp., *Wen Xuan,* 11.4b; trans. Knechtges, *Refined Literature,* vol. 2, 243–44.

36. Xiao Zixian, comp., *Nan Qi Shu* 南齊書 (History of the southern Qi) (Beijing: Zhonghua shuju, 1972), 52.907. This and other examples in this paragraph are cited by Chen Siling, *Wenxin diaolong yilun* 文心雕龍臆論 (Speculative thoughts on *Wenxin diaolong*) (Chengdu: Bashu shushe, 1986), 63, 66.

37. A similar point is made by Chen Siling, *Wenxin diaolong yilun*, 63–65.

Chapter 6

1. James J. Y. Liu has observed: "Various modern scholars have identified Liu Hsieh's 'intuitive thinking' (*shen-ssu*) with 'imagination' or its modern Chinese equivalent, *hsiang-hsiang.*" See *Chinese Theories of Literature*, 125, and 164, note 20.

2. Ronald Egan has noted several early appearances of the term in his paper, "Poet, Mind, and World: A Reconsideration of the 'Shensi' Chapter of *Wenxin diaolong*," Chapter 5 of the present volume.

3. For instance, see Li Zehou and Liu Gangji, *Zhongguo meixueshi* 中國美學史 (A history of Chinese aesthetics) (Taipei: Gufeng chubanshe, 1978), vol. 2, 817.

4. Zhu Xi, *Chuci jizhu* 楚辭集注 (Collected commentaries on the *Songs of Chu*) (Taipei: Wanguo tushu gongsi, 1956), vol. 1, 141.

5. Xiao Tong, *Wen xuan* 文選 (Selections of refined literature) (Taipei: Shangwu yinshuguan, 1960), vol. 1, 405.

6. Ibid., 579.

7. Warnock, *Imagination*, 10. Her other book on imagination is *Imagination and Time* (Oxford: Blackwell Publishers, 1994).

8. I. A. Richards, *Principles of Literary Criticism* (London: Routledge & Kegan Paul LTD, 1924), 239.

9. Alex Preminger, ed., *The Princeton Handbook of Poetic Terms* (Princeton, N.J.: Princeton University Press, 1986), 98.

10. Warnock, *Imagination*, 10.

11. Preminger, *The Princeton Handbook of Poetic Terms*, 98.

12. Ibid.

13. Johnson, *The Body in the Mind*, 141. Here Johnson follows the observation made by Harold Osborne in *Aesthetics and Art Theory: An Historical Introduction* (New York: E. P. Dutton, 1968), 208. Osborne defines our modern usage of imagination as "a power of the mind to mold experience into something new, to create fictive situations and by sympathetic feeling to put oneself into the other man's place." Mary Warnock also begins her discussions of the subject with John Locke (1632–1704), George Berkeley (1685–1753), David

Hume (1711–76), and Immanuel Kant (1724–1804) in her two books, *Imagination* and *Imagination and Time*.

14. Johnson, *The Body in the Mind*, 141.

15. Ibid., 141–44.

16. Ibid., 143–44.

17. Ibid., 144.

18. Ibid.

19. Ibid., 145.

20. M. H. Abrams, *The Mirror and the Lamp: Romantic Theory and the Critical Tradition* (New York: W. W. Norton & Company, Inc., 1953), vi.

21. Ibid.

22. This has been touched upon in Abrams, *The Mirror and the Lamp*, 64–68; Warnock, *Imagination and Time*, 1–16; and Johnson, *The Body in the Mind*, 25–29.

23. Samuel Taylor Coleridge, "Dejection: An Ode," in I. A. Richards, ed., *The Portable Coleridge* (New York: The Viking Press, 1950), 172.

24. Ibid., 170.

25. Abrams, *The Mirror and the Lamp*, 67.

26. Abrams has pointed this out. See *The Mirror and the Lamp*, 66–67. The metaphors can be found in the third and fourth stanzas of Coleridge's "Dejection." See Richards, *The Portable Coleridge*, 170–71.

27. Warnock, *Imagination and Time*, 33.

28. Quoted in Warnock, *Imagination*, 78.

29. Walter Jackson Bate, ed., *Criticism: The Major Texts* (New York: Harcourt, Brace & World, 1952), 379.

30. Ibid., 387.

31. Warnock, *Imagination and Time*, 12–15, 41–42.

32. Ibid., 13.

33. Ibid. Mark Johnson has provided a brilliant detailed analysis of Kant's theory of the imagination, including Kant's ideas about the "schematizing activity of the imagination." See *The Body in the Mind*, 147–70.

34. Warnock, *Imagination and Time*, 14.

35. Kant's phrase is quoted in *Imagination and Time*, 30.

36. Ibid., 42.

37. Mark Johnson, *The Body in the Mind*, 155.

38. Li Zehou and Liu Gangji have noted this in their *Zhongguo meixueshi*, vol. 2, 818.

39. Zhu Xi, *Sishu jizhu* 四書集注 (Collected commentaries on the four books) (Taipei: Xuehai chubanshe, 1989), 64.

40. Qu Wanli, *Shijing quanshi* 詩經詮釋 (Annotated *Book of Songs*) (Taipei: Lianjing chubanshe, 1983), 151, 339.

41. Xiao Yan's "Xiaosifu" 孝思賦 (Rhapsody on filial thought) can be found in Yan Kejun, *Quan shanggu sandai qinhan sanguo liuchao wen*, vol. 7, *Quanliangwen* 全梁文, juan 1, 1, 3.

42. Li Zehou and Liu Gangji, *Zhongguo meixueshi*, vol. 2, 818.

43. Warnock, *Imagination and Time*, 6.

44. Li Zehou and Liu Gangji, *Zhongguo meixueshi*, vol. 2, 818.

45. Ruan Yuan 阮元, *Shisanjing zhushu* 十三經注疏 (Commentaries on the thirteen classics) (Taipei: Yiwen yinshuguan, 1965), 166. My translation of the passage is adapted from *I Ching, or Book of Changes*, translated into English by Cary F. Baynes from the German translation of Richard Wilhelm, 328–29.

46. Ibid.

47. A. C. Graham, trans., *Chuang-tzu: The Inner Chapters* (London: Mandala, 1986), 18.

48. Ibid., 35.

49. Ibid.

50. Ibid., 18.

51. Ibid.

52. "Yangqi," *WXDL*, 42/4–5, 358.

53. A. C. Graham translates Prince Mou's remark as follows: "My body is here by the river and the sea, but my heart lingers on under the city gate-towers of Wei." See Graham, *Chuang-tzu*, 229. "The city gate-towers of Wei" is Graham's rendering of 魏闕. This certainly makes sense because Prince Mou was from the State of Wei 魏國. However, according to good ancient commentaries, 魏 here is supposed to be a loan word for 巍, meaning "lofty." "Lofty" is used to qualify the life of wealth, prestige, and status that Prince Mou is reminiscing about while he is in retirement. See the discussion of the meaning of 魏闕 in Wang Shumin 王叔岷, *Zhuangzi jiaoquan* 莊子校詮 (A collated commentary on *Zhuangzi*) (Taipei: Zhongyang yanjiuyuan lishi yuyan yanjiusuo, 1988), vol. 3, 1148–49. In translating passages from *WXDL*, I have consulted the translations by Vincent Yu-chung Shih (*The Literary Mind and the Carving of Dragons*), Stephen Owen (*Readings in Chinese Literary Thought*), and Ronald Egan (Chapter 5 in this volume). It goes without saying that I have benefited from their translations.

54. Zhang Shuxiang, "Shensi yu xiangxiang" 神思與想像 (Daimonic thinking and imagination), in *Zhonghua wenhua fuxing yuekan* 中華文化復興月刊 (Chinese cultural renaissance monthly) 8, no. 8 (1975), 43–49. This is a remarkably thorough and insightful article comparing "daimonic think-

ing" with the Western concept of "imagination." I shall refer extensively to Professor Zhang's findings in this article. See p. 43 in the article for the current reference.

55. Ibid.

56. Egan has already commented on this in Chapter 5.

57. Zhang Shuxiang, "Shensi yu xiangxiang," 44. My discussion of "literary thinking" in this paragraph and the following are heavily drawn from Professor Zhang's article. See especially 44–45.

58. *WXDL* 26/30, p. 338.

59. Shih, *The Literary Mind and the Carving of Dragons*, 216.

60. Zhou Zhenfu, *Wenxin diaolong xuanyi*, 130.

61. Stephen Owen's translation can be found in *Readings*, 201, and in Chapter 5 in this volume.

62. Zhang Shuxiang, "Shensi yu xiangxiang."

63. *WXDL* 8/66, 310; 22/159, 331; and 1/8, 301.

64. *WXDL* 47/214, 367.

65. The seven emotions are joy, anger, sorrow, fear, love, hatred, and desire.

66. I have consulted James J. Y. Liu's translation of this passage, along with translations by Vincent Shih, Stephen Owen, and Ronald Egan. Liu's translation can be found in his book *Chinese Theories of Literature*, 75. Passage 1 is from "Mingshi" 明 詩 (An exegesis of poetry), passage 2, from "Wuse" 物 色 (The colors of things), and passage 3 from "Tixing" 體 性 (Style and nature).

67. William Wordsworth, "Preface to the Second Edition of the *Lyrical Ballads*" in Walter Jackson Bate, ed., *Criticism*, 344.

68. Xu Fuguan has reviewed the early usage of the term in these ancient texts in his article "Zhongguo wenxuezhong de qi de wenti—*Wenxin diaolong* fenggupian shubu" 中 國 文 學 中 的 氣 的 問 題——文 心 雕 龍 風 骨 篇 疏 補 (The issue of *qi* in Chinese literature—a supplementary commentary on the "Wind and Bone" chapter of *Wenxin diaolong*), in *Zhongguo wenxue lunji* 中 國 文 學 論 集 (Critical essays on Chinese literature) (Taizhong: Minzhu pinglunshe, 1966), 297–98.

69. A brief discussion of *qi* in *Wenxin diaolong* can be found in David Pollard, "Ch'i [i.e., *Qi*] in Chinese Literary Theory," in Adele Austin Rickett, ed., *Chinese Approaches to Literature from Confucius to Liang Ch'i-ch'ao* (Princeton: Princeton University Press, 1978), 50–51. Pollard has acknowledged that his article "was chiefly inspired by, and is greatly indebted to" Xu Fuguan's article "Zhongguo wenxuezhong de qi de wenti—*Wenxin diaolong* fenggupian shubu."

70. Susan Bush has suggested this in her book *The Chinese Literati on Painting: Su Shih (1037–1101) to Tung Ch'i-ch'ang (1555–1636)* (Cambridge, Mass.: Harvard University Press, 1971), 16.

71. Zhu Xi, *Sishu jizhu*, 234–35.

72. Liu, *Chinese Theories of Literature*, 68.

73. Xu Fuguan, "Zhongguo wenxuezhong de qi de wenti—*Wenxin diaolong* fenggupian shubu," 303–4.

74. I borrow this rendering from Stephen Owen, *Readings*, 210.

75. Wang Yuanhua mentions numerous scholars including Zhang Heng Zheng Xuan, Lu Ji, Xi Kang, and Shen Yue, who have used the term *qingzhi* 情志 in their writings. See his book *Wenxin diaolong jiangshu* 文心雕龍講疏 (Explications of *Wenxin diaolong*) (Taipei: Shulin chubanshe, 1993), 186–87.

76. This is to be found in the "Fuhui" 附會 chapter. (*WXDL* 43/12).

77. This conception of the origin of poetry and literature is naturalistic because the poet or writer is not viewed as being inspired by the muses or other supernatural powers.

78. Sun Yaoyu presents this argument in his article "*Wenxin diaolong* shenyongxiangtong shuo tanxi" 文心雕龍神用象通說探析 (An inquiry into the theory of 'When the daimon is at work, images are accomplished' in *Wenxin diaolong*), in *Wenxin diaolong xuekan*, 6 (1992), 206–15, especially 209–11. Stephen Owen also recognizes the difference between the *wu* in the "Shensi" chapter and that in the "Wuse" chapter. Owen says, "In 'Spirit Thought' [i.e., 'daimonic thinking'] [Liu] had used the term *wu* in the broader philosophical sense of 'object,' meaning whatever might be encountered by mind in the spirit journey. Here [in the "Wuse" chapter] *wu* are the preeminently physical things of the natural world, sensuous presences." See Owen, *Readings*, 277.

79. Sun Yaoyu, "*Wenxin diaolong* shenyongxiangtong shuo tanxi," 206–7. Here I follow Sun Yaoyu's adoption of Wang Yuanhua's interpretation of *shen yong xiang tong* 神用象通 and read *yong* 用 as "to be applied" rather than "to use" and *tong* as "to accomplish." This line is usually read by scholars as: "The daimon uses images to get through." See Wang Yuanhua's interpretation in *Wenxin diaolong jiangshu*, 111, 205.

80. Wang Shumin, *Zhuangzi jiaoquan*, vol. 1, 181.

81. Ibid., vol. 3, 1331. The rendering of this phrase as "rolling smoothly along with things" can be found in A. C. Graham, *Chuang-tzu: The Inner Chapters*, 279.

82. I am indebted to Wang Yuanhua for identifying and explaining the allusion. See *Wenxin diaolong jiangshu*, 90–91.

83. Shih, *The Literary Mind and the Carving of Dragons*, 217. Stephen Owen also takes the line as an allusion to the Cook Ding story. See *Readings*, 204, 610, note 76.

84. The meaning of the line Zhou Zhenfu gives can be found in his *Wenxin diaolong xuanyi*, 131. He cites the allusion to *Zhuangzi* in his other book, *Wenxin diaolong zhushi*, 298. However, the source of the original line is from the "What matters in the nurture of life" chapter and not from the "The world of men" chapter, as Zhou indicates.

85. See Guo Qingfan, *Zhuangzi jishi* 莊子集釋 (Collected annotations on *Zhuangzi*) (Taipei: Shijie shuju, 1962), vol. 1, 129.

86. See Owen, *Readings*, 610, note 76.

87. Zhang Shuxiang, "Shensi yu xiangxiang," 49.

88. Xiao Tong, *Wenxuan*, vol. 2, 1128.

89. Xu Fuguan, "Zhongguo wenxuezhong de qi de wenti—*Wenxin diaolong* fenggupian shubu," 302, 304. Xu thinks that Liu Xie's distinction between "the firm and the yielding" in pneuma is an improvement from Cao Pi's original distinction.

90. Johnson, *The Body in the Mind*, xv.

91. Ibid., 29.

92. Ibid., xiv.

93. Ibid.

94. Ibid., 169.

95. This is a modified version of the English translation of the passage from Wilhelm's German translation of *The I Ching, or Book of Changes*, 328–29.

96. Ibid., l. To restore Wilhelm's own rendering, I have substituted the word "trigrams" in Baynes's English translation with "signs."

97. Ibid., l–li.

98. Owen, *Readings*, 277.

99. Ibid.

100. Zong-qi Cai has already noted this in his article "Huazihuasi he Liu Xie de wenxue chuangzao shixue" 華茲華斯和劉勰的文學創造詩學 (The poetics of literary creation in William Wordsworth and Liu Xie) in *Wenxin diaolong yanjiu* 文心雕龍研究 (Research on *Wenxin diaolong*) (Beijing: Beijing University Press, 1998), vol. 3, 218–19.

101. This is modified from Stephen Owen's translation in *Readings*, 286.

102. Shih, *The Literary Mind and the Carving of Dragons*, 353–54.

103. Li Zehou and Liu Gangji, *Zhongguo meixueshi*, vol. 2, 826. The last two lines of this passage are difficult and ambiguous. Scholars have offered various interpretations of them. For the second to last line, I follow Zhou

Zhenfu in reading *yan* 研 as *yanjiu* 研究 (study, investigate), *yue* 閱 as *yueli* 閱歷 (experience), and *zhao* 照 as *guanzhao* 觀照 (observation, reflection). See Zhou Zhenfu, *Wenxin diaolong xuanyi*, 131. For the last line, I follow Li Zehou and Liu Gangji in reading *xun* 馴 as *shi . . . pinghe* 使 . . . 平和 (to make calm) and *zhi* 致 as *xinsi, qingzhi* 心思、情致 (mental, emotional state). See Li Zehou and Liu Gangji, *Zhongguo meixueshi*, vol. 2, 826.

104. Zhou Zhenfu, Li Zehou, and Liu Gangji have observed this. See Zhou Zhenfu, *Wenxin diaolong zhushi*, 304–5; Li Zehou and Liu Gangji, *Zhongguo meixueshi*, vol. 2, 826.

105. Zhou Zhenfu has briefly discussed this in *Wenxin diaolong zhushi*, 303–4.

106. Ma Xulun 馬敘倫, *Laozi jiaogu* 老子校詁 (A collated commentary on *Laozi*) (Hong Kong: Wanguo chubanshe, 1983), 63. The English translation is from D. C. Lau, *Lao Tzu: Tao Te Ching* (New York: Penguin Books, 1963), 72.

107. Wang Shumin, *Zhuangzi jiaoquan*, vol. 2, 818.

108. Scholars in the past, such as Wang Fuzhi and Yao Nai 姚鼐 (1732–1815), have pointed out that "Knowledge roams north" is close to "The great and venerable teacher" chapter in meaning and content. See Wang Shumin, *Zhuangzi jiaoquan*, vol. 2, 805.

109. Ibid., vol. 1, 130. My translation is adapted from the renderings by A. C. Graham and Burton Watson. For Graham's translation, see A. C. Graham, *Chuang-tzu: The Inner Chapters*, 68. For Watson's translation, see *The Complete Works of Chuang Tzu* (New York: Columbia University Press, 1968), 57–58.

110. Wang Shumin, *Zhuangzi jiaoquan*, vol. 1, 268. The English translation is from A. C. Graham, *Chuang-tzu: The Inner Chapters*, 92.

111. Chen Guying, *Zhuangzi jinzhu jinyi* 莊子今注今譯 (Zhuangzi: a modern commentary and translation) (Beijing: Zhonghua shuju, 1983), 117.

112. Wang Shumin, *Zhuangzi jiaoquan*, vol. 1, 132.

113. Ibid., 105.

114. Lu Ji, "Wen fu" 文賦 (Rhapsody on literature) in Xiao Tong, *Wenxuan*, vol. 1, 350. Stephen Owen has discussed this passage in some detail; see *Readings*, 96–98.

115. The term *xujing* appears twice in "The way of heaven" 天道 chapter in the Outer Chapters section of *Zhuangzi*. Both *xu* and *jing* also appear separately numerous other times in this chapter. Wang Fuzhi has pointed out that many of the ideas in this chapter conflict with the philosophy of Zhuangzi, the author of the Inner Chapters and some other portions of the text. He

thinks that the chapter is an expansion on Laozi's idea of "adhering to stillness" [守靜]. He suspects that the chapter was written by somebody during the Qin or early Han dynasties. See Wang Shumin, *Zhuangzi jiaoquan*, vol. 1, 471.

116. Watson, trans., *Hsun Tzu: Basic Writings* (New York: Columbia University Press, 1963), 127.

117. Li Zehou and Liu Gangji, *Zhongguo meixueshi*, vol. 2, 824. Wang Yuanhua thinks that Liu Xie's concept of "emptiness and stillness" is not derived from Laozi and Zhuangzi but from Xunzi. See Wang Yuanhua, *Wenxin diaolong jiangshu*, 118–21.

118. A. C. Graham, *Chuang-tzu: The Inner Chapters*, 98.

119. Ibid., 19.

Chapter 7

1. Among these chapters, I count "Yuan Dao" 原道, "Shensi" 神思, "Tixing" 體性, "Tongbian" 通變, "Fenggu" 風骨, "Dingshi" 定勢, "Qingcai" 情采, "Yinxiu" 隱秀, "Yangqi" 養氣, "Fuhui" 附會, "Zongshu" 總術, "Shixu" 時序, "Wuse" 物色, "Cailüe" 才略, "Zhiyin" 知音, "Chengqi" 程器, and "Xuzhi" 序志.

2. The "genre" chapters run from chapter 2 to chapter 25. Chapter 47, "Cailüe," is also essentially a review of authors and their primary genres of composition.

3. These include "Rongcai" 鎔裁, "Shenglü" 聲律, "Zhangju" 章句, "Lici" 麗辭, "Bixing" 比興, "Kuashi" 夸飾, "Shilei" 事類, "Lianzi" 練字, and "Zhixia" 指瑕.

4. Liu Xie distances himself from the pejorative connotations of *diaolong* in "Xuzhi," opening paragraphs. See also Owen, *Readings*, 185.

5. See also François Jullien, "Théorie du parallélisme littéraire, d'aprés Liu Xie," *Extrême-Orient Extrême-Occident* 2 (1989): 99–109. My article, entitled "Where the Lines Meet: Parallelism in Chinese and Western Literatures," appeared in *CLEAR* 10, nos. 1–2 (July 1988), 43–60; and in *Poetics Today* 11, no. 3 (fall 1990), 523–46.

6. As far as I have been able to determine (with the help of Willard Peterson), the expression "correlative thinking" was first introduced by Joseph Needham in *Science and Civilization in China* (Cambridge: Cambridge University Press, 1959), vol. 2, 279–91 passim. It is, of course, A. C. Graham who should be credited with turning it into a staple of studies of Chinese thought. See, for example, his *Yin-Yang and the Nature of Correlative Thinking* (Singapore: Institute of East Asian Philosophies, 1986), and *Disputers*

of the Tao (La Salle, Ill.: Open Court, 1989), 319–56, 389–428. An enlightening review of comparable tendencies in early Greek thought can be found in Geoffrey Lloyd's *Polarity and Analogy* (Cambridge: Cambridge University Press, 1966).

7. See, for example, Fan Wenlan, ed., *Wenxin diaolong zhu*, "Tixing," 505, "Qingcai," 537, "Fuhui," 650, "Zongshu," 655, "Wuse," 693. On the significance of Liu Xie's own style for this argument, see Owen, *Readings*, 184f.

8. See below, and note 31. See also "Xuzhi," 726.

9. For the basic distinction between *wen* and *bi*, see "Zongshu," 655. See also the opening discussion in the "Fenggu" chapter, 513, and the notion of parallelism as a marker of closure in double *ju*-units, in "Zhangjü," 571. See Owen, *Readings*, 252.

10. For Owen's comment, see *Readings*, 256.

11. See "Yidui," 439.

12. This use of the word *xian* can be seen in this chapter, 588, line 4. See also "Zongjing," 23.

13. See, for example, "Rongcai," 543f. See Owen, *Readings*, 249.

14. Compare with the use of the character *li* 儷 in "Mingshi" p. 67. The poetic pairing of *li* and *qi* goes back at least as far as "Zhaohun" 招魂 in *Chuci*: "麗而不奇些."

15. The precise meaning of the phrase 高下相須 remains unclear to me. Most modern Chinese and Western translations tend to gloss over it in the simple sense of paired opposites.

16. Both passages from the *Shang shu* are found in the sections combined in modern editions under the heading "Dayu mo" 大禹謨. See D. C. Lau et al., ed., *Shangshu zhuzi suoyin* 尚書逐字索引 (Concordance to the *Book of Documents*) (Hong Kong: Commercial Press, 1995), 5, 6.

17. The *Wenyan* commentary is generally ascribed to the late Warring States or early Han periods. Our text of "Xici zhuan" almost certainly dates from the Western Han. See Michael Lowe, ed., *Early Chinese Texts: A Bibliographic Guide* (Berkeley, Calif.: Institute of East Asian Studies, 1993), 221.

18. All commentators take the ambiguous expression "the paired speeches of the great officers" [大夫聯辭] as a clear reference to the *Zuo zhuan* text.

19. It is not irrelevant to recall here the additional meaning of the paired terms *qi* and *ou*, in the alternate reading *ji ou*, i.e., "odd" and "even."

20. The four Han poets are, of course, Yang Xiong 揚雄 (53 B.C.–18 A.D.), Sima Xiangru 司馬相如 (179–117 B.C.), Zhang Heng 張衡 (78–139), and Cai Yong 蔡邕 (133–192). Note that the author does not bother to specify the Wei and Jin authors he has in mind.

21. The distinction between verbal and semantic parallelism also under-lies many passages in the *Wen fu*, where the crucial pair of terms tends to be *ci* and *li* 辭理. (For example, *Wenxuan*, juan 17, 5a, 7b. See translation by David R. Knechtges, *Wen Xuan*, vol. 3, 221, 227.) Compare also the catego-ries of *shidui* 事對, *yidui* 意對, and so on, in the *Wenjing mifulun*. The same variable can be seen in other places in the *Wenxin diaolong* text, e.g., "Lunshuo" 論説, 328, and "Zhangbiao" 章表, 407 [⋯理周辭要，引義比事，必得其偶].

22. See "Tongbianlun" 通變論 (On conformance and divergence), a chapter in *Gongsunlongzi*, *SBBY* ed., 8a.

23. Aristotle, *Rhetoric* 3:9 (1410a); see George A. Kennedy, *Aristotle: On Rhetoric* (New York: Oxford University Press, 1991), 243. See also Wang Li's analysis of the same relations in *Hanyu shiluxue* 漢語詩律學 (Chinese pros-ody) (Shanghai: Xin zhishi chubanshe, 1958), 153–82.

24. See Zhou Zhenfu 周振甫, *Wenxin diaolong xuanyi*, also cited in Furuta Keiichi 古田敬一, *Chūgoku bungaku ni okeru tsuiku to tsuiku-ron* 中國文學における對句と對句論 (Parallel lines and parallelism in Chinese lit-erature) (Tokyo: Kazama shobo, 1982), 39.

25. See *Wenxuan* 文選, juan 8, 14b and juan 19, 8a. The pronoun *zhi* 之 in the line is somewhat ambiguous in reference.

26. For the Wang Can lines, see *Wenxuan*, juan 11, 2b. The citation from Zhang Zai (ca. 289) does not seem to appear in the text included in *Wenxuan*, nor in Ding Fubao 丁福保, ed., *Quan Han Sanguo Jin Nanbeichao shi* 全漢三國晉南北朝詩 (The complete poetry of the Han, Sanguo, Jin, and Nan-beichao Periods) (Taipei: Shijie shuju, 1969). For the Zhang Hua and Liu Kun pieces, below, see Ding Fubao, ed., *Quan Han Sanguo Jin Nanbeichao shi*, vol. 1, 284, 416.

27. The line ⋯指類而求⋯ is often taken as referring simply to the dif-ferent categories of *dui* presented in the essay, but I believe the point is as I have rendered it.

28. The "'syntactic' slippage" I have in mind refers to the matching of the expression *biyi* 比翼 (adv.) + *xiang* 翔 (v.) in the first line with *zhi* 知 (v.) + *jiehe* 接翩 (o.) in the second. For the idea of "chiasmus" in Chinese poetics, see Qian Zhongshu 錢鍾書, *Guanzhuibian* 管錐編 (Collected insights through a gimlet hole) (Beijing: Zhonghua shuju, 1979), vol. 1, 66; vol. 3, 858 f. Qian brilliantly translates chiasmus as *yacha jufa* 丫叉句法. The allu-sion, of course, is to Zhuangzi's "Pianmu" 駢拇 chapter in the appended (外篇) collection. Compare with the use of the same metaphor in this book in the "Yidui" chapter, 438, the "Rongcai" chapter, 543, and so on.

29. That is, he is apparently describing the conjoining of elements of uneven quality and not contrasting instances of *zhengdui* and *fandui*.

30. The use of the word *li* 理 here is ambiguous. It is generally taken in the various modern Chinese translations as simply the "basic sense" (*daoli*) of a given passage, but I believe it must in this context carry a broader meaning of the analogical reasoning underlying complex parallelism. See Fan Wenlan *Wenxin diaolong zhu*, 596, note 12. If this reading is correct, it would make of the apparently innocuous use of the word *lei* 類 in the preceding line, at the very least, a play on words. Compare with the *Wenjing mifu* analytical heading *leidui*.

31. See extensive critical comments on this variable attached to Fan Wenlan's notes, 596–604. Note the implicit opposition between *qi* and *li* 奇麗 in this passage. In other passages in the book, the word *qi* may mean little more than "excellent." See, for example, "Mingshi," 67, "Tixing," 505, "Fenggu," 514, and "Dingshi," 531. Compare with the *Wenjing mifu* category *qidui* 奇對.

32. For this assessment, see Knechtges, *Wen Xuan*, vol. 1, 45 ff., and Owen, *Readings*, 251. See also Chinese references in my "Where the Lines Meet," 527.

33. See a similar comment by Zhou Zhenfu in *Wenxin diaolong jinyi*, 312.

Chapter 8

1. Reading 究 rather than 追. The "determinate" (literally, "having number" [*youshu* 有 數]), suggests the "divisions" of analytical exposition.

2. No English term works quite like *tong* 通. Rather than the three-dimensional space implied in "comprehensiveness," *tong* is linear, "getting through from beginning to end." Variations on "comprehension" are chosen because it is a term that combines understanding and making understood.

3. The "fish-trap and snare" are the familiar figures from *Zhuangzi*'s "external things" (外 物): They are the words that get the meaning and are then abandoned.

4. The only plausible alternative is that "carving dragons" (*diaolong*) is in all cases a pejorative term, which would lead to a translation of the title as "Mind in literature versus dragon-carving."

5. A less colorful version of this is given in chapter 34, "Zhangju" 章 句: "If a phrase loses its companion, it is on a journey without company; matters go awry from their sequence and drift aimlessly without coming to rest" [若 辭 失 其 朋 ，則 羈 旅 而 無 友 ，事 乖 其 次 ，則 飄 寓 而 不 安] (*WXDL* 34/ 55–58).

6. If the problematic claim of the priority of pattern is a hopping *Kui* considered alone, joined with its examples and yoked to the parallel case, it pro-

duces another situation described in "Parallel Phrasing": "If two matters are matched together, yet are unbalanced in quality, then you have a fine steed in harness on the left and a nag hitched up on the right" [若兩事相配，而優劣不均，是驥在左驂，駑為右服也] (*WXDL* 35/101–4). This makes for troubled driving.

7. That is, a "good" analysis means a correct analysis of how things are; "good" [*bian*], however, may be rhetorically appealing, yet far from the truth.

8. For example, "All cats sing gray; San Francisco is a cat; therefore San Francisco sings gray." The logic is correct. Since "division" has more semantic content than logic, it cannot produce such statements.

9. Contrast the very different meaning of *bian* in the phrasing 文辭之變.

10. Perhaps because a problematic choice of words on Liu Xie's part led to a copyist's confusion.

11. I would suggest that *cai* 財 is a sound loan rather than a miswritten graph. This would produce a still problematic 志合文才 (aims matched literary talents). The advantage of this is that the phrase *wencai* 文才 is attested elsewhere (chapter 41, "Zhixia" 指暇 [Criticizing faults]).

12. Compare with Yang Xiong's distinction between *li yi ze* 以則 (lovely and thereby giving a norm) and *li yi yin* 麗以淫 (lovely and thereby leading to debauchery). That distinction, made between the Shi poets and the poets of Chu and Han, corresponds exactly to Liu Xie's passage from an age of positive style to decadence.

13. For the relation of the terms paired by *er* 而, I suggest observing what happens when the negative is inserted: *er bu* 而不. If one wrote 質而不辨, these would be unsurprising; there is no difficulty distinguishing the terms. If, however, one wrote 淳而不質, it would be very hard to know what was meant. Much the same would be true of 侈而不豔. One might be able to tease a subtle distinction out of 淺而不綺, but the distinction would be very fine.

14. Liu Xie was quite aware of this. In the "Yinxiu" 隱秀 chapter he refers to to the *bianhu ti* 變互體 (*WXDL* 40/19).

Chapter 9

1. Stephen Owen's translation in *Readings in Chinese Literary Thought* (hereafter *Readings*). Translations in this paper, when not cited from *Readings*, are my own.

2. Most scholars acknowledge the echoes of the "Appended Commentary" (*Xici*) to *Changes*, but they differ on the "content" of the Tao. For example, Huang Kan and Liu Yongji link Tao to "the way things naturally are [*ziran*],"

cited in Zhan Ying, ed., *Wenxin diaolong yizheng*, vol. 1, 1–2, 4, 7–8. Xu Fuguan emphasizes Confucian themes in *Zhongguo wenxue lunji*, 385–99. Current opinions tend toward Liu Xie's eclecticism. For a good summary of the
genealogy of the idea of *yuan Tao* and similar formulations, see Zhang Shaokang 張少康, *Wenxin diaolong xintan* 文心雕龍新探 (New investigations
on *Wenxin diaolong*) in *Wenshizhe xue jicheng* 文史哲學集成 (Collection of
studies on literature, history, and philosophy), 232 (Taipei: Wenshizhe chubanshe, 1996), 23–41.

3. For example, Zihan, minister of Song, says, "Weaponry has been established for long, it displays authority against the unlawful, and makes clear the
virtue of civil instruction" [兵之設久矣，所以威不軌而昭文德也] (*Zuo
zhuan*, Xiang 27.6, in *Chun qiu Zuo zhuan zhu*, Yang Bojun, ed. [Beijing:
Zhonghua shuju, 1981], 4 vols.); Kongzi 孔子, *Lunyu* 論語 (The analects),
Zhu Xi 朱熹, annot., *Sishu Jizhu* 四書集注 (Four books, with collected
commentaries) (Shanghai: Zhonghua shuju, 1927), 16.1: "That is why when
those afar do not submit, one should cultivate the virtue of civil instruction
to make them come" [故遠人不服，則修文德以來之]; *Classic of Poetry*
(*Shijing* 262, "*Jiang Han*" 江漢): "Direct his power of civil instruction,/
Spread it to the four realms" [矢其文德，洽治四國]; image of hexagram
no. 9, "Xiaochu" 小畜: "The superior person glorifies the power of civil instruction" [君子以懿文德]. These examples are cited in Liao Weiqing 廖蔚
卿, *Liu chao wenlun* 六朝文論 (Writings on literature in the Six Dynasties)
(Taipei: Lianjing chuban gongsi, 1978), 11.

4. See Yang Xiong 揚雄, *Yangzi fayan* 揚子法言 (Model sayings of Master Yang) (Shanghai: Zhonghua shuju, 1927), "Junzi," and Wang Chong,
Lunheng (Balanced inquiries), "Shujie." Both are cited in Liao Weiqing, *Liu
chao wenlun*, 12.

5. The allusion is to *Zhuangzi*, "Lie Yukou." See also Cheng Xuan Ying's
annotation: "Feathers have natural patterns, to decorate and paint them is to
strive for human cleverness," [羽有自然之文采，飾而畫之，則務人
巧], in Qian Mu, comp., *Zhuangzi zhuanjian* (Hong Kong: Dongnan yinwu
chubanshe, 1956), 246.

6. Although most Six Dynasties writers acknowledge the Classics as the
origins of later literary genres, there are disagreements on whether they embody ideal *wen*. For example, Yan Yannian claims in his *Tinggao* (Family in-
structions) that the *Classic of Poetry* is the ancestor of all poetry and that the
Spring and Autumn Annals is the highest example of "books of praise and
blame." See Guo and Wang, *Zhongguo lidai wenlun xuan*, vol. 1, 312–25.
However, in a passage cited in *Wenxin diaolong*, chapter 44, "Zongshu" 總述
(General technique), Yan identifies the Classics with plain spoken words

(*yan*) and opposed them to written texts, which inevitably involve patterning, whether rhymed (*wen*) or unrhymed (*bi* 筆). (In doing so, Yan effectively effaces the distinctions between *wen* and *bi*.) "Yan Yannian considers *bi*, as normative form, to be the patterning of spoken words. The classics are thus [based on] spoken words and not on words patterned through being written down [*bi*], traditions and records are [based on] words patterned through being written down and not on spoken words" [顏延年以為‥「筆之為體，言之文也；經典則言而非筆，傳記則筆而非言] (*WXDL* 44/9–12). For a discussion of Yan Yannian's literary thought, see Wang Kaiyun 王闓運 and Yang Ming 楊明, *Wei Jin Nanbei chao piping shi* 魏晉南北朝文學批評史 (A history of literary criticism in Wei, Jin, and Nanbeichao periods) (Shanghai: Shanghai guji chubanshe, 1989), 206–9.

7. An obvious allusion to Yang Xiong's criticism of *fu* (poetic exposition): "The *fu* of the poets [in the *Classic of Poetry*] are beautiful yet regulated; the *fu* of the [latter-day] court poets are beautiful but excessive" [詩人之賦麗以則，辭人之賦麗以淫] in *Yangzi fayan*, 2/2a.

8. *Readings* 77, Guo and Wang 1:170. The Chinese text refers to Guo Shaoyu and Wang Wenshang, eds., *Zhongguo lidai wenlun xuan* (An anthology of writings on literature through the ages), 3 vols. (Shanghai: Shanghai guji chubanshe, 1979).

9. Most scholars believe that *Wenxin diaolong* was completed before the end of the fifth century, in the last years of the Qi dynasty, adducing as evidence the eulogies to Qi in chapter 45 of *Wenxin diaolong*. In the biography of Liu Xie in *Liang shu*, Xiao Tong is said to have "received Liu as one with whom he had deep affinities" [*shen aijie zhi* 深愛接之]. (See Yang Mingzhao, "Liang shu Liu Xie zhuan jian zhu" [Annotations on the biography of Liu Xie in the *History of Liang*], in *Wenxin diaolong zhu shiyi* [Supplements to the collation and commentary on *Wenxin diaolong*], 385–413.) However, although Liu Xie held the post of Xiao Tong's secretary (*donggong tongshi she-ren* 東宮通事舍人) for about seven years (511–19), he probably resided in the Eastern Palace for no more than two years (517–19). Among Xiao Tong's numerous works addressed to the men of letters he associated with, none were addressed to Liu Xie, which raises doubts regarding his supposed deep appreciation of Liu Xie. For discussions of the connection between Xiao Tong and Liu Xie, see Wang Yuanhua, *Wenxin diaolong chuangzuo lun*, and Mou Shijin 牟世金, *Wenxin diaolong yanjiu* 文心雕龍研究 (Studies on *Wenxin diaolong*) (Beijing: Renmin wenxue chubanshe, 1995), 46–83.

10. Xiao Gang quotes the same passage in his preface to Xiao Tong's collected writings ("Zhaoming taizi ji xu"). See XiaoTong, *Zhaoming taizi ji* (n.p., n.d., Zhonghua shuju, sibu beiyao edition), 1a.

11. See *Wenxin diaolong*, chapter 3, "Zongjing" (Honoring the Classics), chapter 4, "Zhengwei" (Rectifying the classical apocrypha), chapter 16, "Shizhuan" (Historical traditions), and chapter 17, "Zhuzi" (Various philosophers). Many "functional genres" appear in both *Wen xuan* and *WXDL*, a notable exception is *WXDL*, chapter 15, "Xieyin" (Jests and riddles), which probably violates notions of decorum embodied in *Wen xuan*.

12. *Liulian aisi*; *aisi* means literally "thoughts of lament."

13. Guo and Wang 1:340. Liu Xie discusses the distinctions between *wen* and *bi* in chapter 44, "Zongshu". Zhan Ying cites most of the better-known arguments on the subject in *Wenxin diaolong yizheng*, 1622–27; see also Guo and Wang, *Zhongguo lidai wenlun xuan,* vol. 1, 344–49.

14. A line from the *Classic of Poetry*, 154.

15. *Guizang, Lianshan*, and *Zhouyi* are mentioned in *Zhouli* ("Chunguan taipu") as "San Yi" (The three changes). The divinatory tradition of *Guizang*, probably an imitation of the *Zhouyi* from the Spring and Autumn or Warring States periods, is lost by the Han, since it is not mentioned in the "Yiwenzhi" of *Han shu* ("Treatise on arts and letters" in *History of Han*). For a brief account of Han and Jin fabrications that claim to be the ancient *Guizang*, see Qu Wanli 屈萬里, *Xian Qin wenshi ziliao kaobian* 先秦文史資料考辨 (Researches on the literary and historical sources from the pre-Qin period) (Taipei: Lianjing chuban gongsi, 1983), 465–66.

16. A line from "Zhao hun" (Summoning the soul) in *Chuci*. See also Ruan Ji, "Yong huai," no. 11, in *Ruan Ji ji jiaozhu*, ed. Chen Bojun (Beijing: Zhonghua shuju, 1987), 251–56.

17. For example, Jian'an literature was widely regarded as the "new canon" in fifth- and sixth-century literary thought. Liu Xie joins the general chorus of praise, especially in "Mingshi" 明詩 (Illuminating poetry) (*WXDL* 6/93–108) and "Shixu" 時序 (Times and changes) (*WXDL* 45/155–79), and more briefly in "Zhaoce" 詔策 (Decrees and petitions) (*WXDL* 19/91–94) and "Qizou" 啓奏 (Memorials and submissions) (*WXDL* 23/41–47). However, he also criticizes the *yuefu* poems of the period for their emotional and musical excesses (*WXDL* 7/70–81). Cao Zhi is warmly praised in chapters 6 and 45, but he is also chided for misuse of allusions (*WXDL* 38/116–24), improper levity in referring to rulers (*WXDL* 41/15–24), verbosity and diffusion (*WXDL* 12/56–59).

18. They are also defending or justifying their own styles. Unlike these figures, Liu Xie was not the major poet of his day.

19. Some twentieth century scholars classify "Biansao" 辨騷 as the first of twenty-one chapters (i.e., chapters 5 to 25) on genres. See, for example, Fan Wenlan, *Wenxin diaolong zhu*, 4–5, and Liu Dajie 劉大杰, *Zhongguo wenxue fazhan shi* 中國文學發展史 (A history of the development of Chinese lit-

erature) (Hong Kong: Zhonghua shuju, 1969), 229. However, given Liu Xie's emphasis in "Telling of my intent" on the arguments linking the first five chapters, and since the *Chuci* as genre is included in chapter 8, "Quanfu" 詮 賦 (Explaining the *fu*), it seems that "Biansao" should be read as a discussion of the role of intensity, excesses, and filiation with tradition in the rise of imaginative literature. For incisive discussions of this chapter's classification, see Xu Fuguan, *Zhongguo wenxue lunji*, 425–36, and Mou Shijin, *Wenxin diaolong yanjiu*, 110–24.

20. The Han exegete Wang Yi was the first to designate *Encountering Sorrow* as *The Classic of Encountering Sorrow* (*Lisao jung*). The appellation implies filiation from the canonical Classics.

21. In chapter 1, however, Liu Xie asserts that by the Shang and Zhou times, "patterning predominated over substance."

22. "But up until Sima Xiangru and Wang Bao, in most cases poets used their great native talent and did not apply themselves to learning. After Yang Xiong and Liu Xiang, many cited books to add to their writing. This was the great divide of give and take, the demarcation should not be confused" (*WXDL* 47/136–41). In chapter 38, "Shilei" 事 類 (Categories of events), Liu Xie asserts that allusions first appeared in the works of Jia Yi and Sima Xiangru, and the practice became widespread with Yang Xiong and Liu Xin (*WXDL* 38/26–42).

23. See Fan Wenlan, *Wenxin diaolong zhu*, 521–23.

24. Liu Xie believes that the five poets cited here—Mei Sheng, Sima Xiangru, Ma Rong, Yang Xiong, Zhang Heng—"are as one" (*ruyi* 如 一). Zhou Zhenfu has tried to make a case for heightening particularization, concreteness, and inwardness. Citing Wang Shizhen's *Yiyuan zhiyan* (Goblet words from the garden of literature), Zhou Zhenfu suggests that Cao Cao's "Guan Canghai" (Watching the blue sea), also derived from the examples of *fu* cited by Liu Xie, takes the interiorization one step further (*Shici lihua* [Discourses on poetry], quoted in *Wenxin diaolong yizheng*, 1093).

25. For Six Dynasties examples of the view of literary history as progress, see Ge Hong 葛 洪 (284–363), *Baopu zi* 抱 朴 子 (Master who embraces simplicity), "Junshi" 鈞 世 and "Shangbo" 尚 博 (in Guo and Wang, *Zhongguo lidai wenlun xuan*, vol. 1, 206–13), and see Xiao Tong's preface to the *Wen xuan* (in Guo and Wang, *Zhongguo lidai wenlun xuan*, vol. 1, 329–35). Xiao Zixian 蕭 子 顯 (489–537) also affirms the necessity of change (*bian*) in literary history in *Nan Qi shu* (History of the southern Qi), 52.908; see Guo and Wang, *Zhongguo lidai wenlun xuan*, vol. 1, 264–65.

26. Sima Qian writes that the lofty intent and aspirations of Qu Yuan "can be said to rival even the sun and moon in brightness" [雖 與 日 月 爭 光 可

也] (*Shiji* 84.2482). According to Ban Gu, the passage that includes this line is taken from Liu An's (d. 122 B.C.) "Lisao xu" (Introduction to "Lisao"). See Ban Gu, "Lisao xu," in Guo and Wang, eds., *Zhongguo lidai wenlun xuan*, vol. 1, 120. Liu An might have been inspired by the same metaphors in works attributed to Qu Yuan. The line "In brightness he equals sun and moon" [與 日月兮齊光，與日月兮同光] appears in both "Yun zhong jun" (Lord in the clouds) from "Jui ge" (Nine songs) and "Xisong" (Declaration of regrets) ("Xisong" 惜頌) from "Jiu zhang" (Nine works). The phrase "wind and clouds" (*fengyun* 風雲) refers to "*Fu* on the Wind" ("Feng fu" 風賦) and the goddess Morning Cloud (*zhaoyun* 朝雲) in "*Fu* on Gaotang" ("Gaotang fu" 高唐賦), both attributed to Song Yu.

27. In chapter 17, "Zhuzi," Liu Xie describes Zou Yan as "nourishing his political thought with the pattern of heaven" [*yangzheng yu tianwen* 養政於 天文] (*WXDL* 17/38).

28. Sima Qian, *Shiji*, 46.1895.

29. *Quan Liang wen* (Complete prose of the Liang dynasty), 11/1a, in Yan Kejun, comp., *Quan shanggu sandai Qin Han sanguo liuchao wen*.

30. For discussions of the variations of this expressve-affective axis, see Wang Jinling 王金凌 *Zhongguo wenxue lilun shi (Liuchao pian)* 中國文學 理論史 (六朝篇) (A history of Chinese theories of literature: the Six Dynasties volume) (Taipei: Huazheng shuju, 1988), 267–90; Wang Kaiyun and Yang Ming, *Wei Jin Nanbeichao piping shi*, 493–570.

31. For the provenance and other instances of the "sickness of the clam" metaphor, see Zhan Ying, ed., *Wenxin diaolong yizheng*, 1784.

32. "The beginning of the pivotal point attains the center of the ring, in order to respond to the endless [transformations]." See Zhuangzi, "Qiwu lun" 齊物論 in *Zhuangzi jishi*, 66.

33. See, for example, Xu Fuguan, *Zhongguo wenxue lunji*, 18–37; Wang Jinling, *Zhongguo wenxue lilun shi (Liuchao pian)*, 23–50.

34. This idea is also developed in Cao Pi, *Dianlun lunwen* (A discourse on literature), and in Lu Ji, "Wen fu" (A poetic exposition on literature). See Guo and Weng, eds., *Zhongguo lidai wenlun xuan*, vol. 1, 124–30.

35. Liu Xie sometimes uses the word *qi* as a term of praise and approbation, and sometimes as a disparaging term.

36. See Zhuangzi, chapter 28, "Rangwang" 讓王 (Yielding rulership), in *Zhuangzi jishi*, vol. 4, 979.

37. Aside from obvious references in chapter 1, "Xiaoyao you" (Free and easy wandering), wandering also marks supreme spiritual attainment in other chapters. The following are some examples. "[T]he supreme being . . . wanders beyond the four seas" [至人 ⋯ 遊乎四海之外] (chapter 2, "Qiwi lun"

[On seeing things as equal]). Zhuangzi is said to "wander with the Creator above" [上與造物者遊] (chapter 33, "Tianxia" [All under heaven]). "To ride on the way and its power so as to drift and wander . . . drift and wander with the ancestor of the myriad things" [若夫乘道德以浮遊⋯浮游乎萬物之祖] (chapter 20, "Shanmu" [The mountain tree]). "I wander in the beginning of things. . . . He who attains supreme beauty and wanders in supreme joy is called the supreme being" [吾遊於物之初⋯得至美而遊乎至樂，謂之至人] (chapter 21, "Tian Zifang" 田子方). Hongmeng (primal breath) playfully wanders, slaps his thighs, hops like a bird, claims transcendence of knowledge, and urges forgetfulness in chapter 11, "Zaiyou" (Let it be). For a perceptive discussion of the idea of *you* in *Zhuangzi*, see Xu Fuguan 徐復觀, *Zhongguo yishu jingshen* 中國藝術精神 (The spirit of Chinese aesthetics) (Taizhong: Donghai Daxue, 1966), 45–134. Lu Ji also speaks of "the mind roaming over ten thousand *ren*" [*xinyou wanren* 心遊萬仞] in literary creation.

38. In *Mengzi*, intent controls energy, and energy infuses the physical form with emotions [夫志、氣之帥也，氣、體之充也，夫志至焉，氣次焉⋯志壹則動氣，氣壹則動志] (*Mengzi*, 2A.2).

39. See also "Jiebi" 解蔽 (Removing obstacles to understanding) in *Xunzi*; chapter 16 in *Laozi*; "TianTao" 天道 (Way of heaven) in *Zhuangzi*; "Jingshen xun" 精神訓 (Lesson on the spirit) in *Huainanzi*; Lu Ji, "Wen Fu". These sources are quoted in Zhan Ying, ed., *Wenxin diaolong yizheng*, 979.

40. One is reminded of Lu Ji's lines: "Trying out the void to demand forms,/Knocking on silence to seek sounds."

41. Lu Ji's "Wen Fu" also begins and ends with similar ideas. He points to the residue not assimilated by his own exposition and articulates his self-doubts from his writing experience.

42. The analogy between the human body and literary works is also developed in *WXDL* 5/95–96 and 43/11–14.

43. Yang Xiong develops this analogy in his comparison of Han *fu* rhetoric to an excessivly adorned woman: "Or put it this way: a woman has beauty; does writing have beauty also? The answer is yes. The worst thing for a woman is to have her inner beauty beclouded by cosmetics; the worst thing for a piece of writing to have is rules and proportions confounded by excessive rhetoric" [或曰，女有色，書亦有色乎，曰有，女惡華丹之亂窈窕也，書惡淫辭之淈法度也]. See *Yangzi fayan*, 2/1b–2/2a.

44. "The Way of Heaven" in *Zhuangzi jishi*, 465.

45. Han feizi, "Wai chu shuo zuo shang" in Wang Xianshen, ed., *Hanfeizi jijie* 韓非子集解 (*Hanfei zi*, with collected annotations and commentaries) (Taipei: Shangwu, 1970), chapter 32, 24.

46. Some scholars assert that Liu Xie is implicitly endorsing the idea of phonal rules because he is seeking the patronage of Shen Yue who formalized phonal rules and gave them currency. See Zhan Ying, ed., *Wenxin diaolong yizheng*, 1209.

47. Quoted in *Zhengyi*, in Zhan Ying, ed., *Wenxin diaolong yizheng*, 172–73.

48. Liu Xizai, "Shigai," in *Yigai*, quoted in Zhan Ying, ed., *Wenxin diaolong yizheng*, 173.

49. Variations and nuances depend on the restraining factor—that is, on where one puts the brake on dangerous passions. For example, Zhu Xi breaks away from the Mao-Zheng tradition in more literalist readings and boldly characterizes some poems in the *Classic of Poetry* as "licentious" (*yinshi* 淫 詩). However, he reinstates the moral purpose of the poems by claiming in his preface that Confucius, as editor, includes such negative examples as warnings. The basic proposition has not changed. The burden of moral purpose has simply shifted to the textual labor of Confucius, who in editing the *Classic of Poetry* has sifted out "those poems whose good does not suffice as example or whose evil does not suffice as warning" (preface to *Shi ji zhuan*). For an informed analysis of the principles guiding the interpretation of the *Classic of Poetry* from Han to Song, see Stephen Van Zoeren, *Poetry and Personality*.

50. Thus Zhu Xi urges us to discard the Han commentary, just as, five centuries later, some Ming thinkers deem it necessary to put aside Zhu Xi's commentary (e.g., Zhang Dai in *Sishu yu* [Encounter with the four books]). In *Gushi bian*, Gu Jiegang describes his work on the *Classic of Poetry* as reconstruction: He wants to "wash and rinse out the true face (of the classics)." See Gu Jiegang 顧頡剛, *Gushi bian* 古史辨 (An analysis of ancient histories) (Taipei: Landeng chubanshe, 1993), vol. 3, 1.

51. For a comprehensive list of the usages of the phrase "carving dragons" and its interpretations, see Zhan Ying, ed., *Wenxin diaolong yizheng*, 1901–2. Wang Liqi, Li Qingjia, and Zhou Zhenfu read the word *qi* 豈 as meaning "more or less" and understand the comparison with Zou Shi as broadly affirmative. I think the reading of the line as a rhetorical question implying differences is more convincing.

Chapter 10

Editor's note: Full citations for all works mentioned in this article are given in "Works Cited."

Works Cited

Works in Western Languages

Abrams, M. H. *The Mirror and the Lamp: Romantic Theory and the Critical Tradition.* New York: W. W. Norton & Company, Inc., 1953.

Adams, Hazard. "Canons: Literary Critical Power Criteria." *Critical Inquiry* 14 (1988): 748–64.

————, ed. *Critical Theory Since Plato.* New York: Harcourt Brace Jovanovich, 1971.

Altieri, Charles. "An Idea and Ideal of a Literary Canon." In *Canons*, edited by Robert von Hallberg, 41–64. Chicago: University of Chicago Press, 1984.

Bate, Walter Jackson, ed. *Criticism: The Major Texts.* New York: Harcourt, Brace & Co., 1952.

Bennet, Andrew, ed. *Readers and Reading.* London: Longman, 1995.

Bloom, Harold. *The Western Canon.* New York: Harcourt, Brace & Co., 1994.

Bush, Susan. *The Chinese Literati on Painting: Su Shih (1037–1101) to Tung Ch'i-ch'ang (1555–1636).* Cambridge, Mass.: Harvard University Press, 1971.

Chang, Chang-yue. "The Metaphysics of Wang Pi (226–249)." Ph.D. diss., University of Pennsylvania, 1979.

Chow, Tse-tsung. "Ancient Chinese Views of Literature, the Tao, and Their Relationship." *Chinese Literature: Essays, Articles, Reviews* 1, no. 1 (1979): 3–29.

Coleridge, Samuel Taylor. "Dejection: An Ode." In *The Portable Coleridge*, edited by I. A. Richards. New York: Viking Press, 1950.

Dasgupta, S. N., and S. K. De. *History of Alakra Literature and History of Kvya Literature.* Vol. 1 of *A History of Sanskrit Literature: Classical Period*, edited by S. N. Dasgupta. Calcutta: University of Calcutta, 1947.

De, Sushil Dumar, ed. *History of Sanskrit Poetics.* 2d ed. 2 vols. Calcutta: K. L. Mukhopadhyay, 1960.

Deutsch, Eliot. *On Truth: An Ontological Theory.* Honolulu: University of Hawaii Press, 1979.

DeWoskin, Kenneth. *A Song for One or Two: Music and the Concepts of Art in Early China.* Ann Arbor, Mich.: Center for Chinese Studies, University of Michigan, 1982.

Dreyfus, Hubert L., and Paul Rabinow. *Michel Foucault: Beyond Structuralism and Hermeneutics.* 2d ed. Chicago: University of Chicago Press, 1983.

Eliot, T. S. *On Poetry and Poets.* New York: Noonday Press, 1961.

————. *Selected Essays, 1917–1932.* New York: Harcourt Brace Jovanovich, 1932.

Foucault, Michel. *The Archaeology of Knowledge.* Trans. A. M. Sheridan Smith. New York: Colophon, 1972.

Fung, Yu-lan. *A History of Chinese Philosophy.* Trans. Derk Bodde. Princeton, N.J.: Princeton University Press, 1953.

Gerow, Edwin. *Indian Poetics.* In *A History of Indian Literature*, edited by Jan Gonda, vol. 5, fasc. 3. Wiesbaden: Otto Harrassowitz, 1977.

Graham, A. C. *Chuang-tzu: The Seven Inner Chapters and Other Writings from the Book Chuang-tzu.* London: George Allen & Unwin, 1981. Paperback edition published as *Chuang-tzu: The Inner Chapters.* London: Mandala, 1986.

————, ed. *Disputers of the Tao.* La Salle, Ill.: Open Court, 1989.

————. *Yin-Yang and the Nature of Correlative Thinking.* Singapore: Institute of East Asian Philosophies, 1986.

Harris, Wendell V. "Canonicity." *PMLA* (January 1991): 110–121.

Hart, James A. "The Speech of Prince Chin: A Study of Early Chinese Cosmology." *Explorations in Early Chinese Cosmology*, edited by Henry Rosemont, 35–65. Chico, Calif.: Scholar Press, 1984.

Hawkes, David, trans. and annot. *The Songs of the South, by Qu Yuan and Other Poets.* Rev. ed. New York: Penguin Books, 1985.

Iser, Wolfgang. *The Act of Reading: a Theory of Aesthetic Response.* Baltimore, Md.: Johns Hopkins University Press, 1978.

Johnson, Mark. *The Body in the Mind: The Bodily Basis of Meaning, Imagination, and Reason.* Chicago: University of Chicago Press, 1987.

Jowett, Benjamin. *The Dialogues of Plato.* 2 vols. New York: Random House, 1937.

Jullien, François. "Théorie du parallélisme littéraire, d'aprés Liu Xie." *Extrême-Orient Extrême-Occident* 2 (1989): 99–109.

Kane, P. V. *History of Sanskrit Poetics.* 3rd rev. ed. Delhi: Motilal Banarsidass, 1961.

Kennedy, George A. *Aristotle: On Rhetoric.* New York: Oxford University Press, 1991.

Knechtges, David R., trans. *Wen Xuan, or Selections of Refined Literature.* 3 vols. Chinese original compiled by Xiao Tong. Princeton, N.J.: Princeton University Press, 1982–1996.

Lau, D. C. *Lao Tzu: Tao Te Ching.* New York: Penguin Books, 1963.

Legge, James, trans. and annot. *The Ch'un Ts'ew with the Tso Chuen.* Vol. 5 of *The Chinese Classics.* Hong Kong: Hong Kong University Press, 1960.

———, trans. and annot. *The Chinese Classics.* 5 vols. Hong Kong: Hong Kong University Press, 1960.

———, trans. and annot. *The Shoo King or the Book of Historical Documents.* Vol. 3 of *The Chinese Classics.* Hong Kong: Hong Kong University Press, 1960.

Liu, James J. Y. *Chinese Theories of Literature.* Chicago: University of Chicago Press, 1975.

———. *Language—Paradox—Poetics: A Chinese Perspective,* edited by Richard John Lynn. Princeton, N.J.: Princeton University Press, 1988.

Lloyd, Geoffrey. *Polarity and Analogy.* Cambridge: Cambridge University Press, 1966.

Longinus. "On the Sublime." Trans. W. R. Roberts. In *Critical Theory Since Plato,* edited by Hazard Adams. New York: Harcourt Brace Jovanovich, 1971.

Lowe, Michael, ed. *Early Chinese Texts: A Bibliographic Guide.* Berkeley, Calif.: Institute of East Asian Studies, University of California, Berkeley, 1993.

Lynn, Richard John, trans. *The Classic of Changes: A New Translation of the I Ching As Interpreted by Wang Bi.* New York: Columbia University Press, 1994.

———. *The Classic of The Way and Virtue: A New Translation of the Tao-te ching of Laozi as Interpreted by Wang Bi.* New York: Columbia University Press, 1999.

Mair, Victor H., ed. *The Columbia Anthology of Traditional Chinese Literature.* New York: Columbia University Press, 1994.

———. "Ma Jianzhong and the Invention of Chinese Grammar." In *Studies on the History of Chinese Syntax,* edited by Chaofen Sun. Journal of Chinese Linguistics Monograph Series, no. 10 (1997): 5–26.

———, trans. and annot. *Tao Te Ching: The Classic Book of Integrity and the Way.* New York: Bantam, 1990.

————, trans. and annot. *Wandering on the Way: Early Taoist Tales and Parables of Chuang Tzu*. New York: Bantam, 1994; Honolulu: University of Hawaii Press, 1998.

Mair, Victor H., and Tsu-Lin Mei. "The Sanskrit Origins of Recent Style Prosody." *Harvard Journal of Asiatic Studies* 51, no. 2 (December 1991): 375–470.

Makeham, John. *Name and Actuality in Early Chinese Thought*. Albany, N.Y.: State University of New York Press, 1994.

Mather, Richard B. *The Poet Shen Yüeh (441–513): The Reticent Marquis*. Princeton, N.J.: Princeton University Press, 1988.

Needham, Joseph. *Science and Civilization in China*. Vol. 2.2. Cambridge: Cambridge University Press, 1959.

Nienhauser, William H., Jr., ed. *The Indiana Companion to Traditional Chinese Literature*. Bloomington, Ind.: Indiana University Press, 1986.

Osborne, Harold. *Aesthetics and Art Theory: An Historical Introduction*. New York: E. P. Dutton, 1968.

Owen, Stephen. *Readings in Chinese Literary Thought*. Cambridge, Mass.: Harvard University Press, 1992.

————. *Traditional Chinese Poetry and Poetics: Omen of the World*. Madison, Wisc.: University of Wisconsin Press, 1985.

Plaks, A. H. "Where the Lines Meet: Parallelism in Chinese and Western Literatures." *CLEAR* 10, no. 1–2 (1988–1989): 43–60. Reprinted in *Poetics Today* 11, no. 3 (fall 1990): 523–46.

Pollard, David. "Ch'i in Chinese Literary Theory." In *Chinese Approaches to Literature from Confucius to Liang Ch'i-ch'ao*, edited by Adele Austin Rickett, 43–66. Princeton, N.J.: Princeton University Press, 1978.

Poulet, Georges. "Criticism and the Experience of Interiority." In *Reader Response Criticism, From Formalism to Post-Structuralism*, edited by Jane P. Tompkins. Baltimore, Md.: Johns Hopkins University Press, 1980.

Preminger, Alex, ed. *The Princeton Handbook of Poetic Terms*. Princeton, N.J.: Princeton University Press, 1986.

Richards, I. A., ed. *The Portable Coleridge*. New York: Viking Press, 1950.

————. *Principles of Literary Criticism*. London: Routledge & Kegan Paul LTD, 1924.

Rickett, Adele Austin, ed. *Chinese Approaches to Literature from Confucius to Liang Ch'i-ch'ao*. Princeton, N.J.: Princeton University Press, 1978.

Robinet, Isabelle. *Taoism: Growth of a Religion*. Trans. and adapt. Phyllis Brooks. Stanford, Calif.: Stanford University Press, 1997. Originally published as *Histoire du Taoïsme des origines au XIVe siècle*. Paris: Cerf, 1992.

Sastry, P. V. Naganatha, ed., trans., and annot. *Kāvyālaṃkāra of Bhāmaha*. 2d ed. Delhi: Motilal Banarsidass, 1970.

Saussy, Haun. *The Problem of a Chinese Aesthetic*. Stanford, Calif.: Stanford University Press, 1993.

Schipper, Kristofer. *The Taoist Body*, trans. Karen C. Duval. Berkeley, Calif.: University of California Press, 1993. First published as *Le corps taoïste*. Paris: Librairie Arthème Fayard, 1982.

Schwarz, Wolfgang. *Rückläufiges Wörterbuch des Altindischen*. Wiesbaden: Otto Harrassowitz, 1978.

Shih, Vincent Yu-chung, trans. and annot. *The Literary Mind and the Carving of Dragons: A Study of Thought and Pattern in Chinese Literature*. Rev. ed. Hong Kong: Chinese University Press, 1983. Originally published by Columbia University Press, 1959.

Spariosu, Mihail I. *The God of Many Names: Play, Poetry, and Power in Hellenic Thought from Homer to Aristotle*. Durham, N.C.: Duke University Press, 1991.

Storch, Tanya. "Chinese Buddhist Historiography and Orality." *Sino-Platonic Papers* 37 (March 1993): 1–16.

Van Zoeren, Steven. *Poetry and Personality: Reading, Exegesis, and Hermeneutics in Traditional China*. Stanford, Calif.: Stanford University Press, 1991.

von Hallberg, Robert, ed. *Canons*. Chicago: University of Chicago Press, 1984.

Warnock, Mary. *Imagination*. London: Faber and Faber, 1976.

———. *Imagination and Time*. Oxford: Blackwell Publishers, 1994.

Watson, Burton, trans. *The Complete Works of Chuang Tzu*. New York: Columbia University Press, 1968.

———, trans. *Hsun Tzu: Basic Writings*. New York: Columbia University Press, 1963.

Wilhelm, Richard, trans. *The I Ching, or Book of Changes*. Trans. from German into English, Cary F. Baynes. Princeton, N.J.: Princeton University Press, 1950.

Winternitz, M. *History of Indian Literature*. Vol. III. Part One: *Classical Sanskrit Literature*, Part Two: *Scientific Literature*, trans. Subhadra Jha. Delhi: Motilal Banarsidass, 1985.

Wordsworth, William. "Preface to the Second Edition of the *lyrical ballads*." In *Criticism: The Major Texts*, edited by Walter Jackson Bate, 335–46. New York: Harcourt, Brace & Co., 1952.

Wu, Pei-yi. "Self-examination and Confession of Sins in Traditional China." *Harvard Journal of Asiatic Studies*, 39.1 (July 1979): 5–38.

Yu, Pauline. *The Reading of Imagery in the Chinese Poetic Tradition*. Princeton, N.J.: Princeton University Press, 1987.

Chinese and Japanese Works

Ban Gu 班固, comp. *Han shu* 漢書 (History of the Han). Beijing: Zhong-hua shuju, 1962.

Cai Zhongxiang 蔡鍾翔, and Yuan Jixi 袁濟喜. "*Wenxin diaolong* yu Wei-Jin xuanxue" 文心雕龍與魏晉玄學 (*Wenxin diaolong* and abstruse learning of the Wei and Jin). *Wenxin diaolong xuekan* 文心雕龍學刊 (The *Wenxin diaolong* journal) 3 (1986): 19–42.

Cai Zong-qi 蔡宗齊. "Huazihuasi he Liu Xie de wenxue chuangzao shixue" 華茲華斯和劉勰的文學創造詩學 (The poetics of literary creation in William Wordsworth and Liu Xie). *Wenxin diaolong yanjiu* 文心雕龍研究 (Studies on *Wenxin diaolong*) 3 (1998): 205–29.

Cao Zhi 曹植. *Cao Zhi ji jiaozhu* 曹植集校 (Collation and annotation of the works of Cao Zhi). Beijing: Renmin wenxue chubanshe, 1984.

Chen Mengjia 陳夢家. "Shangdai shenhua yu wushu" 商代神話與巫術 (Myths and shamanistic arts in the Shang dynasty). *Yanjing xuebao* 燕京學報 (Journal of the Yenching University) 20 (1936): 572–74.

Chen Shou 陳壽, comp. *Sanguo zhi* 三國志 (Memoirs of the three king-doms). Beijing: Zhonghua shuju, 1959.

Chen Siling 陳思苓. *Wenxin diaolong yilun* 文心雕龍臆論 (Speculative thoughts on *Wenxin diaolong*). Chengdu: Bashu shushe, 1986.

Cheng Tianhu 程天祜 and Meng Erdong 孟二冬. "*Wenxin diaolong* zhi 'shenli' bian—yu Ma Hongshan tongzhi shangque" 文心雕龍之'神理'辨與馬宏山同志商榷 (An analysis of 'spiritual principle' in *Wenxin diaolong*—an exchange of opinion with comrade Ma Hongshan), edited by Qi-Lu shushe. *Wenxin diaolong xuekan* 文心雕龍學刊 (The *Wenxin diaolong* journal) 1 (1983): 185–99.

Chunqiu Zuo zhuan zhengyi 春秋左傳正義 (Correct meanings of the Zou commentary to Spring and Autumn annals). Shisanjing Zhushu 十三經注疏 (Commentary and subcommentary on the thirteen classics), com-piled by Ruan Yuan 阮元 2 vols. Beijing: Zhonghua shuju, 1979.

Ding Fubao 丁福保, ed. *Quan Han Sanguo Jin Nanbeichao shi* 全漢三國晉南北朝詩 (The complete poetry of the Han, Sanguo, Jin, and Nanbei-chao periods). 3 vols. Taipei: Shijie shuju, 1969.

Dong Zhi'an 董治安. *Xian Qin wenxuan yu xian Qin wenxue* 先秦文獻與先秦文學 (Pre-Qin texts and pre-Qin literature). Jinan: Qi Lu shushe, 1994.

Du Lijun 杜黎均. *Wenxin diaolong wenxue lilun yanjiu he yishi* 文心雕龍文學理論研究和譯釋 (Translation, annotation, and study of the literary theory in *Wenxin diaolong*). Beijing: Beijing chubanshe, 1981.

Fan Wenlan 范文瀾. *Wenxin diaolong zhu* 文心雕龍註 (Annotated edition of *Wenxin diaolong*). 2 vols. Beijing: Renmin wenxue chubanshe, 1978.

Fan Ye 范曄, comp. *Hou Han shu* 後漢書 (History of the later Han). Beijing: Zhonghua shuju, 1965.

Fang Yuanzhen 方元珍. *Wenxin diaolong yu Fojiao guanxi zhi kaobian* 文心雕龍與佛教關係之考辨 (An examination of the relationship between *Wenxin diaolong* and Buddhism). *Wenshizhe Xue Jicheng* 文史哲學集成 (Studies on literature, history, and philosophy), 161. Taipei: Wenshizhe chubanshe, 1987.

Feng Chuntian 馮春田. *Wenxin diaolong yuci tongshi* 文心雕龍語詞通釋 (A comprehensive glossary of terms in *Wenxin diaolong*). Jinan: Mingtian chubanshe, 1990.

Furuta Keiichi 古田敬一. *Chūgoku bungaku ni okeru tsuiku to tsuiku-ron* 中國文學における對句と對句論 (Parallel lines and parallelism in Chinese literature). Tokyo: Kazama shobo, 1982.

Gao You 高誘. "Huainanzi xu" 淮南子序 (Preface to *Huainanzi*). *Quan Hou Han wen* 全後漢文. *Quan shanggu Sandai Qin Han Sanguo Liuchao wen* 全上古三代秦漢三國六朝文, compiled by Yan Kejun. In *Quan shanggu Sandai Qin Han Sanguo Liuchao wen*. 5 vols. Beijing: Zhonghua shuju, 1965.

Gu Jiegang 顧頡剛. *Gushi bian* 古史辨 (Analysis of ancient histories). 7 vols. Taipei: Landeng chubanshe, 1993.

———. "Lun jinwen *Shangshu* zhuzuo shidai shu" 論今文尚書著作時代書 (A letter on the date of the composition of *Shang shu*). *Gushi Bian*, 200–206. Taipei: Landeng chubanshe, 1993.

Guo Jinxi 郭晉稀. *Wenxin diaolong zhuyi* 文心雕龍注譯 (Annotation and translation of *Wenxin diaolong*). Lanzhou: Kansu renmin chubanshe, 1982.

Guo Qingfan 郭慶藩, comp. *Zhuangzi jishi* 莊子集釋 (Collected annotations on *Zhuangzi*). Taipei: Shijie shuju, 1962.

Guo Shaoyu 郭紹虞. "Zhongguo wenxue piping lilun zhong 'Dao' di wenti" 中國文學批評理論中道的問題 (The issue of "the Tao" in Chinese theories of literary criticism). *Zhaoyushi gudian wenxue lunji* 照隅室古典文學論集 (Collected writings on classical Chinese literature from the Zhaoyu Studio), 34–65. Vol. 2. Shanghai: Shanghai guji chubanshe, 1983.

———. *Zhongguo wenxue piping shi* 中國文學批評史 (A history of Chinese literary criticism). Shanghai: Shanghai shudian, 1989.

Guo Shaoyu 郭紹虞 and Wang Wensheng 王文生, eds. *Zhongguo lidai wenlun xuan* 中國歷代文論選 (An anthology of writings on literature through the ages). 3 vols. Shanghai: Shanghai guji chubanshe, 1979.

Gyakubiki Bukkyōgo jiten 逆引佛教語辭典 (Reverse dictionary of Buddhist terms), compiled by Gyakubiki Bukkyōgo jiten hensan iinkai 逆引佛教語辭典編纂委員會 (Editorial committee for the reverse dictionary of Buddhist terms). Tokyo: Hakushobō, 1995.

Harvard-Yenching Institute Sinological Index Series, comp. *Lunyu yinde* 論語引得 (Concordance to the *Analects*). Beijing: Harvard-Yenching Institute, 1940.

Harvard-Yenching Institute Sinological Index Series. *Zhuangzi yinde* 莊子引得 (A concordance to *Zhuangzi*), supplement no. 20. Cambridge: Harvard University Press, 1956.

He Suishi 賀綏世. *Wenxin diaolong jindu* 文心雕龍今讀 (A modern reading of *Wenxin diaolong*). Henan: Wenxin chubanshe, 1987.

He Yi 何懿. "Yuan Tao" 原道 (The Tao as the source). *Wenxin diaolong xue zonglan* 文心雕龍學綜覽 (A comprehensive survey of studies on *Wenxin diaolong*), edited by *Wenxin diaolong* xue zonglan bianweihu, 137–47. Shanghai: Shanghai shudian chubanshe, 1995.

Hou Naihui 侯迺慧. "Cong 'qi' de yiyi yu liucheng kan *Wenxin diaolong* de chuangzuo lilun" 由氣的意義與流程看文心雕龍的創作理論 (Theory of literary creation in *Wenxin diaolong*: a view from the perspective of the idea of *Qi* as a process). In *Wenxin diaolong zonglun* 文心雕龍綜論 (Comprehensive discussions of *Wenxin diaolong*), 241–83.

Huan Tan 桓譚. "Xin lun" 新論 (New treatise). *Quan Hou Han wen* 全後漢文 (Complete prose of the later Han). In *Quan shanggu Sandai Qin Han Sanguo Liuchao wen*, compiled by Yan Kejun. Beijing: Zhonghua shuju, 1965.

Huang Jichi (Wong Kai-chee) 黃繼持. "Liu Xie de 'Mie huo lun'" 劉勰的滅惑論 (On Liu Xie's "Treatise on the eradication of doubts"). *Xiangang daxue Zhongwen xuehui* (Journal of the Chinese Society), *Wenxin diaolong yanjiu zhuanhao* (Special issue on the study of *Wenxin diaolong*) (December 1962): 28–34.

Huang Jinhong 黃錦鋐. *Yushi xiangzhu Wenxin diaolong* 語釋詳注文心雕龍. Taipei: HongTao wenhua shiye youxian gongsi, 1976.

Huang Kan 黃侃. *Wenxin diaolong zhaji* 文心雕龍札記 (Notes on *Wenxin diaolong*). Beijing: Zhonghua shuju, 1962.

Jao Tsung-i. *See* Rao Zongyi.

Kim Min-na 金民那. *Wenxin diaolong de meixue* 文心雕龍的美學 (The aesthetics of *Wenxin diaolong*). Taiwan: Wenshizhe chubanshe, 1993.

Kimura Kiyota 木村清孝. "Ryu Kyo ni okeru 'Bukkyo' no yakuwari" 劉勰にあける「佛教」の役割 (The role of Buddhism in the thought of Liu-Ssu [*sic*]). *Shūkyō kenkyū* 宗教研究 (Journal of religious studies) 42, no. 4 (June 1969): 71–73. Translation into Chinese by Ichimura Itsuko 市村伊都子 as "'Fojiao' dui Liu Xie suo qi de zuoyong" (The effect of "Buddhism" upon Liu-Ssu [*sic*]) 佛教對劉勰所起的作用. *Wenxin diaolong xuekan* 文心雕龍學刊 (The *Wenxin diaolong* journal) 4 (1986): 415–17.

Kong Fan 孔繁. "Liu Xie yu Fojiao" 劉勰與佛教 (Liu Xie and Buddhism). In Qi-Lu Shushe, ed., *Wenxin diaolong xuekan* 文心雕龍學刊, 1 (1983): 414–33.

Kong Yanzhi 孔延之, comp. *Guiji duo ying zong ji* 會稽掇英總集 (General collection of gathered flowers from Guiji). Taipei, Taiwan: Shangwu yinshuguan, 1973.

Kong Yingda 孔穎達, annot. *Liji zhengyi* 禮記正義 (Correct meanings of the *Book of Rites*). Vol. 2. *Shisanjing zhushu* 十三經注疏 (Commentary and subcommentary on the thirteen classics), compiled by Ruan Yuan. 2 vols. Beijing: Zhonghua shuju, 1977.

———. *Commentary to Shang shu zhengyi* 尚書正義 (Correct meanings of *Shang shu*). *Shisanjing zhushu* 十三經注疏 (Commentary and subcommentary to the thirteen classics), compiled by Ruan Yuan. 2 vols. Beijing: Zhonghua shuju, 1977.

———, annot. *Mao shi zhengyi* 毛詩正義 (Correct meanings of the Mao text of the *Book of Poetry*). In *Shisanjing zhushu* 十三經注疏 (Commentary and subcommentary on the thirteen classics), compiled by Ruan Yuan. 2 vols. Beijing: Zhonghua shuju, 1977.

Kou Xiaoxin 寇效信. *Wenxin diaolong meixue fanchu yanjiu* 文心雕龍美學範疇研究 (Studies on aesthetic categories in *Wenxin diaolong*). Xian: Renmin chubanshe, 1997.

Kōzen Hiroshi 興膳宏. "Bunshin chōryō to Shutsu-sanzō-kishū-sono himerareta kōsho megutte" 文心雕龍と出三藏記集—その秘められた交渉をめぐつて (*Wenxin diaolong* and collected notes on the production of the tripiṭaka—concerning their hidden connections), edited by Fukunaga Mitsuji 福永光司. *Chūgoku chūsei no shokyo to bunka* 中國中世の宗教と文化 (Chinese medieval religion and culture) (1983): 127–238.

———. "*Wenxin diaolong* de ziran guan" 文心雕龍的自然觀 (The concepts of *ziran* in *Wenxin diaolong*). *Wenyi luncong* 文藝論叢 (Forum on art and literature) 16 (1982).

———, trans. *Bunshin choryo* 文心雕龍 (*Wenxin diaolong*). Tokyo: Chikuma shobo, 1968.

Kūkai 空海. *Bunkyō hifuron* 文鏡秘府論 (Treatises from the secret repository of the literary mirror). Beijing: Renmin wenxue chubanshe, 1975.

Lau, D. C. et al., ed. *Lüshi chunqiu zhuzi suoyin* 呂氏春秋逐字索引 (A concordance to *Spring and Autumn Annals of Master Lü*). The ICS Ancient Chinese Texts Concordance Series, no. 12. Hong Kong: Commercial Press, 1994.

———. *Shangshu zhuzi suoyin* 尚書逐字索引 (A concordance to the *Book of Documents*). Hong Kong: Commercial Press, 1995.

Li Jingrong 李景燦. *Wenxin diaolong xinjie* 文心雕龍新解 (New explanations of *Wenxin diaolong*). Taipei: Hanlin chubanshe, 1968.

Li Miao 李淼. "Xingzhe, jiegou, lilun tixi" 性質、結構、理論體系 (Essential qualities, structure, and theoretical system). *Wenxin diaolong xue zonglan* 文心雕龍學綜覽 (A comprehensive survey of studies on *Wenxin diaolong*), 86–90. Shanghai: Shanghai shudian chubanshe, 1995.

Li Qingjia 李慶甲. *Wenxin diaolong shiyuji* 文心雕龍識隅集 (Collected random thoughts on *Wenxin diaolong*). Shanghai: Guji chubanshe, 1989.

———. "*Wenxin diaolong* yu Foxue sixiang" 文心雕龍與佛學思想 (*Wenxin diaolong* and Buddhist thought). *Wenxue pinglun congkan* 文學評論叢刊 (Collected papers on literary criticism) 13 (1982): 263–94. Reprinted as Vol. 1 in *Wenxin diaolong yanjiu lunwen xuan* (A selection of research papers on *Wenxin diaolong*) 文心雕龍研究論文選 (1949–1982), 135–65. Jinan: Qi-Lu shushe, 1988.

Li Yuegang 李曰剛. *Wenxin diaolong jiaoquan* 文心雕龍斠詮 (Comprehensive collation and commentary on *Wenxin diaolong*). Taipei: Guoli bianyiguan, 1982.

Li Zehou 李澤厚 and Liu Gangji 劉剛紀. *Zhongguo meixueshi* 中國美學史 (A history of Chinese aesthetics). Vol. 2. Taipei: Gufeng chubanshe, 1978.

Liang Qichao 梁啓超. "Shi sishi mingyi" 釋四詩名義 (An explanation of the meanings of the four poetic genres). In *Yinbingshi heji: zhuanji* 飲冰室合集 (專集) (A combined edition of collected writings from the Yinbing Studio. Part II: specialized writings), vol. 10, juan 74, 92–97. Shanghai: Zhonghua shuju, 1936.

Liao Weiqing 廖蔚卿. *Liuchao wenlun* 六朝文論 (Writings on literature in the Six Dynasties). Taipei: Lianjing chuban gongsi, 1978.

Liu Dajie 劉大杰. *Zhongguo wenxue fazhan shi* 中國文學發展史 (A history of the development of Chinese literature). Hong Kong: Zhonghua shuju, 1969.

Liu Gangji 劉綱紀. *Liu Xie* 劉勰. *Shijie Zhexuejia Congshu* 世界哲學家叢書 (World philosophers series). Taipei: Dongda tushu gongsi, 1989.

Liu Mengxi 劉夢溪. "Han yi Fodian yu Zhongguo de wenti liubian" 漢譯佛典與中國的文體流變 (The Chinese translation of the Buddhist canon and developments of Chinese literary genres). In *Chuantong de wudu* 傳統的誤讀 (Misreadings of tradition). Shijiazhuang: Hebei jiaoyu chubanshe, 1996.

Liu Shipei 劉師培. "Wenxue chuyu wuzhu zhi guan shuo" 文學出於巫祝之官說 (An explanation: literature came from the officials in charge of shamanistic incantations). In *Zuo An waiji* 左盒外集 (Supplementary collection of Zuo An). Taipei: Huashi, 1975.

Liu Yongji 劉永濟. *Wenxin dialong jiaoshi* 心雕龍校釋 (Collation and explanations of *Wenxin diaolong*). Beijing: Zhonghua shuju, 1962.

Lo Genze 羅根澤. *Zhongguo wenxue piping shi* 中國文學批評史 (A history of Chinese literary criticism). 3 vols. Shanghai: Gudian wenxue chubanshe, 1957–1961.

Lou Yulie 樓宇烈, ed. *Wang Bi ji jiaoshi* 王弼集校釋 (Critical edition of the works of Wang Bi with explanatory notes). 2 vols. Beijing: Zhonghua shuju, 1980.

Lu Ji 陸機. "Wen Fu" 文賦 (Discourse on literature). *Lu Ji ji* 陸機集 (Collected works of Lu Ji), edited by Jin Taosheng 金濤聲. Beijing: Zhonghua shuju, 1982.

Lu Kanru 陸侃如 and Mou Shijin 牟世金, eds. *Wenxin diaolong yizhu* 文心雕龍譯 (Translation and annotation of *Wenxin diaolong*). 2 vols. Jinan: Qi-Lu shushe, 1981.

Lu Xun 魯迅. "Chi jiao" 吃教 (Feeding off doctrine). *Lu Xun quan ji* 魯迅全集 (Complete works of Lu Xun), vol. 5, 310–11. Beijing: Renmin wenxue chubanshe, 1981.

Ma Hongshan 馬宏山. "Dui Liu Xie 'jia pin bu hunqu' he 'yi shamen Sengyou' de kanfa" 對劉勰 "家貧不婚娶" 和 "依沙門僧佑" 的看法 (An opinion on Liu Xie's "not getting married because he came from a poor family" and "attaching himself to the Śramaṇa Sengyou"). *Wenxin diaolong xuekan* 文心雕龍學刊 (The *Wenxin diaolong* journal) 1 (1983): 434–46.

———. "Liu Xie qianhou qi sixiang 'cunzai yuanze fenqi' ma?" 劉勰前後期思想 "存在原則分歧" 嗎? (Were there any differences in principle between Liu Xie's earlier and later ideas?). *Lishi yanjiu* 歷史研究 (Historical researches) 5 (1980): 117–30.

———. "Lun *Wenxin diaolong* de gang" 論《文心雕龍》的網 (On the framework of *Wenxin diaolong*). *Zhongguo shehui kexue* 中國社會科學 (Social sciences in China) 4 (1980): 177–95.

———. *Wenxin diaolong san lun* 文心雕龍散論 (Essays on *Wenxin diaolong*). Ürümchi: Xinjiang renmin chubanshe, 1982.

———. "*Wenxin diaolong* zhi 'Dao' bian—jian lun Liu Xie de zhexue sixiang"

文心雕龍之 "道" 辨——兼論劉勰的哲學思想 (An analysis of the "Way" in *Wenxin diaolong*—together with a discussion on Liu Xie's philosophical thought). *Zhexue yanjiu* 哲學研究 (Philosophical Research) 7 (1979): 74–78.

Ma Xulun 馬敍倫. *Laozi jiaogu* 老子校詁 (A collated commentary on *Laozi*). Hong Kong: Wanguo chubanshe, 1983.

Mekada Makoto 目加田誠, trans. *Bunshin chōryō* 文心雕龍 (*Wenxin diaolong*). Tokyo: Ryokei Shosha, 1986.

———. "Ryu Kyo No Hukotsuron" 劉勰の風骨論 (A study on the "wind and the bone"). 洛神の賦 (Rhapsody on the goddess of the Luo River). Tokyo: Musashino Shoin, 1989.

Mengzi 孟子. *Menzi* 孟子 (The book of Mencius). *Sishu Jizhu* 四書集註 (Collected commentaries to the four books), annotated by Zhu Xi 朱熹. Shanghai: Zhonghua shuju, 1927.

Mou Shijin 牟世金. *Liu Xie nianpu huikao* 劉勰年譜匯考 (A study of collected chronological tables of Liu Xie). Sichuan: Ba Shu shushse, 1988.

———. *Wenxin diaolong yanjiu* 文心雕龍研究 (Studies on *Wenxin diaolong*). Beijing: Renmin wenxue chubanshe, 1995.

Mu Kehong 穆克宏. "Lun *Wenxin diaolong* yu rujia sixiang guanxi" 論文心雕龍與儒家思想的關係 (On the relationship between *Wenxin diaolong* and Confucian thought). In *Wenxin diaolong Yanjiu Lunwen Xuan* 文心雕龍研究論文選 (A selection of research papers on *Wenxin diaolong*), vol. 1, 104–25. Jinan: Qi-Lu shushe, 1988.

Ouyang Xun 歐陽詢, comp. *Yiwen leiju* 藝文類聚 (Classified compilation of belles lettres), collated by Wang Shaoying 汪紹楹, 2 vols. Hong Kong: Zhonghua shuju, 1973.

Pan Chonggui (P'an Ch'ung-kuei) 潘重規. "Liu Xie wenyi sixiang yi Foxue wei gendi bian" 劉勰文藝思想以佛學為根底辨 (An argument over Liu Hsieh's basing his literary thought on Buddhism). *You shi xuezhi* 幼獅學誌 (Youth quarterly) 15, no. 3 (1979): 100–111. Reprinted in *Wenxin tongdiao ji* 文心同雕集 (A collection of shared carvings on the literary mind), edited by Cao Shunqing 曹順慶, 78–94. Chengdu: Chengdu chubanshe, 1990.

Peng Enhua 彭恩華, comp. and trans. *Xingshan Hong Wenxin diaolong lunwen ji* 興膳宏文心雕龍論文集 (Collected articles of Kōzen Hiroshi on *Wenxin diaolong*). Jinan: Qi-Lu shushe, 1984. Especially important is the long article on pp. 5–108 entitled "*Wenxin diaolong* yu Chu Sanzang ji ji" (*Wenxin diaolong* and collected notes on the production of the tripiṭaka) 文心雕龍與出三藏記集. It was originally published in Japanese as "*Bunshin chōryō* to Shutsu-sanzō-kishū-sono himerareta koosh o megutte"

文心雕龍と出三藏記集——その秘められた交渉をめぐつて (*Wenxin diaolong* and collected notes on the production of the tripiṭaka—concerning their hidden connections) *Chūgoku chūsei no shokyo to bunka* 中國中世の宗教と文化 (Chinese medieval religion and culture), ed. Fukunaga Mitsuja 福永光司, 127–238. Kyoto: Kyoto daigaku Jinbun kagaku kankyo, 1982.

Peng Huizi 彭會資. *Zhongguo wenlun da cidian* 中國文論大辭典 (Comprehensive dictionary of Chinese literary criticism). Guangxi: Baihua wenyi chubanshe, 1990.

Qian Mu 錢穆, comp. *Zhuangzi zhuanjian* 莊子纂箋 (Commentaries and annotations on *Zhuangzi*). Hong King: Dongnan Yinwu chubanshe, 1951.

Qian Zhonglian 錢仲聯. "Shi *qi*" 釋氣 (An explanation of *Qi*). *Gudai wenxue lilun yanjiu* 古代文學理論研究 (Research on classical Chinese literary theory) 5 (1981): 129–50.

Qian Zhongshu 錢鍾書. *Guanzhuibian* 管錐編 (Collected insights through a gimlet hole). 4 vols. Beijing: Zhonghua shuju, 1979.

Qi-Lu shushe 齊魯書社, ed. *Wenxin diaolong xuekan* 文心雕龍學刊 (Studies on *Wenxin diaolong*), no. 1 (1983).

Qiu Shiyou 邱世友. "Liu Xie lun wenxue de buoruo juejing" 劉勰論文學的般若絕境 (Liu Xie on the incomparable literary realm of prajñā). In *Wenxin diaolong yanjiu* 文心雕龍研究 (Studies on *Wenxin diaolong*), no. 3 (Beijing: Beijing University Press, 1998), 21–41.

Qu Wanli 屈萬里. "*Shang shu* bu ke jin xin di cailiao" 尚書不可盡信的材料 (Material in *Shang shu* that is not fully trustworthy). *Xin shidai* 新時代 (New era) 1, no. 3 (1964): 23–25.

———. *Shijing quanshi* 詩經詮釋 (Annotated *Book of Songs*). Taipei: Lianjing chubanshe, 1983.

———. *Xian Qin wenshi ziliao kaobian* 先秦文史資料考辨 (Researches on the literary and historical sources from the pre-Qin period). Taipei: Lianjing chuban gongsi, 1983.

Rao Pengzi 饒芃子, ed. *Wenxin diaolong yanjiu huicui* 文心雕龍研究薈萃 (Collected studies on *Wenxin diaolong*). Shanghai: Shanghai shudian, 1992.

Rao Zongyi (Jao Tsung-i) 饒宗頤. *Fanxue ji* 梵學記 (Indological studies). *Zhonghua xueshu congshu* 中華學術叢刊 (Chinese studies series). Shanghai: Shanghai guji chubanshe, 1993.

———. "Liu Xie wenyi sixiang yu Fojiao" 劉勰文藝思想與佛教 (The literary thoughts of Liu Xie as adapted from Buddhism). *Xiangang daxue Zhongwen xuehui* (Journal of the Chinese Society), *Wenxin diaolong yanjiu zhuanhao* 文心雕龍研究專號 (Special issue on the study of *Wenxin diaolong*), edited by Rao Zongyi (December 1962): 17–19.

————. "*Wenxin Diaolong* 'Shenglü Pian' yu Jiumoluoshi tongyun—lun 'Sisheng Shuo' yu Xitan zhi guanxi jian tan Wang Bin, Liu Shanjing, Shen Yue youguan zhu wenti" 文心雕龍聲律篇與鳩摩羅什通韻——論四聲說與悉曇之關係兼談王斌，劉善經，沈約有關諸問題 (The 'chapter on prosody' in *Wenxin diaolong* and Kumārajīva's *Comprehensive Rhymes*—a discussion of the relationship between the theory of the four tones and the Siddham script, together with a discussion of various questions relating to Wang Bin, Liu Shanjing, and Shen Yue). *Fanxue ji*, edited by Rao Zongyi, 93–120. Originally appeared in *Zhonghua wenshi luncong* 中華文史論叢 (Chinese literature and history series) 3 (1985).

————. "*Wenxin diaolong* tan yuan." 文心雕龍探源 *Xiangang daxue Zhongwen xuehui* (Journal of the Chinese Society), *Wenxin diaolong yanjiu zhuanhao* 文心雕龍研究專號 (Special issue on the study of *Wenxin diaolong*), edited by Rao Zongyi (December 1962): 1–12.

————, ed. *Wenxin diaolong yanjiu zhuanhao* 文心雕龍研究專號 (Special issue on the study of *Wenxin diaolong*). *Xiangang daxue Zhongwen xuehui nian kan* 香港大學中文學會年刊 (Annual Publication of the Chinese Society, the University of Hong Kong) (December 1962).

————. "*Wenxin yu Apitanxin*" 文心與阿毗曇心 (Literary mind and Abhidharma mind). In *Fanxue ji*, edited by Rao Zongyi, 179–85. Also in *Wenxin diaolong Yanjiu Huicui* 文心雕龍研究薈萃 (Collected studies on *Wenxin diaolong*), edited by Rao Pengzi 饒芃子, 339–43. Shanghai: Shanghai shudian, 1992.

Ruan Yuan 阮元. *Yanjingshi yiji* 揅經室一集 (A collection from the Yanjing Studio). *SBCK* 四部叢刊.

————, comp. *Shisanjing zhushu* 十三經注疏 (Commentary and subcommentary on the thirteen classics). 2 vols. Beijing: Zhonghua shuju, 1977.

Shen Qian 沈謙. *Wenxin diaolong pipinglun fawei* 文心雕龍批評論發微 (On the subtle meanings of the theory of criticism in *Wenxin diaolong*). Taipei: Lianjing chuban gongsi, 1977.

Shen Yue 沈約, comp. *Song shu* 宋書 (History of the Song). Beijing: Zhonghua shuju, 1974.

Shi Lei (Leei Shih) 石壘. *Wenxin diaolong yuan dao yu Fo Tao yi shuzheng* 文心雕龍原道與佛道義疏證 (A comparative study of truth as the source of aesthetic phenomena in *Wenxin diaolong* and Buddhism). Hong Kong: Yunzai shuwu, 1971. Republished as the first half of Shi Lei, *Wenxin diaolong yu Fo Ru er jiao yi li lun ji* 文心雕龍與佛儒二教義理論集 (Collection of papers on *Wenxin diaolong* and the principles of Buddhist and Confucian doctrines). Hong Kong: Yunzai shuwu, 1977.

Sima Qian 司馬遷, comp. *Shiji* 史記 (Records of the grand historian). Beijing: Zhonghua shuju, 1975.

Su Zhaoqing 蘇兆慶. "Liu Xie wannian beigui he Fulaiha Dinglin si de chuangjian" 劉勰晚年北歸和浮來山定林寺的創建. *Beijing daxue xuebao* 3 (1997): 98–102.

Sun Changwu 孫昌武. *Fojiao yu Zhongguo wenxue* 佛教與中國文學 (Buddhism and Chinese literature). *Zhongguo wenhua shi congshu* 中國文化史叢書 (Chinese cultural history series). Shanghai: Shanghai renmin chubanshe, 1988.

Sun Rongrong 孫蓉蓉. *Wenxin diaolong yanjiu* 文心雕龍研究 (Studies on *Wenxin diaolong*). Nanjing: Jiangsu chubanshe, 1983. Nanking: Jiangsu jiaoyu chubanshe, 1994.

Sun Yaoyu 孫耀煜. "*Wenxin diaolong* shenyongxiangtong shuo tanxi" 文心雕龍神用象通說探析 (An inquiry into the theory of "when the daimon is at work, images are accomplished" in *Wenxin diaolong*). *Wenxin diaolong xuekan* 文心雕龍學刊 (The *Wenxin diaolong* journal), vol. 6 (1992): 206–15.

Tang Junyi 唐君毅. *Zhongguo zhexue yuanlun: yuan dao pian* 中國哲學原論：原道篇 (Fundamental discourses on Chinese philosophy: the Tao as source). Hong Kong: Xinya yanjiusuo, 1973.

Toda Kogyo 戶田浩曉, trans. *Bunshin choryo* 文心雕龍 (*Wenxin diaolong*). 2 vols. Tokyo: Meitoku Shuppansha, 1972.

Wang Bi 王弼 and Kong Yingda 孔穎達, annot. *Zhou yi zhengyi* 周易正義 (Correct meaning of the *Book of Changes*). juan 8, in SSJZ, vol. 1. *Shisanjing zhushu* 十三經注疏, compiled by Ruan Yuan, 2 vols. Beijing: Zhonghua shuju, 1977.

Wang Chunhong 汪春泓. "Guanyu *Wenxin diaolong* zhi Fojiao yuanyuan de xin sikao" 關於文心雕龍之佛教淵源的新思考 (New reflections concerning the Buddhist origins of *Wenxin diaolong*). *Wenxin diaolong yanjiu* 文心雕龍研究 (Studies on *Wenxin diaolong*), vol. 2. Beijing: Beijing daxue chubanshe, (1996): 126–54.

Wang Dajin 王達津. "Lun *Wenxin diaolong* de wenti lun" 論文心雕龍的文體論 (On the theory of genres in *Wenxin diaolong*). *Wenxin diaolong yanjiu lunwenji* 文心雕龍研究論文集 (Collected essays on *Wenxin diaolong*), edited by Zhongguo *Wenxin diaolong* Xuehui. Beijing: Renmin wenxue chubanshe, 1990.

———. "Yetan 'Cong Handai guanyu Qu Yuan de lunzheng dao Liu Xie de Biansao" 也談從漢代關於屈原的論爭到劉勰的辨騷 (Another discussion on the development from the debate on Qu Yuan to Liu Xie's "Biansao"). *Zhongguo wenxue piping yanjiu lunwen ji: Wenxin diaolong yanjiu zhuanji* 中國文學批評研究論文集: 文心雕龍研究專集, edited by Zhongguo yuwen xueshe, 22–26. Beijing: Zhongguo yuwen xueshe, 1969.

Wang Gengsheng 王更生. *Wenxin diaolong duben* 文心雕龍讀本 (*Wenxin diaolong*: a reader). Taipei: Wen shi zhe chubanshe, 1985.

———. *Wenxin diaolong daodu* 文心雕龍導讀 (Guided readings in *Wenxin diaolong*). Taipei: Hauzheng shuju, 1983.

———. *Wenxin diaolong xinlun* 文心雕龍新論 (New discussions on *Wenxin diaolong*). Taipei: Wen shi zhe chubanshe, 1991.

———. *Wenxin diaolong yanjiu* 文心雕龍研究 (Studies on *Wenxin diaolong*). Taipei: Wen shi zhe chubanshe, 1979.

Wang Guowei 王國維. *Song Yuan xiju kao* 宋元戲劇攷 (Study of Song and Yuan drama). Taipei: Yiwen yinshuguan, 1964.

Wang Jinling 王金凌. *Wenxin diaolong wenlun shuyu xilun* 文心雕龍文論術語析論 (An analysis of critical terminologies in *Wenxin diaolong*). Taipei: Huazheng shuju, 1981.

———. *Zhongguo wenxue lilun shi (Liuchao pian)* 中國文學理論史 (六朝篇) (A history of Chinese theory of literature: the Six Dynasties volume). Taipei: Huazheng shuju, 1988.

Wang Kaiyun 王闓運 and Yang Ming 楊明. *Wei Jin Nanbeichao wenxue piping shi* 魏晉南北朝文學批評史 (A history of literary criticism in Wei, Jin, and Nanbeichao periods). Shanghai: Shanghai guji chubanshe, 1989.

Wang Li. *Hanyu shilüxue* 漢語詩律學 (Chinese prosody). Shanghai: Xin zhishi chubanshe, 1958.

Wang Liqi 王利器, ed. *Wenxin diaolong xin shu* 文心雕龍新書 (New edition of *Wenxin diaolong*). Hong Kong: Longmen shudian, 1967. Revised as *Wenxin diaolong jiaozheng* 文心雕龍校證 (Collation and verification of *Wenxin diaolong*). Shanghai: Shanghai guji chubanshe, 1980.

Wang Meng'ou 王夢鷗. *Gudian wenxuelun tansuo* 古典文學論探索 (Explorations of classical literature). Taipei: Zhengzhong shuju, 1984.

Wang Shumin 王叔岷. *Wenxin diaolong zhuibu* 文心雕龍綴補 (Emandations to *Wenxin diaolong*). Taipei: Yiwen yinshuguan, 1975.

———. *Zhuangzi jiaoquan* 莊子校詮 (A collated commentary on *Zhuangzi*). Vol. 3. Taipei: Zhongyang yanjiuyuan lishi yuyan yanjiusuo, 1988.

Wang Xianshen 王先慎, ed., *Hanfeizi jijie* 韓非子集解 (*Hanfei zi*, with collected annotations and commentaries). Taipei: Shangwu, 1970.

Wang Yi 王逸, ed. *Chuci buzhu* 楚辭補注 (Supplementary commentary to *Chuci*). *SBBY* 四部備要.

Wang Yuanhua 王元化. "'Mie Huo Lun' yu Liu Xie de qianhouqi sixiang bianhua" 滅惑論與劉勰的前後期思想變化 ("Treatise on the eradication of doubts" and the transformation of Liu Xie's thinking in its earlier and later stages). *Wenxin diaolong jiangshu* 文心雕龍講疏 (Lectures and notes on *Wenxin diaolong*), 27–52. Also in *Wenxin diaolong yanjiu lunwen xuan* 文心雕龍研究論文選 (A selection of research papers on *Wenxin diaolong*), vol. 1 (1949–1982), 83–103. Jinan: Qi-Lu shushe, 1988. Also in Wang Yuanhua, *Wenxin diaolong chuangzuo lun* 文心雕龍創作論 (The theory of literary creation in *Wenxin diaolong*), 22–40. Shanghai: Shanghai guji chubanshe, 1979.

———. *Wenxin diaolong jiangshu* 文心雕龍講疏 (Lectures and notes on *Wenxin diaolong*). Shanghai: Shanghai guji chubanshe, 1992.

———. *Wenxin diaolong chuangzuo lun* 文心雕龍創作論 (The theory of literary creation in *Wenxin diaolong*). Shanghai: Shanghai guji chubanshe, 1979.

Wei Zhao 韋昭, annot. *Guo yu* 國語 (Speeches of the states). 2 vols. Shanghai: Shanghai guji chubanshe, 1978.

Wei Zheng 魏徵, et al., eds. *Sui shu* 隋書 (History of the Sui). Shanghai: Zhonghua shuju, 1973.

Wenxin diaolong xue zonglan bianweihui, ed. *Wenxin diaolong xue zonglan* 文心雕龍學綜覽 (A comprehensive survey of studies on *Wenxin diaolong*). Shanghai: Shanghai shudian chubanshe, 1995.

Xi Kang 嵇康. "Qin fu" 琴賦 (A rhapsody on the lute). *Xi Kang ji jiaozhu* 嵇康集校注 (Collation and commentary on the works of Xi Kang), edited by Dai Mingyang 戴明揚. Beijing: Renmin wenxue chubanshe, 1962.

Xia Chengtao 夏承燾. "'Caishi' yu 'fushi'" 采詩與賦詩 (On collected poetry and presented poetry). *Zhonghua wenshi luncong* 中華文史論叢 (Forum on Chinese literature and history) 1 (1962): 171–82.

Xiao Tong 蕭統, comp. *Wen xuan* 文選 (Selections of refined literature), ed. Hu Kejia 胡克家. Taipei: Zhengzhong shuju, 1971.

Xiao Yan 蕭衍. "Xiaosifu" 孝思賦 (Rhapsody on filial thought). In *Quan shanggu Sandai Qin Han Sanguo Liuchao wen* 全上古三代秦漢三國六朝文 (Complete prose writings of the ancient Three Dynasties, Qin, Han, Three Kingdoms, and Six Dynasties), edited by Yan Kejun 嚴可均. (Taipei: Shijie shuju, 1963), vol. 7, *Quanliangwen* 全梁文, juan 1, 1–3.

Xiao Zixian 蕭子顯, comp. *Nan Qi shu* 南齊書 (History of the southern Qi). Beijing: Zhonghua shuju, 1972.

Xiong Lihui 熊黎輝. "Chuangzuo lun" 創作論 (Theory of literary creation). *Wenxin diaolong xue zonglan* 文心雕龍學綜覽 (A comprehensive survey of studies on *Wenxin dialong*), edited by *Wenxin diaolong* xue zonglan bianweihu, 98–105. Shanghai: Shanghai shudian chubanshe, 1995.

Xu Fuguan 徐復觀. *Zhongguo wenxue lunji* 中國文學論集 (Collected works on Chinese literature). Taipei: Xuesheng shuju, 1974.

Xu Fuguan 徐復觀. *Zhongguo yishu jingshen* 中國藝術精神 (The spirit of Chinese aesthetics). Taizhong: Donghai Daxue, 1966.

Xunzi yinde 荀子引得. Taipei: Chengwen Publishing Company, 1966.

Xu Shen 許慎. *Shuowen jiezi* 説文解字 (Explanations of simple and compound characters), annot. by Duan Yucai 段玉裁. Taipei: Yiwen yinshuguan, 1974.

Yan Kejun 嚴可均, comp. *Quan shanggu Sandai Qin Han Sanguo Liuchao wen* 全上古三代秦漢三國六朝文 (Complete prose of antiquity, the Three Dynasties, Qin, Han, the Three Kingdoms, and the Six Dynasties). 5 vols. Beijing: Zhonghua shuju, 1965.

Yang Mingzhao 楊明照. "Liang shu Liu Xie zhuan jian zhu" 梁書劉勰傳箋注 (Annotations on the biography of Liu Xie in the *History of Liang*). In *Wenxin diaolong zhu shiyi* 文心雕龍校注 (Collation and commentary on *Wenxin diaolong*), 385–413. Shanghai: Shanghai guji chubanshe, 1982.

———. *Wenxin diaolong zhu shiyi* 文心雕龍校注拾遺 (Collation and commentary on *Wenxin diaolong*). Shanghai: Kuji chubanshe, 1982.

Yang Xiong 揚雄. *Yangzi fayan* 揚子法言 (Model sayings of Master Yang). Shanghai: Zhonghua shuju, 1927.

Ye Shuxian 葉舒憲. *Shi jing di wenhua chanshi: Zhongguo shige de fasheng yanjiu* 詩經的文化闡釋——中國詩歌的發生研究 (A cultural exegesis of *Shi jing*: studies on the genesis of Chinese poetry). Wuhan: Hubei renmin chubashe, 1994.

Yong Rong 永瑢 et al., ed. *Siku quanshu zongmu* 四庫全書總目 (General catalog of the Imperial Library). 2 vols. Beijing: Zhonghua shuju, 1965.

Zhan Ying 詹鍈. *Wenxin diaolong fengge xue* 文心雕龍風格學 (The theory of styles in *Wenxin diaolong*). Beijing: Renmin wenxue chubanshe, 1982.

———, ed. *Wenxin diaolong yizheng* 文心雕龍義證 (Investigation of the meanings of *Wenxin diaolong*). 3 vols. Shanghai: Shanghai guji chubanshe, 1989.

Zhang Binglin 章炳麟. *Wenshi* 文始 (Genesis of *Wen*). Taipei: Taiwan Zhonghua shuju, 1970.

Zhang Dai 張岱. *Sishu yu* 四書遇 (Encounter the four books), edited by Zhu Hongda 朱宏達. Hangzhou: Zhejiang guji chubanshe, 1985.

Zhang Lizai 張立齋. *Wenxin diaolong zhuding* 文心雕龍注訂 (Annotations and emendations of *Wenxin diaolong*). Taipei: Zhengzhong shuju, 1967.

Zhang Qicheng 張啓成. "*Wenxin diaolong* zhong de daojia sixiang" 文心雕龍中的道家思想 (Taoist thought in *Wenxin diaolong*). *Wenxin diaolong yanjiu lunwen xuan (1949–1982)* 文心雕龍研究論文選 (A selection of research papers on *Wenxin diaolong*), vol. 1, 126–34. Jinan: Qi-Lu shushe, 1988.

Zhang Shaokang 張少康. "Liu Xie weishenme yao 'yi shamen Sengyou'?—du *Liang shu*, 'Liu Xie zhuan' zhaji" 劉勰為什麼要 "依沙門僧佑" ——讀《梁書‧劉勰傳》札記 (Why did Liu Xie want to "attach himself to the Śramaṇa Sengyou"?—notes on reading "The Biography of Liu Xie" in the *Liang History*). *Beijing Daxue xuebao* 北京大學學報 (Journal of Beijing University) 6 (1981): 91–93, 10.

———. "*Wenxin diaolong* de yuanTao lun—Liu Xie wenxue sixiang de lishi yuanyuan yanjiu zhi yi"《文心雕龍》的原道論——劉勰文學思想的歷史淵源研究之一 (Discussion of the original way in *Wenxin diaolong*—one in a series of studies on the sources of Liu Xie's literary thought). *Wenxin diaolong xuekan* 文心雕龍學刊 (The *Wenxin diaolong* journal) 1 (1983): 156–70.

———. *Wenxin diaolong xintan* 文心雕龍新探 (New investigations on *Wenxin diaolong*). *Wenshizhe xue jicheng* 文史哲學集成 (Collection of studies on literature, history, and philosophy), no. 232. Taipei: Wen shi zhe chubanshe, 1996.

Zhang Shuxiang 張淑香. "Shensi yu xiangxiang" 神思與想像 (Daimonic thinking and imagination). *Zhonghua wenhua fuxing yuekan* 中華文化復興月刊 (Chinese cultural renaissance monthly) 8, no. 8 (1975): 43–49.

Zhang Wenxun 張文勛. *Liu Xie de wenxueshi lun* 劉勰的文學史論 (Liu Xie's theory of literary history). Beijing: Remin wenxue chubanshe, 1984.

Zhang Yan 張嚴. *Wenxin diaolong tongshi* 文心雕龍通識 (General thoughts on *Wenxin diaolong*). Taipei: Shangwu shuju, 1969.

Zhang Zhiyue 張志岳. "*Wenxin diaolong* Biansao pian' fawei" 文心雕龍辨騷偏發微 (On the subtle meanings of the "Biansao" chapter of *Wenxin diaolong*). *Wenxin diaolong yanjiu lunwenji* 文心雕龍研究論文集 (Collected essays on *Wenxin diaolong*), edited by Zhongguo *Wenxin diaolong* xuehui, 394–409. Beijing: Remin wenxue chubanshe, 1990.

Zhao Zhongyi 趙仲邑, ed. *Wenxin diaolong yizhu* 文心雕龍譯注 (Translation and annotation of *Wenxin diaolong*). Taipei: Guanya wenhua shiye youxian gongsi, 1991.

Zheng Xuan 鄭玄, comp. *Zhou li zhushu* 周禮注疏 (Commentary on the rituals of Zhou). In *Shisanjing Zhushu* 十三經注疏 (Commentary and subcommentary on the thirteen classics), comp. Ruan Yuan. 2 vols. Beijing: Zhonghua shuju, 1979.

Zhong Rong 鍾嶸. *Shipin* 詩品 (Classes of poetry), edited by Cheng Yanjie 陳延傑. Beijing: Renmin wenxue chubanshe, 1980.

Zhongguo gudian wenxue yanjiuhui, ed. *Wenxin diaolong zonglun* 文心雕龍綜論 (Comprehensive discussions on *Wenxin diaolong*). Taipei: Taiwan xuesheng shuju, 1988.

Zhongguo *Wenxin diaolong* xuehui, ed. *Wenxin diaolong yanjiu lunwenji* 文心雕龍研究論文集 (Collected essays on *Wenxin diaolong*). Beijing: Renmin wenxue chubanshe, 1990.

Zhongguo yuwen xueshe 中國語文學社, ed. *Zhongguo wenxue piping yanjiu lunwen ji: Wenxin diaolong yanjiu zhuanji* 中國文學批評研究論文集: 文心雕龍研究專集 (Collected essays on Chinese literary criticism: a special volume in the studies of *Wenxin diaolong*). Beijing: Zhongguo yuwen xueshe, 1969.

Zhou Cezong (Chow Tse-tsung) 周策縱. *Gu wuyi yu liushi kao* 古巫醫與六詩攷 (Study of ancient shaman-doctors and the six poetic genres and modes). Taipei: Jinglian chubanshe, 1986.

Zhou Zhenfu 周振甫. *Wenxin diaolong jinyi* 文心雕龍今譯 (A modern translation of *Wenxin diaolong*). Beijing: Zhonghua shuju, 1986.

———. *Wenxin diaolong xuanyi* 文心雕龍選譯 (Translated selections from *Wenxin diaolong*). Beijing: Zhonghua shuju, 1980.

———. *Wenxin diaolong zhushi* 文心雕龍注釋 (Commentaries and explanations on *Wenxin diaolong*). Beijing: Renmin wenxue chubanshe, 1983.

Zhu Xi 朱熹. *Chuci jizhu* 楚辭集注 (Collected commentaries on the *Songs of Chu*). Vol. 1. Taipei: Wanguo tushu gongsi, 1956.

———. *Sishu jizhu* 四書集注 (Collected commentaries on the four books). Taipei: Xuehai chubanshe, 1989.

Zhu Xi 朱熹, annot. *Lunyu* 論語 (The analects). In *Sishu Jizhu* 四書集注 (Collected commentaries to the four books). Shanghai: Zhonghua shuju, 1927.

Zhu Yingping 朱迎平, ed. *Wenxin diaolong suoyin* 文心雕龍索引 (Indexes to *Wenxin diaolong*). Shanghai: Shanghai guji chubanshe, 1987.

Zhu Ziqing 朱自清. *Shi yan zhi bian* 詩言志辨 (An analysis of "Poetry expresses the heart's intent"). Beijing: Guji chubanshe, 1956.

Index